Offenders on Offending

Offenders on Offending

Learning about crime from criminals

Edited by
Wim Bernasco

WILLAN
PUBLISHING

Published by
Willan Publishing
Culmcott House
Mill Street, Uffculme
Cullompton, Devon
EX15 3AT, UK
Tel: +44(0)1884 840337
Fax: +44(0)1884 840251
e-mail: info@willanpublishing.co.uk
Website: www.willanpublishing.co.uk

Published simultaneously in the USA and Canada by

Willan Publishing
c/o ISBS, 920 NE 58th Ave, Suite 300,
Portland, Oregon 97213-3786, USA
Tel: +001(0)503 287 3093
Fax: +001(0)503 280 8832
e-mail: info@isbs.com
Website: www.isbs.com

First published 2010

ISBN   978-1-84392-776-1 paperback
       978-1-84392-777-8 hardback

British Library Cataloguing-in-Publication Data

A catalogue record for this book is available from the British Library

FSC
Mixed Sources
Product group from well-managed
forests and other controlled sources

Cert no. SGS-COC-2482
www.fsc.org
© 1996 Forest Stewardship Council

Project managed by Deer Park Productions, Tavistock, Devon
Typeset by TW Typesetting, Plymouth, Devon
Printed and bound by T J International Ltd, Trecerus Industrial Estate, Padstow, Cornwall

Contents

Figures and tables

Figures

Tables

List of abbreviations

BBC	British Broadcasting Corporation
BCS	British Crime Survey
CCTV	closed-circuit television
CSEC	'commercially sexually exploited children'
FCI	federal correctional institution (US)
GIS	geographical information system
HIV	human immunodefficiency virus
HSV	herpes simplex virus
HTLV	human T-cell lymphotropic virus
ICE	Immigration and Customs Enforcement (US)
ICVS	International Crime Victim Survey
IRB	institutional review board
KfV	Austrian Road Safety Board
LEC	life-events calendar
NCVS	National Crime Victimisation Survey
NIJ	National Institute of Justice (US)
NSCR	Netherlands Institute for the Study of Crime and Law Enforcement
NYC	New York City
RDS	respondent driven sampling
SFHR	Social Factors in HIV Risk project
UPI	United Press International

Notes on contributors

Wim Bernasco is a Senior Researcher at the Netherlands Institute for the Study of Crime and Law Enforcement (NSCR). He has an MSc in psychology from Leiden University and a PhD in sociology from Utrecht University. His main research interest is environmental criminology, in particular offender travel and target selection, and he has written about these topics in various international crime and criminal justice journals. He organised the workshop where the authors in this volume discussed their contributions.

Fiona Brookman is Reader in Criminology and Deputy Director of the Centre for Criminology, University of Glamorgan, in South Wales, which she helped to establish in 2001. Dr Brookman received her PhD from Cardiff University in 2000. Her research and publications generally revolve around homicide and other forms of violence (such as street robbery) and she is author of *Understanding Homicide* (Sage, 2005) and numerous articles and book chapters. She is currently undertaking research into difficult to detect and unsolved homicides. Her research on homicide forms part of the British Murder Investigation Manual.

Heith Copes is Associate Professor of Criminal Justice at the University of Alabama at Birmingham. His primary research combines symbolic interactionism and rational choice theory to better understand the criminal decision-making process. His recent publications appear in the *British Journal of Criminology, Crime and Justice: A Review of Research, Criminology and Public Policy* and *Social Problems*. He recently received funding from the National Institute of Justice to conduct a qualitative study of identity thieves.

Ric Curtis is a Professor and Chair of the Anthropology Department at John Jay College of Criminal Justice in New York City. Over the last 30 years, his work has primarily focused on crime, drugs, disease and gangs. He is also on the Board of Directors of several harm reduction programmes in New York City.

Henk Elffers graduated in mathematical statistics at the University of Amsterdam and got his PhD at Erasmus University, Rotterdam on a thesis about measuring tax evasion by various methods. Presently he is a Senior Researcher at the Netherlands Institute for the Study of Crime and Law Enforcement (NSCR), Amsterdam, and has a professorship in empirical research into criminal law enforcement at Vrije Universiteit, Amsterdam. His research interests encompass measurement problems in spatial criminology, rational choice theory of criminal decision-making and the relationship between public opinion and the administration of criminal justice.

Matthias Gaderer has been a research fellow at the Austrian Road Safety Board (KfV) since 2006. Based in Vienna, the KfV is Austria's largest institution for research in the fields of road safety, leisure injuries and property crime. Mr Gaderer holds a master's degree from the University of Vienna in Sociology and Communication Sciences. Currently he is working on his doctoral thesis. His research interests are burglary, victims of crime, robbery and surveillance.

Frank van Gemert studied Cultural Anthropology and is currently working at the department of Criminology of VU University in Amsterdam, The Netherlands. Over the years he has been involved in a variety of qualitative research, including projects on street dealers, gangs, homicides and squatters. He is a member of the steering group of Eurogang, an international network for comparative research on gangs, and a board member of KWALON, a platform for qualitative research in the Netherlands.

Andy Hochstetler is Associate Professor of Sociology at Iowa State University. His interests focus primarily on offender self-conception or identities, offender narratives and foreground dynamics of criminal decision-making. Hochstetler addresses these subjects using a variety of methodologies and sources of data including secondary analyses of survey data, the collection of survey data and qualitative interviews. He is co-author of one book with Professor Neal Shover, *Choosing White-Collar Crime*, which applies an analysis of choice and opportunity to these crimes. He also has written numerous articles and chapters that examine offender accounts and claims about self and situations and the links between backgrounds and other parts of storylines that lead to crime.

Ben W. Hunter is a Research Associate based in the School of Law at the University of Sheffield. He is currently involved in the project Tracking Progress on Probation: Long-Term Patterns of Desistance, due to end April 2012. His main research interests are white-collar crime, desistance from crime and resettlement after conviction and his PhD thesis explored white-collar offenders' stories of resettlement as told through their autobiographies. More general research interests include a focus on the existential aspects of offending and the use of existentialism and existential sociology for an understanding of offenders' experiences.

Scott Jacques is a PhD candidate in the Department of Criminology and Criminal Justice at the University of Missouri – St Louis, and a researcher at the Netherlands Institute for the Study of Crime and Law Enforcement. In the fall of 2010 he will begin an assistant professor position in the School of Criminal Justice at the University of Cincinnati. In addition to his field-based research on drug dealing, Scott and Richard Wright are currently developing a falsifiable theory of method. This work has been published in the *Journal of Research in Crime and Delinquency*, the *Journal of Criminal Justice Education* and *Crime, Law and Social Change*.

Shane D. Johnson is a Reader at the UCL Jill Dando Institute of Crime Science, University College London, England. He has a PhD and an MA in Psychology and a BSc in Computer Science. He has particular interests in the spatial and temporal distribution of crime, computer simulation, evaluation methods and design against crime. His work has been funded by sponsors including the Arts and Humanities Research Council, the Engineering and Physical Science Research Council, the British Academy and the Home Office. He has published over 50 original research papers in journals including the *Journal of Quantitative Criminology and Criminology and Public Policy*.

Marie Rosenkrantz Lindegaard is a postdoctoral fellow at the Netherlands Institute for the Study of Crime and Law Enforcement (NSCR) in Amsterdam. She obtained her Master degree in anthropology from the University of Copenhagen and her PhD from the University of Amsterdam. She conducted extensive fieldwork among adolescents in Cape Town, South Africa, where she investigated how male youngsters avoid violence, and how they experience it if they cannot or do not want to avoid it. A part of the study was conducted in prison. In her current work she explores the meaning of social and spatial mobility for the way that young males in the Netherlands negotiate situations of violence.

Jody Miller is Professor of Criminology and Criminal Justice at the University of Missouri – St Louis. She specialises in feminist theory and qualitative research methods. Her research focuses on gender, crime and victimisation in the context of urban communities, offender networks and the commercial sex industry. Dr Miller is author of *Getting Played: African American Girls, Urban Inequality, and Gendered Violence* (New York University Press, 2008) – a finalist for the 2008 C. Wright Mills Award – and *One* *of the Guys: Girls, Gangs, and Gender* (Oxford University Press), as well as numerous articles and book chapters.

Carlo Morselli is an Associate Professor at the School of Criminology and researcher at the International Centre for Comparative Criminology, Université de Montréal. Aside from research on criminal earnings and achievement, his current work lies primarily in the fields of criminal networks and organised crime. In 2005 he published *Contacts, Opportunities, and Criminal Enterprise* (University of Toronto Press). In 2009, he published *Inside Criminal Networks* (Springer).

Claire Nee is Reader in Forensic Psychology at the University of Portsmouth where she is also Director of the International Centre for Research in Forensic Psychology. She graduated in Applied Psychology and undertook her PhD on a situational analysis of residential burglary in Ireland at University College, Cork. She worked for many years as a criminal policy researcher at the Home Office Research and Planning Unit in the UK. Her research interests encompass offender decision-making, child criminality and personality disorder in women offenders.

Veronika A. Polišenská is a Postdoctoral Fellow at the Institute of Psychology of the Academy of Sciences of the Czech Republic. She specialises in the study of property offenders and mainly conducts her research in penitentiary facilities. Her theoretical background primarily lies within the realm of environmental criminology. She is particularly interested in the criminal mobility of offenders, studying criminal mobility in conjunction with offenders' personality, motivation, aggression and other factors.

George F. Rengert is Professor of Criminal Justice at Temple University in Philadelphia. His area of specialty is the spatial and temporal behaviour of property criminals. His books include: *Suburban Burglary: A Time and a Place for Everything* (Charles Thomas), *Metropolitan Crime Patterns* (Criminal Justice Press), *Crime Spillover* (Sage), *Suburban Burglary: A Tale of Two Suburbs* (Charles Thomas), *Campus Security: Situational Crime Prevention in High-Density Environments* (Criminal Justice Press), and *The Geography of Illegal Drugs* (Westview Press). Currently he is working on the application of geographic information systems to urban crime control.

Neal Shover is Professor of Sociology at the University of Tennessee, Knoxville. His areas of expertise and interest include white-collar crime, criminal careers and ethnographic research methods. His most recent book (co-authored with Andy Hochstetler) is *Choosing White-Collar Crime* (Cambridge University Press, 2006). Professor Shover has been a visiting fellow at the US Department of Justice and a visiting scholar at several universities both in the US and abroad.

Lucía Summers is a Research Fellow at the UCL Jill Dando Institute of Crime Science, University College London, England. She has a BSc in Experimental Psychology, an MSc in Forensic Psychology and an MSc in Research Methods. She is currently completing her PhD in Crime Science. Her interests mainly lie in the prevention of serious violence although she has researched other topics, such as the spatio-temporal patterns of property crime. Her work has been published both in English (e.g. *Journal of Quantitative Criminology*) and Spanish language journals (e.g. *Revista de Derecho Penal y Criminología*).

Pierre Tremblay is a Professor at the School of Criminology, Université de Montréal. He received his PhD in criminology from the Université de Montréal. His current interests include the size of active offender populations, diffusion of criminal innovations and the linking anomie and criminal achievement theories of crime.

Richard Wright is Curators' Professor and Chair of the Department of Criminology and Criminal Justice at the University of Missouri – St Louis, and Editor-in-Chief of the *British Journal of Sociology*. He has co-authored numerous books on the offender's perspective, including *Burglars on Burglary* (Gower, 1984), *Burglars on the Job* (Northeastern University Press, 1994), *Armed Robbers in Action* (Northeastern University Press, 1997) and *Street Justice* (Cambridge University Press, 2006). In addition, he has co-edited *The Sage Handbook of Fieldwork* (Sage, 2006).

Sheldon X. Zhang is Professor of Sociology at San Diego State University. He has spent more than a decade conducting research on transnational criminal activities, particularly in the areas of human smuggling and sex trafficking. His research on human smuggling appeared in such journals as *Criminology, British Journal of Criminology* and *Crime, Law, and Social Change*. He has published two books on human smuggling and trafficking topics: *Chinese Human Smuggling Organizations – Families, Social Networks, and Cultural Imperatives* (Stanford University Press, 2008) and *Smuggling and Trafficking in Human Beings: All Roads Lead to America* (Praeger, 2007).

Birgit Zetinigg is Head of the Department of 'Property and Fire' at the Austrian Road Safety Board (KfV). Based in Vienna, the KfV is Austria's largest institution for research in the fields of road safety, leisure injuries and property crime. Ms Zetinigg holds a Master's degree in Criminal Justice Policy (London School of Economics and Political Science). Her major research interests include burglary, fear of crime, youth crime and robbery.

Foreword

Michael Tonry

According to the *Oxford English Dictionary*, the term 'criminology' first appeared in English in the pages of the *Athenænum* in September 1890: 'We share Dr Topinard's dislike of the term "criminal anthropology", and may adopt the term "criminology" till better can be found.' The same article attempted to define 'criminologist'.

Cesare Lombroso's *L'uomo delinquente*, published in 1876, is the first book that most criminologists retrospectively claim as one of their own, even if in its time it was the founding document of the criminal anthropology the *Athenænum* disdained, and even if most twenty-first-century criminologists distance themselves from its analyses and conclusions.

The roots of criminology go deeper – into what we, but not the early excavators, would describe as quantitative and qualitative research. The numerical pioneers were Adolphe Quételet and André-Michel Guerry, the Belgian and French statisticians who, beginning in the 1820s, laid the foundations for modern social statistics. They demonstrated that patterns and levels of criminality varied from place to place but were relatively stable over time in any one place. The storytelling pioneers included great novelists like Charles Dickens, who daily walked the streets of London watching and listening, to give verisimilitude to *Oliver Twist* and other of his descriptions of London life high and low. They also included great journalists like Henry Mayhew who, among many other accomplishments, founded the still-surviving humorous British magazine *Punch*. Mayhew is most famous, however, for his four-volume *London Labour and the London Poor*, based on innumerable interviews with and lengthy observations of poor people. The fourth volume documented the lives of thieves, prostitutes and beggars.

I rehearse these nineteenth-century developments to offer two observations about Wim Bernasco's fine collection of essays on qualitative research about crime and criminals. The first is that quantitative and qualitative research, at least in their purer forms, are separate kinds of enterprise. Quételet and Guerry were active and influential in the 1840s and 1850s when Mayhew was working on his classic – today we might say ethnographic – work. Quételet and Guerry would have been astonished to be told that they were in some way in competition with Mayhew, and that one enterprise was better, or more valuable, than the other.

The same thing is true of the major figures in the first celebrated English-language criminology programme at the University of Chicago. Ernest W. Burgess was laying a foundation for 50 years of quantitative research on parole decision-making and recidivism prediction that provided PhD topics for three generations of celebrated sociologists – Lloyd Ohlin, Daniel Glaser, Dudley Duncan and Albert J. Reiss, Jr prominent among them. At the same time, Robert E. Park, Frederick Thrasher, Clifford Shaw and William F. Whyte were writing classic works on gangs and on individual offenders based on the use of qualitative methods. Shaw and Benjamin McKay combined both approaches.

The second observation derives from the first: quantitative research is neither better nor worse than qualitative research. Which is more appropriate depends on the subjects being examined and the methods being employed, and often they are complementary. Sometimes, qualitative research is a necessary preliminary step in designing surveys and questionnaires, and a necessary follow-up in explaining the patterns quantitative analyses appear to reveal. Sometimes, contrariwise, quantitative analyses reveal patterns in data generated from qualitative work that would otherwise pass unobserved.

Both observations should go without saying, but in some times and places they are not seen as self-evident or they get overlooked. Much of British criminology in the 1980s and 1990s, for example, was afflicted by a Luddite rejection of new technologies and characterised by the peculiar belief that quantitative research was 'positivist', 'managerial' or 'administrative', and inherently inferior to qualitative work. Similar attitudes were less evident but not absent from continental Europe and Commonwealth countries. Criminology and criminological research suffered.

Much of contemporary American criminology is sometimes, by contrast, said to be so mesmerised by quantitative technique that it sometimes loses sight of the subjects being studied, and especially loses sight of theory. Reference is regularly made to researchers setting out carrying quantitative hammers and looking for nails to hit.

Both mindsets are wrong. Different questions require different methods and styles, and all methods and styles require constant re-examination.

The questions *Offenders on Offending* addresses are older than criminology and as new as tomorrow, and they are the right questions. How do we learn things about crime and criminals, and how confident can we be about what we think we have learned? For so long as those questions have been asked, some people have sought insight from patterns revealed by numbers, and others have sought insight directly or indirectly from offenders themselves.

Two premises of *Offenders on Offending* are that quantitative researchers need to draw more heavily on the fruits of qualitative work and that questions of reliability, validity and generalisability lurk everywhere. This fine volume offers insights from pioneering qualitative researchers of the past 40 years and the innovative ideas of comparative youngsters. It contains articles on work done inside prisons and on work done in the community. The animating questions are what do we know, how confidently do we know it and how can we do better next time?

Wim Bernasco has provided an important service, and a valuable new resource and reference work, to researchers of very stripe. People working primarily within qualitative traditions will find here work at the cutting edge of methodological self-inquiry. People working primarily within quantitative traditions will see what they have been missing and how, by drawing on it, they can make their own work richer in nature and more nuanced in understanding.

Preface

Wim Bernasco

There are many things about crime that we can only learn from offenders. It is, however, not at all easy to find them and persuade them openly and truthfully to discuss their crimes. Most are difficult to reach, and many are unable or unwilling to provide the answers we need. This book is about the methodology of offender-based research. It is about what we can learn from criminals about crime and about what we can do to find them, to obtain their cooperation, to help them provide relevant and truthful answers, and to assess the validity of their accounts. The articles have been written by renowned scholars who have conducted offender-based research in a variety of settings. They share with us the lessons they have learned, discussing the many challenges of offender-based research but always keeping a clear focus on providing solutions. I hope and think the volume will appeal as much to experienced researchers as to students who are starting to find their way in offender-based research.

The book is the result of a three-day workshop held 8–10 October 2008 at the Netherlands Institute for the Study of Crime and Law Enforcement (NSCR), where the first drafts of the chapters were presented and discussed. After rewriting, the chapters were reviewed (single-blind) by two or three reviewers and the editor. The reviewers included authors, workshop participants and other researchers with relevant research expertise. They all greatly contributed to this volume by investing their time and effort. For this, I thank Margit Averdijk, Arjan Blokland, Fiona Brookman, Gerben Bruinsma, Heith Copes, Ric Curtis, Henk Elffers, Frank van Gemert, Barbra Van Gestel, Ben Hunter, Andy Hochstetler, Scott Jacques, Vere van Koppen, Joanne van der Leun, Marie Lindegaard, Jody Miller, Carlo Morselli, Claire Nee, George Rengert, Danielle Reynald, Neal Shover, Melvin Soudijn, Richard Staring, Lucía Summers, Isabel Verwee, Frank Weerman, Johan van Wilsem, Richard Wright, Birgit Zetinigg and Sheldon Zhang. At the NSCR, Ariena van Poppel helped organise the workshop smoothly, skilfully and cheerfully arranging accommodation, meals and local transport.

Throughout the project, Michael Tonry's coaching was essential. He provided help, feedback and support, and chaired the workshop in his usual professional and charming style.

Part 1
Setting the stage

Chapter 1

Learning about crime from criminals: editor's introduction

Wim Bernasco

There are many ways to learn about crime and about criminals. We can analyse criminal justice records, we can analyse data from surveys, and we can analyse the accounts of the offenders in their own words. The latter approach is referred to as 'offender-based research'. It usually involves talking to offenders and observing them in their own environment. Although offenders are potentially the richest source of information on their crimes and on their lives, offender-based research is difficult. Many offenders are hard to find, and many are unable or unwilling to tell us what we would like to know. Nevertheless, the offenders' perspective is vital to knowing and understanding crime.

Offender-based research evolved during the founding era of modern criminology, where it was at the heart of the Chicago School studies of crime. Already in the first decades of the past century, offender-based research included observational studies and case studies based on interviewing. For example, *The Gang* (Thrasher 1927) and *Street Corner Society* (Whyte 1937) are excellent examples of early ethnographic field-work. In *The Jack-Roller* (1930), *The Natural History of a Delinquent Career* (1931) and *Brothers in Crime* (1938), Shaw and his colleagues give book-length accounts of the lives of young offenders in the form of autobiographies – thus written in the first person – that were based on interviews with the boys and others acquainted with them, but also on official police records and newspaper stories.

The autobiographical style did not mean that Shaw and others took the boys' words for granted. There were clear concerns about the veracity and truthfulness of the accounts of these offenders. After stressing the importance of including other verifiable supplementary materials to evaluate and interpret more accurately the personal document, Shaw nevertheless underlines the value of subjectivity.

> It should be pointed out, also, that the validity and value of the personal documents are not dependent on its objectivity or veracity. It is not expected that the delinquent will necessarily describe his life-experiences objectively. On the contrary, it is desired that his story will reflect his own personal attitudes and interpretations, for it is just these personal factors which are so important in the study and treatment of the case. Thus, rationalizations, fabrications, prejudices, exaggerations are quite as valuable as objective descriptions, provided, of course, that these reactions be properly identified and classified. (Shaw 1930: 2–3)

Note that in the last sentence of the quotation, Shaw makes the subtle point that rationalisations and other distortions are important to record provided *they are recognised as such*. Obviously, this implies that it is possible to separate the objective event from the presentation of that event by the individuals involved. To claim that a person exaggerates a situation requires that we know what the situation actually was like.

In his Editor's Preface to 'The Natural History of a Delinquent Career', Ernest W. Burgess (1931) articulates a somewhat more critical attitude regarding the validity of the offenders' accounts, as he notes:

> Granted that the life-history possesses this unique human value, what if any is its function as an instrument of scientific inquiry? Is the writer of the document telling the truth? Is he not influenced, consciously or unconsciously, by his conception of his audience? Does any person know sufficiently well the causes of his own behavior for his statement, sincere though it may be, to be given full credence? These and other questions must be squarely faced before any final decision may be made upon the merits of the life-history as an instrument of scientific research. (Burgess 1931: xi)

Burgess went on to prescribe that the offenders' accounts were to be checked by 'interviews with parents, brothers and sisters, friends, gang associates, school teachers and principals, probation officers and social workers' (p. xii) and against official records of their crimes. In other words, he was emphasising the need for cross-validation of the data.

These quotations from early offender-based studies demonstrate that from the very beginnings, the veracity and validity of offender accounts have been issues concerning researchers working in the offender-based tradition.

Although offender-based research has always been an important branch of criminology, the last three decades have witnessed increasing streams of data originating from the criminal justice system and from victimisation surveys. In many parts of the world, criminal justice systems produce increasing streams of data on crime that are often accessible to researchers, including forensic evidence, CCTV footage and geocoded police reported crime incidents. The discovery of the victimisation survey has greatly impacted our knowledge of crime. The National Crime Victimisation Survey(NCVS) and the British Crime Survey (BCS) are large-scale surveys that have been around for decades, and the latest wave of the International Crime Victimisation Survey (ICVS) includes data from residents of 30 nations and 33 main cities all over the world.

Although it has never been absent from criminology, offender-based research has not gained a comparable increase in interest or dissemination. This is unfortunate, because if anyone can provide first-hand information on offending, offenders can. How did a person learn to commit an offence? How precisely was a specific crime enacted? What made the person commit the offence? What made the offender decide in favour of a particular target? What were his or her emotions like when committing the offence? Because the offenders' perspective is vital to knowing and understanding crime, to answer these questions researchers need to leave their desks and offices and go out onto the streets and into the bars, shops, schools, boardrooms and prisons, to talk to offenders and see them in their own environment.

Outside of their offices, the researchers that conduct offender-based research have to struggle with many issues and concerns. Offenders are difficult to reach, and many are unable or unwilling to provide the answers we need. A special concern of the researchers is the veracity of what they are being told by the people they are interviewing or hanging out with. Are they speaking 'the' truth or 'their' truth? While this holds true for any person that we involve as subjects in research, it may be of particular relevance for offenders, as we ask them detailed questions on their stigmatised and sanctioned behaviours. There are myriads of reasons to lie or misrepresent information, if only for the purpose of creating an impression of respectability. There are just as many ways in which the findings are biased because of miscommunications and misunderstandings between the researcher and the offenders, who often come from different social worlds. How can we prevent this from happening, and how can we detect it and correct it when it happens?

This book is about what we can do to maximise the validity of what offenders tell us about their offending. Offending is broadly defined to include not only criminal and deviant acts, but also the emotions and cognitions that play a role before, during or after the act. We will take stock of various methods to elicit information on offending from offenders, addressing the strengths and weaknesses of each of these methods, and discussing strategies to obtain the collaboration of offenders and to maximise the validity and reliability of the data. The emphasis will be on methods that aim to collect tangible information on the behaviour of offenders in general and on their criminal behaviour in particular.

In the following 15 contributions, researchers from around the world share their experiences and insights, all with a clear focus

5

on methodological issues of fieldwork among various types of offender populations. Each contribution deals with a few central issues:

- Where, when and how can we obtain information from offenders on offending?

- What can we learn from offenders that cannot be accessed from other sources?

- How can offenders be motivated to participate in research?

- How can offenders be motivated and helped to provide valid accounts of their offending?

- How can the information that offenders provide be checked and validated?

The remainder of this chapter is a concise overview that serves to introduce the other chapters by sketching their subject matter and role in the context of this book. The chapters are ordered in five parts that roughly correspond to the settings of offender-based research (Part 2, 'Prison settings' and Part 3, 'Field settings'), the people involved in offender-based research (Part 4, 'Social categories of offenders and researchers') and what many see as the subject matter of offender-based research (Part 5, 'Learning about the act'). This editor's introduction and the next two chapters together form Part 1 ('Setting the stage') and serve as a broad introduction to the theme of this volume.

In the second chapter, *Henk Elffers* develops a simple but very useful taxonomy of the mechanisms that can threaten the validity of the offender interview. He discusses misinformation, misunderstanding and misleading, and makes recommendations on how to minimise the bias and distortions that may result from these mechanisms. One of the recommendations is to have a strict interview protocol with detailed interviewer instructions regarding appropriate and inappropriate questions and responses, a recommendation that follows from the observation that interviewers may easily spoil the validity of the data by posing suggestive questions or by failing to ask questions because they draw premature conclusions. Remarkably, this recommendation seems to contrast with the tendency in offender-based research to have the interview proceed informally – in the style of a normal conversation – in order to make the interviewed person feel at ease and 'open up'.

In the third chapter, *Scott Jacques* and *Richard Wright* extend the theory of offender-based method that they started to develop in earlier work. In that work, they discussed the hypothesised effects of relational distance between researcher and research subject on the amount of recruitment, the required remuneration and the quantity and quality of information provided (Jacques and Wright 2008). In their contribution to this volume,

Jacques and Wright use Donald Black's pure sociology approach to argue that offenders to whom more law has been applied (in particular institutionalised offenders) participate more in research, require less remuneration and provide lower quantity and quality of information than offenders to whom less law has been applied (in this case non-institutionalised offenders).

The core issue in the three chapters in Part 2, 'Prison settings', is how the prison setting influences various aspects of offender-based research. Of particular concern is the validity of findings that are obtained by interviewing offenders about their offending behaviour outside prison.

In strong defence of the prison interviews, *Heith Copes* and *Andy Hochstetler* offer counterarguments to Jacques and Wright's hypothesis that institutionalised offenders provide lower quantity and quality of information than those who are non-institutionalised. Acknowledging the possible selectivity of the population of detained offenders, their plea in favour of prison interviews is not just an opinion but is based on a comprehensive argument backed up by a considerable body of literature that seems to underline the advantages of conducting offender-based research in prisons or other closed institutions.

Implicitly supporting this point of view, *Carlo Morselli* and *Pierre Tremblay* report on their research on criminal achievement among offenders incarcerated in Canadian penitentiaries. They provide a detailed account of how they and their interview team managed to set up the research in the penitentiaries and learned practical methods of obtaining cooperation and trust from the respondents. The study's main dependent variable was a highly quantifiable variable: self-reported criminal earnings before incarceration. Arguably, criminal earnings is a challenging variable to measure, one that is potentially fraught with the risks that Elffers describes as misinformation, misunderstanding and misleading. Morselli and Tremblay demonstrate how the consistency of such a complex measure can be successfully assessed in various ways. They conclude that the measurement of criminal achievement among prisoners is a tractable and promising approach. It even yielded positive reactions from the respondents, in part because the form and content of the questionnaires (crime inventory, calendar, accounting of legitimate and criminal earnings) surprised and intrigued many of them.

In the concluding chapter of Part 2, *Fiona Brookman* provides an exceptionally complete overview, not only of the challenges associated with offender-based research in prison and how they may be handled, but also of how interview data obtained in this way might be enhanced with other forms of information or insight. She addresses the ways in which written documents (police files, newspaper reports), accounts of other people (victims, witnesses, co-offenders, family), group interviews, follow-up interviews and visual data (photographs and CCTV footage) can be used to assess the validity and enhance the insights gained from a 'standard' interview. In doing so, she not only provides many examples of how these enhancements have been utilised in offender-based research and in other contexts, she also warns of relying too heavily on each of these triangulation methods.

Learning about crime from criminals does not only take place in the setting of an interview. The three chapters in Part 3, 'Field settings', are written by researchers, all three anthropologists, who have conducted offender-based research by going out into the streets to talk to offenders and observe them in their own environment. Field settings provide many opportunities for learning about crime in more diverse ways and more directly than through the verbal accounts of the offenders themselves.

The possibility of triangulation – the validation of findings by using multiple sources of information or multiple methods to obtain or analyse them – is considered one of the main advantages of ethnographic fieldwork. In the opening chapter of this part, *Marie Rosenkrantz Lindegaard* makes an argument in favour not only of multiple methods but in favour of multiple triangulations. She distinguishes between triangulation of methods (whereby the same phenomenon is studied by multiple methods), actor triangulation (multiple persons give an account of the same events) and triangulation of context (the same person is observed in various geographical places and social contexts). Her chapter is a comprehensive account of how she used these three triangulations in her ethnographic research among young men in South Africa, in which she explored how they, as a perpetrator or as a victim, got involved in violence or managed to evade involvement.

In the second chapter, *Frank van Gemert* makes a plea for ethnography. One of his observations is that in ethnography researchers are sometimes initially fooled and told lies, but that such lies seldom survive repeated observation. As a consequence, repeated measurement of the same phenomena is one of the pillars of ethnographic validity claims, besides triangulation to multiple sources and continuous reflections of the researcher. In line with this argument, van Gemert argues that the single-shot interview is not always the most effective way to obtain reliable and truthful information from offenders.

In the third chapter of this part, *Ric Curtis* explores how existing methods can help to ascertain validity in ethnographic fieldwork among hard-to-reach and hidden populations. This includes locating eligible respondents, recruiting them into research, eliciting accurate and credible information from them, and assessing the veracity of their accounts. Where Van Gemert's emphasis on repeated measurement and triangulation of sources presupposes a researcher who is sufficiently embedded in the community and has gone through a lengthy period of gaining acceptance, Curtis discusses methods of verification that are useful when triangulation is not feasible. Many of these methods reconstruct part of the social networks among the population studied, sometimes using information gained through the recruitment process, whereby respondents recruit other eligible research participants for their network. Although Curtis provides more examples of clear-cut lying and deceit than most other contributors do, his conclusion is remarkably optimistic: there are various ways to overcome problems of validity, and it is often our own preconceived ideas about what is possible that is the biggest impediment to what we want.

Offender-based research does not take place in a social vacuum. It involves researchers and respondents (and often also other persons such as prison warders or field recruiters) who often have very different social and cultural backgrounds. As a consequence, the issues of gender, social class and ethnicity that shape our interactions in daily life also play a role in the interactions between the participants in offender-based research. In passing, Morselli and Tremblay noted the reactions of respondents to their mixed-gender student interviewer team.

Offender-based researchers have to deal practically with issues of gender, social class and ethnicity. Not only must they take into account that their own gender, class and ethnicity (and those of their co-workers) may work in favour or against their recruitment attempts, they must also be aware of how the validity of their findings may be endangered by the biases caused by gender, class and ethnic differences or preoccupations. The three chapters in Part 4, 'Social categories of offenders and researchers', address the roles of gender, class and ethnicity in offender-based research.

Jody Miller reflects on the various ways in which the gender of the interviewer and the person interviewed may influence the style, length and content of interviews with offenders, very often in combination with other aspects of both persons' social positions, such as class, age and ethnicity. Although she remains profoundly skeptical about the extent to which interviews provide access to unmediated 'truth' about experiences, actions and motives, her analysis clearly shows that paying attention to the role of gender in interviews can reveal a great deal about how individuals construct accounts of their offending and about the contexts and meanings of offending. Drawing from three of her major studies, including both male and female offenders and male and female interviewers, she argues that interview-based research on offending is enhanced when research teams are diverse and when this diversity is taken into account when the data is analysed.

While the social positions of interviewer and interviewee without doubt affect the content of interviews, they can also strongly influence the recruitment process. This is clearly demonstrated in the contribution by *Sheldon Zhang*. It shows how he, as a researcher of Chinese descent, successfully gained and maintained access to Chinese human smuggling groups by making use of the large-role that social networks play in the Chinese community, both in the United States and in China. Ethnic and cultural proximity can help to gain trust. The networks not only facilitated recruitment, they also helped to validate data from different sources.

Of the various sources of information on crime that we have access to, the autobiography is probably the most curious and maybe also the most suspect. Against all odds, *Neal Shover* and *Ben Hunter* build their arguments on autobiographies of criminals or former criminals, and with remarkable results. Is there any reason to rely on the trustworthiness of the autobiography? If only because the writer has an obvious interest in presenting himself or herself positively, and enough time and opportunity to create a plausible story, autobiographies are usually taken with a grain of salt. But Shover and Hunter do not analyse the autobiography as a factual account of criminal behaviour. They read it as an apology, and an apology provides an interesting view on the thinking of the white-collar criminal. The authors' words echo Shaw's words that 'rationalizations, fabrications, prejudices, exaggerations are quite as valuable as objective descriptions, provided, of course, that these reactions be properly identified and classified'. An interesting observation is that white-collar criminals actually are good sources of information on white-collar crimes, precisely because they often lack a sense of guilt. They are not at all reluctant to talk about what they did and how they did it, because they do not see it as wrong. Consequently, those who interview white-collar criminals should be prepared to conform their vocabulary to the frames of their respondents, and avoid using words like 'offending', 'crime' and 'criminal'.

The chapters in Part 5, 'Learning about the act', have in common their strong focus on the act of offending itself. This interest includes observable behaviour, but certainly does not imply a narrow focus on it. Indeed, observable behaviour is something that can be registered and is often witnessed by victims or bystanders, or which can be derived from evidence on the scene. On the other hand, what goes on in the minds of offenders when they plan their act, when they choose their targets and when they make numerous other choices before, during and after the event is much more relevant to understanding the act of offending than the simple description of acts. Many offender-based researchers are essentially interested in offenders as experts in offending, and their task is to learn from the experts. Because many experts rely on automated routines and judgments, the art of learning from offenders is the art of learning from experts.

In the opening chapter of this part, *Claire Nee* reviews the offender-based literature on burglary, showing that a considerable amount of triangulated evidence has emerged over past decades on how the act of burglary is committed, and arguing that together these studies exemplify Glaser and Strauss's grounded theory, albeit realised not within a single study but within a series of subsequent studies, each one building on the results of prior studies. Nee describes a new method in which committing a burglary can be simulated with a computer program. The program is used to track the movements and choices of respondents inside burgled houses. This method, more than did prior methods, comes close to watching a real burglary in progress.

In an attempt to reveal information about offenders' spatial cognition and decision-making that would be difficult to elicit otherwise, *Lucía Summers*, *Shane Johnson* and *George Rengert* used two types of mapping tasks in offender interview. For various reasons, sketch mapping tasks, in which subjects are asked to draw maps that represent their knowledge of their physical environment, proved to be less useful than cartographic maps, which are actual topographical maps of a specific geographical area. Besides providing information on offenders' spatial cognitions, the mapping tasks also enhanced the subjects' ability to articulate their spatial decision-making. In line with Nee's description of current developments in the use of computer technology, the authors suggest that mapping tasks in offender interviews be extended to include Google Earth and other spatially informed technologies.

Sketch mapping tasks were also used by *Veronika A. Polišenská* in her research among burglars. She provides a comprehensive discussion of the possibilities and limitations of mental maps in general and in offender-based research in particular. One of the interesting aspects of her research among Czech burglars is the distinction between detailed local sketch maps and schematic travel maps. The first depict the burglar's knowledge of a specific local situation and are used by burglars who target properties in a limited area (possibly near their own residence); the latter resemble travel plans that link origins, destinations and major transit stops, and are typically drawn by burglars whose journey-to-crime is associated with extended travel beyond the boundaries of their city or town of residence. In addition to providing insights in how we can learn about concrete offending behaviour in offender-based research, Polišenská's chapter is also very useful in broadening our understanding of the conditions of offender-based research in prison in the Czech Republic.

In the last contribution to this part 'Learning about the act', *Birgit Zetinigg* and *Matthias Gaderer* describe their research among incarcerated bank robbers. They validated the robbers' accounts of their robberies not only with official files, but also with newspaper clippings describing these robberies, and with the results of site visits, where they talked to bank managers and clerks who witnessed the robbery, and where they took photos inside and outside the bank branch to record the physical characteristics of the site.

These five parts of the book, taken together, give a comprehensive overview of the challenges and possible solutions to issues of validity in offender-based research. As new issues are raised and new challenges are identified, the contributions will stimulate discussion about future directions in offender-based research. Most importantly, the accounts of the authors who have written this book show that offender-based research is a thriving field where exciting developments are taking place.

References

Burgess, Ernest W. (1931) 'Editor's preface', in C. R. Shaw and M. E. Moore, *The Natural History of a Delinquent Career*. Chicago: University of Chicago Press, pp. xi–xii.

Jacques, S. and Wright, R. (2008) 'Intimacy with outlaws: the role of relational distance in recruiting, paying, and interviewing underworld research participants', *Journal of Research in Crime and Delinquency*, 45: 22–38.

Shaw, C. R. (1930) *The Jack-Roller – A Delinquent Boy's Own Story*. Chicago: University of Chicago Press.

Shaw, C. R. (1938) *Brothers in Crime*. Chicago: University of Chicago Press.

Shaw, C. R. and Moore, M. E. (1931) *The Natural History of a Delinquent Career*. Chicago: University of Chicago Press.

Thrasher, F. (1927) *The Gang*. Chicago: University of Chicago Press.

Whyte, W. F. (1937) *Street Corner Society*. Chicago: University of Chicago Press.

Chapter 2

Misinformation, misunderstanding and misleading as validity threats to offenders' accounts of offending

Henk Elffers

Abstract

Approaching offenders in order to use them as a source of information on their offences obviously poses validity concerns. The present chapter reviews a number of validity threats: problems of misinformation, of misunderstanding and of misleading, and it looks into possible ways of addressing these problems.

When we contemplate the use of statements of offenders about the way they have committed an offence, we find ourselves right in the middle of the long-standing and ongoing debate on validity problems with self-reports on behaviour. For some research questions, the statements of offenders may be interesting *as such*, e.g. when we try to gauge the way they perceive their situation as offenders. However, when we intend to use offenders' statements as a source of information about their past behaviour, the validity question takes centre stage: to what degree can we interpret offenders' statements on their behaviour as a true representation of what has happened in the past, around the time they contemplated and actually committed an offence? In such cases, we are not interested in the offender as such, but we treat him as an instrument that makes available information about that offence and its associated decision-making.

The chapter has a modest aim: providing a short and systematic list of validity threats in the context of self-reports as can be found in the literature on validity problems, but with the explicit goal to take validity problems as seriously as we can and go a step further than a ritual writing down that the problem exists: 'Most investigators using such measures have simply acknowledged an awareness of the skepticism surrounding the reliability and validity of self-reported data', as Sobell (1976) formulated it. We should try and counteract validity problems as well as we can. Though I couch the discussion here in terms of the validity of reports about offending, many considerations remain valid in a general self-report context (Wentland and Smith 1993).

The basic structure of the problem recognises three entities: the researcher, the offender and the offence, the last seen as a behavioural act of the offender. The researcher asks the offender to inform him of certain characteristics of the offence. I use 'offence characteristics' in a rather broad sense; offender's decisions about the offence are also seen as offence characteristics. So, we are interested in offenders' accounts of their own actions, cognitions and emotions, as well as in what they can report about the situation in which the offence occurred, e.g. what others (co-offenders, victims, guardians) did or did not do around the moment of the offence.

By discussing validity problems, I will silently pass over a number of other problems that may hamper the use of offenders' statements, i.e. cases where the respondent does not provide any information. I will just mention a few here: the offender refuses outright to give an answer to the question; the person interviewed is innocent of the offence, hence cannot inform you about it at all; the offender is physically or mentally not fit for answering questions; the authorities prohibit interviewing the offender; the offender is no longer available for interviewing. Such problems may well be very relevant and unpleasant, but I will not treat them here as they are not validity problems.

Let us consider for what reasons the information being provided by the offender can misrepresent the offence characteristics. Three types of problems may be identified:

- *Misinformation* – the respondent himself does not have access to the sought for information.

- *Misunderstanding* – there is mutual misunderstanding between offender and researcher about what is communicated: the respondent answers a different question than was intended by the researcher, while neither respondent nor researcher is aware of it.

- *Misleading* – there is unwillingness from the side of the offender to tell the truth to an outsider; the respondent is actually trying to mislead the researcher by knowingly returning an incorrect answer.

Misinformation

Even if it is beyond all doubt that a person participated in an event, it does by no means follow that he can inform us about each and every detail of what happened: he may after all *not be well informed* himself. There may be two reasons for that: either the respondent has never had access to the information sought for (e.g. he has never reflected on his role in an offence at all), or he indeed may have possessed the relevant information but has meanwhile *forgotten* it.

Misinformation: being uninformed

The first of these – never having possessed the information – may be on a trivial level, such as when the informant simply did not get information that in principle was available but somehow not picked up by the respondent. An offender cannot inform in a trustworthy way about the time his co-offender left the scene of the crime if he did not see him leaving during the actual event itself. It is very important to distinguish between factual and counterfactual reports. Factual questions address what has happened or what the respondent actually was aware of or thought and argued. Counterfactual questions address what the respondent would have done or thought if he – counterfactually – had been aware or had been informed. In ordinary conversation we switch easily between those two, without much consequence. If a friend has bought a red sweater in a shop where you know they also sell purple ones, you may remark 'So you did not like the purple one?' and get as an answer 'I really prefer red', which may mean: 'Indeed, I compared the red and purple sweaters, and I happened to prefer the red one', but also 'I have not seen a purple one, but anyway in general I like red more than purple' or perhaps 'I was immediately so much taken by this red one that I did not care for any other, purple or not'. So it remains wholly unclear whether the person actually has observed that purple sweaters were on sale or not. In everyday conversation we usually do not sort out such ambiguous statements, but when gathering information in a research context it pays to be more alert. The *lesson to learn* from this is that we should meticulously work out the formulation of our questions in order to be able to take the respondent by the hand and guide him through the interview so that we get exactly the detailed information we need.

In many a case, however, it may be argued that it is useless to ask people certain questions because they simply cannot have access to the relevant process. Nisbett and Wilson (1977) in their famous article 'Telling more than we can know' are very critical where reports about *motivations* are concerned ('why did you do this or that'). They hold that it is useless to ask people about their motivations, arguing that they are generally unaware of *why* they did something. The argument largely hinges on the suggestion that many choices are made unconsciously, and that asking people to explain the why's of a choice only leads to the construction of a rationalisation tale that is made up after the fact. Following Calahan (1968), Nisbett and Wilson (1977) point out that people sometimes even do not know that they have made a choice or even that they have displayed a certain behaviour. The *lesson* here is that forcing people to give answers on motivation questions may well force them to return answers that have only a feeble relation to reality. Bluntly summarised: do not expect useful information on motivation from interviewing offenders on their motives.

Misinformation: memory problems

The second problem about not being able to give an informative answer on questions about offences is the memory problem. It is well documented that memory about offences is lacking in precision. Medanik (1982) has already shown that accuracy of verbal statements about problem behaviour deteriorates with time, and the feared telescoping effect (people remembering events either much too early or much too late in time) is usually formidable in size (e.g. Elffers and Averdijk 2007). In any event, reports about offences seem to be rather dependent on the time elapsed between behaviour and questioning (e.g. Farrington 1973; Elffers 1991: 28).

Psychology has produced an impressive literature about memory and memory lapses (e.g. Cohen 1996; Stein *et al.* 1997; Wolters 2002). One of the phenomena that is of interest for offender interviewing is the *consistency bias*: memories about former feelings and attitudes tend to be biased towards present-day feelings and attitudes. This is of course especially problematic when we interview offenders during detention about events that have led to their convictions. For example, looking backwards, they may well remember that they had already evaluated the crime as a rather risky one, even when that had not been true in the moment itself. They will tend to report about what happened with the hindsight that it happened to go wrong. Moreover, people tend to remember events and behaviours often by adapting them to so called *schemata*: events will be remembered according to what people perceive as a normal or model *schema* of such an event. So people may report that a dog in the house where they broke in looks like their schematised image of a watch dog (large, fierce, barking hard), even when it was a dwarf pinscher. Such adaptive recollection is most likely to occur in peripheral details that do not take centre stage in the event being questioned and recollected.

One of the great problems with memory in this context is that people usually suffer from inadequate *source monitoring*, i.e. knowing where a remembered detail comes from. In the literature about police interrogation and false memories it has been shown that repeatedly talking about an event, such as occurs in often repeated interrogations, may bring details into somebody's memory, not because he remembers it from the event itself, but because he remembers it from a previous session in which that element has been discussed between him and the investigators. For example, the suspect says he does not know in what type of car his victim arrived, but then the officers say 'Come on, man, all witnesses say it was a grey Ford Transit'. The suspect then may, in a subsequent session, honestly but erroneously think that he remembers that detail. Actually he does remember it, but is not able to recognise that it comes from a different source (the former interrogation session) rather than from his own observation during the crime.

A *lesson to be learned* here is that these points must be taken into consideration when we talk with offenders on past offences. We ought to be very conscious not to plant cues into the offender's memory by talking about various aspects of the offence that we may know already from other sources, and we must be aware of consistency bias. In my opinion these problems point to the requirement for a rather strict protocol on the interviewer's side. By specifying meticulously what should be asked and said, we do not run the risk of inadvertently issuing information to the respondent. Rather paradoxically, specifying what should be said is indeed necessary for making clear what not to say. A less formal interview style (open interviewing, in which the researcher is free in reacting on what the respondent says) may be much more dangerous, as exactly this natural interplay between questions and answers issues memory implant cues that are hard to discover, even when the interview is fully recorded. The literature on police interrogation should be a warning here (e.g. Ost *et al.* 2002). On the other hand, using closed answer formats will certainly be instrumental in getting distorted or imagined versions of reported events. So it is my impression that a rather strict protocol on the interviewer's side, and an open answer format for the offender, preferably in one session only, should be seen as the least problematic with respect to memory problems.

Misunderstanding

Under the misunderstanding heading we can classify the problem of mismatching reference frames (e.g. 'violence' meaning something different to the respondent than to the interviewer). A good example is from my own interviewing of people about tax fraud (Elffers 1991; cf. Webley *et al.* 2006). One of my respondents was a successful plumber who was adamant: he would pay every cent of his taxes, otherwise he would loose his self-respect, he said. Later on it turned out that he had an active moonlighting business on the side for which he paid no tax of course. Confronted with that, he was truly (at least, I thought he was stating the truth about that) surprised about my questioning that practice: 'That is not tax dodging. Tax fraud is if you do not pay over your 9–5 business'. Tax inspectors will not agree, I am afraid. Such mismatching definitional problems will occur quite often in offender interviewing, as long as the interviewer has not fully grasped the offender's perspective. In fact many white-collar offenders – just as this plumber did – do not perceive themselves as offenders at all. Shover and Hunter (this volume) argue that data provided by white-collar criminals may be reliable because their belief in their own innocence gives them little reason to mislead. Consequently, using words that imply guilt in the interview, such as 'offence' or 'crime', should be discouraged. In their experience such offenders have no problem in talking about their actions as long as we do not call these actions offences or crimes. The *lesson* here is that this seems to call for a rather open interview style, in which it is first of all left to the respondent to retell his story in his own words, and then probe into what exactly is meant by terms and so on. Notice that this advice is contrary to that in the section on memory!

Under the misunderstanding heading we should of course also attend to common 'good questioning practice' as taught in any standard methods book in interviewing, in order to safeguard ourselves against common errors like not listening, taking undeserved short cuts, misunderstanding of questions or answers. A special problem is that, at least in Dutch practice, a large proportion of the detainee population does not speak Dutch very well, or not at all. Widespread misunderstanding will be an acute threat then, and it seems necessary to use native speakers of the mother tongues of the offenders in such a case.

Misleading

People may actively or passively try to give a wrong picture to the interviewer. In the case of reporting about offences this may go both ways. It could be denying that any offence has taken place or at least underplaying the role of the respondent in it making the behaviour appear less immoral, or other neutralisation techniques. It could, on the contrary, also be bragging about criminal adventures or reporting non-existing or overstated offences. Both of these fall under the denominator of social desirability (Crowne and Marlowe 1960; Edwards 1990). Paulhus (1984) showed that social desirability may come in two varieties: either the wish to deceive the interviewer, or, more fundamentally, the wish to present a picture to oneself, and therefore also to the outside world, that is more in accordance to what the reporter would wish it to be, i.e. the unwillingness to tell the truth to oneself. In such a case the offender may prefer to reinterpret events within the coveted frame of his self-image (self-presentational concern: Baumeister 1982; dissonance reduction: Bem and McConnell 1970; life as a story: Goffman 1959), which, as said, may go both ways: understating or overstating. Calahan (1968) summed up this problem nicely: 'it may well be that certain questions on past behavior do not lend themselves to accurate measurement through survey research approaches, not because people do not want to tell the truth to others, but because they cannot tell the truth to themselves.' The *lesson* here is that we must face the possibility that offenders sometimes cannot help us at all with relevant information.

A special case may take the form of *momentary consistency bias*, i.e. that people in an interview do not like to give an inconsistent picture of themselves and therefore bring their later answers in line with previous ones. People like to be – in fact need to be – consistent in the way they see themselves. They cannot imagine themselves doing things that are not in accordance with their self-image, hence they will bring their answers in line with their self-image. Deviating from this course would imply a major restructuring of the way they see themselves. It is unlikely that a simple interview could trigger such a profound exercise (Hessing *et al.* 1988). Goffman (1959) argued that people perceive their life as stories, in which they may be motivated to increase the 'shapeliness' of their personal stories to protect their self-image. Momentary consistency will be acted out when in the same session we first ask an offender whether he has committed a certain offence, and then later on in the session we ask about his attitudes with respect to this offence. It is rather inconsistent, and therefore unattractive to the speaker, to describe oneself as a street robber and at the same time have a very negative attitude with respect to street robbery. People carry on in the mood that they have adopted in the beginning of an interview. A *lesson to be learned* may be that it sometimes is wise to consider multiple interview session well apart in time, one session focusing on what actually happened, another on attitudes and judgments. Momentary consistency may be less important then, though it will presumably not be totally absent either.

The problem of misleading reports by the respondent is perhaps the hardest of all to tackle. Of course, obvious prerequisites, like convincing assurance of anonymity, are important. Some researchers hope that being interviewed is to prisoners such a welcome break from dull prison life that they will be more open. However, it is hard to believe that the self-presentation problem will be completely overcome this way. Can lie detection techniques be of help here? I doubt it. Forensic psychological literature has indeed demonstrated that lies are associated with certain observable characteristics, but the scientific literature (as opposed to some police literature – for a discussion see National Research Council 2003) pretty unequivocally denies the possibility of classifying statements as lies in a reliable way (Vrij 2008) if no data independent of the respondent are available. Moreover, lie detection techniques are usually geared to a situation where interrogator and respondent have a quite different relationship from that of a research setting, that is a naturally antagonistic one. Though various instruments to measure social desirability tendencies have been proposed (Paulhus 1991; Tourangeau and Smith 1990; cf. also Wentland and Smith 1993), an operational strategy to apply 'corrections' to answers has not emerged (Harteveld 2005).

Linking offenders' self-reports to other information

Indeed, in a number of studies it has been shown that careful question-naires or interviews on such different behaviours as traffic offences, tax evasion, social security fraud and dog fouling returned answers that had very low to no correlation with observational measures from a different source (Van Giels *et al.* 1990; Elffers 1991; Hessing *et al.* 1993; Webley and Siviter 2000). Low correlation may be the consequence of any one or more of the three problems signalled here: misleading, misinformation or misunderstanding. The *lesson* here is that it seems always advisable to get outside information to compare with self-reports, and if these cannot be obtained – which often will be the case – a researcher should consider refraining from using self-reports on offending. Perhaps, however, this advice is a bit too gloomy. Many of the concerns voiced here address the direct admission or denial of an offence. In much offender-based research on offending we may hope that the fact that an offence has taken place is granted by the offender, especially if he is going to be interviewed when in custody, as he very well knows then that the interview is because of his offence. The focus of such an interview is on the ways and means, the choices and deliberations, and may, hopefully, be understood by the offender as addressing him in his professional capacity as offender. Will this improve the situation? It may well be helpful against underreporting, but on the other side of the coin it may well enhance bragging.

Summing up

Validity concerns are at the heart of interviewing offenders on past offending, and any researcher should feel encouraged to look the problem in the eyes and at least check for himself where he stands with respect to the various problematic aspects identified above: misinformation (not knowing, memory problems), misunderstanding (different interpretations of questions and answers between interviewer and respondent) and misleading (under-reporting, over-reporting, self-presentation).

Listing possibly threatening factors by no means demonstrates that self-reports are useless. In any given case, a threat may not materialise, or it will affect responses only marginally, or no other method will do better. However, I would like to challenge all researchers using offenders' statements about their past offences to address why their approach may be vulnerable or resistant to such problems. Any one who admits that interviewing offenders on past offending behaviour is perhaps in his case too vulnerable to the serious threat from validity factors should consider instead whether it is possible to extract information on offending by different methods, or consider combining various methods where feasible. Perhaps some research questions would be better answered through observations, through interrogating offenders on different hypothetical scenarios or through discussing with offenders in the real world how they would operate if contemplating an offence. All these methods have their own validity concerns which must be thought through as well, of course.

References

Baumeister, R. F. (1982) 'A self presentational view of social phenomena', *Psychological Bulletin*, 91: 3–26.

Bem, C. G. and McConnell, H. K. (1970) 'Testing the self-perception explanation of dissonance phenomena: on the salience of premanipulation attitudes', *Journal of Personality and Social Psychology*, 14: 23–31.

Calahan, D. (1968) 'Correlates of respondent accuracy in the Denver reliability survey', *Public Opinion Quarterly*, 32: 608–21.

Cohen, G. (1996) *Memory in the Real World* (2nd edn). Hove: Psychology Press.

Crowne, D. P. and Marlowe, D. (1960) 'A new scale of social desirability independent of psychopathology', *Journal of Consulting Psychology*, 24: 349–54.

Edwards, A. L. (1990) 'Construct validity and social desirability', *American Psychologist*, 45: 287–9.

Elffers, H. (1991) *Income Tax Evasion. Theory and Measurement*. Deventer: Kluwer.

Elffers, H. and Averdijk, M. D. E. (2007) *Aangeven aan te geven? [Reporting Having Reported]*. NSCR Report 2007/5. Leiden: NSCR.

Farrington, D. P. (1973) 'Self-reports of deviant behaviour: predictive and stable?', *Journal of Criminal Law and Criminology*, 64: 99–110

Goffman, E. (1959) *The Presentation of Everyday Self in Everyday Life*. New York: Doubleday.

Harteveld, A. (2005) 'De raadselachtige werking van de randomized response: het effect van impression management op het rapporteren van gevoelige gedragingen' ('The mysterious functioning of the randomized response method: the effect of impression management on reporting sensitive behaviour') in J. Blad (ed.), *Rijzende sterren in het veiligheidsonderzoek (Rising Stars in Safety and Security Research)*. Den Haag: Boom Juridische uitgevers, pp. 177–88.

Hessing, D. J., Elffers, H. and Weigel, R. H. (1988) 'Exploring the limits of self-reports and reasoned action: an investigation of the psychology of tax evasion behavior', *Journal of Personality and Social Psychology*, 54: 405–13.

Hessing, D. J., Elffers, H., Robben, S. J. and Webley, P. (1993) 'Needy or greedy? The social psychology of individuals who fraudulently claim unemployment benefits', *Journal of Applied Social Psychology*, 23(3): 226–43.

Medanik, L. (1982) 'The validity of self-reported alcohol consumption and alcohol problems: a literature review', *British Journal of Addiction*, 77: 357–82.

National Research Council (2003) *The Polygraph and Lie Detection*. Washington, DC: National Academies Press.

Nisbett, R. E. and Wilson, T. D. (1977) 'Telling more than we can know: verbal reports of mental processes', *Psychological Bulletin*, 84: 231–57.

Ost, J., Vrij, A., Costall, A. and Bull, R. (2002) 'Crashing memories and reality monitoring. Distinguishing between perceptions, imaginations and "false memories"', *Applied Cognitive Psychology*, 16: 125–34.

Paulhus, D. L. (1984) 'Two-component models of socially desirable responding', *Journal of Personality and Social Psychology*, 46(3): 598–609.

Paulhus, D. L. (1991). 'Measurement and control of response bias', in J. Robinson, P. Shaver and L. Wrightman (eds), *Measures of Personality and Social Psychological Attitudes*. San Diego, CA: Academic Press, pp. 17–60.

Sobell, L. C. (1976) 'The Validity of Self-Reports. Towards a Predictive Model'. Unpublished dissertation, University of California, Irvine.

Shover, N. and Hunter, B. W. (2010) 'Blue-collar, white-collar: crimes and mistakes', in W. Bernasco (ed.), *Offenders on Offending: Learning About Crime from Criminals*. Cullompton: Willan.

Stein, N. L., Ornstein, P. A., Tversky, B. and Brainerd, C. (eds) (1997) *Memory for Everyday and Emotional Events*. Mahwah, NJ: Laurence Erlbaum Associates.

Tourangeau, R. and Smith, T. W. (1996) 'Asking sensitive questions: the impact of data collection mode, question format, and question context', *Public Opinion Quarterly*, 60: 275–304.

Van Giels, B., Hessing, D. J. and Elffers, H. (1990) *Rood Rijden: Determinanten van het rijden door rood onder automobilisten* [*Determinants of Red Light Jumping by Motorists*]. Rotterdam: ECSTR.

Vrij, A. (2008) *Detecting Lies and Deceit: Pitfalls and Opportunities* (2nd edn). Chichester: John Wiley & Sons.

Webley, P. and Siviter, C. (2000) 'Why do some dog owners allow their dogs to foul the pavement? The social psychology of minor rule transgression', *Journal of Applied Social Psychology*, 30: 1371–80.

Webley, P., Adams, C. and Elffers, H. (2006) 'Value added tax compliance', in E. J. McCaffery and J. Slemrod (eds), *Behavioral Public Finance*. New York: Russell Sage Foundation, pp. 175–205.

Wentland, E. J. and Smith, K. W. (1993) *Survey Responses: An Evaluation of Their Validity*. San Diego, CA: Academic Press.

Wolters, G. (2002) 'Herinneren door getuigen' ['Eyewitness memory'], in P. J. van Koppen, D. J. Hessing, H. L. G. J. Merckelbach and H. F. M. Crombag (eds), *Het Recht van Binnen. Psychologie van het Recht* (*Handbook of Psychology of Law*). Deventer: Kluwer, pp. 397–415.

Chapter 3

Apprehending criminals: the impact of law on offender-based research

Scott Jacques and Richard Wright

Abstract

The past quarter century has witnessed the emergence of a rich methodological literature devoted to various ways of tapping into the offender's perspective on crime. Whatever its virtues, that literature has remained almost wholly atheoretical. We recently introduced a preliminary theory of research grounded in the perspective of pure sociology. In this chapter we seek to extend that theory by examining how law and normative status affect offender-based research. We argue that as more law is applied to actors (i.e. as the normative status of persons or groups declines), the probability that those actors are recruited for offender-based research increases, the amount of remuneration provided to them for participation decreases and the quality of data obtained from them decreases. We conclude by offering theoretically situated, practical advice about the ways in which criminologists might maximise data while minimising costs associated with recruitment and remuneration.

Criminologists require data collected via fieldwork, interviews and experiments with offenders in order to understand fully the factors that influence lawbreaking (see, for example, Brookman *et al.* 2007; Carr 2005; Copes *et al.* 2007; Curtis 2003; Jacobs and Wright 2006; Jacques and Wright, forthcoming; Jacques and Wright 2008a, 2008b; Morselli 2001; Nee and Meenaghan 2006; Shover 1996; St Jean 2007; Venkatesh 2006; Zhang *et al.* 2007). Research has shown conclusively that criminals know things about crime that others do not (see, for example, Wright *et al.* 1995; Logie *et al.* 1992), and this makes them a valuable source of information about lawbreaking. The challenge for methodologists and criminologists is to determine how best to access that information. What sort of research strategies yield the most valid and plentiful data at the lowest cost?

The past quarter century has witnessed the emergence of a rich methodological literature devoted to various ways of tapping into the offender's perspective on crime (see, among many others, Adler 1990; Dunlap and Johnson 1999; Ferrell and Hamm 1998; Glassner and Carpenter 1985; Jacobs 1998, 2006; Mieczkowski 1988; Williams *et al.* 1992; Venkatesh 2008; Wright *et al.* 1992). Whatever its technical merits, this literature has remained strikingly atheoretical. The advance of methodology and criminology is slowed by atheoretical ideas because they are difficult to falsify through empirical research (see Popper 2002).

Without a theory of offender-based research, the task of finding the most economical strategy for accessing information held by criminals is, at best, foggy and inefficient or, at worst, practically impossible. This is true because if recommendations for improving research are not deduced from a falsifiable theory, then those recommendations cannot be shown to be wrong with empirical data. And if recommendations cannot be falsified, then bad advice may linger longer than it should and good advice may not be adopted at the rate or magnitude it deserves. Even if a theory of offender-based research is eventually disproved through empirical research, both the theory and the research benefit methodology and criminology by revealing what factors do not produce more valid and plentiful data at a lower cost.

With the limits of atheoretical method in mind, we recently introduced a preliminary theory of research (Jacques and Wright 2008c). In this chapter, we seek to extend our theory by examining how law and normative status affect offender-based research. In turn, we review the current state of our conceptualising and theorising on offender-based research, define the concepts of law and normative status, hypothesise the impact of those variables on offender-based research and conclude by offering theoretically situated, practical advice about the ways in which criminologists might maximise data while minimising the costs associated with recruitment and remuneration.

Toward a theory of offender-based research

There are at least two *first* steps in developing a theory of offender-based research. The first step is to specify what is being explained. What *is* 'offender-based research'? The next step is to make predictions regarding how offender-based research is affected by any given variable. What *causes* 'offender-based research'?

What is offender-based research?

Research, or *method*, is a social behaviour defined as the process of recording or analysing information. Research is a quantitative variable: it increases with every additional datum collected or analysed. Because research can be quantified, measured and empirically observed, it is theoretically explainable. In other words, we can predict what situations, persons and groups are most likely to be involved in surveys, interviews, experiments, observations or analyses.

Offender-based research is defined here as the process of obtaining information about crime through conversation with or observation of persons who have personally engaged in crime (at least once). More narrowly, there are at least three distinct parts of collecting information from offenders: recruitment, remuneration and data collection (Jacques and Wright 2008c; also see Dunlap and Johnson 1999; Wright *et al.* 1992).

Recruitment is defined as the process of interacting with criminals and convincing them to provide data. *Remuneration* is defined as payment for participation in research. *Data collection*, or *data quality*, is defined as the process whereby knowledge about crime is ascertained by criminologists through conversation with or observation of criminals.

Defined thusly, offender-based research is a social, empirical and quantifiable variable measured by: (1) the number of recruitments or the amount of effort (e.g. time) spent on recruitment; (2) the number of remuneration payments or the amount of remuneration provided; and (3) the number of data collection sessions (e.g. interviews) or the amount of valid data collected. *More recruitment of, remuneration of, or data collection with offenders* is equivalent to *more offender-based research*.

A purely sociological perspective

Although offender-based research is first and foremost a means of knowledge production, it is also a quantitative variable and therefore it should be theoretically explainable. This raises the question: *What factors affect the amount of recruitment, remuneration, and data quality in offender-based research across situations, people or groups?* Although many theoretical perspectives may have the ability to explain research, our theory draws on the orienting paradigm known as *pure sociology* (see, especially, Black 1976, 1995, 1998, 2000; Cooney 2006).

Social structure = social status + social distance → social behaviour

The goal of pure sociology is to understand how the quality (type) and quantity (amount) of social behaviour is affected by social structure. *Social structure* is defined as the relative social status of and also social distance between every actor in a particular situation.

Actors, meaning individuals or groups, vary in *social status*, meaning their position in a social hierarchy. There are at least five forms of social status: *vertical status*, measured by wealth; *radial status*, measured by community involvement and production; *corporate status*, measured by memberships and organisation; *symbolic status*, measured by knowledge and conventionality; and *normative status*, measured by freedom from social control. *Higher* social status is equivalent to more wealth, community involvement, production, memberships, organisation, knowledge, conventionality and freedom.

Actors also vary in *social distance*. Whereas social status is the characteristic of one actor, social distance may be thought of as the characteristic of (at least) two actors. There are at least three forms of social distance: *relational distance*, measured by the amount of interaction between two actors; *corporate distance*, measured by the number of common memberships; and *social distance*, measured by the number of cultural similarities. *Closer* social distance is equivalent to more prior interaction between actors, more common memberships held by them and more similarities in their ideas and forms of expression.

Pure sociologists attempt to specify how variability in the social status of and social distance between actors involved in a situation affect their social behaviour. There are many different kinds of social behaviour. Broadly speaking, however, pure sociology is used to explain the social behaviours of resource transfer and accumulation, interaction, organization, culture and social control. In short, the goal is to determine how variability in social structure causes variability in the kind and amount of social behaviour that occurs.

For instance, Black (1976) theorises that – all else equal – crimes by lower-status persons against higher-status persons are more likely to be punished by the government than are similar crimes by higher-status persons against lower-status persons. Related to this idea, Black (1983) also argues that retaliation – or justice without the government – is more likely to occur as access to law decreases, and so the social structures least likely to lead to law are most likely to result in vengeance. The perspective of pure sociology has also been used to explain a number of other behaviours, including avoidance (Baumgartner 1988), retaliation (Black 1983, 1998; Cooney 1998), ideas (Black 2000), welfare (Michalski 2003), art (Black 1998: 168–9), predation (Cooney 2006), genocide (Campbell 2009) and victimisation related to active offender research (Jacques and Wright forthcoming).

It is possible to develop purely sociological theories in several ways. One way is to look at the available data on a behaviour and attempt to identify its patterning with social status and social distance. If patterns are found then they might provide a good start toward a more comprehensive and nuanced theoretical understanding. This is what we might call a 'mining' approach to theory development. Another way, however, is to specify a theory – meaning to make predictions about how variability in

26

social structure affects behaviour – with nothing but intuition, which may or may not be built on years of experience with the topic being theorised. This is what we might call an 'intuitive' approach to theory development. The predictions produced by both forms of theory development, mining and intuitive, will ultimately require formal testing to ascertain their worth. How theories are 'made' is distinct from – and less important than – whether theories are 'good', meaning relatively valid, simple, general, testable and original (see Black 1995).

The epistemology and perspective of pure sociology

As a theoretical perspective, the value of pure sociology is its generality, simplicity, testability and originality (for details, see Black 1995). The paradigm is original because it intentionally disregards what other sociological perspectives find key: motivations and emotions. By disregarding those factors, purely sociological theories become more testable because motivations and emotions are subjective and so beyond *direct* empirical measurement. Although motivations and emotions often are construed to explain 'why' behaviour happens, the concepts of motivation and emotion are, at best, unobservable or, at worst, nothing real at all; thus their inclusion in theoretical models makes them less simple and, again, less testable than theories that eschew such explanatory variables. Perhaps in the end, however, the ultimate question is whether any given theory is valid. Although empirical data and statistics can be used to test pure sociological theories and directly falsify them, theories concerned with motivations and emotions can never be directly falsified because those factors are subjective. Therefore the validity of such theories will forever remain opaque.

An important point to clarify is that even if a purely sociological *theory* – such as Black's (1976, 1983) well-known theory of law or theory of self-help – was falsified through empirical testing, this does *not* mean that the purely sociological *perspective* is falsified or invalid. A perspective, or paradigm, is a way of conceptualising the world and a strategy for explaining it (e.g. social structure). On the other hand, a theory is a statement that specifies how concepts are causally related to each other. Thus a purely sociological theory may be incorrect (falsified) if it does not significantly predict how sociological factors affect each other, but this does not necessarily mean that those sociological factors do not exist or affect each other in different ways. For example, even if more intimate relationships do not in fact reduce retaliation (which is a theory – see Black 1998), this does not necessarily mean that there are no real things such as 'intimacy' and 'retaliation' (which are concepts) or that they have no causal relationship. Note, however, that if there are no such real things as 'intimacy' and 'relational distance' then a theory that uses them as independent or dependent variables will be necessarily invalid, at least in part.

A preliminary theory of method

We have begun to develop a preliminary 'theory of method', or 'theory of research', nested in the paradigm of pure sociology (Jacques and Wright 2008c, forthcoming). Although the theory we are developing may eventually be falsified, our ultimate goal is to stimulate a debate in science, especially criminology, which leads to greater *theoretical understanding* of research. As discussed above, a valid theory of research would be useful because its implications could be adopted to improve research and, in turn, the findings that emerge from it.

In our initial attempt to explain research, we restricted our theoretical attention to *active offender research* and the explanatory variable known as *relational distance* or intimacy. By definition, the relational distance between a researcher, liaison (e.g. a recruiter) and offender decreases as the amount of prior contact between them increases (see Black 1976). Two persons, for example, who drink alcohol or smoke marijuana together are closer in relational distance to each other than are two people who do not. Likewise, two persons who have a mutual friend, acquaintance or colleague are closer in relational distance than two people without such a contact. We addressed the question: how does relational distance affect the process of obtaining information from unincarcerated criminals?

Our own experiences in recruiting, paying and interviewing drug dealers (Jacques and Wright 2008c) alongside those of other criminologists (Bourgois 2003; Hoffer 2006; Mieczkowski 1988) led to the following hypotheses. As the relational distance between a researcher, liaison and offender decreases: (1) the likelihood that the offender will be recruited increases; (2) the amount of remuneration provided to the offender decreases; and (3) the quality of data collected increases. For example, our theory predicts that a researcher's criminal-friend or family member is more likely than a stranger to agree to participate in research, to do so for little or no compensation and to be honest.

We concluded our initial attempt at theorising method by observing that relational distance is not the sole factor influencing method. Among other possibilities, we speculated that the quantity of law applied to offenders represents an especially strong candidate in this regard (Jacques and Wright 2008c: 34). In this chapter, we seek to extend our preliminary theory of research by examining how law and normative status affect recruitment, remuneration and data quality in offender-based research.

Law and normative status

Social control refers to 'the normative aspect of social life. It defines and responds to deviant behaviour ... Social control is found wherever and whenever people hold each other to standards [whether] on the street, in prison, [or] at home' (Black 1976: 105). Social control is found among many living organisms including, for example, insects (Wenseleers and Ratnieks 2006), non-human primates (de Waal 1989), archaic tribes (see Boehm 2000), modern suburbanites (see Baumgartner 1988) and gang members (see Decker and Van Winkle 1996). The concept of social control encompasses many kinds of behaviours (see Black 1998; Horwitz 1990; Jacques and Wright 2008b), such as law, retaliation, avoidance, negotiation, humiliation, gossip, protest, apology and suicide.

Law is 'governmental social control' (Black 1976: 2). Put differently, law 'is ... the normative life of a state and its citizens, such as legislation, litigation, and adjudication' (p. 2). We can theorise law because it is a quantitative variable – some situations involve more law than others. Law increases with every additional prohibition, arrest, indictment, prosecution, fine or imprisonment.

Actors vary in the amount of law that has been applied to them in the past. Law 'divides people into those who are *respectable* and those who are not' (Black 1976: 105, emphasis added). *Normative status*, or what is also called *respectability*, is a 'record' of an actor's subjection to social control (Black 1976, 1998). The more law that has been applied to an actor in the past, the lower that actor's *formal* normative status. For example, a person who has been arrested, indicted, prosecuted, fined or imprisoned is lower in normative status than someone who has not been subjected to those kinds of formal social control. On the other hand, an actor's *informal* normative status decreases as more informal social control (e.g. vengeance or avoidance) is applied to that actor.

Law and normative status are important variables to explain, but they are also explanatory factors that influence social life. Theory and research suggest, for instance, that actors who are poor, unemployed, unmarried and uneducated not only are more likely to be punished with formal control, but also that actors who have been punished by formal control are *subsequently more likely* to be poor, unemployed, unmarried and uneducated (Black 1976, 1998; Cooney 1998; Western 2006; Wilson 1987, 1996). The point here is that a number of factors determine the variable amounts of law applied across situations, persons and groups, and that this variability in the application of law has consequences for subsequent behaviour.

A theory of normative status and offender-based research

We now propose a theory comprised of a series of propositions that use the explanatory variable of formal normative status to predict variability in offender-based research. To empirically illustrate the theory and suggest how to test it, the propositions are directly followed by hypotheses – or empirical predictions – about the way in which normative status, as measured by institutionalisation, affects recruitment, remuneration and data quality.

There are many measures of formal normative status, such as the number of times a person has engaged in crime or been arrested, prosecuted or punished, or the amount of punishment received in any particular case (Black 1976). For purposes of clarity and brevity, however, this chapter focuses on normative status as measured by government institutionalisation, such as confinement in a jail or prison. All else equal, a person who is confined in a government institution has lower normative status than a person who is free. In other words, criminals who are free have higher normative status than those who are institutionalised, all else equal (e.g. their arrest record or the amount of time they are institutionalised).

To be clear, the purpose of this theoretical exercise is to stimulate a discussion regarding which empirically measurable factors have a statistically significant and substantial impact on the various parts of offender-based research.

Normative status and recruitment

Recruitment is the process by which a researcher goes about locating criminals and convincing them to cooperate in data collection. Recruitment is a quantitative variable measurable by the amount of social interaction devoted to convincing actors to participate in research. Recruitment can last minutes, days or longer, and the number of actors recruited could be one, one hundred or more.

Most offender-based research relies on criteria-based sampling to locate criminals, meaning only those individuals who possess the social, psychological or biological characteristics relevant to research are recruited. The recruitment of offenders for research can take place within the walls of a government institution or in the free world. In both settings, researchers often depend on a liaison, or 'broker', to recruit criminals for participation. In government institutions, a researcher relies on what could be called a 'gatekeeper', that is a person who works for a government institution and has the 'right' to grant researchers access to persons residing therein. In the free world, a researcher depends on what is commonly called a 'recruiter', who is in a position to connect criminals to researchers because of her or his personal and professional ties to both groups.

Just as there are two locales in which criminals can be recruited, so too there are two 'kinds' of criminals: institutionalised and 'free' (i.e. not institutionalised). As relates to law and normative status, institutionalised criminals by definition are lower in normative status than free criminals because they are subject to more law (holding constant other past subjections to law). This conceptual distinction raises the empirical and theoretical question: does normative status, as measured by institutionalisation, affect recruitment in offender-based research?

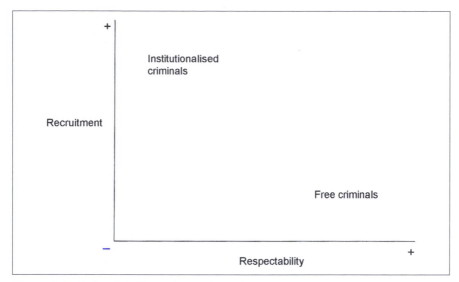

Figure 3.1   Respectability and recruitment

We speculate that it does and offer the following proposition: *Recruitment to offender-based research increases as the normative status of a criminal decreases.* In other words, a criminal is more likely to be recruited for research as more law is applied to that criminal (cf. Black 2000: 350). We hypothesise, then, that offender-based research has more often recruited institutionalised criminals than free ones (see Figure 3.1).

The proposition and hypothesis predict that throughout the history of offender-based research, there have been more recruitments of institutionalised than free criminals. For studies that collect data from institutionalised criminals *or* free criminals (but not both), the above proposition predicts institutionalised criminals are more likely to be recruited. And for studies that collect data from both kinds of offenders, the proposition predicts a larger number of recruited institutionalised offenders per study and on average.

Normative status and remuneration

Remuneration refers to objects and services given to a criminal in return for participation in research. Remuneration is perhaps the most straightforward, generalisable and successful strategy for convincing persons to provide data (see Dunlap and Johnson 1999). Like recruitment, remuneration is a quantitative variable, and is measurable by the amount of resources (objects or services) provided to a criminal as compensation for taking part in research. For instance, a researcher can compensate a participant with no money, £50 or £100.

Does normative status, as measured by institutionalisation, affect

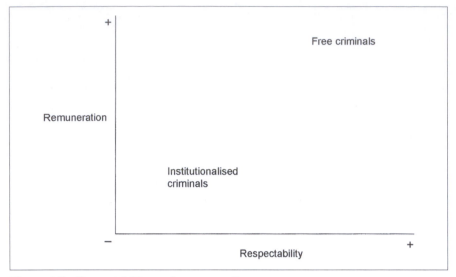

Figure 3.2   Respectability and remuneration

remuneration in offender-based research? We believe that it does and suggest the following proposition: *Remuneration for participation in offender-based research increases as the normative status of a criminal increases.* Stated differently, criminals will receive greater remuneration as less law is applied to them. As relates to institutionalised versus free criminals, then, we hypothesise that the latter group typically receives more compensation than the former for participation (see Figure 3.2).

The above proposition and hypothesis predict that, on average, institutionalised participants have been remunerated less than free-ranging ones. For studies that collect data from institutionalised criminals *or* free criminals, the above proposition predicts a larger *average* remuneration fee in studies of free criminals. For studies that collect data from both kinds of criminals, the proposition predicts larger remuneration for the free-ranging participants, both on average and per study.

Normative status and data quality

The time, effort and resources devoted to recruitment and remuneration are squandered if the resultant data are sparse or false. *Data quality* is defined as the amount of valid information collected from an offender and is a quantitative variable measurable by the amount of data produced and the truthfulness of that information. For example, some offenders never stop talking but others never start, and some interviewees never tell the truth, others tell half of it and still others are almost wholly forthright and honest.

Does normative status, as measured by institutionalisation, affect the quality of data produced in offender-based research? We hypothesise that

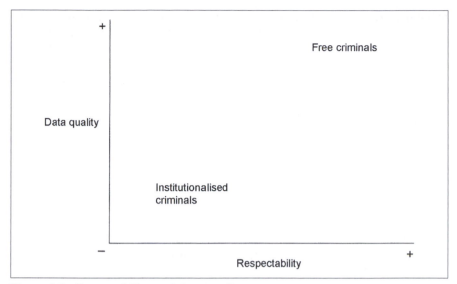

Figure 3.3 Respectability and data quality

it does and offer the following proposition: *Data quality in offender-based research increases as the normative status of a criminal increases.* What this means is that a criminal provides more plentiful and valid data as less law is applied to that criminal. If we compare free criminals to those who are institutionalised, we hypothesise that institutionalised offenders provide less valid data than do free-ranging ones (see Figure 3.3).

The proposition predicts that, on average, institutionalised research participants have provided lower-quality data than have free participants. For studies that collect data from institutionalised criminals *or* free-ranging ones, the above proposition predicts that *per participant*, studies of free offenders produce higher-quality data. For studies that collect data from both kinds of criminals, the proposition predicts that per participant, less valid and truthful data are provided by the institutionalised participants than by the free-ranging ones.

Summary and future directions

Above, we propose a preliminary theory of how research with offenders 'behaves'. Actors' normative status increases as less law is applied to their behaviour, and we have addressed the question: how do law and normative status affect recruitment, remuneration and the quality of data produced in offender-based research? We theorise that as criminals become lower in normative status then they become more likely to be recruited for research, less likely to receive remuneration if they are recruited and less likely to provide valid and plentiful data. Empirically speaking, this theory suggests the following hypotheses: compared to free criminals, institutionalised offenders are more likely to be recruited for research, to receive less remuneration and to provide less valid information.

It is important to note, however, that the purpose of this chapter is to stimulate an academic debate surrounding what factors influence the quality and quantity of research, especially of the offender-based variety. With that said, it is obvious that there is much more to understanding variability in recruitment, remuneration and data quality in research than can be explained solely as a function of formal normative status and government institutionalisation.

Therefore substantial work remains to be done by theorists and researchers before methodologists, including criminologists, will have produced a clear picture of what factors influence variability in research. At present, advancing a theoretical understanding of method requires theorists to develop explanations that can be falsified empirically, and researchers to put those theories to the test with empirical data and statistical analyses.

Formal testing

Science advances by falsifying or supporting theory through empirical testing (Popper 2002). As mentioned above, the two *first* steps in developing a theory of offender-based research are to specify what it *is* and then to make predictions about what *causes* it. The next step in developing a theory of method is testing it with empirical data and then refining or discarding it based on those findings, if necessary.

At present, we – as a field – have practically no readily available empirical information bearing on how offender-based research behaves. Of course, it would have been possible for us to provide anecdotal evidence for our proposed hypotheses (see, for example, the history of burglary research provided by Nee, this book), but doing so would be haphazard. We urge researchers to compile a 'purpose-built' data set and use statistical analyses to determine what empirical factors do or do not influence offender-based research.

Throughout this chapter we have alluded to how our theory might be tested: count and statistically analyse whether, in comparison to free offenders, institutionalised offenders are: (1) more likely to be recruited for research; (2) less likely to be remunerated for participating; and (3) more likely to provide lower quality data. There are many conceivable research designs through which empirical data bearing on these hypotheses might be obtained.

Although we do not want to stymie researchers' creativity, allow us to outline two possible methods for testing our theory of method. The first empirical test would survey criminologists and collect information on the following:

- The number of institutionalised criminals and free criminals recruited for research *interviews* in a specific time span, such as over the past calendar year. The theory is supported if, controlling for all other influences (including their relative population size), institutionalised criminals are, statistically speaking, significantly more likely than free criminals to be recruited for research. The theory is falsified if institutionalised criminals are less likely than free criminals to be recruited or if there is no difference.

- For each interview, the amount of remuneration offered to the participant concerned. The theory is supported if, controlling for all other influences (including the quality of the data provided), institutionalised criminals receive significantly less remuneration than free criminals for participation. The theory is falsified if institutionalised criminals receive more remuneration than free criminals or if there is no difference.

- For each interview, its length. The theory is supported if, controlling for all other influences (including the amount of remuneration), interviews with institutionalised criminals are significantly shorter than interviews with free criminals. The theory is falsified if interviews with institutionalised offenders are longer or if there is no difference.

- For each interview, the number of questions asked by the researcher(s) *in relation to* the number answered by the participant(s). The theory is supported if, controlling for all other influences (including the amount of remuneration and time length), interviews with institutionalised offenders have a significantly lower rate of response than interviews with free criminals. The theory is falsified if interviews with institutionalised offenders have a higher rate of response or there is no difference.

Such a research design would provide empirical evidence on how institutionalisation affects recruitment, remuneration and data quantity in the real world of offender-based research.

What that research design would not tell us, however, is whether institutionalisation affects data *validity*. Given the problems inherent in measuring validity (especially in a field such as criminology), an experimental design is probably the best option for determining the validity of our theory of method. One conceivable experiment is outlined below:

- To control for the influence of recruitment, remuneration and data quantity:

  - Use purposive sampling to recruit one armed robber who is institutionalised and one who is free, and then use snowball sampling to recruit a sample of institutionalised and free armed robbers (e.g. a total of 30 for each group).

- Participants will not receive remuneration directly, but £100 in cash will be delivered to a non-institutionalised person of their choosing following completion of the interview.

- Promise all participants that the interview will take approximately 5 minutes to complete and consists of four questions. To avoid or minimise travel costs and time for the participant, the interview can take place at any time and place of their choosing (given necessary constraints, such as being inside the institution).

• To determine the relationship between institutionalisation and data validity, ask each participant the following questions:

- What is your birth name?

- In which city were you born?

- What is your date of birth?

- What is your mother's year of birth?

• Using the answers to those questions, attempt to obtain a birth certificate for each participant. If an adequate number of birth certificates can be obtained for both institutionalised and free armed robbers *and* they do not significantly differ in this regard, then a test of validity may be made.

- The theory is supported if, controlling for all other influences, institutionalised offenders provide a significantly less valid – meaning less accurate – answer regarding their mother's year of birth than do free criminals.

- The theory is falsified if institutionalised criminals provide a significantly more accurate answer regarding their mother's year birth than do free criminals or there is no difference.

It will not be possible to test the theory based on the answers to the first three questions because institutions often have such information readily available for each offender and, knowing this, such persons are, we theorise, more likely to provide valid information on those topics than free offenders (for details see the section, 'Toward a purely sociological theory of research', below). This is why it is necessary to first determine whether the two groups are equally likely to provide enough information to obtain a birth certificate; again, if they differ in this regard than the following test cannot proceed.

The experiment just described is just an example of how to test whether institutionalisation affects the validity of findings in offender-based research. Whatever research design is used to test our theory of validity, the key will be to ask questions that have independently verifiable answers, such as those found on birth certificates or in official (and accurate) records.

Before tests take place, however, we recommend the development of theories – from various perspectives – to guide the process.

Theory development

Testing requires controlling for extraneous factors. Therefore when testing theories of method it is important to control for the predictions of alternative perspectives. Unfortunately, and as discussed above, there are practically no other theories of offender-based research. As far as we are concerned, it is better to have empirically untested (yet falsifiable) theories of offender-based research than it is to have no such theories at all. *Before the study of offender-based research can progress with tests, we must first create theories to test.* This is not a venture that can be accomplished overnight. Yet until accomplished, research on offender-based research will be crippled for lack of the orienting force of theory. It is analogous to searching in the dark.

What we are saying here is that the field is best off if we *first* produce theories of offender-based research and *then* test them with empirical data and statistical analyses. We can no longer wait for theory development, but holding off on formal testing is perhaps prudent at this time because theory on offender-based research is virtually non-existent. Economically speaking, it is less costly to develop and then test theories than it is to collect data, mine them to form a theory and then test that theory with other data. This is especially true when you consider that the invalidation of theories – so long as they are falsifiable – provides knowledge by telling us what factors *do not* influence a particular behaviour, such as research.

Toward variegated perspectives on offender-based research

The necessity of theory development before testing becomes clear when considering the implications of *perspectives* for the factors being explained. Perspectives are abstract ways of understanding the empirical world around us. Whereas theories differ in their predictions, perspectives differ in their conceptualisations and strategies for forming predictions. The way a perspective conceptualises the world will affect how we *define* offender-based research and its component parts. For instance, a purely sociological theory of research defines 'data quality' as an entirely objective measure: the amount of information (whether obtained through sight, taste, smell, touch or hearing) that is true, meaning congruent with empirical, social events as they actually happened. Because (1) pure sociology is only concerned with objective, social variables, and (2) information on those variables is obtained through empirical observations (including communication with offenders), which themselves are social behaviours, then data quality is entirely objective according to this perspective – it is the *amount* of information that accurately describes *what actually happened* (validity).

On the other hand, there are other perspectives, such as ethnography, that view 'validity' as subjective and not empirical. Thus a theory of validity can never itself be valid because there is no such thing as validity. If a theoretical perspective takes the view that there is no such empirical thing as validity, then a theory of offender-based research grounded in that perspective will, perhaps, have a qualitatively different set of behaviours to explain than the ones explained in this chapter (recruitment, remuneration and data quantity and validity).

These conceptual differences make clear that a theoretical understanding of offender-based research must first be preceded by definitions. Not all perspectives will have the same conception of offender-based research. Methodologists and criminologists should view the behaviour of offender-based research through the 'lens' of various perspectives in order to define it so that theories grounded in those perspectives can be developed. Not only different theories – but also different conceptions – of research may serve to improve our scientific understanding of how data is obtained.

Toward a purely sociological theory of research

The theory proposed in this chapter is preliminary and builds on our earlier work (Jacques and Wright, 2008c). When combined with our initial work on the impact of relational distance on offender-based research (Jacques and Wright 2008c), our current theory is comprised of six propositions that explain three behaviours:

1. Recruitment to a study increases as criminals lose normative status and become closer in relational distance to researchers.

2. Remuneration for participation increases as criminals gain normative status and increase in relational distance from researchers.

3. Data quality increases as criminals gain normative status and reduce relational distance from researchers.

There is much more to social structure than normative status or relational distance, and so future work should specify what other factors may affect the quality and quantity of method. For instance, variability in *knowledge* – which is an aspect of *symbolic status* – stands out as being particularly promising. After all, the goal of science is to produce knowledge.

Knowledge about crime is what criminologists are attempting to generate, and offender-based research is one way of doing so. Knowledge is a quantitative variable, and is measurable by the total and relative number of ideas a person possesses (Black 1976). For instance, some people know more things than others (e.g. the difference between a professor and a college student) and some things are more widely known than others (e.g. more people know how to drive a car than fly a plane).

It seems to us that research may behave as a function of knowledge. For example, one conceivable hypothesis is that recruitment, remuneration and data quality increase as the knowledge of a criminal increases. In other words, the more a criminal knows about a certain behaviour (e.g. robbery or murder) and the less others know about that behaviour, the more likely that criminal is to be recruited for research, to be paid more for doing so and to provide a substantial amount of truthful information. This hypothesis predicts, for instance, that a murderer may receive greater remuneration for participation in research than a robber for the reason murderers and murders are less common than robbers and robbery.

The theory that knowledge affects method is important because, among other things, the effect of normative status on method may otherwise be distorted when analysed empirically. If knowledge is not simultaneously considered, for example, it might *appear* that the relationship between normative status and remuneration is U-curved rather than linear (see Figure 3.4).

It seems eminently plausible that convicted criminals typically are paid less than non-convicted persons for doing exactly the same work. This pattern in life, we suggest above, also applies to remunerating criminals in offender-based research. At the same time, however, we might ask: why would a person who has never committed a crime be paid for providing information about how to commit crimes? The proposition above suggests that because non-criminals know less about crime – and not because they

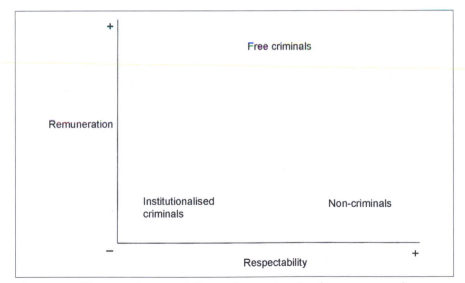

Figure 3.4 U-curve of respectability and remuneration (consequence of not controlling for knowledge)

have more normative status – they are relatively unlikely to be recruited and remunerated because they are relatively unlikely to provide useful data.

All of the above is simply to say that the purely sociological theory of research is in its infancy and requires further elaboration for the *total* effect of social structure to be understood.

Related to this point, it is important to recognise that there are many different ways of operationalising the concept of 'normative status'. This chapter has focused on how institutionalised offenders are more likely than free criminals to be recruited for research, less likely to receive remuneration for taking part and less likely to provide high-quality data. However, our theory of normative status and offender-based research also predicts, for instance, that a person who has committed 100 robberies is more likely to be recruited for research than is a person who has committed just one robbery, that a criminal who has been arrested many times should receive less remuneration for participation than does an offender who never been arrested, and that a murderer is less likely to provide a plentiful amount of valid information about her or his crime than is a burglar. The point here is that different operationalisations of normative status may lead to different albeit similar predictions, and that the full range of these predictions should be specified and examined in future work.

Toward alternative theories of offender-based research

Although our theory is grounded in the paradigm of pure sociology, there are other theoretical perspectives that could be and *should be* employed to explain method. To be sure, method is a complex behaviour that is likely affected by a broad range of factors, such as rationality, learning and opportunity, among others. Methodologists and criminologists should explore the potential of all theoretical perspectives for understanding and improving the process that produces much of the data used in criminological research. We must begin to take atheoretical ideas about how method behaves and turn them into falsifiable predictions that can be tested with empirical research. Even better yet would be to have a coherent theoretical perspective to organise those predictions.

Copes and Hochstetler (this volume), for instance, suggest a number of hypotheses (some more falsifiable than others) that may explain variation in data quality. Their review suggests that the quantity and validity of data obtained from offenders may increase as:

1. therapeutic benefits for participation increase;

2. perceived restitution for participation increases;

3. free time for an offender increases (i.e. as boredom increases);

4. admiration held by an offender for a researcher increases;

5. costs for participation decrease or benefits increase;

6. trust for a researcher held by an offender increases;

7. social distance between a researcher and government officials increases;

8. intoxication of an offender decreases; and

9. the amount of time between an offender's action and the researcher's questions about the action decreases.

Other contributions to this book may move the field toward a comprehensive theory of offender-based research. For example, Shover and Hunter (this volume) provide good reasons for why the validity of data provided by white-collar criminals may vary substantially from the data provided by lower-class criminals. Zhang (this volume) is in some respects suggesting that as the amount of *guanxi* between a researcher and participant increases, then so too should the validity and quantity of information obtained from that participant. And Miller's (this volume) insights provide a starting point for a gendered theory of offender-based research (but also see Weinreb 2006). These theoretical alternatives should be fully developed.

Recommendations

With that in mind, we remind ourselves that an important challenge for criminologists is to determine how best to access the undoubtedly valuable information possessed by criminals. What sort of methodological strategies yield the most valid and plentiful data at the lowest cost? The idea that method can be theorised is important because explanations of method can be used to generate practical strategies for improving it, whether by increasing recruitment success, reducing remuneration payments or enhancing data quality. Regardless of what factors are found to affect method, it should be possible to manipulate them in order to achieve our desired goals. The findings of science are themselves objective factors that influence the world. For example, criminologists have found that governments sometimes discriminate against minorities (Phillips 2009), and this 'finding' is itself a 'social fact' – it exists in the real world; it is read, heard and spoken about. This social fact, in turn, has changed the real world to the degree that it has reduced such forms of government discrimination against minorities. In other words, the goal of science is to produce findings about the real world, and those findings become real things that themselves feed back and affect that world.

Allow us to conclude, then, by suggesting three pieces of practical advice deduced from the theory developed in this chapter:

- Criminals can be more easily recruited from institutions than from the free world.

- Criminals can be paid less for providing data in an institution than in the free world.

- Criminals provide more valid data when they are free than when they are institutionalised.

These practical suggestions tell us that while it may be easier and cheaper to interview institutionalised criminals, on the whole they may be less valuable informants than active criminals.

Whatever the validity of the above assertions, the key takeaway point is that because this chapter makes falsifiable predictions regarding the effect of law on offender-based research, the practical advice suggested herein can be discarded or adapted according to the findings of empirical research that tests the theory. Before testing our theory, however, we hope that competitors will emerge who provide their own falsifiable theories that shed additional light on the behaviour of offender-based research.

Acknowledgments

We wish to thank Eric Baumer, Mark Cooney and Lucía Summers for their comments on an earlier draft. The work on which this chapter is based was supported in part by a Research Grant Award from the National Science Foundation, Division of Social and Economic Sciences, Law and Social Sciences Program (NSF ID #: 0819090), and by a Graduate School Dissertation Fellowship from the University of Missouri – St Louis. Direct correspondence to: Scott Jacques, Department of Criminology and Criminal Justice, University of Missouri – St Louis, One University Boulevard, St Louis, MO 63121 (e-mail: scottjacques@umsl.edu).

References

Adler, P. (1990) *Ethnographic Research on Hidden Populations: Penetrating the Drug World*, NIDA Monograph, 98: 96–111.

Adler, P. (1993) *Wheeling and Dealing: An Ethnography of an Upper-Level Drug Dealing and Smuggling Community* (2nd edn). New York: Colombia University Press.

Baumgartner, M. P. (1988) *The Moral Order of a Suburb*. New York: Oxford University Press.

Black, D. (1976) *The Behavior of Law*. New York: Academic Press.

Black, D. (1983) 'Crime as social control', *American Sociological Review*, 48: 34–45.

Black, D. (1995) 'The epistemology of pure sociology', *Law and Social Inquiry*, 20: 829–70.

Black, D. (1998) *The Social Structure of Right and Wrong* (rev. edn). San Diego, CA: Academic Press.

Black, D. (2000) 'Dreams of pure sociology', *Sociological Theory*, 18 (3): 343–67.

Boehm, C. (2000) 'Conflict and the evolution of social control', in L. D. Katz (ed.), *Evolutionary Origins of Morality: Cross-Disciplinary Perspectives*. Exeter: Imprint Academic.

Bourgois, P. (2003) *In Search of Respect: Selling Crack in El Barrio* (2nd edn). New York: Cambridge University Press.

Brookman, F., Mullins, C., Bennett, T. and Wright, R. (2007) 'Gender, motivation and the accomplishment of street robbery in the United Kingdom', *British Journal of Criminology*, 47 (6): 861–84.

Campbell, B. (2009) 'Genocide as social control', *Sociological Theory*, 27: 150–72.

Carr, P. J. (2005) *Clean Streets: Controlling Crime, Maintaining Order, and Building Community Activism*. New York: New York University Press.

Cooney, M. (1998) *Warriors and Peacemakers: How Third Parties Shape Violence*. New York: New York University Press.

Cooney, M. (2006) 'The criminological potential of pure sociology', *Crime, Law, and Social Change*, 46: 51–63.

Copes, H., Forsyth, C. J. and Brunson, R. K. (2007) 'Rock rentals: the social organization and interpersonal dynamics of crack-for-cars transactions in Louisiana, USA', *British Journal of Criminology*, 47 (6): 885–99.

Curtis, R. (2003) 'Crack, cocaine and heroin: drug eras in Williamsburg, Brooklyn', *Addiction Research and Theory*, 11 (5): 349–66.

de Waal, F. (1989) *Peacemaking Among Primates*. Cambridge, MA: Harvard University Press.

Decker, S. and Van Winkle, B. (1996) *Life in the Gang: Family, Friends, and Violence*. New York: Cambridge University Press.

Dunlap, E. and Johnson, B. D. (1999) 'Gaining access to hidden populations: strategies for gaining cooperation of drug sellers/dealers and their families in ethnographic research', *Drugs and Society*, 14: 127–49.

Ferrell, J. and Hamm, M. S. (1998) *Ethnography at the Edge: Crime, Deviance, and Field Research*. Boston, MA: Northeastern University Press.

Glassner, B. and Carpenter, C. (1985) *The Feasibility of an Ethnographic Study of Property Crime: A Report Prepared for the National Institute of Justice*, mimeo. Washington, DC: National Institute of Justice.

Hoffer, L. D. (2006) *Junkie Business: The Evolution and Operation of a Heroin Dealing Network*. Belmont, CA: Thomson Wadsworth.

Horwitz, A. V. (1990) *The Logic of Social Control*. New York: Plenum Press.

Jacobs, B. A. (1998) 'Researching crack dealers: dilemmas and contradictions', in J. Ferrell and M. S. Hamm (eds), *Ethnography at the Edge: Crime, Deviance, and Field Research*. Boston, MA: Northeastern University Press, pp. 160–77.

Jacobs, B. A. (2006) 'The case for dangerous fieldwork', in D. Hobbs and R. Wright (eds), *The Sage Handbook of Fieldwork*. Thousand Oaks, CA: Sage, pp. 157–68.

Jacobs, B. and Wright, R. (2006) *Street Justice: Retaliation in the Criminal Underworld*. New York: Cambridge University Press.

Jacques, S. (2010) 'The necessary conditions for retaliation: toward a theory of non-violent and violent forms in drug markets', *Justice Quarterly*, 27 (2): 186–205.

Jacques, S. and Wright, R. (2008a) 'The relevance of peace to studies of drug market violence', *Criminology*, 46 (1): 221–53.

Jacques, S. and Wright, R. (2008b) 'The victimization–termination link', *Criminology*, 46 (4): 1009–38.

Jacques, S. and Wright, R. (2008c) 'Intimacy with outlaws: the role of relational distance in recruiting, paying, and interviewing underworld research participants', *Journal of Research in Crime and Delinquency*, 45 (1): 22–38.

Jacques, S. and Wright, R. (forthcoming) 'Dangerous intimacy: toward a theory of violent victimization in active offender research', *Journal of Criminal Justice Education*.

Jansen, A. C. M. (1991) *Cannabis in Amsterdam: A Geography of Hashish and Marihuana*. Amsterdam: Coutinho.

Korf, D. J. (1995) *Dutch Treat: Formal Control and Illicit Drug Use in the Netherlands*. Amsterdam: Thesis Publishers.

Logie, R., Wright, R. and Decker, S. (1992) 'Recognition memory performance and residential burglary', *Applied Cognitive Psychology*, 6: 109–23.

Michalski, J. H. (2003) 'Financial altruism or unilateral resource exchanges? Toward a pure sociology of welfare', *Sociological Theory*, 21 (4): 341–58.

Mieczkowski, T. (1988) 'Studying heroin retailers: a research note', *Criminal Justice Review*, 13: 39–44.

Morselli, C. (2001) 'Structuring Mr Nice: entrepreneurial opportunities and brokerage positioning in the cannabis trade', *Crime, Law, and Social Change*, 35 (3): 203–44.

Nee, C. and Meenaghan, A. (2006) 'Expert decision making in burglars', *British Journal of Criminology*, 46: 935–49.

Phillips, S. (2009) 'Legal disparities in the capital of capital punishment', *Journal of Criminal Law and Criminology*, 99 (3): 717–39.

Popper, K. (2002) *The Logic of Scientific Discovery*. New York: Routledge Classics.

St Jean, P. K. B. (2007) *Pockets of Crime: Broken Windows, Collective Efficacy, and the Criminal Point of View*. Chicago: University of Chicago Press.

Shover, N. (1996) *Great Pretenders: Pursuits and Careers of Persistent Thieves*. Boulder, CO: Westview Press.

Venkatesh, S. A. (2003) 'Review of *Ethnography at the Edge: Crime, Deviance, and Field Research* edited by Jeff Ferrell and Mark S. Hamm', *American Journal of Sociology*, 105 (1): 284–6.

Venkatesh, S. A. (2006) *Off the Books: The Underground Economy of the Urban Poor*. Cambridge, MA: Harvard University Press.

Venkatesh, S. A. (2008) *Gang Leader for a Day: A Rogue Sociologist Takes to the Streets*. New York: Penguin Press.

Weinreb, A. (2006) 'Limitations of stranger-interviewers in rural Kenya', *American Sociological Review*, 71: 1014–39.

Wenseelers, T. and Ratnieks, F. L. W. (2006) 'Enforced altruism in insect societies', *Nature*, 444 (7115): 50.

Western, B. (2006) *Punishment and Inequality in America*. New York: Russell Sage Foundation.

Williams, T., Dunlap, E., Johnson, B. D. and Hamid, A. (1992) 'Personal safety in dangerous places', *Journal of Contemporary Ethnography*, 21 (3): 343–74.

Wilson, W. J. (1987) *The Truly Disadvantaged: The Inner City, the Underclass, and Public Policy*. Chicago: University of Chicago Press.

Wilson, W. J. (1996) *When Work Disappears: The World of the New Urban Poor*. New York: Vintage.

Wright, R., Logie, R. and Decker, S. (1995) 'Criminal expertise and offender decision-making: an experimental study of the target selection process in residential burglary', *Journal of Research in Crime and Delinquency*, 32: 39–53.

Wright, R., Decker, S., Redfern, A. and Smith, D. (1992) 'A snowball's chance in hell: doing fieldwork with active residential burglars', *Journal of Research in Crime and Delinquency*, 29: 148–61.

Zhang, S. X., Chin, K. and Miller, J. (2007) 'Women's participation in Chinese transnational human smuggling: a gendered market perspective', *Criminology*, 45 (3): 699–733.

Part 2
Prison settings

Chapter 4

Interviewing the incarcerated: pitfalls and promises

Heith Copes and Andy Hochstetler

Abstract

Narratives obtained in interviews of offenders provide rich details about the motivations and causes of crime, the nature of criminal calculus and the situational dynamics of the criminal event. There is little question, therefore, that offender accounts have provided criminologists with invaluable insights. Concern does exist, however, about how best to locate and recruit participants to produce the most valid sources of data. One concern focuses on the relative strengths and benefits of recruiting and interviewing incarcerated versus active offenders. In this chapter, we discuss the potential limitations and strengths of prison-based interviews. We begin by examining the criticisms of interviewing in prisons and offer rebuttals to these. We then discuss the various advantages of recruiting and interviewing inmates. The ever-present issue of whether accounts elicited from incarcerated offenders and active offenders vary in significant ways is addressed throughout and reviewed in the conclusion.

Criminologists have a long history of interviewing those engaged in illicit behaviours to gain insights into the nature of crime and criminality (Bennett 1981). Interviews give offenders the opportunity to explain their offences and lifestyles from their own perspective and to elaborate on the motivations and causes of crime, the criminal calculus and the perceived effectiveness of efforts to deter crime. When the voices of those engaged in illicit activity are coupled with the researchers' analyses, academics and law enforcement professionals can get a more realistic glimpse into the world of offenders, move closer toward theoretical explanation of criminal lifestyles and decisions, and better design effective crime control policy (Pogrebin 2004).

Posing open-ended questions to offenders is important for a full understanding of crime and criminality. But, if we are to garner the benefits of the offenders' perspectives, it is necessary that researchers locate these individuals. While there are many places ethnographers can locate offenders (e.g. street corners, bars, shelters, rehabilitation meetings, jails or prison), here we are concerned primarily with the captive audience of incarcerated offenders. When seeking the perspective of inmates, researchers face some challenges that those seeking and interviewing active offenders do not, including scepticism from others about the validity of their findings. Those criticising incarcerated offender samples sometimes repeat the analogy of the animal in the zoo to make the point that one cannot learn about street-life from the incarcerated. According to Polsky (1998: 116), 'We can no longer afford the convenient fiction that in studying criminals in their natural habitat, we would discover nothing really important that could not be discovered from criminals behind bars. What is true for studying the gorilla of zoology is likely to be even truer for studying the gorilla of criminology.' While this colourful metaphor has been repeated by those justifying their research strategy, it may be specious. Currently, we have no empirical evidence that active offenders reveal different aspects about their lives and crimes than do incarcerated ones. In fact, the limited amount of evidence comparing the two types of samples shows consistency in the information they provide (Nee 2003). And, even if accounts do differ between these two groups, it is still not known which is more accurate or rich for qualitative analysis. The lack of empirical validation of the superiority of active-offender research means criminologists risk repeating unsubstantiated conclusions drawn from secondary sources solely because they seem to make sense. At present, there is no convincing reason to jump to the conclusion that the strategy of interviewing the incarcerated about crime should be discarded.

Our goal is to provide an overview of the promises and pitfalls of prison-based interviews for those currently pursuing or contemplating this type of research. We offer rebuttals against critics and point to strengths of the method. This defence hinges on answering the criticisms of inmate-based research and addressing the ever-present issue of whether accounts elicited from incarcerated offenders and active offenders vary in significant ways. Having mounted this defence, we proceed to a discussion of the benefits of inmate interviews. We conclude by proposing a strategy to empirically address this important issue.

Concerning interviews of captive criminals

The academic literature from criminology and sociology is replete with warnings of the potential shortcomings of research based on samples of individuals contacted in prison (Cromwell *et al.* 1991; Glassner and

Carpenter 1985; Jacobs 2000; Polsky 1998; Wright and Decker 1994). Overall, the criticisms of this type of research can be narrowed down to five issues: recruiting unsuccessful offenders, the ulterior motives of inmates, difficulty in establishing rapport, impression management by inmates and difficulty in recall.

Recruiting unsuccessful offenders

A potential problem with relying on imprisoned populations is that the experiences of the captured and confined may not be representative of a population of offenders. Their arrest and conviction are prima facie evidence that they have been unsuccessful and, therefore, they may differ in important ways from offenders who are active. This is important for a study of decision-making because investigators do not want to rely solely on the accounts of offenders who apparently made 'ineffective' or errant decisions and who may be atypical of more successful lawbreakers. This reliance could be devastating for those seeking to design crime prevention efforts based on offenders' perspectives (Piquero and Rengert 1999).

This criticism presents a static portrayal of sampling, contacting and recruiting in prison settings based on official classification that is somewhat artificial. In fact, the bulk of qualitative research on prisoners has used more adaptive techniques. When locating participants it may be best to use a mixed sampling approach that includes snowball sampling. According to Nee (2004: 6–7), 'We found that recommendation by other burglars was more fruitful than using index offence. Many of those serving a sentence for burglary did not consider it the focus of their criminal activity and many more "expert" burglars were serving sentences for other crimes.'

Using a more flexible sampling strategy guards against interviewing only those incarcerated for a particular offence and who apparently have failed to be successful in at least one consequential attempt. Even where offenders are serving time for the offence of interest most researchers are careful to make sure that interviews also contain accounts of successful offences.

Another rebuttal to this criticism is that it is rare for persistent offenders to avoid ensnarement in the criminal justice system over the course of their careers. This is especially true for offenders who venture beyond the security of clandestine drug dealing or who engage in the street-life that is typical of persistent thieves. As Edwin Lemert (1968: 649) stated more than 40 years ago, '[w]hether significant numbers of criminals in the open still lead lives uncomplicated by contacts with law enforcement agencies and large-scale correctional institutions is highly dubious.' There is little reason to doubt that this claim no longer holds true, especially in light of improved investigatory abilities and growth of the criminal justice system. Interviews of active offenders almost always point out that the lifestyle of drug dealing and reckless activities are tied closely to offending for many, and that those close to the drug trade run considerable risk of eventually being captured and confined (Fleisher 1995; Shover 1996).

Apart from their imprisonment, it is possible that there are other indications that imprisoned offenders are less successful than their counterparts; one measure would be the proceeds of crime or other indications of 'effective' decision-making. The notion that active offenders are relatively successful is further undermined by similarity in how active and incarcerated offenders approach crime's risks and rewards. Aside from the fact that prison samples have obviously paid the penalty for their crimes, there is little evidence that theft is more lucrative for active offenders. The amounts that active offenders gain from their crimes do not seem to exceed dramatically those gained by those who are in the criminal justice system. The rewards of any particular crime for all but a few offenders of both 'types' are likely to be small.

The recirculation of offenders between prison and street-life thins cultural boundaries separating the free and the confined. Qualitative research also indicates that prisoners and active offenders are not all that distinct; some active offenders view time behind bars not as indication of criminal failure but as a predictable and manageable cost of continuing in criminal business (Shover 1996: 170). Few active offenders escape occasional moments of clarity where they realise that they will be caught if they continue in crime. Because the borders between imprisoned and active offenders often are thin, it makes as much sense to view a stint in prison or jail as temporary downtime from the streets as it does a marker for criminal failure. Thus there is little reason to think that ensnared offenders differ qualitatively from those not yet caught (Shover 1996).

Ulterior motives

It is a fortunate curiosity that many of those who have engaged in behaviour that society has defined as immoral and illegal would disregard the potential risks and inconveniences and sit down to openly discuss their lives and misdeeds. For present purposes, it is relevant that prisoners located in institutions or through the criminal justice system and offenders unencumbered by criminal justice agencies might decide to participate for different reasons. This potentially leads to findings that differ by context due to systematic variation in samples. The motives individuals have for participating in research also may affect relayed narratives and the type of information withheld. It is necessary, therefore, to understand why offenders agree to tell their stories.

Critics of prison-based research charge that interviews conducted in prison settings restrict participants' candour because they are motivated to join studies due to the mistaken belief that they will accrue benefits (e.g. parole considerations or additional perks). As Richard Wright and Scott

Decker (1997: 4) point out, 'No matter how much inmates are assured otherwise, many will continue to believe what they say to researchers will get back to the authorities and influence their chances for early release.' Similarly, Polsky (1998: 116) claims that data from incarcerated offenders is suspect because it involves the 'kind of "cooperativeness" in which you get told what the criminal thinks you want to hear so you will get off his back or maybe do him some good with the judge or parole board'. The criticism of prison-based research is that the desire to obtain benefits from prison officials is the driving force behind inmates' participation. Consequently, inmates will obscure the truth of their crimes in order to gain favours.

To assess the motives for why inmates agree to interviews, Copes and Hochstetler (2006) inquired of a sample of incarcerated violent offenders. They found that payment for interviews intrigues offenders and whets other motives for participating, but it was uncommon for inmates to state that this was their primary reason for agreeing to be interviewed. It was far more common for offenders to see their participation in the study as a reaffirming or therapeutic exercise. For some, it was a small gesture at restitution by doing something positive. For others, it was an attempt to elicit some understanding from an impartial and attentive outsider. A few saw the decision either as a sign that they were on the right track as evidenced by their ability to admit mistakes or as a chance to explore their motives publicly. For many, there was nothing better to do. Boredom with prison routine and inmate conversations is one of the most commonly cited rationales for participation. No evidence was found that offenders were coerced into participating or that they thought that participation would garner special benefits.

Clearly, for those offenders approached on the street, money is 'critical in generating their interest ... On the streets, money talks; nobody does anything for nothing' (Jacobs 1999: 14). It would appear that remuneration is the primary motive for participation among active offenders, but it was not the only reason. Wright and Decker (1997) stated that they also garnered cooperation by fostering the therapeutic aspect of the interview. In addition, they acknowledged that offenders enjoy sharing information and expertise with those who are strangers to their environments. Finally, they pointed to a practical consideration: many agreed to the interview as a favour for their street recruiter who had vouched for the researcher's credibility and encouraged the decision.

Comparing the writings of those who study active offenders and those who study incarcerated offenders also shows similarity in the motives provided by participants. The primary differences between them appear to be that active offenders are quicker to acknowledge money as their reason, while the incarcerated are more likely to play up the cathartic and therapeutic nature of the interviews and to admit that boredom played a role. Differences appear to be more of proportion than content, however.

More prisoners, first and foremost, are alleviating boredom, and more active offenders seek compensation above other reasons. The question about whether the difference in the distribution of motives leads to deceit from the incarcerated remains.

Rapport

Rapport with participants may be more critical in interviewing about crime than in any other area of inquiry. This is because at least a modicum of trust is required to achieve disclosure of information that has potential risks, and because interviews about potentially stigmatising events lead some participants to deceive or alter their accounts (Berk and Adams 1970). Critics of prison interviews claim that rapport is more difficult to achieve in prison settings than in the free world. Investigators must establish rapport with administrators and staff as well as inmates to successfully acquire data (Patenaude 2004).

As many ethnographers of crime note, among offenders there is a cultural rule 'to treat everyone as a snitch or the man [police] until proven otherwise' (Agar 1973: 26). In prisons, interviewers must contend with this principle not only because inmates are distrustful but because there are potential consequences for appearing to be an informant for law enforcement. Rapport has higher stakes when one respected inmate could feasibly bring other inmates' participation in a research project to a halt or encourage all who are eligible to join a study.

Admittedly, prisons introduce significant social distance between those who are free and the confined. However, we should remember that many persons of interest to criminologists also have considerable distance from conventional and middle-class persons when they are free and entrenched in the spiral of their addictions and other troubles. Just as some prisoners isolate themselves from family and friends when incarcerated, some active offenders are not comfortable near their closest family members when unemployed, strung out, homeless, high, dirty, evading warrants or going through other hard times. This distance suggests that they also may not be comfortable spanning the social distance to converse with criminologists with whom they are likely to share little in common. Establishing rapport is as important and no less difficult outside of prisons.

Communication that clears significant rapport hurdles begins before the interview in the form of invitations to participate and in waivers for human subjects, which necessarily offer little and include warnings about the risks of participation. The remaining reservations can be surpassed by stating directly that participants have no legally supported reason to trust the interviewer, but that measures will be taken to protect them. By telling the participant that they should be careful not to reveal details in the interview that would be helpful to a prosecutor on open cases, trust can be gained. Offenders should be warned to omit crime partners' names, dates, proper nouns of targets, vehicle descriptions, discussion of high-profile crimes or reference to numbers or types of crimes committed but still unsolved. Most anything else they say is useless to those who would punish them further. Offenders surely get the message that their participation is voluntary and there is no surreptitious surveillance goal when a tape recorder is prominently displayed in front of them.

Participants' confidence is aided by the realisation that once they are behind bars the state and its prosecutors are temporarily unconcerned with them and what they did in the past. Only in unusual circumstances is further trouble ensuing or expected. Most know how to speak in generalities when necessary due to the fact that cellmates can inform, phones are tapped and letters are read in prison. So long as they can keep quiet about unsolved high-profile crimes, details of murders, hidden criminal proceeds and crimes for which they are already being investigated, there is little to fear.

Much has been written about the importance of rapport and detailing various strategies for establishing and maintaining it (Berk and Adams 1970). There are only a few devices that may be particular to interviewing in institutions. Researchers in prison may be aided in establishing the right kind of distance despite the setting, because it will be noticeable to inmates that there are no indications that staff have any affinity or show much deference to visiting criminologists. To build on this perception, we have found it helpful to use impersonal pronouns like 'they' when referring to criminal justice functionaries and to show some indication of empathy with gestures and words when possible. Also, it is best to interview inmates in private rooms, alone and without shackles (for obvious reasons). Ultimately, investigators must be casual and seem sufficiently friendly to solicit information, but also able to question or challenge when interviews seem to be going astray or taking a suspicious direction (Miller and Glassner 2004). Some finesse is required on the part of the interviewer. Beyond standard practices for getting along in conversation and specific advice on interviewing in manuals on the subject, maintaining rapport while structuring interviews is artful in all contexts.

Impression management

One impetus for interviewing active offenders is that retrospective accounts might be influenced by impression management in ways that obscure the objective truth or that alter accounts about crimes committed before imprisonment substantively. Concern about inmates' accounts centres on two suspicions. First, it is possible that imprisoned offenders will be embarrassed by their criminal failings and sloppiness and, therefore, will exaggerate the extent to which their crimes were a reasonable result of careful deliberation and executed aptly. Cromwell *et al.* (1991) claimed that burglars interviewed in prison often engage in 'rational reconstructions' of the criminal event. That is, incarcerated burglars reinterpret past behaviour to reflect an overly rational portrait of their crimes. They may describe how ideal crimes should occur and not how they actually happen.

A second and related concern is that 'the prison environment is detached from the temptations and pressures of street life' so that research conducted in this setting misses what is important (Wright and Decker 1994: 213). Presumably, sobriety, remorse and the time that incarcerated men have devoted to contemplation of being caught and imprisoned will lead to new conclusions that would not have been reached were they interviewed elsewhere. These realisations will colour retrospective depictions of crime and result in reconstructions of criminal events that fail to capture what was considered important at the time of the offence. The imprisoned might recall what was thought and done in crime inaccurately because information about consequences is now available that was not available at the time of crime. We term the resultant altered accounts penitent reconstructions.

The rational reconstruction argument rests on the notion that those being interviewed are attempting to avoid looking foolish. While the penitent reconstruction argument has not been fully articulated, it implies that imprisoned offenders have a more thoughtful and potentially more regretful interpretation of their acts than would have been possible soon after recently committed offences. It may also be important for some imprisoned offenders to develop an account where the good person that one is now is reflected in the depiction of self, so that crime is portrayed as out of character. This may lead to excessive justifications and excuses or exaggerated reservations about committing crime (Maruna 2001).

There is scant evidence that interviews of prisoners lead toward the sort of rational reconstruction that criminologists who warn against prison-based sampling frames seem to have in mind. In fact, if using craft, planning, discernment and cool-headedness are the markers of rationality and what we would expect a rationally reconstructed account to contain, there are few differences between prisoners and active offenders in the literature (Nee 2003). To the extent that difference can be found, interviews of active offenders contain depictions indicating slightly more rationality than do those of the imprisoned, undermining the rational reconstruction critique. By comparison, interviews gained from prison-acquired samples are a bit more likely to recount instantaneous drunken episodes; this may be due to the recognition of drug and alcohol problems and the desire to change old habits (Maruna 2001). It is, however, hardly the sort of rational reconstruction that leads to the conclusion that decisions of the imprisoned were more rational and logical than they really were. Nor does it appear that prisoners play at being skilled master criminals or planners inordinately in interviews; they seem to be no better or worse at crime according to their accounts than their active counterparts. Emphasis on being unpredictable and fearless in crime due to an erratic state of mind or entrenchment in street culture is common among all.

Both imprisoned and active offenders report placing their hope of staying free on intuition and luck as much as skill. Emphasis on superstition and fate in determining outcomes means that few need to feel shameful about failing as offenders or pretend that clear reasoning and concern with consequence precipitated their acts. The predominant strategy for preventing an ensuing fall is to luckily time desistance from burglary before a failed crime. Sentiments like 'I hope I stop before they get me' are common. Being fleet of foot and having an intuitive ability to sense danger are assets that offenders also hope will keep them free. Recognition that one gets caught because 'luck runs down' or 'every dog has its day' are common before, during and after imprisonment. We are not claiming that there is not swagger or bragging on the part of active offenders or the incarcerated when it comes to claiming criminal thoughtfulness, only that such claims are rare (Shover 1996), seemingly comparable across contexts and typically unaccompanied by convincing evidence.

Alcohol and drugs figure prominently in accounts of crime provided by active and imprisoned offenders, although slight variations in tense and wording do make acknowledgment of addiction and what it does to decision-making more common in imprisoned samples. Such phrases may begin with 'you have to understand I was an addict' before proceeding to explain a crime or related decision. Active offenders acknowledge that they experienced little guilt during and after crime, imprisoned offenders add the slight disclaimer that 'at the time' they experienced little guilt during or after crime. Narratives of addiction and reform add order to criminal accounts, but do not seem to change the meaning of what is imparted about particular criminal acts.

Distance from crime changes the impressions imparted. Many active offenders enter snowball samples by being criminals of local renown and surely have impressions associated with criminal reputations that they manage. They are likely to have more current investments in street culture than inmates. Presumably, they will want to look tough and will exaggerate personal autonomy and control over their decisions. When imprisonment is predictable as a possible outcome of continued crime, one might be tempted to reconcile criminal persistence by exaggerating imperviousness to consequence (Shover 1996). Active offenders also may see it as more imperative to look and play the violent part of the criminal heavy more than do prisoners. It may be easy to claim in interviews that one will 'blow the head off' victims or have a shootout with police who try to prevent them from escaping. When daily life in prison makes clear the reality of the consequences of punishment and that it can be managed, such expressions of bravado seem ignorant and empty. Claiming to be a killer hardened to consequence obviously does not make one a killer. Impression management is at work when such imperviousness to fear and consequence is expressed.

It has long been recognised that ego-defence can skew qualitative accounts (Maruna and Copes 2005). Little is gained by denying that the interview setting colours narratives, that conversations with the social scientists are not different than what might be said elsewhere, or that recounted events are influenced by the current situation and perspective (Presser 2004). Nevertheless, dampening the criticism that inmate accounts are fundamentally flawed due to impression management is not difficult, especially considering that impression management is a generic aspect of interaction for all.

Recall problems

Critics of samples of prisoners are concerned with inmates' ability to recall the details of their crimes. Absent the prompts and activities that are close at hand when interviewing active offenders, subjects may forget significant events and details as time introduces error in recall. Those researching active offenders have a distinct advantage in that details of crimes are likely to be fresher in participants' memories. The veracity and memories of prisoners can be checked by asking them known facts drawn from the record of their crimes in much the same way that survey researchers assess the accuracy of estimates of self-reported crime. Admittedly, the practice is not often utilised to discount data or exclude participants, so long as interviews are not complete departures from reality.

Altered memories are a risk of all retrospective research, and they occur for many reasons. After decades of analysing panel data, it is well known among psychologists that 'we do not seem to store complete records of events that can be accessed intact ... instead, our memories seem to be largely reconstructed; and our thoughts, feelings, and opinions at the time of recall can have a large impact on the nature of that reconstruction' (Holmberg and Holmes 1994: 264). In addition to how the present biases perception of the past, it is apparent and proven that memories are organised as time passes and people age, so that they can be recalled and presented in coherent and general forms (Cohen 1998). Memory is never possible without the reconstruction of meaning. The story told is always reconstructed from a certain perspective and even changes over the course of time, even if the interview partner tries his best to stay as detailed and truthful as possible (see Berger 1963).

If researchers intend to generalise, they must find ways of making sure offenders are not allowed limitless freedom to be selective about which crimes they recount. This often is done by asking about the last crime for which the offender was not caught or probing to make sure that the crimes recounted are not unusual. Despite these assurances, some details of ordinary offences are lost to memory. Time may fog details of crime and some mundane crimes will be forgotten entirely. Without probing questions about such crimes, an imprisoned offender is unlikely to recall the time they arrived early to friend's house and decided to swipe a gold chain from the counter when asked to recall a burglary. This and other types of memory degradation contribute to scepticism about prison interviews and cast a cloud on works that use them.

A silver lining is that interviews do not often focus on minutiae or detailed conversational information that make recall problems fatal for most purposes in qualitative criminology. Most are focused on understanding the general sense that respondents make of their own environments and behaviour. It is likely that active offenders recalling recent crimes are able to more firmly distinguish what happened exactly, what was considered in a given crime and other precise details but the effect on accounts may not change substantive meaning from what would be gained later. Active offenders also may choose not to bore interviewers by recounting offences they deem uninteresting or petty.

One recall problem with criminal justice samples is that offenders are likely to blend the characteristics of a specific crime with the other crimes they committed. One may hear, for example, that 'Tommy said let's go make some money,' because that's what Tommy usually said when he wanted to commit crime. This may be the offender's generalisation about how crime typically occurs, and interpreted as such it probably is accurate enough for the purposes at hand in qualitative criminology. Nevertheless, the analyst does not have the chance to generalise from the original event data as it has already been done by the interviewed person.

There are steps that might improve validity and confidence in recall. Most of these are standard qualitative techniques. They include triangulation with additional data where it is available; this might include official records or interviews of additional persons knowledgeable of events. Beginning with recent events and stepping backwards improves recall. Calendars are useful, if the research concerns the timing or frequency of events (Nee 2004). In questioning, interviewers can probe about inconsistencies, continually refocus the interview on a discrete event, and ask about larger contexts where details should be known to the subject or could be checked. Interviewers can take pauses where participants are asked to verify how sure they are about their statements and how well they can recall precisely what happened. A brief discussion about why they remember a crime cannot hurt.

Recall is a problem when interviewing those whose crimes may have occurred long ago whether or not they have been incarcerated. This is especially true for those who were intoxicated regularly or who committed so many crimes that it might be difficult for them to remember the details of any single offence. In some cases details from long ago are accurately recalled and offenders can provide some justification for why these memories are salient (Jacobs and Wright 2006). Nevertheless, researchers should be aware of the tendency to generalise in recall and how it colours data even if the consequences seem to have little bearing on what they will find when they make their own generalisations from offenders' statements. If the goal is to minimise interpretation and selective attention to detail, it is safe to assume that it is better to interview about offences that are recent than offences that occurred long ago. Inmates entering prison will recall their last crimes in greater detail than those who are approaching release, for example. For some projects, the inclusion and accuracy of precise details exactly as they happened may be critical to analysis. However, the purposes of most qualitative studies allow that offenders be given considerable liberty to tell it how they now see it and to impart retrospective interpretations and meanings. The rationale for some studies is to get participants to make sense of their lives to this point because what they think is relevant; this goal is only tangentially related to accuracy in the provided sequence of events. Whether these interpretations and meanings are present or distinctive just after an offence and whether or not they should be considered useless material if recently developed are debatable questions.

In favour of prison interviews

Thus far we have elaborated on the potential limitations of prison-based interviews and fortified against critiques of them. Here, we raise our heads above the parapet and counter with some potential benefits to seeking the accounts of the incarcerated. Apart from apparent conveni-ence, we describe several reasons that this approach may be a better strategy than soliciting them on the streets. While their memories may not be as fresh, interviewees from prisons are more likely to be clear headed, contemplative and interested in participating. Consequently, they are also better able to place particular events, decisions and outlooks into the larger contexts that shaped them.

First among the potential advantages of interviewing prisoners is that they are more likely to be motivated and interested participants. Develop-ing rapport with participants is a general rule in qualitative research, but just as important is getting and maintaining interest in the interview. Try interviewing even close friends about topics they are uninterested in discussing to see how rapport is not the only important consideration in getting people to talk for an extended period. Free citizens of all types, especially those with the fast-paced lifestyles characteristic of most persistent offenders, have more pressing things to occupy their time than sitting through an interview answering questions about things they likely have never considered until that very moment. Of course, this is also why remuneration is the key motive for participation by active offenders.

Akerstrom (1985) argues that active offenders often do not make the best study participants because their attention is elsewhere (namely focused on future deals) and, therefore, it is difficult to hold their attention long enough to complete an interview. Jacobs and Wright (2006) acknowledge distractions that impede interviews with active offenders; they were often interrupted by an impatient recruiter who wanted the interview to end early as he had things to do, for example. Some researchers recount stories of those few offenders who were apparently trying to 'hustle' their way through the interview so that they could collect their pay and return to their ordinary affairs (Jacobs 2000). For these reasons interviews with active offenders can be rushed and hurried, and may be relatively shallow by comparison to clear-headed participants with time on their hands. The rationale for qualitative interviews is that they provide insight into the ways in which offenders interpret, assess, organise, perceive and classify their worlds (Lex 1990: 393). Answers cut short or lacking thought potentially betray these benefits by leading to incomplete data, misunderstandings and subsequent misinterpretations of the data.

Certainly, those who interview inmates are not immune to the practical problem of participant interest. In fact, many of those inmates we have interviewed were reluctant to give more than one or two sentence responses to questions where we would have preferred sophisticated and insightful answers or 'thick' descriptions. While it may not be possible to determine if stunted responses are due to personality characteristics of the particular participant, in combination with the reality that we do not interview the 'chattering classes', neither can we rule out the possibility that participants simply wanted to be done. However, the boredom and regularity of prison encourages participation. One positive externality of these features of prison life is that inmates are more likely to be interested in the interview than those who are free to get back to their business. In our experience with inmates, few indicated directly or otherwise that they wanted to have the interview end quickly.

Investigators utilising samples of active offenders also must accept that those they interview might be drunk or high, sleepy, or going through withdrawal, making any meaningful conversation difficult (Akerstrom 1985). Nearly all of those who have interviewed active participants can relay stories of intoxicated participants who are unable to stay focused on the questions and whose statements are indecipherable or inconsistent when they do answer. With admirable honesty about ethnographic contingencies, Jacobs and Wright (2006: 22) report that 'one person we were supposed to interview got so high on drugs before coming to speak with us that he could not climb the hill that leads to our office (we interviewed his associate instead).' In such circumstances, interviews may introduce errors because the respondent simply cannot stick to the point or put the details of the narrative together in a consistent and coherent manner.

It is unclear how many interviews with active offenders are affected by participants' immediate use of drugs or alcohol, as the only guide is common sense when it comes to determining whether participants are intoxicated or otherwise not of sound mind. The addicted usually have learned to converse under the normal effects of drugs and alcohol abuse, but it only takes mild doses of drugs and alcohol to change ordinary interaction. Many active offenders exceed that threshold daily, and also suffer from more intractable effects of addiction on thought and communicative ability. Asking participants directly about their current use of drugs may help researchers make decisions about the accuracy of odd information but may also damage rapport or add to confusion, as it can be difficult to clarify muddled thought. There are no clear guides for discounting information that might be suspect due to drug and alcohol use but it is doubtful that what is added to interviews by capturing the 'normal state' of addicted offenders surpasses the value of what could be added in accuracy and clarity by having a sample of offenders in more steady states of mind. There may be truth in wine, but it contains impatience, incoherence and exaggeration as well. We acknowledge that not all inmates are thinking clearly or are free from prescribed or illicit substances when interviewed, but they certainly are less likely to be high than when free and in many cases medication improves data quality.

A third advantage of prison interviews is that prisoners may be in a better position to interpret their lives than active offenders. Hustling allows little time for reflective moments. While those who interview active offenders often must piece together fragments to interpret what they are told, those who interview prisoners are likely to receive more reflective and cohesive accounts. Prisoners may be more likely to go beyond explaining what happened to explaining what it means and to recounting events as part of larger narratives of life. While these accounts may be formulated into overly coherent forms or structured for other purposes, the insights they provide allow investigators to check conclusions and make sense of the offenders' lives 'through their own eyes' as they see them in relatively contemplative periods and moments. Our inclination is to believe that 'inactive' offenders can present more cohesive and meaningful interpretations of their decisions and lives than can those currently in the chaos and fray associated with active offending. While the interviewer in prison is faced with the possibility that participants are providing narratives of their life organised well after crime, the interviewer of active offenders may face a greater possibility that narratives are not organised into any sensible, self-reflective or cohesive form at all.

A final advantage of prison interviews is that offenders can be purposively sampled to build confidence that the target group is represented and that findings apply widely. This is because it is common for those engaging in interviews with active offenders to rely on snowball samples to locate suitable participants (Biernacki and Waldorf 1981). This style of sampling relies on seeking referrals from a key informant and then soliciting interviews from these individuals. Without a doubt this is an effective strategy for tapping into networks of active criminals and gaining their confidence (Wright *et al.* 1992). When using this method, however, researchers must be aware that they may have difficulty extending beyond one or two social networks and they are reliant on key informants' decisions over whom to refer, which means that generalising is especially hazardous and the structure of the sample is difficult to plan and control. The greatest risk is that informants refer only individuals with whom they share in common important variables (Jacques and Wright 2008).

When conducting prison interviews investigators have more information at the outset that allows creative and intentional structuring of the sample. Systematic sampling frames are much easier to generate and some random selection can be used to reduce the influence of researchers' choices about whom to interview. Official records can provide long lists of prospects and can be used to draw bounds around the population to be studied. One might eliminate all offenders without evidence of a previous criminal record before their last offence to remove incidental or novice offenders, for example.

Even where official records are used to structure a sample, there may be little reason for establishing sample parameters and the categories it contains at inception and adhering rigidly to a design based solely on those inclusion criteria. As research gets under way, one can use official information purposefully and efficiently to make sure that categories that are emerging as potentially significant are explored thoroughly. New variables from records can be used to select potential participants, if the investigator begins to suspect that they are worth exploration. An initial list of potential interview subjects also can be expanded by more informal means as the research proceeds. Hybrid snowball and sampled lists of participants can complement each other, and be used separately or together in analysis. When sampling methods are combined, findings will not be wholly contingent on selection by key informants or the potential biases introduced by using a single recorded offence to define eligible participants. Official records also can help ensure that there is not systematic bias in who decides and refuses to participate in research. If urban respondents are not answering the call to be interviewed as much as rural ones or those who have injured victims are less willing to talk, investigators can discover and purposively attempt to remedy the problems with the sample.

An additional benefit of prison recruitment is the ability to access a wider range of geographies than would be typically available outside of institutions. Investigators are not limited to one community. Stratified samples across locales or samples drawn from national prison systems can yield findings that extend beyond potentially local and idiosyncratic conditions and patterns.

Conclusion

Recall Polsky's metaphor comparing interviews of inmates with observations of caged gorillas to drive home the point that studying inmates will lead to errant conclusions. While numerous scholars repeat Polsky's zoological analogy, it does suffer from a fundamental flaw. Most of the animal kingdom does not have the ability to articulate their thoughts, decision processes or motives in the present or past. Biologists must observe animals directly in the wild because beasts cannot describe why they choose to pick certain prey or verbally interpret why they do so. As criminologists, 'our subjects, unlike chemicals or cells or apes, are perfectly capable of communicating to researchers, explaining what they have been through, what they do, and what they hope to achieve with various behaviours' (Maruna 2006: 274). Because it is clearly unethical to accompany offenders while they commit serious property or violent crimes, we rely on accounts of their thoughts and behaviours. Polsky's metaphor works only for those who watch interaction and action close-up, and breaks down when applied to those who hear about it. No matter the legitimacy of Polsky's device, his general concerns that context can skew results are shared by many – including us.

Before accepting that active offenders will yield a better representation of offenders, we should acknowledge that representative samples of the general population of offenders do not exist in qualitative criminology, as the parameters of this group can only be defined by selecting self-reported offenders from a random sample of the population. Even representative samples of known offenders are rare. Rather than aim at statistical generalisation, investigators often adopt the goal of thematic saturation, an attempt to make sure that discovery covers the important points and relationships likely to occur with additional data. Qualitative investigations in criminology generally, therefore, are ill-suited for the purposes of statistical generalisation or comparison. Sufficient numbers across the ordinary spectrum of offenders may participate to saturate important themes and yield meaningful and accurate qualitative results, no matter the location of offenders. Presently, there is no reason to believe that limitations of sampling active or incarcerated offenders impede analyses so severely that important theoretical distinctions in groups will not be found in some number.

The credibility of prison samples is extremely consequential for all who study crime no matter their methodology. Much of what we know of serious offenders has been garnered from them. At this date, we simply do not know whether one type of sample is better than the other at eliciting accurate and informative interviews. All that has been written, by us and others, is based on hunches and assumptions about how sample construction influences data. Empirical assessments addressing this issue are lacking (see Nee 2003, 2004 for exceptions). Thus before this issue can be put to rest romanticised notions about proximity of investigators to their subject, unsubstantiated justifications that we read in papers and folklore must be set aside and empirical answers pursued. To turn Polsky's phrase, we can no longer afford the convenient fiction that studying active offenders necessarily yields better data than studying them behind bars.

One means of answering the call is for investigators using identical interview guides that generate qualitative loosely structured responses to interview offenders housed in a state prison system and active in the state. These offenders should be matched on gender, age, criminal experience and crime of interest. Active offenders would ideally be drawn proportionately to the composition of the prison system by residence, and would likely heavily represent a few major metropolitan areas of the state with some appearance of inhabitants of rural regions. In addition to interviews, surveys with measures central to criminology should be administered to determine whether there are distinctive psychological and social characteristics among those who are caught and imprisoned. Such a study could address many of the questions raised in this paper about active versus incarcerated interviews, and also would speak to how being incarcerated changes depictions of crime substantively.

Alternatively, qualitative components can be added to longitudinal research where a panel of potential offenders (designated as high risk for continued crime) are contacted and interviewed repeatedly no matter their current status in the criminal justice system. By convincing those who will conduct the next generation of large-scale cohort studies of youths at risk of offending that their work will be strengthened with the addition of qualitative components, strides will occur in the reliability and validity of data as well as in the understanding of contextual influences on research.

Our goal is not to dismiss interviews with free-ranging offenders. To the contrary, we see great value in this type of design and what has been learned by implementing it. We simply point out that both styles of research are subject to attacks grounded only in intuition. More needs to be learned about the pitfalls and promises of each and the place of context in shaping accounts.

References

Agar, M. (1973) *Ripping and Running: A Formal Ethnography of Urban Heroin Addicts*. New York: Seminar Press.

Akerstrom, M. (1985) *Crooks and Squares: Lifestyles of Thieves and Addicts in Comparison to Conventional People*. New Brunswick, NJ: Transaction.

Bennett, J. (1981) *Oral History and Delinquency: The Rhetoric of Criminology*. Chicago: University of Chicago Press.

Berger, P. (1963) *Invitation to Sociology: A Humanistic Perspective*. New York: Anchor Books.

Berk, R. and Adams, J. M. (1970) 'Establishing rapport with deviant groups', *Social Problems*, 18: 102–17.

Biernacki, P. and Waldorf, D. (1981) 'Snowball sampling: problems and techniques of chain referral sampling', *Sociological Methods and Research*, 10: 141–63.

Chambliss, W. (1975) 'On the paucity of original research on organized crime: a footnote to Gallicher and Cain', *American Sociologist*, 10: 36–9.

Cohen, G. (1998) 'The effects of aging on autobiographical memory', in C. P. Thompson, D. J. Herrmann, D. Bruce, J. D. Read, D. G. Payne and M. P. Toglia (eds), *Autobiographical Memory: Theoretical and Applied Perspectives*. Mahwah, NJ: Lawrence Erlbaum Associates, pp. 105–24.

Copes, H. and Hochstetler, A. (2006) 'Why I'll talk: offenders' motives for participating in qualitative research', in P. Cromwell (ed.), *In Their Own Words: Criminals on Crime* (4th edn). Los Angeles: Roxbury, pp. 19–28.

Cromwell, P., Olson, J. N. and Avary, D. W. (1991) *Breaking and Entering: An Ethnographic Analysis of Burglary*. Newbury Park, CA: Sage.

Fleisher, M. S. (1995) *Beggars and Thieves: Lives of Urban Street Criminals*. Madison, WI: University of Wisconsin Press.

Glassner, B. and Carpenter, C. (1985) *The Feasibility of an Ethnographic Study of Property Offenders: A Report Prepared for the National Institute of Justice*. Washington, DC: National Institute of Justice.

Holmberg, D. and Holmes, J. G. (1994) 'Reconstruction of relationship memories: a mental models approach', in N. Shwartz and S. Sudman (eds), *Autobiographical Memory and the Validity of Retrospective Reports*. New York: Springer-Verlag, pp. 267–90.

Jacobs, B. A. (1999) *Dealing Crack: The Social World of Streetcorner Selling*. Boston, MA: Northeastern University Press.

Jacobs, B. A. (2000) *Robbing Drug Dealers: Violence Beyond the Law*. New York: Aldine de Gruyter.

Jacobs, B. A. and Wright, R. (2006) *Street Justice: Retaliation in the Criminal Underworld*. New York: Cambridge University Press.

Jacques, S. and Wright, R. (2008) 'Intimacy with outlaws: the role of relational distance in recruiting, paying, and interviewing underworld research participants', *Journal of Research in Crime and Delinquency*, 45: 22–38.

Lemert, E. (1968) 'Review of *Hustlers, Beats and Others* by Ned Polsky', *American Journal of Sociology*, 73: 649–50.

Lex, B. (1990) 'Narcotics addicts' hustling strategies: creation and manipulation of ambiguity', *Journal of Contemporary Ethnography*, 18: 388–415.

Maruna, S. (2001) *Making Good: How Ex-convicts Reform and Rebuild Their Lives*. Washington, DC: American Psychological Association.

Maruna, S. (2006) 'Review of *In Their Own Words: Criminals on Crime* by Paul Cromwell', *Australian and New Zealand Journal of Criminology*, 39: 274–5.

Maruna, S. and Copes, H. (2005) 'What have we learned from five decades of neutralization research?', *Crime and Justice: An Annual Review of Research*, 32: 221–320.

Miller, J. and Glassner, B. (2004) 'The "inside" and the "outside": finding realities in interviews', in D. Silverman (ed.), *Qualitative Research* (2nd edn). London: Sage, pp. 125–39.

Nee, C. (2003) 'Research on burglary at the end of the millennium: a grounded approach to understanding crime', *Security Journal*, 16: 37–44.

Nee, C. (2004) 'The offender's perspective on crime: methods and principle in data collection', in A. Need and G. Towl (eds), *Applying Psychology to Forensic Practice*. Oxford: Blackwell, pp. 3–17.

Patenaude, A. L. (2004) 'No promises, but I'm willing to listen and tell what I hear: conducting qualitative research among prison inmates and staff', *The Prison Journal*, 84: 69–91.

Piquero, A. R. and Rengert, G. (1999) 'Studying deterrence with active residential burglars', *Justice Quarterly*, 16: 451–61.

Pogrebin, M. (ed.) (2004) *About Criminals: A View of the Offender's World*. Thousand Oaks, CA: Sage.

Polsky, N. (1998) *Hustlers, Beats, and Others* (expanded edn). New York: Lyons Press.

Presser, L. (2004) 'Violent offenders, moral selves: constructing identities and accounts in the research interview', *Social Problems*, 51: 82–102.

Shover, N. (1996) *Great Pretenders: Pursuits and Careers of Persistent Thieves*. Boulder, CO: Westview.

Shover, N. and Honaker, D. (1992) 'The socially bounded decision making of persistent property offenders', *Howard Journal of Criminal Justice*, 31: 276–93.

Wright, R. T. and Decker, S. (1994) *Burglars on the Job: Streetlife and Residential Break-ins*. Boston, MA: Northeastern University Press.

Wright, R. T. and Decker, S. (1997) *Armed Robbers in Action: Stickups and Street Culture*. Boston, MA: Northeastern University Press.

Wright, R., Decker, S., Redfern, A. and Smith, D. L. (1992) 'A snowball's chance in hell: doing field research with residential burglars', *Journal of Research in Crime and Delinquency*, 29: 148–61.

Chapter 5

Interviewing and validity issues in self-report research with incarcerated offenders: the Quebec inmate survey

Carlo Morselli and Pierre Tremblay

Abstract

Self-report research on incarcerated offenders has had its share of support and criticism. The present chapter provides evidence from a survey of over 250 offenders that were incarcerated in federal penitentiaries in Quebec between 2000 and 2001. The principal aim of the survey was to gather data on offenders' criminal earnings during a three-year window period. The focus for this chapter will be on various aspects surrounding the self-report survey. First, site selection and access is discussed, with a particular focus on variations across minimum, medium and maximum security level penitentiaries. Second, the logistics of respondent solicitation are addressed, with a special outlook placed on the more personal techniques for persuading inmates to take part in a survey. Third, the questionnaire and sample designs are outlined. Fourth, key variables, such as the criminal earnings measures, are described. These variables are subsequently validated for their overall form, their internal consistency and their correlation with respondents' self-perceptions and expectations. The chapter concludes with a discussion of the limits surrounding the inmate survey and an overall appraisal of its contribution to criminological research.

The present study begins with the ambitious aims of two inmate surveys conducted by the Rand Corporation during the 1970s and 1980s (Peterson and Braiker 1981; Chaiken and Chaiken 1982). The Rand Corporation's objective was marked heavily by selective incapacitation and 'career criminals' policies that found a prominent place in criminological thought for a brief period during these decades. While our study followed the survey method that was at the base of the Rand studies, we are less concerned with identifying habitual criminals and high crime commission rates. The main focus, instead, is on the criminal earnings of respondents who participated in the survey. The principal inquiry that guided the data-gathering and analytical phases of the research addresses the following straightforward question: why do some offenders make more from crime than others? We have become accustomed to referring to this research as the criminal achievement programme.

This criminal achievement programme is guided by three intertwined assumptions and objectives. The principal assumption is that criminal action is a means to an end. This assumption places us in a purposive action framework and in close association with rational choice approaches to crime. Second, money earned through crime is used as the main indicator for this purposive outcome. We are aware that money is not the only thing that is sought after through criminal action and we acknowledge that status, reputation and prestige may also be indicators of individual achievement. Our decision to focus primarily on the money is based on its tangibility when compared to other possible indicators of achievement and an understanding that, while money may not be the only sought after thing, it is an important thing for most offenders. The final aspect driving the criminal achievement research programme combines these two assumptions and establishes the principal objective to change criminology's traditional dependent variable from participation in crime or frequency of offending to the beneficial outcome of crime (money/criminal earnings).

The present chapter addresses the empirical foundation of the research programme: the 287 offenders who participated in the survey and who shared their experiences in crime with us. The survey was conducted with incarcerated offenders and such a task presented serious challenges for data gathering and eventual analyses. The subsequent sections share our experiences as we made our way toward accessing prison sites, soliciting potential respondents, completing the lengthy questionnaire that was designed for the survey, and scrutinising the responses and variables that have been and will continue to be central in explaining why some offenders make more out of crime than others.

Accessing correctional institutions

Past researchers have emphasised the difficulties for gathering data on crime experiences in correctional settings. Indeed, the first step is probably the hardest in that obtaining authorisation to enter a prison or penitentiary can be more difficult and time-consuming than obtaining volunteers from an inmate population. For another experience with Canadian correctional services, see Desroches (2005). We were allowed access to five Quebec-based penitentiaries in the Canadian correctional service infrastructure. Two were minimum security sites. Two others were medium security sites. The fifth was the federal correctional services' reception centre. Once lengthy bureaucratic demands were met and access was obtained, no major problems were experienced in the minimum and medium security sites. The reception centre, however, did present a series of problems that obliged us to abandon the survey in this site after only 15 interviews. The main problem was due to the heavy demand placed on inmates to participate in research when entering a prison system for a new sentence. Inmates found in the reception centre are new entries who are awaiting referral to minimum, medium or maximum security prisons across the province and country. During this entry phase, inmates are required to pass a series of intense evaluations from practitioners from the correctional services and various university-based research teams. At first, motivation to participate in our survey was low among inmates passing through the reception centre because we were associated with this general evaluation process. Once inmates realised that participation in our survey was on a volunteer basis (which made it distinct from other evaluations at this site), they were even more likely to refuse our invitations in order to avoid one of the many tests that they had to go through. In the end, the reception centre was dropped from the research, leaving the sample's survey composed of inmates residing in minimum and medium security facilities at the time of the interview. Thus one of the first things that we learned is that although there are advantages in recruiting inmates as they enter the correctional system, for volunteer-based research we found recruitment to be more feasible in sites that placed inmates in a more long-term and stable environment at the mid or late stages of their sentences.

Soliciting and motivating respondents

Following recommendations in the literature for improving the quality of data from survey research with inmates (Marquis and Ebener 1981; Horney and Haen-Marshall 1991), all questionnaires were completed in face-to-face sessions with interviewers. Twelve interviewers took part in the data gathering stage of the research. At the time of the interviews, all were graduate students at the School of Criminology, Université de Montréal. Eight were women. Four were men. Interviewers entered each penitentiary site in groups of four or five. On most days, each interviewer would be able to complete two questionnaires (one in the morning and one in the afternoon).

For each site, officials from correctional services supplied a list of names for the entire inmate population. This list also included the inmate's identification number, date of birth, date of most recent entry into the correctional services system and the crime(s) for which he was incarcerated. A random list of 20 inmates was extracted from this population for each interviewer to use during the survey period in a given site.

With a list of inmate names in hand and upon entry into the survey site, each interviewer was ready to solicit respondents for the survey. In general, interviewers were restricted to sectors and rooms in each penitentiary site and interviews were usually conducted in offices that were reserved for meetings between inmates and their lawyers. In minimum security sites, the offices of absent caseload managers were also used for interview purposes.

A telephone was supplied to each interviewer, who would either call a guard designated to assist in the survey for that day or the caseload manager in charge of the inmate who was next on the interviewer's list. The inmate would be called either in private or through a central intercom. While the details of the survey were not provided, inmates were aware beforehand that they had been selected to participate in university research that focused on the *financial situation of inmates prior to their current incarceration*. They were issued half-day passes that excused them of work duties for that period – this usually helped break some ground during the eventual encounter. From the early stages of the interview phase of the research, we asked the guards and caseload managers who were instructed to contact each inmate not to reveal anything about the research in progress. Early experiences revealed that such intermediaries sometimes presented the research objectives in a blunt and misguided manner. Thus inmates would sometimes arrive in the assigned office with an understanding that the survey would call for the revelation of crimes and criminal earnings that were not revealed in official records, but with little understanding of the confidential and independent context in which the research was taking place.

These and other situations led to short periods (one or two days at a time) during which the interview team was less successful in their solicitation efforts. This was particularly the case in medium-security penitentiaries. In such sites, interviewers do not have the same physical access to inmates as in minimum-security penitentiaries. In the minimum-security site, interviewers and inmates were in constant contact with each other beyond the location reserved for the interview. In the medium-security site, interviewers had to rely on guards to make the first contact with the inmate on the sample selection list. Because guards would often present their understanding of the survey to the inmate before interviewers had any chance of meeting them, this led to much confusion and, at times, straightforward refusals even before we were able to present the research. After we realised what was going on, we asked the guards to simply call the inmate and not say anything about our survey. While the guards did not understand why we wanted them to stop 'helping' us, they nevertheless respected our request and we were able to present the research with greater coherence and success. But helpful guards were not the only obstacle. After another two-day period in which our acceptance rate was dropping in a medium-security site, we turned directly to the leaders among the inmates to see what could be the source of our temporary lack of success – our initial feeling was that the word was being spread within the prison for inmates not to participate in our survey. We called all inmates who were part of the inmate council at that medium-security site and asked them if there was any truth to our suspicions. They assured us that they had nothing to do with such things. After a friendly conversation, we asked if they could help us by spreading the word around to encourage inmates to participate in our survey. They agreed and, by the next day, the survey was back on track again.

How each interviewer solicited inmates was also crucial for improving our participation rate. Rather than assign all to a uniform protocol for presenting the research, each interviewer was encouraged to develop her/his own techniques and solicitation strategies that would optimise the chances that an inmate would agree to participate in the survey. Thus, aside from assuring inmates that all information revealed during the interview would remain confidential (confidentiality forms were signed for such purposes), that the survey was not connected to the correctional services sector in any way and that respondents were free to cease the interview at any point, interviewers were instructed to remain straightforward and personal (*to be oneself*) when meeting with potential respondents for the first time. This led to the revelation of distinct personality traits that would come to mark each interviewer. Such typecasting ranged from the anti-authoritarian guy, the nice girl/guy, the straight girl/guy, the naïve girl/guy, the tough girl and 'Lolita'.

Other aspects also facilitated respondent solicitation. The most obvious of these elements was the presence of female graduate students. Most of the inmates (and particularly the younger ones) were eager to spend some time with these members of the team. Some often joked of their disappointment when being called by the few male members of the team. This usually (and memorably) amounted to some initial awkwardness which quickly faded once the interviewer proceeded to explain what the survey was about and what would be required by the respondent. Soliciting inmates typically grew easier as the interview group prolonged their stay in a particular prison. On most days, the interviewer group would have lunch at the same time and in the same mess hall as the inmates. Such proximity got inmates talking about the survey. Inmates who already participated in the survey would often tell of their experience and spread the word that there was nothing to worry about. At times, some inmates would even approach interviewers and present their motivation to take part in the survey. Also, in the minimum-security sites, interviewers were allowed to roam freely in the common grounds of the penitentiary (e.g. television room, pool room, mess hall, recreation yard, gym). This led to some partial deviance from our sampling strategy and, for 23 cases, questionnaires were completed following this more open form of solicitation.

Our various intervention strategies and overall demeanor within the different penitentiary sites appear to have been beneficial, although not without problems. The main obstacle that we faced was that 35 per cent of inmates that we called simply did not show up to the interview location. These absentees were due to many reasons:

1. The inmate was transferred to another penitentiary after we received the sample selection list.

2. The inmate was on an important work duty (e.g. in the kitchen or at a remote site) and was unable to take the time off at the moment of his call.

3. The inmate may have been put off after hearing the guard's presentation of the survey in one of the medium-security sites.

4. The inmate simply did not want to meet with us.

Once we were able to solicit the inmate ourselves, our record was quite good – overall, we had a 76 per cent acceptance rate. We can also maintain that none of the interviewers were treated aggressively or with disrespect by any of the inmates who they solicited (successfully or unsuccessfully).

The questionnaire design

Interviews were conducted immediately after an inmate agreed to participate in the survey. Those who agreed to take part in the survey had the option of completing the questionnaire with an interviewer in either French or English. The length of time to complete a questionnaire varied between two and three hours, depending on the amount of information provided by the respondent. The questionnaire was made up of almost two hundred questions, but most of the time was allotted to two sections aimed at recording criminal and non-criminal patterns during a three-year window period and the set of core contacts making up the respondent's criminal network during this same period. These time-consuming sections were placed in the middle of the questionnaire, following a series of sections in which information on a respondent's socio-demographic and background characteristics were recorded. In the latter portions of the questionnaire, interviewers recorded more general experiences that respondents had during the window period, the cities or larger geographical regions in which they committed their crimes, and a series of self-perception and Likert-scale questions derived from various general theoretical traditions in criminology.

The calendar format and window period

Recording data on criminal and non-criminal earnings is not simply a matter of asking respondents what they were doing and earning during a given period. The calendar format that was integrated in the questionnaire design was based on a similar format in the second Rand inmate survey. The main incentive for including such a format was to facilitate respondents' recall of past events, activities and outcomes during the window period. This window period, as with the Rand survey, was based on the three years preceding the beginning of the incarceration period being served at the time of the interview. To make sure that we were not faced with situations in which respondents were forced to recall events, activities and outcomes from more than ten years in their pasts, we restricted the sample selection to inmates who had been incarcerated for less than seven years at the time of the interview – with the three-year window period, this would assure that we were working with memories within a ten-year time span. Respecting this criterion was not a problem in that 90 per cent of the respondents who took part in the survey had been incarcerated for less than five years; three-quarters had been incarcerated for less than three years.

The window period's 36-month time span was established with the respondent and, for each month, information was recorded on previous incarcerations or arrests, cities of residence, key life events (or potential turning points), legitimate work experiences and earnings, months in which the respondent received social security benefits, undeclared jobs and income, and, finally, criminal activities and earnings. We began with what we believed to be the easiest detail for inmates to remember – past incarceration spells. Indeed, our expectations were confirmed in that respondents found it very easy to recall past sequences in the window period during which they were incarcerated. With this simple task, the calendar segment of the questionnaire was underway and before we completed this segment by asking respondents to declare their criminal or non-criminal earnings, we had already established their criminal justice experiences, the cities in which they were living and what key life events had occurred across each month in the window period. Such cues facilitate recall in that while it would be unrealistic to expect respondents (in any criminal or non-criminal survey sample) to clearly remember the details surrounding their activities and wages during a given phase of their lives, asking them to do so after reconstructing other life circumstances allowed them to associate and spark the finer details that are generally more difficult to remember. For example, a respondent found it easier to remember what he was doing and how much he was earning after he situated himself in the context of a month (or sequence of months) in which he had just moved to Montreal, two months before a short prison spell, following the month that his first child was born, and during which he was working 40 hours per week as a janitor for about twelve dollars an hour. The respondent would more easily recall that he was also making about $300 per week selling cannabis to a small clientele during this month and the two months that followed, just before his arrest and incarceration for drug dealing.

To structure the recall of past criminal activities and earnings, we proceeded with a crime-by-crime method. The questionnaire was designed so that interviewers could guide the respondent toward remembering past predatory and market crimes and the details surrounding them. Thus, rather than ask a respondent to remember his crimes and the months for which he was active, we would first ask if he committed any robberies during the window period. If he had, the month or sequence of months for which he was committing robberies was recorded as were a series of details concerning his experiences with robberies. Such details included the status and prestige that he assigned to such an activity, the number of crimes that he would commit on a monthly basis (when active), information on the types and scope of accomplices that he turned to for such crimes, and an estimate of how much he would personally earn from such crime on an average basis. This last item was included in the survey for validation purposes and will be compared with the monthly earnings recorded in the calendar for the same crimes. Aside from robbery, other predatory crimes that were suggested to the respondent by the interviewer were burglary, auto-theft, theft, fraud and cons/swindles. The last category of these predatory crime categories was largely misunderstood by the respondents and was eventually dropped from the analytical portion of the study. Note that respondents also had the option of including any other predatory crime during this segment of the interview.

Once the predatory crime segment was completed, the interviewer oriented the respondent toward recalling any possible market crimes that occurred during the window period. Such crimes included participation in drug dealing and distribution, contraband (of non-drug products), loansharking, sex-related markets, illegal gambling, fencing of stolen goods and any other market offences that the respondent could think of and add to the set of responses. As with the predatory crimes, respondents were asked to identify the months during which they were active in these market crimes as well as providing similar details on their rate of crime commission, their network of accomplices and criminal contacts, and personal gains from such crimes. Thus it was only after reconstructing all these elements of the window periods that we asked respondents to provide us with the monthly earnings that they were making for each of the criminal activities that they reported.

Starting and working samples

Respondents were, on average, 34 years of age at the time of the interview. In terms of education, 82 per cent had not completed their high school and 7 per cent of this substantial majority did not have more than a primary-level education.

On average, respondents were serving sentences of 64 months (or just over five years). The breakdown for main crimes for which respondents were convicted was consistent with the overall population of federal inmates in Quebec prisons. We distinguish crimes of a predatory nature (e.g. robbery or burglary) from market crimes which are typically transactional or consensual (drug dealing or illegal gambling operating). The majority of sample members were incarcerated for robbery (31 per cent) or drug dealing/trafficking (27 per cent). The remainder of the sample was incarcerated for theft or burglary (17 per cent), violent crimes (10 per cent), other criminal market activities (7 per cent), fraud (6 per cent) or other predatory crimes (2 per cent). The self-report format of the survey was indeed effective in that respondents did not deny committing crimes and they regularly reported crimes for which they were not convicted.

While 287 inmates participated in the survey, most of our analyses are based on a restricted sample. For present purposes, we work with a sample of 214 inmates that was derived after two sets of extractions. First, 25 questionnaires were removed from the sample because they were too incomplete and of poor quality. Second, 48 questionnaires were completed by respondents who were not incarcerated for money-oriented crimes and who did not report participation in any money-oriented crimes during the window period. Most of this latter group, which will be used as a comparison group for various analyses in the research, were incarcerated for violent acts (e.g. homicide or assault), sex crimes (e.g. sexual aggression, pedophile acts) and various cases of criminal negligence (e.g. drunk driving).

The criminal earnings variable

The study's dependent variable compiles all criminal earnings reported for the window period by 214 respondents. Overall, respondents combined to report a sum of $117,582,889 in criminal earnings – 31 respondents had no criminal earnings to declare from their criminal actions during the window period. Median criminal earnings for the sample during the three-year period is $105,949 (or an annual median of $35,316). The mean for the criminal earnings distribution is much higher at $549,453 (standard deviation = $1,739,541).

Because this distribution is highly skewed, we reshaped the variable with a logarithmic (base 10) transformation. Such a decision has been encouraged in past research that included a criminal earnings variable[1] and is firmly entrenched in a theoretical justification that necessitates the logarithmic transformation of money. The logic of the argument follows the principle of decreasing marginal utility. Money is consistent with this principle in that an addition of $100 is perceived with decreasing value at higher levels of a given distribution. In short, giving someone who has $100 another $100 will be of greater value than giving $100 to someone who has $100,000 – we also assume that the first person will be more satisfied than the second. Thus, applying a logarithmic transformation compresses higher values more heavily than lower values: a value of 1 becomes 0; a value of 10 becomes 1; a value of 100 becomes 2; a value of 1,000 becomes 3; and so on. Aside from this theoretical fit, this logarithmic transformation option is more feasible than alternative methods (truncation or deletion of extreme values) in that it disproportionately compresses higher values while not completely discarding them. Furthermore, such a transformation maintains the proportional scale while normalising the distribution. For interpreting results, an antilog conversion is required and a geomean (the antilog of the mean for a logged distribution) is generally used to offer a more sensible result (for example, a mean of 3,4 for the logged distribution will be converted into $2,512).

Before transforming the criminal earnings variable with a logarithmic transformation, the 31 respondents who declared no criminal earnings were given one dollar each so as to retain them after the logarithmic transformation was applied, whereupon they returned to a status of $0 earners. A geomean of $19,208 in criminal earnings for the three-year window period was obtained for the entire sample. If we remove the $0 respondents from the sample, the geomean is much closer to the original distribution's median ($102,118).

Validating the criminal earnings estimate

How accurate are our estimations of criminal earnings? We developed four strategies for assessing consistency across variables. The first assesses the overall distribution in a stratification pattern that is akin to non-criminal income distributions. The second assesses consistency across two different measures of criminal earnings. The third and fourth introduce self-perception and expectation variables to assess the level of coherence that respondents displayed in regard to what they gained from crime.

The 20/80 rule

The first 'validation' strategy addresses the assumption that incarcerated offenders are typically failed offenders. Whether incarcerated offenders are more or less 'successful' than free offenders is still up for debate and little evidence has been provided to settle this issue. After surveying almost 2,000 federal inmates in the United States for their firearm possession patterns and criminal activities, Wright and Rossi maintained that their sample was more likely representative of hard-core or serious offenders (Wright and Rossi 1986). After interviewing free robbers in St Louis, Wright and Decker argued that 'by definition inmates are failed criminals' (Wright and Decker 1997: 7).

It would be difficult to choose a side in this debate. Instead, we prefer to emphasise that our survey may have relied on incarcerated offenders, but because we gathered information for the three-year window period preceding their incarceration at the time of the interview, our survey focuses on the criminal experiences of these inmates when they were free and active offenders.

The irrelevance of the 'free versus incarcerated offender' debate also emerges when examining our survey results, which illustrate to what extent an inmate population is made up of both 'failed' and 'serious' offenders (serious in the sense that they take crime seriously enough to achieve something out of it). Using a Lorenz curve (Lorenz 1905), Figure 5.1 relates the cumulative distribution of offenders to the cumulative distribution of criminal earnings, illustrating the inequality of criminal earnings across the offender population. The pattern is consistent with the 20/80 division that is sometimes referred to as the 'Pareto principle' and which follows the observation that in societies tainted by inequality, 80 per cent of the wealth will be possessed by 20 per cent of the population.

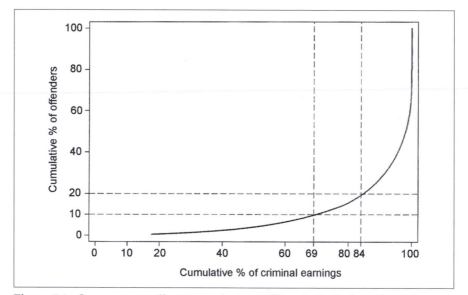

Figure 5.1 Lorenz curve illustrating the inequality of criminal earnings (Pareto principle)

The 20/80 pattern applies to the criminal earnings distribution that we obtained from the survey. Of the total sum of roughly 120 million dollars reported by respondents, the top 10 per cent of criminal earners accounted for 69 per cent of that sum; the top 20 per cent of criminal earners accounted for 84 per cent of the total (see the reference lines in Figure 5.1). This distribution and its salient division between haves and have-nots illustrate the extent to which a criminal 'population' may be stratified.

While, in itself, such a finding does not provide a sufficient validation for our criminal earnings estimate, the fact that it is consistent with this well-established pattern does provide some level of assurance that our sample members were at least consistent with past assessments of collective income and wealth patterns. The subsequent validation strategies increase our trust in the information that our respondents' shared during the survey.

Consistency across criminal earning estimations

The second validation strategy compared two criminal earnings measures. The first was the sum of overall monthly criminal earnings gathered from the calendar section of the questionnaire. The second was the sum of crime-specific monthly earnings that respondents reported making in their personal gains across individual crimes. There were some discrepancies between the two variables, but the scope of this difference depended on whether the initial or logged versions of each variable were applied. For the original variables, a moderate correlation ($r = 0.45$) was obtained between the criminal earnings measures. Logging both variables considerably improved the correlation ($r = 0.93$) and the validation of criminal earnings estimates.

Self-perceptions of criminal success and criminal earnings

For the third strategy, we analysed to what extent respondents' self-perceptions were coherent with the criminal earnings they reported. Past research has demonstrated that offenders are quite realistic about their likelihood of achieving some level of success through crime (Levitt and Venkatesh 2000) and in their personal assessments of past accomplishments. In previous work, we referred to this strategy as the 'bragging effect' (Tremblay and Morselli 2000), referring to cases in which low-earning respondents perceived themselves as successful in crime. During the latter portion of each interview, and following a similar question from the Rand surveys, respondents were asked to estimate the level of success they felt that they had in doing crime. For the 162 inmates who responded to this question, 34 per cent perceived themselves as having high success, 27 per cent as having average success, 16 per cent perceived themselves as having low success and 23 per cent felt that they had no success whatsoever in crime during the window period. Geomean comparisons of criminal earnings for the entire window period across these self-perception categories are consistent in that respondents who perceived themselves as having no success in crime reported the lowest criminal earnings ($34), followed by those who perceived little success ($1,612), moderate success ($54,532) and high success in crime ($223,358). In addition, the 0$ earners were appropriately concentrated among those who considered having attained 'no success' (69 per cent) and 'little success' (19 per cent) in crime – the remainder (12 per cent) could be described as misperceiving themselves as average or highly successful offenders.

Life expectations and criminal earnings

The fourth validation strategy that we derived examined whether respondents maintained reasonable ideals for a life without crime. Immediately following the question addressing personal success in crime, we asked respondents the following question: 'What annual legitimate revenue would incite you to completely stop your criminal activities?' Indeed, financial desires were reasonable and consistent with self-perceptions of success in crime. For the 194 respondents who provided a response to this question, ideal annual legitimate earnings were established at a geomean of $35,658. This variable was correlated with the logged version of the criminal earnings variable ($r = 0.25$; $\alpha < 0.05$). More consistency was found when crossing the ideal legitimate earnings variable with the self-perception of criminal success variable. Those with high self-perceptions asked for $65,471; those with moderate self-perceptions asked for $47,498; those with low self-perceptions were satisfied with $25,522; and those perceiving no success from crime requested $6,265. These findings evoke not only the coherent and reasonable grasp that offenders have when it comes to money issues, but also the substantial lucidity that they have in regard to their own personal achievements.

Problems estimating criminal earnings

While we were satisfied with the consistency between variables within the survey, we did identify two areas that appear to influence our criminal earnings estimate. Both are associated with the interview format.

Variations across site security levels

The security level of the survey site influenced criminal earnings – geomeans for respondents surveyed across different sites illustrate that those in minimum-level security sites at the time of the survey reported significantly lower criminal earnings than those in medium-level security sites ($5,187 versus $72,825). The small group of 15 respondents who were surveyed while passing through the correctional services' reception centre also reported relatively low criminal earnings (geomean=$6,235). That offenders incarcerated in medium-security institutions are higher earners is consistent with the common-sense contention that incarcerated offenders are more likely serious offenders. The follow-up to this assumption would be that offenders in higher-security correctional institutions would be even more serious.

This contention and its follow-up may apply here, but we must also consider that referral to a minimum-security institution could be decided at different points throughout an inmate's incarceration spell. Thus, whereas some offenders may be referred to minimum-security sites at the beginning of their incarceration term, others will be referred only after residing in higher-level security institutions over an extended period – placement in a minimum-security site is often reserved for inmates who have records of good behaviour throughout their time in prison. In short, at some earlier point during their incarceration term at the time of the survey, many of the inmates interviewed in minimum security sites were also incarcerated in medium-security sites.

With this said, it may be that medium-security sites were more likely populated by higher-earners because in as much as less serious offenders residing in medium-security prisons will eventually be transferred to the minimum level, the more serious offenders are more likely to stay at the medium level – thus a higher proportion of more serious offenders are always present at the medium level.

A second reason for this difference may be due to statistical problems, particularly in terms of variable composition. The higher earnings reported by those interviewed in medium-level security sites may be influenced by extreme outliers at the higher levels of the criminal earnings continuum. But this is not the case. In fact, the inverse is true: less variation is found for the medium-security category (coefficient of variation=33 per cent) than for the minimum-security category (coefficient of variation=59 per cent).

Interviewer bias

The second (and minor) problem with the criminal earnings variable concerns slight variations among interviewers, and with one interviewer in particular. Three-quarters of the interviews were conducted by women. We did not identify any significant gender biases in regard to reported criminal earnings. Respondents who conducted interviewers with female interviewers did report criminal earnings that were slightly higher than those who conducted interviews with male interviewers, but the difference was not significant (geomeans of $23,408 for female interviewers and $10,994 for male interviewers). Variation was higher for males than for female interviewers (coefficients of variation of 53 per cent for males and 44 per cent for female interviewers).

There was one apparent discrepancy when we compared reported criminal earnings across individual interviewers. One of our female interviewers, who joined the team during the final months of the survey and completed 19 questionnaires, stood out from the rest of the interviewing team. On average (geomean), her respondents reported criminal earnings ($396,199) that were much higher than for any other interviewer. Criminal earning geomeans for the remaining eleven interviewers ranged from $1,347 to $207,684. Variations for each interviewer depended on the number of interviews that were completed and the presence of high earners who would influence the average for the group of respondents interviewed by each of the team members.

Conclusions

For this chapter, we establish that surveying incarcerated offenders for information on their criminal experiences is indeed a rich and valid approach – one that is unfortunately avoided by many criminologists and other students of crime. Too often we are trapped in a debate that has us siding with either the advantages of surveying the free and active offender or accessing a stable pool of incarcerated offenders. When choosing a side in this debate or simply ignoring the debate altogether, it is important to remember that most persistent offenders will experience an incarceration term at some point in their careers and that all incarcerated offenders were free and active at some point in their pasts.

Our experiences with the inmate sample allow us to state and conclude with a series of observations. First, respondents did not deny committing crimes and they did not only report crimes for which they were serving prison terms. Face-to-face interviews with offenders have the advantage of creating an ongoing dialogue between interviewee and interviewer. When conducted properly, the interview process embeds these two parties in a trustful exchange. This is particularly the case when the research instrument carries the respondent beyond the many superficial, typical and repetitive questions that are asked of him at many instances throughout his incarceration. Because our questionnaire was designed to keep this dialogue dynamic and because we were seeking very detailed data on various features of a respondent's criminal experiences, respondents themselves became curious of what was the overall outcome was of their criminal pasts. This is the impression that we, as interviewers, had when we would complete various segments of the questionnaire (the inventory of crimes, the calendar, the accounting of legitimate and criminal earnings) and then present the overall result to the respondent and ask if the details made sense to him. Responses would vary from 'yeah, I wasn't too good' to 'not bad, eh?'

Such impressions are validated by respondents themselves who, as a group, showed consistency across different questions that gathered information on their criminal earnings. Respondents were not concentrated among failed or overly successful offenders – instead, a sensible mix was found. Respondents did not appear to be exaggerating their criminal experiences or achievements – instead, they were quite coherent in evaluating their own criminal outcomes. They could also be described as reasonable in their expectations from a life without crime and such expectations are consistent with their self-perceptions of what they achieved from crime in their pasts.

Note

1 See McCarthy and Hagan (2001) and Matsueda *et al.* (1992).

References

Chaiken, J. M. and Chaiken, M. R. (1982) *Varieties of Criminal Behavior*. Santa Monica, CA: Rand Corporation

Desroches, F. (2005) *The Crime That Pays: Drug Trafficking and Organized Crime in Canada*. Toronto: Canadian Scholars' Press.

Horney, J. and Haen-Marshall, I. (1991) 'Measuring lambda through self-reports', *Criminology*, 29: 471–95.

Levitt, S. D. and Venkatesh, S. A. (2000) 'An economic analysis of a drug-selling gang's finances', *Quarterly Journal of Economics*, 115: 755–89.

Lorenz, M. O. (1905) 'Methods of measuring the concentration of wealth', *Publications of the American Statistical Association*, 9: 209–19.

McCarthy, B. and Hagan, J. (2001) 'When crime pays: capital, competence, and criminal success', *Social Forces*, 79: 1035–59.

Marquis, K. H. and Ebener, P. (1981) *The Quality of Prisoner Self-Reports*. Santa Monica, CA: Rand Corporation.

Matsueda, R. L., Gartner, R., Piliavin, I. and Polakowski, M. (1992) 'The prestige of criminal and conventional occupations: a subcultural model of criminal activity', *American Sociological Review*, 57: 752–70.

Peterson, M. A. and Braiker, H. B. (1981) *Who Commits Crimes: A Survey of Prison Inmates*. Cambridge, MA: Oelgeschlager, Gunn & Hain.

Tremblay, P. and Morselli, C. (2000) 'Patterns in criminal achievement: Wilson and Abrahamse revisited', *Criminology*, 38: 633–59.

Wright, J. D. and Rossi, P. H. (1986) *Armed and Considered Dangerous: A Survey of Felons and their Firearms*. Hawthorne, NY: Aldine de Gruyter.

Wright, R. T. and Decker, S. H. (1997) *Armed Robbers in Action: Stickups and Street Culture*. Boston, MA: Northeastern University Press.

Chapter 6

Beyond the interview: complementing and validating accounts of incarcerated violent offenders

Fiona Brookman

Abstract

Speaking to offenders in detail about their offending and related issues is a complex yet increasingly routine feature of criminological research. There is little doubt that the rich narratives often gathered are invaluable to the criminological endeavour. However, it is not always clear how to elicit detailed and 'credible' information from offenders or when and how to supplement accounts either to corroborate certain 'facts' or to enrich the data already gleaned. Drawing upon examples from my own research with murderers and street robbers, as well as the experiences of other researchers, this chapter represents an attempt to appraise the process of planning, undertaking and making sense of qualitative interviews with violent offenders in a prison context. I will suggest that in interpreting interview data researchers need to be mindful of the distinction between 'fact-seeking' and 'meaning-seeking'.

Social scientists have been gathering and analysing the accounts of offenders for over a century in a variety of settings and contexts. There is now a considerable body of literature acknowledging that research involving offender narratives can provide a far richer and deeper understanding of criminal behaviour than other sources. This is not to suggest, however, that offender accounts are unproblematic. Many researchers have reflected upon the credibility of the accounts that they elicit and have demonstrated the various ways in which offenders excuse, justify and minimise their offences as part of their 'vocabulary of motive' (Sykes and Matza 1957; Taylor 1972; Cromwell and Thurman 2003; Davidson 2006). There is seemingly less literature on how offenders exaggerate or glamorise their offences or their own skill and daring (see, though, Maguire and Bennett 1982 and Irwin 1987). Some researchers have been particularly scathing about the validity of accounts provided by incarcerated offenders suggesting that this context is not conducive to gaining 'truthful' accounts (see Wright and Bennett 1990).

This chapter represents an attempt to appraise the process of planning, undertaking and making sense of qualitative interviews with violent offenders in a prison context. I will suggest that it is particularly important to keep in mind the overall objectives of the research and the kinds of research questions being asked when making any kind of appraisal as to the value of the data elicited. At the most fundamental level this includes a need for clarity about the basic epistemological assumptions that are being made. Positivist and constructivist approaches are clearly quite different in this respect.

The positivistic position pivots around the objective gathering of verifiable data. To these ends, positivists would wish to create a 'pure' interview 'enacted in a sterilized context, in such a way that it comes as close as possible to providing a "mirror reflection" of the reality that exists in the social world' (Miller and Glassner 1997: 99). As Miller and Glassner (1997: 99) point out, 'this position has been thoroughly critiqued over the years in terms of both its feasibility and its desirability'. At the opposite end of the spectrum from the 'purist positivists' are radical social constructionists who hold that it is not possible to capture the reality of the complex social world in an interview. Somewhere in between are those who believe that good quality data can be elicited using interviews but that it must be treated with an appropriate level of appreciation for what is being revealed.

At a practical level, researchers need to be aware of what it is they are seeking from their interviewees (i.e. what questions and why) before an assessment of the credibility of the data elicited is even attempted. For example, if researchers are essentially 'fact-seeking' and interested to investigate certain behavioural or factual details gathered during interview (such as the extent and nature of a person's criminal convictions or how often he or she frequents certain pubs in the neighbourhood) then it is possible to conduct validity checks using various documents or other evidence (such as prison and court records or by speaking to close associates). If, on the other hand, the primary objective of the research is 'meaning-seeking', i.e. to unravel perceptual issues (such as offenders' motivations for committing crime or their decision-making processes during the commission of crime), then one needs to adopt a more interpretative approach. Recourse to additional data or particular techniques under this model could help to attain the richest, most complete and genuine picture of that person's offending. However, the idea of an absolute truth would be rejected.

The chapter is split into two substantive sections, beginning, in part 1, with an exploration of some of the specific challenges of interview-based research with violent offenders and how these might be overcome. I pay particular attention to imprisoned offenders as this has tended, in the UK at least, to be a popular means to accessing offenders. This is followed, in part 2, by a consideration of the extent to which a broader research strategy that incorporates additional forms of data and methodological approaches can be useful. This section is somewhat more speculative in 'offering up' a number of possible examples of useful data combinations while acknowledging the problems that triangulation can generate.

Part 1: Interviewing in prison – overcoming some unique challenges

Incarcerated offenders represent an ideal 'captive audience' for the purposes of social science research. Prisoners are generally very receptive to the idea of speaking to researchers about their offending (see Copes and Hochstetler 2006 and this volume). However, they are also a peculiar sub-set of offenders in that they have been caught and are undergoing what is in most countries the severest kind of penalty available for their offending. The nature of the total institution of the prison setting along with the status of violent offender bring with them unique challenges that need to be taken into account when planning, undertaking and making sense of the research.

Access

One of the immediate challenges associated with prison-based research is gaining access – an extremely time consuming and increasingly bureaucratic process. For example, in England and Wales, accessing prisoners generally involves negotiating with multiple gatekeepers (including HM Prison Service in London, prison governors and psychology staff) and involves completing detailed forms, providing copies of research instruments and, on occasion, being interviewed. As criminology has grown as a discipline, the Prison Service now receives an increasing volume of requests to access prisoners, further raising the chances of refusal to enter certain establishments. Research has important costs for prison staff and prisoners and inevitably disrupts normal prison activities (see Noaks and Wincup 2004: ch. 4). Hence, access is rarely a one-off event. Rather, negotiations are most often characterised as a complex, dynamic and ongoing process.

Selection techniques

Once access is approved via key 'gatekeepers' the next potential difficulty is actually recruiting willing participants who meet the necessary research criteria. Who solicits the inmates affects their decision to agree. For example, prison staff generally have no real investment in the project and may not 'sell' it to inmates in a way that the researcher would. The ideal scenario would be to identify the particular inmates who were appropriate to take part in the study (this could be any prisoners or a specific sub-category of offenders), undertake some kind of sampling technique and then approach prisoners directly. In reality, it is often not possible to follow such a format. Rather, one has to rely upon a prison psychologist or prison officer to pass information (perhaps in the form of letters, information sheets, consent forms and so forth) to those they identify (via computer or paper-based records or first-hand knowledge) as fitting the criteria and then simply take whoever happens to volunteer. Where prison staff agree to assist in gaining willing participants they can, of course, inadvertently skew the selection process. For example, it is more likely that inmates will perceive that they will receive some kind of benefit or advantage by agreeing (or suffer some disadvantage if they refuse) when approached by the administration.

While not ideal, there are measures that the research team can take to optimise this process such as ensuring that the information being provided regarding the research project (to both staff and prospective interviewees) is clear, concise and honest so that potential interviewees are able to make truly informed judgments about whether or not to become involved. In addition, it is possible to devise ways in which suitable offenders are located by approaching inmates and by inmates approaching the research team. For example, in order to access violent street offenders (as part of the Street Violence Project[1]), we asked prison staff to highlight the research to inmates and ask for volunteers but also devised large posters that were placed on each wing asking for volunteers (Wright *et al.* 2006). In order to access violent men as part of my doctoral research I was given the opportunity, at one of the prisons, to actually address a group of around 20 men, all of whom fitted the criteria, explain to them the nature and purpose of the research and ask them to sign up to take part over the next few days if they were interested. The benefits of meeting potential interviewees beforehand is that the researcher can take the time to carefully explain the aims of the research, to emphasise that information will be treated confidentially and more generally to demonstrate that the research is ethical (see http://www.britsoccrim.org/ethical.htm). Also, any misconceptions can be dealt with – such as ensuring that volunteers understand that they will not gain any advantage in terms of their treatment within the prison by taking part, nor will they suffer any disadvantage by not taking part.

The ideal should be that one is continually striving to ensure that the right sort of offenders are invited to take part in the study and that they have complete and open information about the study so that they make truly informed decisions about whether or not to be interviewed.

Research scheduling: the need to be flexible

The regime of prison is such that time is carefully managed and there are only a few key windows of opportunity to conduct uninterrupted interviews throughout the day. Moreover, it is not uncommon to find, after arriving at a prison, that planned interviews cannot go ahead because the potential interviewee may be receiving a visit from a solicitor, family member or friend (all of which will be a priority over involvement in research) or may simply have changed his or her mind. Alternatively, prison staff may not be available to escort the researcher or inmates around the prison.

Once interviews are underway there are still many factors, both routine and unexpected, that disrupt their smooth running. For example, Copes and Hochstetler had to stop interviews because of fog alerts and lockdowns (personal communication) and I have had to cut short interviews due to security alerts. Lunch, recreation and educational classes and training also disrupt interviews. Hence the researcher has to be adaptable and flexible and build in ample research time to overcome these difficulties.

The interview process

A crucial aspect in relation to the issue of optimising interview data is the actual interview process. It is often assumed that as long as access has been secured and ethical principles carefully considered that a good interview will somehow follow. Moreover, on large research projects it is often the case that the principal researchers who have actually designed the research are not heavily involved in the actual interviews due to other work and research commitments. Therefore more junior, less experienced research assistants are drafted in who are not necessarily sufficiently embedded into the project and sometimes have a lack of experience and training in undertaking interviews with offenders.

Facilitating free expression: honesty is the best policy

Many researchers recognise that it is vital to maintain an open and honest relationship in interviews and to avoid deception. Some feminists in particular emphasise solidarity and empathy in the research and are committed to 'emancipating the oppressed'. As such, deception would be diametrically opposed to their ideology and methods (Punch 1994: 89). Williamson (2004: 22) aptly states, 'trust is a necessary precursor to "truth"'. Of course, those who are incarcerated may be especially cynical and suspicious as to the 'real' agenda of researchers and therefore be less willing to agree to be interviewed or to 'open up' in an interview setting. This is a further challenge to prison-based research.

There are, however, numerous ways in which the researcher can try to create an open exchange. Of critical importance is to ensure the honest articulation of the aims of the project, the manner in which the data will be used and the extent to which assurances of anonymity and confidentiality apply. Singer *et al.* (1995) found that when research involves sensitive information, confidentiality assurances improve responses. Moreover, they suggest that the higher the degree of confidentiality the better the data received (see also Singer *et al.* 2003). Aside from assurances of confidentiality, the use of pseudonyms, chosen by the offender, is a useful approach that I have always adopted. In addition, consent forms can be carefully designed to assure the interviewee that only in exceptional circumstances would total confidentiality not apply. For example, assurances can extend to discussions of crimes for which the offender has never been caught by stressing the importance of speaking in general as opposed to specific terms in relation to such offences (i.e. avoiding dates, place names and so forth).

In order to promote an open, conversational-style interview process, all interviews need to begin with an introduction, where the full aims of the research are explained to the interviewee as well as the ethical principles being adopted. Throughout my projects I have always told participants about the data that I have already analysed and why it is important for me to speak to them and to obtain their frank and honest opinions and insights into violence generally and their own involvement in it. Frequently interviewees begin to express their views at this point, before I have actually asked the first question. Hence a good introductory talk can lead, quite naturally, into the interview. In addition, adopting the stance of curious questioner throughout is a useful approach. This means probing and asking for clarification if in any doubt as to what an interviewee means. Moreover, as Oakley (1981: 49) points out, in interviewing there is 'no intimacy without reciprocity'. Sharing experiences and stories (within reason) is, therefore, a useful interview approach but also a natural way to undertake an exchange of views.

Finally, in terms of physical setting, it is important that the researcher try to negotiate the best possible private space for conducting interviews. I have almost always managed to secure private space but am aware of other researchers who have had to settle for semi-private rooms within prisons and, as a consequence, have experienced interruptions and noise, all of which have a negative impact upon the interview process. Moreover, the chances of an interviewee 'opening up' are clearly compromised if he or she can be overheard.

Status of the researcher and researched

The impact of gender, age, social class and race on the research process has been discussed by a number of researchers (see Miller this volume). For example, female researchers including Easterday *et al.* (1982), Gelsthorpe (1990), Gurney (1991) and Ackers (1993) have focused in particular on the gender and age issue. The consensus is that being a young female can be both enabling and constraining. It has been argued, for example, that personable young women make more empathic interviewers than men (Dingwall 1980: 881). Whatever the case, it is clear that within the prison setting more than most others, the researcher needs to be sensitive to the power imbalance between researcher and researched and to reflect upon the various ways in which gender, age, race, social class, appearance, demeanour and accent, among other factors, can impact upon the kind of data retrieved (see Webb *et al.* 2000: 20). One way to counteract any bias produced by the biography of the researcher is to use different interviewers and to then undertake a systematic comparison of different researchers' influences upon the information retrieved (see Denzin 1989 on 'investigator triangulation').

Capturing the conversation

Prisons are not the most ideal location for the use of recording equipment. Carrying such equipment into the prison can lead to additional security checks and hence delays but also, unless the equipment is of very good quality, it may not capture the conversation well due to lots of background noise and poor acoustics. That said, there is little doubt that the use of an unobtrusive (ideally high-quality digital) recording device is important as it allows one to capture every word of the conversation and not be distracted by note taking. It is common practice to turn this audio data into verbatim interview transcripts and to rely upon this data when undertaking analysis. Yet, as Kvale (1996: 166–7) aptly notes, transcripts are 'decontextualized conversations' ('to *trans*cribe means to *trans*form'). Hence, the auditory account should be revisited during the analysis of the research as it contains rich data, such as laughter, tone of voice and so forth, that cannot be adequately captured in textual form. It is important, of course, that the interviewee is comfortable with having the conversation recorded and that it does not inhibit free expression. It is always advisable, even where an interviewee consents to having the interview recorded, to stress that it can be turned off at any time if that would make the offender more comfortable in revealing certain aspects of their offending career. A perceptive and sensitive interviewer invariably knows when it might be appropriate to reiterate that offer during interview. For example, an interviewee's body language can illustrate when he or she is feeling uncomfortable, restless or bored or whether the person has become agitated or excitable (see Webb *et al.* 2000: 152). Certainly during interviews that I have conducted it has become necessary to occasionally pause the recording device in order that the interviewee is more comfortable discussing sensitive issues. One question in particular has almost always led to such caution, namely 'what offences have you committed that have not come to the knowledge of the police or other agents of the CJS?' Noaks and Wincup (2004: 86) recommend that the interviewee be given control of the recording device and its on/off switch in order to go some way to 'redressing the inherent power imbalance between interviewer and interviewee'.

The nature and ordering of questions

The nature and ordering of questions can have a significant impact upon the quality of information received. This is particularly pertinent when dealing with sensitive topics such as violent crime, not least because reflecting back upon a murder or violent robbery committed can lead to strong emotions. There is some evidence that in order to enhance recall, researchers should focus upon events closest in time. For good discussions regarding intentional and unintentional retrospective distortion, see Beauregard *et al.* (2007) and Progrebin *et al.* (2006).

Aside from the issue of enhancing recall, researchers often debate the relative merits of asking closed factual questions first or more open and detailed questions. There seems to be something of a consensus that it is appropriate to commence with less emotive issues and lead up to sensitive topics, and researchers often design interview schedules with this in mind. However, there are other more subtle ways in which the quality and quantity of information retrieved can be affected. For example, during the street violence project (Brookman *et al.* 2007; Wright *et al.* 2006) over 130 offenders were interviewed across six different prisons in England and Wales and a total of four different researchers conducted the interviews. A fairly lengthy semi-structured interview schedule was adopted. However, the information gleaned varied quite considerably due to interviewer style and technique. For example, one of the sections focused specifically on the decisions made during the actual commission of a violent street event (such as a robbery), including how the target was approached, whether and how weapons were used and how the event unfolded. Most interviewees provided very detailed accounts but it was also often necessary to go back over the detail and seek further elaboration. However, one of the interviewers was apt to move very quickly from the answers provided in this section to the next section – which focused upon whether and how the offender had got caught. It became noticeable that this approach led to a significant decrease in further detailed information. It is possible that taking the offender abruptly from the account of their crime (which they often discussed with some excitement) to the negative experience of being caught led to the stunted flow.

Related to this is the issue of the use of multiple questions on the same topic. Dean and Foote Whyte (1969: 107) note that it is important to ask questions in many different ways so that 'the complex configuration that a person's sentiments represent can be more accurately understood'. To illustrate, as part of my doctoral research into homicide and sub-lethal violence in the UK I interviewed 20 men who had been incarcerated for homicide or sub-lethal violence. They were asked a series of questions about violence. One set asked them to provide narratives of the most recent violent event they had been involved in. Another set asked them more generally and abstractly about the causes of this sort of violence (e.g. murder or assault). A final set asked them to consider whether violence was ever useful or necessary. Unsurprisingly perhaps, I uncovered what appeared to be a fundamental contradiction between the men's accounts of particular acts of violence and their reflections upon the reasons for violence more generally. Specifically, the men tended to explain their recourse to violence essentially by 'blaming' the victim. By focusing upon the inappropriate behaviour of the victim, the men excluded reference to external factors (either social or situational), or factors specific to themselves as violent offenders (such as biological or psychological predispositions to violence). In contrast, when the men were asked to consider the causes of violence among men on a more general level, they drew upon the very issues that they formerly neglected to mention, i.e. the role of alcohol, the families in which they were raised and the kinds of environments in which they lived. Some even suggested that violence was part and parcel of some men's 'makeup', others that it was a pleasurable pursuit and linked to feelings of power. Clearly the use of different styles of questions demonstrates the complexity and diverseness of human explanations.

Flick (2006) has designed a method – known as the episodic interview – which he claims is capable of revealing both episodic knowledge linked to experiences and concrete situations and circumstances and semantic knowledge, which is more abstract and generalised. Essentially, episodic knowledge is retrieved using narratives (e.g. 'Looking back, what was your first encounter with violence? Could you recount the situation for me?'). Semantic knowledge, on the other hand, is retrieved through 'concrete pointed questions' (Flick 2006: 181). In short, it is increasingly being recognised that the specific nature of questions used in an interview setting impacts in important ways upon the kind of data retrieved (see also Flick 1994).

Techniques of neutralisation

There is a substantial body of literature that highlights questions surrounding the validity and veracity of offender accounts and self-reports (among others, Henning and Holdford 2006; Davidson 2006). These concerns focus on issues with retrospective accounts, exaggeration, minimisation, distortion, justification, neutralisation, denial, preservation of favourable self-images and so on. See Maruna and Copes (2005) for an excellent appraisal of neutralisation research over the past five decades.

An overwhelming observation regarding the reliability of offender accounts relates to the linguistic mechanisms that respondents often employ. As C. Wright Mills (1940: 904) put it, 'the differing reasons men give for their actions are not themselves without meaning' (see Presser 2009 for an exemplary discussion of the ways in which offender narratives might be reconceptualised in criminology).

Violent offenders have often undergone 'training' or 'cognitive behavioural therapy' (for example an 'anger management' course) within the prison setting and their accounts may be 'glossed' or couched in therapy language. Over half of the violent men I interviewed as part of my PhD had recounted details of their most recent violent offence to a prison or probation officer and undergone a process of considerable reflection about their violent offending – the purpose being to ascertain whether these men were sufficiently motivated to begin to address their offending behaviour through attendance at such programmes. There is little doubt that these interviews may have impacted upon the kinds of accounts these men drew upon to explain their violence to me during interview. The task for the researcher is to take such processes into consideration when formulating research questions and analysing the narratives received. So while the possibility of concealment, embellishment, exaggeration or outright deception cannot be overlooked in any conversation (criminal or otherwise), there may be particular challenges posed in the case of interviews with violent offenders who are being 'trained' to view their attitudes to, and use of violence, in new ways (see Copes and Hochstetler this volume on 'penitent' reconstructions and Peräkylä 1997 and Miller and Glassner 1997 for a comprehensive discussion of the problem of eliciting reality in interviewing).

Of course, prison-based treatment programmes are just one way in which offenders may come to develop a particular way of articulating their offending and offences. Incarcerated offenders are (usually) exposed to the wider culture via contact with prison staff, visitors, television and radio and a high turnaround of new prisoners with more recent exposure to the outside world. Offenders, therefore, become exposed to wider societal norms regarding acceptable 'vocabularies of motive' (see Mills 1940; Taylor 1972; Scully and Marolla 1984).

This is not, moreover, an issue that is confined to the accounts of violent offenders or to those who are interviewed in prison. Many accounts from a range of criminals elicited in a variety of settings exhibit such tendencies. For example, Carl Klockars' (1974) study *The Professional Fence* demonstrates the ability of the protagonist, Vincent Swaggi, to assuage his guilt by adopting techniques of neutralisation. Although he received and sold stolen goods he asserted that he had never stolen anything in his life and made, what was for him, an important distinction between stealing and receiving. He reasoned that stealing would continue even if he were not there to receive the goods. Furthermore, it was very important for Vincent to present himself as a businessman. He took great pride in his 'work' and tended to elevate himself above other fences whom he regarded as inferior and less expert in their criminal enterprises than himself. Similar examples can be found in Philippe Bourgois' (2003) *In Search of Respect: Selling Crack in El'Barrio.*

In short, while techniques of neutralisation are not unique to imprisoned violent offenders,[2] there are certain distinctive factors that may lead this group to be particularly susceptible to minimising and distorting their accounts. These include the effects of any programmes of reform they may have undergone, the extent to which their offences are perceived, within wider society and among offenders, as particularly serious (e.g. child sex offenders are considered especially deviant in Western culture and afforded the lowest status among other prisoners). In addition, the very status of inmate, coupled with the effects of prison subculture, will likely impact upon offenders' views of the world and colour the language adopted and explanations provided.

Discourse and linguistic analysis

Timor and Weiss (2008) recommend exploring the linguistic devices used by offenders. As a result of the ability of the offender to minimise the harm they have caused, researchers must take into account 'more than just the manifest content of verbal statements, as a person can purposefully conceal certain components of his perception or deny them' (Timor and Weiss 2008: 112). Researchers should also take latent messages into consideration, which are decipherable by examining certain grammatical tools that the offender may employ. These may include discomfort with the criminal acts they have committed, the use of minimising techniques and tag questions ('do you know what I mean?' 'You understand don't you?').

Discourse analysis is somewhat broader in scope in that it focuses upon the social rather than purely linguistic organisation of talk (or text). For example, it focuses upon the construction of versions of events and the 'interpretive repertoires' that are used in such constructions (see Flick 2006: 324). There are many different forms of discourse analysis with varying dimensions of analysis and methodologies. For example, critical (or Foucauldian) discourse analysis focuses upon the ways in which social and political ideology and power is reproduced by text and talk. Discourse analysis clearly offers a further means of unravelling meaning and, in particular, can help to make sense of what might at first appear to be contradictory attitudes or sentiments by placing them in context (see Potter and Wetherell 1987).

Summary

Thus far I have considered some of the particular challenges associated with prison-based interviews with violent offenders and how these difficulties might be tackled. A broader strategy would include enhancing interview data with other forms of information or insight – to which I now turn.

Part 2: Methodological triangulation

Denzin (1989) distinguishes between four broad types of triangulation: (1) data; (2) investigator; (3) theory; and (4) methodological. In this part of the chapter I focus, in the main, upon methodological triangulation (specifically between-method triangulation).

The use of multiple methods within the social sciences is generally regarded as a useful strategy in that the weaknesses of one method are, arguably, overcome by the strengths of another (Denzin 1989). As Webb *et al.* (2000: xiii) put it: 'multiple methods – properly used in combination – help to overcome threats to validity'.

While there is both an intuitive and scientific appeal to such cross-validation, this approach often assumes some universal 'truth' awaiting discovery by the researcher. In contrast, human behaviour, interpretation and sentiment are complex, multi-faceted and rarely static. Hence, as Flick (2006: 390) notes, the focus of triangulation 'has shifted increasingly towards further enriching and complementing knowledge and towards transgressing the (always limited) epistemological potentials of the individual method'. Moreover, as indicated in the introduction, the extent to which one can corroborate or complement interview data depends crucially upon the research questions being addressed and hence the particular kind of information being sought. Arguably, the further one moves from observable, factual events towards internal thoughts and perceptions, the less feasible and desirable validation becomes. With this in mind I now consider some of the techniques that could be adopted to complement interview data.

Official documents

Many researchers who conduct offender interviews perform validation checks of the information they elicit in order to gauge how truthful or otherwise their respondents have been (Athens 1980; Ray and Simons 1987). Porter and Woodworth (2007) compared official and self-reported homicide descriptions of psychopaths and non-psychopaths.

They discovered that both groups tended to minimise the instrumentality and exaggerate the reactivity of their homicides in a 'self-exculpating fashion' (though psychopaths did so to a greater degree). The authors suggest that their research is the first to examine the manner in which offenders describe their violence relative to official files. In fact, in 1990 Scully interviewed men convicted of rape and used pre-sentence reports to verify their accounts. This allowed Scully to distinguish between three distinct types of rapist – those who admitted the rape (admitters), but who systematically understated the amount of force and violence used; those who denied they had committed any rape (deniers) and whose accounts differed markedly from the victim's and police's version of what had taken place; and finally those who denied any contact at all with their victims. In addition, Klockars (1974) supplemented interviews with 'Vincent' (a professional fence) with orphanage records, probation records and other miscellaneous documents in order to corroborate interview information.

There are certainly a wealth of documents available that are often not used at all or to their full potential by researchers that can add to – and sometimes challenge – information already received. However, there are two important notes of caution. Firstly, it is not correct to assume that official documents are necessarily more valid than the reports of offenders themselves. Researchers have to assess the credibility of official documents in much the same way as they assess offender accounts. For example, during my analysis of police murder files (as part of a multi-method approach to exploring homicide) I discovered that parts of these documents had been written, essentially, to persuade the Crown Prosecution Service to prosecute the defendant. Particular sorts of language were adopted in order to make some witness accounts seem more credible than others and to discredit other accounts. In short, the context in which these documents were written and their overall aim meant that they had to be viewed with caution in much the same way as verbal accounts need to be interpreted carefully (Brookman 1999). Further, while it is possible to validate or corroborate factual data (such as an offender's criminal history via official records), it is difficult to validate people's feelings, perceptions, motives or opinions. Yet it is the latter that researchers are often keen to unravel.

Other documents

Aside from official documents there are a host of other potentially valuable materials – both historic and contemporary – that social scientists can draw upon to complement interview data. These include diaries, letters, autobiographies and so forth (see Barbour 2008: ch. 1). Offender biographies, for example, represent an underused resource within criminology, despite their use by pioneering Chicago criminologist Clifford

Shaw in the 1930s (see Goodey 2000). Nellis (2002) discusses the value of using prisoner autobiographies in the training of probation officers and focuses, in particular, upon what they reveal about desistance from crime and the penal system. Clearly though, their value is even broader and can be extended to explorations of, for example, lifestyle and motives for offending. Shover (1996) made extensive use of the autobiographies of offenders and ex-offenders (in combination with offender interviews, ethnographic research and survey data) to excellent effect. As he aptly acknowledges, the interpretations found in such accounts benefit from the extended length of time that the authors have spent making sense of their lives: 'Men who spend years in prison characteristically devote hours to examining their pasts, the forces that shaped them and significant contingencies in their lives. Published autobiographies are storehouses of these interpretations and other materials' (Shover 1996: 190; Shover and Hunter, this volume). Further, autobiographical accounts engage with emotion in a way that is much more difficult, if not impossible, to reveal in an interview setting. As Priestley (1989 cited in Nellis 2002: 437) notes: 'although there may well be distortions, deceptions and misperceptions in any one particular prisoner autobiography, the whole corpus of work presents a picture in which the main outlines are clearly confirmed from many sources'. In a slightly different vein, Cohen and Taylor (1977) supplemented interviews and conversations with inmates by asking them to produce stories, essays and poems on particular topics. These data then formed the basis for 'further talk and exchange of mutual interpretations' (cited in Jupp 1989: 141). Similarly diaries can be used to provide powerful insights into what is happening in respondents' lives between interviews and can be used to identify issues to explore in further interviews. As Barbour (2008: 18) notes, diaries 'can provide scope for articulating issues that might not be picked up in interviews and for accessing what would otherwise remain "hidden" or "muted" accounts'. Finally, some researchers have made use of newspaper reports to good effect. For example, Copes and Hochstetler, as part of their identity theft research, used newspapers to locate participants. When they then interviewed the offenders they took the newspaper story to explain how the individual had been chosen but also used it as a launching pad for discussion, as many of the interviewees wanted to correct the story (personal communication).

Other 'key' individuals

Beyond official documentation, researchers can draw upon the accounts of other individuals who may be in a position to offer a valuable additional perspective to the main interviewees. Key individuals in this context might include ex-offenders, co-offenders, victims, witnesses or, in order to gain a broader perspective of the social world that offenders inhabit, family and friends. Once again, of course, we cannot assume that these informants offer more valid information. Rather, the information needs to be taken as part of the tapestry being woven – to help to refine interpretations and generalisations already made or assist in the generation of fresh ideas.

Victim, witness and co-offender accounts

Symbolic interactionists have always recognised the importance of acknowledging the relationship between the offender and the victim of crime and how they interact with one another before and during the criminal event.

> It would not be correct nor complete to speak of a carnivorous animal, its habits and characteristics, without looking at the prey on which it lives ... Although it looks one-sided as far as the final outcome goes, it is not a totally unilateral form of relationship. They work upon each other profoundly and continuously, even before the moment of disaster. To know one we must be acquainted with the complementary partner. (Von Hentig 1948: 385)

From this perspective, one could argue that it would make sense to always try to gather the perspectives of all of the 'players' involved in a criminal event. This could include the offender, co-offenders, the victim(s) and any witnesses. In reality this is not always possible. For example, in the case of homicide there is no victim remaining to interview and it would be difficult and ethically problematic to trace and interview witnesses most of the time (if there were any). However, for other offences this may be less tricky. For example, in the case of assaults or street robbery one may be able to use official documents (such as police files) to trace the relevant victims and seek their willingness to take part. Wright and Decker (1997) explored the dynamics of offender–victim confrontations in armed robbery but relied exclusively on the accounts of offenders. Juxtaposing offender accounts with those of the victims or witnesses would presumably have provided some interesting alternative accounts and shed additional light on the phenomenon.

Relatives and friends

Similarly, speaking to relatives and friends of offenders can allow the researcher to capture different perspectives on the same issue. A classic study that adopted such an approach is Klockars' (1974) *The Professional Fence*. Klockars undertook corroborative interviews with the friends and family of 'Vincent' (as well as observing his dealings with criminals and others and making use of documents – as discussed above). Marie Lindegaard (this volume), during her ethnographic fieldwork in South

Africa, compared young juveniles' explanations of how and why they were involved in crime with explanations from friends and family. In short, while it may be difficult to achieve in practice certain research projects would undoubtedly benefit by gathering information from other 'actors' who are part of the wider social network of the offender.

Group interviews and focus groups

Given that there are various individuals who may have valuable information and insights in relation to crime, it may also be beneficial to bring these various informants together and undertake group interviews or focus groups. Focus groups differ, subtly, from group interviews in that 'the researcher is actively encouraging of, and attentive to, the group interaction' (Kitzinger and Barbour 1999: 20, cited in Barbour 2007). People's views and perceptions often develop in a social context, via interactions with family, friends, neighbours and colleagues. Focus groups and group interviews can help researchers to unravel these processes and enable the researcher to 'get closer to the to-and-fro social exchanges that take place in everyday life' (Crow and Semmens 2008: 124). While focus groups provide a more dynamic picture than the static result of one-to-one interviews, they are, nevertheless, difficult to manage and the very dynamics that prove so valuable to explore can also present real challenges, with some group members dominating discussions and others becoming uncomfortable and unwilling to take part in an exchange.

Multiple and follow-up interviews

There is some evidence that the more familiar the respondent is with the researcher the more honest he or she is likely to be (Jacques and Wright 2008; Bourgois 2003; Davidson 2006; Williamson 2004). For example, Davidson (2006) found that interviewees provided more honest accounts in later interviews and Williamson (2004) has argued that his long-term contact with 'the Miltown Boys' (originally interviewed when they were teenagers and then again some twenty years later) helped to secure open and honest accounts not least because of the trust that had developed between himself and the boys/men. If verified through further study, it would be important for researchers to try to arrange follow-up interviews with incarcerated offenders over more extended periods of time than is often the case with short-term research projects.

Multiple interviews allow one to capture the changing views or sentiments of individuals in a way that is not possible in one interview. In addition, it allows one more scope to alter the setting and context of the interview. As Dean and Foote Whyte (1969: 113) put it, 'informants can and do hold conflicting sentiments at one time and they hold varying sentiments according to the situation in which they find themselves'. Hence the importance of repeated interviews in different contexts.

Lindegaard (this volume) followed the stories of young offenders from one social setting to another (e.g. prison, home, street). She convincingly argues that by gathering accounts in different contexts from different actors (see above) one gains a much more sophisticated appreciation of how and why offenders construct accounts in particular ways.

Collaborative interpretations

Multiple interviews allow for a more collaborative process to emerge between the researcher and the researched. For example, Cohen and Taylor (1977), during their prison-based research, engaged in a form of collaborative research in which the inmates and researchers were viewed as equal partners with an equivalent contribution to the final product. The rationale for such collaboration is that 'if subjects recognise themselves in research accounts this provides one way of establishing the validity of such accounts' (Jupp 1989: 141). Along similar lines, Kvale (1996: 247) advocates 'reversing the direction' in research to allow the subjects to comment on researchers' interpretation of the interview. This might include allowing subjects to listen to researchers' conversations about their interviews or allowing them to read through the transcripts and early analysis and offer their views (see also Flick 2006 on 'communicative validation'). Moreover, Kvale notes that 'what is relatively new in qualitative research in the social sciences is the emphasis on truth as negotiated in a local context, with extensions of the interpretive community to include the subjects investigated and the lay public' (Kvale 1996: 247).

Visual data

Another possible way to supplement or corroborate interview data is by use of visual data. For example, depending upon the nature of the research project, it could be possible to use CCTV to supplement and even inform interview data. For example, assaults and street robberies are increasingly captured on CCTV due to the proliferation of cameras across cities and towns. These images will often have been seized by the police as part of their evidence and so it is possible that a researcher could try to match up offenders to CCTV footage and then make use of this visual data prior to, during or after conducting interviews in such a way as to cross check the details provided by offenders regarding their actions – including their specific role in the robbery, the level of violence adopted and so forth.

While unlikely to be an option with prison-based research, there is clearly scope for ethnographic researchers to encourage interviewees to make use of video and photographs to capture 'their world'. For example, those taking part in the study can be asked to take (or have someone else take) photographs or video footage that illustrate who they are and their lifestyle (see Dabbs 1982; St Jean 2007). The images can be used as data in their own right and/or to inform and stimulate interviews. Like interview data, however, photographic images have also been scrutinised for their validity with the old adage 'the camera never lies' being challenged. Becker (1986), for example, suggests that photographs may not 'tell the truth' and recommends questioning what is in the picture? what is focused on? and what is left out? Similar objections have been raised regarding video footage (see Flick 2006: ch. 18).

Finally, researchers could make use of visual information to help to validate accounts of violence. Specifically, exterior physical signs (such as scars) are often presented as war wounds to interviewers and tattoos similarly can validate offenders' claims regarding their membership in, or association with, certain gangs.

Conclusion

Throughout this chapter I have considered the various difficulties associated with gleaning full and frank information from incarcerated violent offenders and the extent to which it is possible to build effectively upon offender accounts with alternative forms of data. While the prison setting naturally imposes various constraints, there are measures that one can adopt to minimise their impact upon the research process and, ultimately, the quality of data obtained. In addition, researchers have at their disposal a diverse range of alternative methods and data sources that can be drawn upon to corroborate or further enrich interview data. However, as indicated earlier, the extent to which it is necessary or useful to adopt a broader strategy depends upon the kinds of research questions being posed.

For example, if one wishes to discover 'what happened' during a street robbery then it is perfectly feasible to use multiple sources and, in effect, cross check the offender's version of events (e.g. by using information from witnesses, the victim and perhaps CCTV). While one would not expect to gain a definitive account of what happened it would, nevertheless, be possible to establish a fairly credible version of events based upon multiple evidence. If, on the other hand, the objective of the research is to uncover and explain the offender's motivation for committing crime (i.e. to get at his or her 'truth') then going beyond accounts is less helpful. However, there are still techniques that can be employed to 'dig deep', unravel and build upon the offender's account. These include discourse analysis, the use of different question styles, probing for inconsistencies, the use of multiple interviews, the use of different interviewers and interviewing the offender in different contexts (e.g. prison, home, the street). Each of these techniques can, in different ways, help to illuminate the offender's meaning.

However much there is to be gained by supplementing offender accounts with other forms of data, the offenders' 'take' on their offending and their social world ought still to take centre stage for those of us who are interested in unravelling the motives for offending. There is no one better placed to articulate his or her thoughts, emotions, decisions, objectives, goals, hopes and fears than the offender him/herself.

Acknowledgments

Special thanks to Professor Mike Maguire, Professor Trevor Bennett and Assistant Professor Heith Copes for their guidance and invaluable comments on an earlier draft of this chapter.

Notes

1 A qualitative study of the role of violence in street crime funded by the Economic and Social research Council for England and Wales (Award Number: RES-000-22-0398).
2 In addition, there is no compelling evidence to date that accounts provided by incarcerated offenders are any less reliable or valid than those provided by 'active' offenders (see Copes and Hochstetler this volume).

References

Ackers, H. L. (1993) 'Racism, sexuality, and the process of ethnographic research', in D. Hobbs and T. May (eds), *Interpreting the Field: Accounts of Ethnography*. Oxford: Clarendon Press.

Agnew, R. (1990) 'The origins of delinquent events: an examination of offender accounts', *Journal of Research in Crime and Delinquency*, 27: 267–94.

Athens, L. H. (1980) *Violent Criminal Acts and Actors: A Symbolic Interactionist Study*. London: Routledge & Kegan Paul.

Barbour, R. (2007) *Doing Focus Groups*. London: Sage.

Barbour, R. (2008) *Introducing Qualitative Research*. London: Sage.

Beauregard, E., Rossmo, D. K. and Proulx, J. (2007) 'A descriptive model of the hunting process of serial sex offenders: a rational choice perspective', *Journal of Family Violence*, 22 (6): 449–63.

Becker, H. (1986) 'Do photographs tell the truth?', in *Doing Things Together*. Evanston, IL: Northwestern University Press, pp. 273–92.

Bourgois, P. (2003) *In Search of Respect: Selling Crack in El'Barrio*. New York: Cambridge University Press.

Brookman, F. (1999) 'Accessing and analysing police murder files', in F. Brookman, L. Noaks and E. Wincup (eds), *Qualitative Research in Criminology*. Aldershot: Ashgate.

Brookman, F., Bennett, T. H., Mullins, C. and Wright, R. (2007) 'Gender, motivation and the accomplishment of street robbery in the United Kingdom', *British Journal of Criminology*, 47 (6): 861–84.

Coates, L. and Wade, A. (2007) 'Language and violence: analysis of four discursive operations', *Journal of Family Violence*, 22 (7): 511–22.

Cohen, S. and Taylor, L. (1975) 'Prison research: a cautionary tale', *New Society*, 31 (643): 253–5

Cohen, S. and Taylor, L. (1977) 'Talking about prison blues', in C. Bell and H. Newby (eds), *Doing Sociological Research*. London: Allen & Unwin.

Copes, H. and Hochstetler, A. (2006) 'Why I'll talk: offenders' motives for participating in qualitative research', in P. Cromwell (ed.), *In Their Own Words: Criminals on Crime. An Anthology* (4th edn). London: Oxford University Press.

Cromwell, P. (ed.) (2006) *In Their Own Words: Criminals on Crime. An Anthology* (4th edn). London: Oxford University Press.

Cromwell, P. and Thurman, Q. (2003) 'The devil made me do it: use of neutralizations by shoplifters', *Deviant Behaviour*, 24 (6): 535–50.

Crow, I. and Semmens, N. (2008), *Researching Criminology*. Maidenhead: Open University Press.

Dabbs, J. M. (1982) 'Making things visible', in J. Van Maanen, J. M. Dabbs and R. Faulkner (eds), *Varieties of Qualitative Research*. London: Sage.

Davidson, J. (2006) 'Victims speak: comparing child sexual abusers' and child victims' accounts, perceptions, and interpretations of sexual abuse', *Victims and Offenders*, 1 (2): 159–74.

Dean, J. P. and Foote Whyte, W. (1969) 'How do you know if the informant is telling the truth?', in G. J. McCall and J. L. Simmons (eds), *Issues in Participant Observation*. London: Addison-Wesley.

Denzin, N. K. (1989) *The Research Act* (3rd edn). Englewood Cliffs, NJ: Prentice Hall.

Dingwall, R. (1980) 'Ethics and ethnography', *Sociological Review*, 28 (4): 871–91.

Easterday, L., Papademas, D., Schorr, L. and Valentine, C. (1982) 'The making of a female researcher: some role problems in fieldwork', in R. Burgess (ed.), *Field Research: A Sourcebook and Field Manual*. London: Allen & Unwin.

Flick, U. (1994) 'Social representations and the social construction of everyday knowledge: theoretical and methodological queries', *Social Science Information*, 33: 179–97.

Flick, U. (2000) 'Episodic interviewing', in M. Bauer and G. Gaskell (eds), *Qualitative Researching with Text, Image and Sound: A Practical Handbook*. London: Sage.

Flick, U. (2006) *An Introduction to Qualitative Research* (3rd edn). London: Sage.

Gelsthorpe, L. (1990) 'Feminist methodologies in criminology: a new approach or old wine in new bottles', in L. Gelsthorpe and A. Morris (eds), *Feminist Perspectives in Criminology*. Milton Keynes: Open University Press.

Goodey, J. (2000) 'Biographical lessons for criminology', *Theoretical Criminology*, 4 (4): 473–98.

Green, G., South, N. and Smith, R. (2006) 'They say you are a danger but you are not: representations and construction of the moral self in narratives of dangerous individuals', *Deviant Behaviour*, 27 (3): 299–328.

Gurney, J. N. (1991) 'Female researchers in male-dominated settings', in W. B. Schaffir and R. A. Strebbins (eds), *Experiencing Fieldwork: An Inside View of Qualitative Research*. Newbury Park, CA: Sage.

Hammersley, M. and Atkinson, P. (1995) *Ethnography: Principles in Practice*. London: Routledge.

Henning, K. and Holdford, R. (2006) 'Minimization, denial, and victim blaming by batterers: how much does the truth matter?', *Criminal Justice and Behaviour*, 33 (1): 110–30.

Irwin, J. (1987) *The Felon*. Berkeley, CA: University of California Press.

Jacobs, B. A. (2006) 'The case for dangerous fieldwork', in D. Hobbs and R. Wright (eds), *The Sage Handbook of Fieldwork*. Thousand Oaks, CA: Sage, pp. 147–68.

Jacques, S. and Wright, R. (2008) 'Intimacy with outlaws: the role of relational distance in recruiting, paying, and interviewing underworld research participants', *Journal of Research in Crime and Delinquency*, 45 (1): 22–38.

Jupp, V. (1989) *Methods of Criminological Research*. London: Routledge.

Klockars, C. B. (1974) *The Professional Fence*. London: Tavistock.

Kvale, S. (1996) *Interviews: An Introduction to Qualitative Research Interviewing*. Thousand Oaks, CA: Sage.

Maguire, M. and Bennett, T. (1982) *Burglary in a Dwelling – The Offence, the Offender and the Victim*. London: Heinemann.

Martin, C. (2000) 'Doing research in a prison setting', in V. Jupp, P. Davies and P. Francis (eds), *Doing Criminological Research*. London: Sage.

Maruna, S. and Copes, H. (2005) 'What have we learned from fifty years of neutralization research?', *Crime and Justice: A Review of Research*, 32: 221–320.

Miller, J. and Glassner, B. (1997) 'The "inside" and the "outside": finding realities', in D. Silverman (ed.), *Qualitative Research: Theory, Method and Practice*. London: Sage.

Mills, C. W. (1940) 'Situated actions and vocabularies of motive', *American Sociological Review*, V (December): 904–13

Nellis, M. (2002) 'Prose and cons: offender auto/biographies, penal reform and probation training', *Howard Journal*, 41 (5): 434–68.

Noaks, L. and Wincup, E. (2004) *Criminological Research: Understanding Qualitative Methods*. London: Sage.

Oakley, A. (1981) 'Interviewing women: a contradiction in terms', in H. Roberts (ed.), *Doing Feminist Research*. London: Routledge & Kegan Paul.

Peräkylä, A. (1997) 'Reliability and validity in research based on tapes and transcripts', in D. Silverman (ed.), *Qualitative Research: Theory, Method and Practice*. London: Sage.

Pogrebin, M., Stretesky, P. B. and Unnithan, N. P. (2006) 'Retrospective accounts of violent events by gun offenders', *Deviant Behavior*, 27 (4): 479–501.

Porter, S. and Woodworth, M. (2007) 'I'm sorry I did it ... but he started it: a comparison of the official and self-reported homicide descriptions of psychopaths and nonpsychopaths', *Law and Human Behaviour*, 31 (1): 91–107.

Potter, J. and Wetherell, M. (1987) *Discourse and Social Psychology: Beyond Attitudes and Behaviour*. London: Sage.

Presser, L. (2009) 'The narratives of offenders', *Theoretical Criminology*, 13 (2): 177–200.

Punch, M. (1994) 'Politics and ethics in qualitative research', in N. K. Denzin and Y. S. Lincoln (eds), *Handbook of Qualitative Research*. London: Sage.

Ray, M. C. (1986) *Convicted Offenders' Vocabulary of Motive: Truth or Consequences*, Ann Arbor, MI: University Microfilms International.

Ray, M. C. and Simons, R. L. (1987) 'Convicted murderers accounts of their crimes: a study of homicide in small communities', *Symbolic Interactionism*, 10 (1): 57–70.

Scully, D. (1990) *Understanding Sexual Violence*. London: Harper Collins.

Scully, D. and Marolla, J. (1984) 'Convicted rapists' vocabulary of motives: excuses and justifications', *Social Problems*, 31 (5): 530–44.

Shaw, C. (1930), *The Jack-Roller: A Delinquent Boy's Own Story*. Chicago: University of Chicago Press.

Shover, N. (1996), *Great Pretenders: Pursuits and Careers of Persistent Thieves*. Boulder, CO: Westview.

Singer, E., Van Hoewyk, J. and Neugebauer, R. J. (2003) 'Attitudes and behavior – the impact of privacy and confidentiality concerns on participation in the 2000 Census', *Public Opinion Quarterly*, 67 (3): 368–84.

Singer, E., Von Thurn, D. and Miller, E. (1995) 'Confidentiality assurances and response: a quantitative review of the experimental literature', *Public Opinion Quarterly*, 59 (1): 66–77.

St Jean, P. K. B. (2007) *Pockets of Crime*. Chicago: University of Chicago Press.

Sykes, G. and Matza, D. (1957) 'Techniques of neutralization', *American Sociological Review*, 22: 664–70.

Taylor, L. (1972) 'The significance and interpretation of replies to motivational questions: the case of sex offenders', *Sociology*, 6 (1): 23–39.

Timor, U. and Weiss, J. M. (2008) 'Sociolinguistic and psycholinguistic indications of behaviour disorders: analysis of a prisoner's discourse', *International Journal of Offender Therapy and Comparative Criminology*, 52 (1): 112–26.

Von Hentig, H. (1948) *The Criminal and His Victim: Studies in the Sociobiology of Crime*. New Haven, CT: Yale University Press.

Webb, E. J., Donald T., Campbell, R., Schwartz, D. and Sechrest, L. (2000) *Unobtrusive Measures: Nonreactive Research in the Social Sciences* (rev. edn). Chicago: Rand McNally.

Williamson, H. (2004) *The Milltown Boys Revisited*. Oxford: Berg.

Wright, R. and Bennett, T. (1990) 'Exploring the offender's perspective: observing and interviewing criminals', in L. Kimberly and F. Kemp (eds), *Measurement Issues in Criminology*. London: Springer-Verlag.

Wright, R. and Decker, S. (1997) *Armed Robbers in Action: Stickups and Street Culture*. Boston, MA: Northeastern University Press.

Wright, R., Brookman, F. and Bennett, T. (2006) 'The foreground dynamics of street robbery in Britain', *British Journal of Criminology*, 46 (1): 1–15.

Part 3
Field settings

Chapter 7

Method, actor and context triangulations: knowing what happened during criminal events and the motivations for getting involved

Marie Rosenkrantz Lindegaard

Abstract

Based on ethnographic research inside and outside a South African juvenile prison, I argue that asking offenders about their perspectives on their offences brings about a one-sided version both of what happened during a criminal event and of the motivation for getting involved in such events. The knowledge generated through the offender's perspective can be evaluated for its validity through triangulation of methods, actors and contexts. These triangulations bring about various perspectives on the criminal event and the motivations for becoming a part of it, and by combining and comparing those perspectives it becomes possible to evaluate their relative validity. I illustrate this point through an analysis of a South African male youngster who committed a murder, got sentenced for it for five years and was released from prison during my fieldwork. The chapter unpacks what is meant by 'ethnographic research' and shows how validity is created in such kind of research.

Criminologists know very little about what really happens during criminal events (Collins 2008; Katz 1988; Lindegaard 2009; Schinkel 2004). Most research on crime is based on statistical calculations about what *might* have happened. It is known what kinds of factors could have played a role in the occurrences of crime; it is not known whether these factors actually played a role in specific incidences. Recently a considerable amount of studies have been conducted in which the researcher interviews offenders about what happened during criminal events (see this volume). This body of literature has contributed fascinating insights into how offenders perceive the crimes they have committed and what happened during those events according to their memories and interpretations. Due to the relatively limited, often one-time and one-sided interaction between the offender and the researcher, I suggest interviews with offenders are not a useful method when applied alone. When the aim is to know what happened during a criminal event and the motivations for getting involved as offender, interviews need to form part of various kinds of methodological triangulations in order to generate valid knowledge. I illustrate this point through ethnographic data collected in Cape Town.

Triangulations

Hastrup (1995) suggests that validity of ethnographic data is established through the consistency of the perspectives collected. This argument is based on the idea that perspectives on the world are not true or false but more or less probable. The task of social scientists is to figure out which perspectives are most probable and to make the structure of those probabilities clear (Bourdieu 1984; Hastrup 1995). I propose that combining different kinds of triangulation is a way to systematically figure out the probability of a certain perspective.

The chapter puts forward three types of triangulation which will bring about a fuller picture of what happened during criminal events and what the motivation of the offender might be to become part of such events. The first triangulation I suggest is common practice in ethnographic research (Hammersley and Atkinson 1995): combining three different methods (methods). The second triangulation is often used by ethnographers but rarely reflected upon (Hannerz 2003): three different actors' perspectives, in this case on the criminal event and on the offender (actors). The third triangulation could be seen as a development of what Marcus (1995) defined as 'multi-sited ethnography': three different contexts in which the offender tells about the criminal event and interacts with different kinds of people (contexts). The principle of 'triangulation' could as well include two, four or five methods, actors or contexts; it does not necessarily have to be three.

Background of the research

The aim of the research I conducted was to find out why, how and when male youngsters became involved as perpetrators in violent criminal events. I did not try to find out what really happened in those moments in the sense that I wanted to know specific details about, for instance, the roles of the perpetrator, victim and bystander during those events. My interest was to understand the events from the perspective of male youngsters. I focused both on what happened in the criminal events a male youngster became a part of, and on what his motivation to become a part of such events might be. As will become clear from the chapter, I approached all perspectives as 'true' in the moment they were expressed but through the means of triangulation of methods, actors and contexts it became clear that some perspectives were more probable than others.

Background of the case

I will focus on one youngster as an illustration of my methodological point. He refers to himself with the pseudonym Drégan. The first time I met him was in 2004 in Pollsmoor prison where he was incarcerated for a murder he committed when he was 17 years old. He took part in a conflict resolution programme I facilitated for an NGO.[1] When he was released from prison the first time, he became a part of my PhD research. That practically meant allowing me to become a part of different aspects of his life, getting to know his friends and family and bringing me along to the places he went to. It also meant giving interviews, participating in group discussions, filling in a questionnaire and taking pictures with a disposable camera.

Through my fieldwork I triangulated methods but also actors and contexts, which in practice meant that I conducted different perspectives on the criminal events Drégan sometimes became a part of and on his motivations for becoming a part of such events. These perspectives helped me to answer the question: how, why and when did Drégan become a part of criminal events?

I will now go through the different kinds of triangulation and describe the kind of perspectives I conducted on Drégan and the violent situations he became a part of. As the case illustrates, the triangulations allowed me to validate the data I conducted. By 'validate' I mean figure out which perspectives were most probable.

Methods

The three types of methods I will describe are: interviews, observation and photos (Figure 7.1). While interviewing offenders is arguably the most direct way to learn about offenders' motivations for getting involved in criminal events, interview results depend on various aspects of the interview situation and the interaction between interviewer and interviewee (Bourdieu 1999; Kvale 1996; Lindegaard 2007; Spradley 1979;

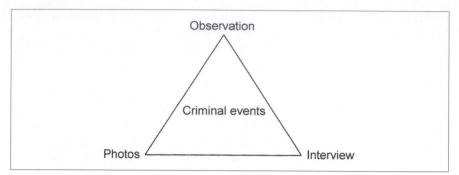

Figure 7.1   Triangulation of methods

Tankink 2007; Vysma and Tankink 2006). Observing what is going on during those events is the most obvious way of getting to know what happened during criminal events but observation results also depend on a variety of factors such as the extent to which the researcher becomes emotionally involved in what is going on (Collins 2008; Lindegaard 2009). While the relational aspect of the production of knowledge is not immediately an issue with the method of providing informants with cameras and asking them to take pictures of themes related to the research since the informant is taking photos when the researcher is not there, the photos are nevertheless produced in a relationship with the researcher and the topic of the research. Photos are therefore not less 'biased' than interviews or observation. I will now illustrate what kind of information I got about the criminal events Drégan became a part of from applying these methods. The triangulation of methods helped me to get closer to an understanding of the question of *how* Drégan got involved in criminal events.

Interviews

I conducted four formal interviews with Drégan in four different contexts. They provided slightly different versions of what was at stake for him in situations where he perpetrated 'violence', which is here understood as physically aggressive reactions aimed at hurting someone. In one of the interviews he elaborated in detail on the moment where he killed a guy with an axe. The interview was conducted in his mother's living room a month after he was released from prison. I will now provide an extensive part of his elaboration on the killing in order to show how he got involved in this act.

A part of the interview with Drégan:

> *Drégan:* One evening, I was sitting in the shebeen, this guy asks me for a kiss. I tell him, are you crazy, are you fucking crazy. The guy

hits me with a beer bottle. I carried an axe at that time, a small axe. If it was not an axe it was a tagger [sharp, thin knife-like instrument] or a knife, just something, always armed. It was part of the dress code. I take out the axe. Hit this guy but the guy is not alone. Now I am crazy and there is this whole gang. But I have a friend with me as well. He also has an axe but he is crumpling. I come back to that guy that I already knocked out. He is already away. When they see the state he is in, they get crazy. And they see I am all alone.

Marie: Can you explain, I would very much like to hear every detail of when you hit this guy.

Drégan: I was like crazy . . .

Marie: So what do you remember?

Drégan: Like I say, I cannot even remember any of their faces man. The moment when that guy hit me with a beer bottle and I stood up and I hit the first person that I see. I just stood up with my axe. I do not even know if the guy that I hit was the guy that hit me with the beer bottle. They were like a group and I just hit the first guy.

Marie: And what do you remember from the moment where you hit him?

Drégan: It just feels like everything goes slow.

Marie: What clothes did he have on?

Drégan: I cannot remember any of that. Because two weeks after that incident. I went back there to look for the guys and we wanted to shoot them. But I did not know who these people were so I had to ask around. I probably spoke with them but I was like gone [the first time he met them]. I was drunk. I did not notice anybody. I am just in love with myself at the time [of the killing].

Marie: So where did you hit him?

Drégan: In here (points at his neck). In his face.

Marie: How hard?

Drégan: Joh, very hard (laughs nervously). With all the anger and power you have in your body.

Marie: And how does that feel?

Drégan: Joh . . . powerful man (silence). At that time it felt good . . . It felt very good.

Marie: What can you compare this feeling to?

Drégan: (Silence) It is almost like an orgasm, something like that. It is a very good feeling.

Marie: So you get a kick?

Drégan: Yes! It is really a kick. It is almost like stress relief. Major stress relief, because the adrenaline is pumping. Everything is wild and you are in control. You destroy. Your mind is racing, blood flowing, senses are high and you are alert and joh, mad.

Marie: How does it feel in your body?

Drégan: You are warm and shaking . . . I do not even want to get into that zone again. It is a 'dark side'. It is a very dark place to be. You go over to a 'dark side'. Your mood automatically changes like you activate yourself into battle mode. First you are into party mode, then you are automatically into battle mode because your body is familiar with that mode, you understand? Because it is a mode that it [his body] usually gets into; into battle mode . . . Joh, everything you do, the way you think, the way you speak, you speak louder, more aggressive. Your eyes are more aggressive. The person you are fighting can almost see the death in your eyes because your whole body etches, it radiates evil.

Marie: How do you look at him? What does he become to you?

Drégan: Like a cockroach. Because you do not have any fear at the time because if you have fear, somehow you will feel inferior man. You have to go up against him. You do not fear, nothing. You do not see this guy as a threat. You do not even consider him. You are actually surprised if this guy reacts. He must just fear you. He must just prepare to die now. There is no defence of yourself, nothing. Many times I was surprised when somebody hit me back. I do that see him retaliating. I do not contribute stuff like that. It is not a part of the game.

In this narrative Drégan suggests that it is a conflict with the victim which leads to the murder. The conflict starts with the victim provoking Drégan and hitting him with a beer bottle. He describes himself as 'crazy' which seems to suggest being out of control and not thinking through what he is doing. When he first gets into what he calls 'battle mode' he describes being 'in love with myself'. He is not busy with his victim but with his own emotional experience of overcoming fear and feeling a rush of adrenaline (see also Lindegaard forthcoming). The moment he kills feels 'very good', 'almost like an orgasm' and 'stress relief'. It is also described as moving to a 'dark side' characterised by the absence of fear. It is somehow a fascinating side but also a side he is afraid of entering because he does not know what it makes him capable of doing.

Later in the interview Drégan describes how this aggressive way of reacting predominantly occurs when he has been drinking and when he interacts with guys involved in gangsterism. He has never been a part of a gang himself but before he went to prison he was busy with criminal activities similar to guys involved in gangs. His independence from a gang required that he was even tougher than these guys. The advantage of not being in a gang was that he had a feeling of being able to do what he wanted without being pressured into it like many guys involved in gangs. Later during my fieldwork I realise that Drégan's explanation of his aggressive reactions as exclusive for his interaction with gangster types is not probable. I am never there in a situation where he kills but I am there during a fight with his uncle.

Observation

During my fieldwork, I observed Drégan in many different contexts where he changed his behaviour and adapted to what people expected of him. When we were hanging out with his friends he would be tough and sometimes threaten people. With his girlfriend and family he was soft, elaborated on his emotions and tried to be caring. In prison his body language was similar to when he was hanging out with his friends outside: he clearly tried to be a tough guy who did not tolerate disrespect. When we were driving in my car or walking around in a shopping mall he always took off his cap and explained to me that otherwise people would think he was a gangster and then they might think he had kidnapped me or something. He told me about many fight situations but I only observed him in one and that was when I went back to Cape Town to discuss my chapters with the youngsters I wrote about, before my dissertation was published. After a fight with his mother Drégan had moved to his grandmother's house in another part of the city where his uncle also stayed. His uncle had an alcohol problem and the fight occurred in Drégan's room while we were busy discussing the things I had written about him. I described it in the following way in my fieldwork notes:

When I arrived at Drégan's grandmother's house Drégan quickly came to my car to say hallo and explained I had to walk fast from the car to her front door to avoid being seen by his uncle who was hanging out drinking outside the house of the neighbour. We sat down in the living room and started chatting. After about half an hour his uncle entered the front door. He was drunk in the way someone is drunk if he has been drinking heavily for days in a row without making a break. His eyes were red, his body out of balance, and he smelled overwhelmingly like alcohol. When he saw me on the couch he fell down next to me and put his hand on my leg. I moved his hand immediately and asked him to sit in another chair. He did not listen also not when Drégan asked him to leave. After arguing with him Drégan stood up and pushed him out of the front door and locked it behind him. We decided to move upstairs to Drégan's room in order to avoid the noise of the uncle now banging on the door and screaming. After about an hour where Drégan had been busy reconstructing a situation where he stabbed a guy so severely that he almost died by acting it in front of me, the uncle had found his way upstairs and now entered the room. Drégan immediately pushed him out of the room, smacked him towards the frame of the door and kicked him while he was lying on the floor. Fortunately the uncle was too drunk to fight back and Drégan came back to the room which he locked behind him. He fell down on the bed, his eyes wide open, his face red and his body shaking. He looked at me and said: 'this feeling in the body, this rush, this heart beat, that was just what I was trying to explain to you. Now you saw it in action.' I had difficulties doing as if I was causal about the situation. I felt my own heart beat and sweat in my hands. Drégan looked intensely at me and said: 'it shocked you a little didn't it Marie? I can see it on your face! I wish you had not been exposed to this.'

The situation illustrated exactly what it meant to move to what Drégan had described as the 'dark side' during our interview. I could see how he moved into himself and forgot about people around him while he was busy with his uncle. I experienced the emotional rush of the fight myself and I was able to observe how long it took for both of us to get out of that mood again. Drégan opened a window and lit a cigarette, which seemed to calm him down. I only managed to get out of the emotional rush when I was back in my friend's house where I was staying.

Drégan had not been drinking nor was he interacting with guys in a gang. He was not in a situation where his body language had changed into gangster behaviour like I had seen when he interacted with his friends and in prison. His reaction had occurred in a moment which during interviews he had described as moments where he would not move into 'battle mode'. His uncle's provocations had nevertheless triggered something in him. It therefore seemed that the emotional reaction he had described during interviews as the 'dark side' was less exclusive than he had suggested. It seemed that emotionally tense situations triggered him to move to the 'dark side'. What is not clear from these conclusions is whether Drégan would respond aggressively in all emotional situations no matter what kind of people he was interacting with. Would he, for instance, also beat up his girlfriend in such a situation? From the photos he took he proposed an answer to that question.

Photos

Drégan was asked to take photos of people and places which made him comfortable or uncomfortable. Most of his photos were taken during parties, a few during his working hours as a construction worker. In the description of the photos afterwards it became clear that he used the photos to tell certain stories about himself. Photo one shows one of his female friends (Sharon) and her boyfriend posing with their arms around each other in front of the cupboard in their living room. Photo two portrays a drug dealer who has also been to prison like Drégan. He wears sunglasses and is standing in front of the fridge in his kitchen. Drégan describes the photos in the following way afterwards:

Photo one

This is Sharon's boyfriend [pointing at the man]. It looks like a happy couple right? But it is not! He abuses her a lot. He seems to be a soft and relaxed guy but he can be evil. He even smacked her in front of us [Drégan and his friends] last week so apparently he does not mind. We did not ask for the reason. It is their business. We cannot intervene.

Photo two

This guy is a drug dealer. He has also been to prison and he also likes hanging out with younger people like I do. You do not grow up when you are in prison. Sharon [on photo one], my friend, gets her drugs from him. Sometimes she pays but not always! I do not want to know why she sometimes gets it for free . . . I mean what does she give him back? I do not even want to think about it!

In the description of photo one Drégan clearly positions himself as different from Sharon's boyfriend. He is not someone who would abuse his girlfriend and certainly not while other people are watching. Letting others watch means that you do not care. This comment indirectly suggests that his own aggressive behaviour is not related to women. Abuse of women is not OK and makes a guy 'evil'. This perspective confirms Drégan's claim that his aggressive behaviour is related to interaction with other males. The description of photo two shows that Drégan perceives himself as not fully grown up. This perception comes back in other contexts and is expressed by other actors as well, which will become clear in the following sections. Like the drug dealer who has also missed out on things in his life by being in prison, Drégan is also someone who hangs out with younger people because those of his own age live a life different from his own: 'You do not grow up when you are in prison.' Drégan indirectly suggests that the drug dealer misuses Sharon to have sex with him through providing drugs for her, which is again something he distinguishes himself from. Women seem to be of a different kind: you do not take advantage of, abuse or become aggressive towards them. As I will show now, Drégan's mother confirms this finding about Drégan.

Actors

The three types of actors I will refer to are: warder, mother and uncle (Figure 7.2). Drégan's own perspective and my perspective are included

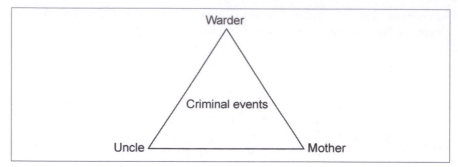

Figure 7.2 Triangulation of actors

in the analysis as well and could be seen as a fourth and fifth perspective. The perspectives the three other actors provide are not so much focused on the criminal events Drégan becomes a part of but more on him and his life in general. These perspectives therefore deal with the question of *why* he might become involved in criminal events rather than how and when.

Warder

I chat to the head of the school inside Pollsmoor prison on my way down to one of the sections. He is very engaged in his work and truly believes that education and good influence from him and the other warders can make a difference for the youngsters being incarcerated. He proudly tells me about the first inmate who ever got a teacher college diploma inside prison and after a while I realise that he is talking about Drégan:

> Oh, so you know Drégan? I am very curious to hear what he is doing! I was warder in his section for a long time and I got to know him really well. He is a VERY intelligent guy. In fact I cannot remember having worked with anyone like him before or ever since. You probably know he was the first one to get a high school diploma and a teacher college diploma inside prison? I was so proud of him. I really hope I will never see him in here again.

Drégan has not told me about this diploma himself. The fact that he is intelligent is no surprise to me. When he got out of prison he did not feel like talking too much about his experiences in there and if he mentioned it I mainly heard about the friends he made and the difficulties with interacting with the gangs without becoming a part of them. I ask him about the diploma next time I see him. He proudly shows me the papers and explains that he has not mentioned it before because he becomes depressed by thinking about it. When he was still in prison he expected that the diploma would help him to work things out outside. Being outside he realised the diploma was not of much help. The only jobs he had managed to get were construction worker jobs and they were really badly paid. Better jobs required a transcript of your criminal record which meant no chance of getting the job.

The perspective provided by the warder therefore gave me insights into an aspect of Drégan which he had not revealed for me because it made him depressed thinking about it. It gave me a better understanding of his stay in prison and what it meant for his life afterwards. It also showed why Drégan might have difficulties avoiding criminal events to come. The feeling of powerlessness in terms of changing the criminal path he had gotten himself into might make it less attractive to stop carrying a gun or another weapon and stop reacting aggressively in moments of tension.

Mother

Whenever I speak to Drégan's mother she complains about her son. She is unemployed, recently got herself a sewing machine and is now trying to earn an income by repairing other people's clothes. She has been married twice and in both her marriages she has been physically abused by her husbands. Her second husband moved out of the house the year before Drégan got out of prison and has recently filed for divorce. Drégan's sister who was 17 at that time had a baby and Drégan's mother explains to me many times that she is frustrated about the fact that Drégan does not take on responsibility as the head of the household. In her eyes the oldest male is supposed to provide for the household. After Drégan violated his parole and was sent back to prison, I decide to visit him with his mother. When we are sitting in the car she describes Drégan in the following way:

> He is such a smooth talker! Now this girl, Neewal he is with, she is a really nice girl. You can see she got manners. He always manages to get girls like that because he can speak so smoothly. Uh, the girls like him. He twists their minds. But I know his tricks! He can talk and talk but it does not change the fact that he is not working, he drinks on weekends, and he violated his parole. That is the story of his life. I don't know how many times I had to pick him up at the police station. He has always been into trouble and I had to deal with all of it. But now it is really time for him to grow up. He is a grown up man now and that means taking responsibility otherwise I will throw him out of the house. I already told him that.

Drégan's mother here explains that getting into trouble is 'the story of his life'. Since he has now reached an age which normally means taking responsibility it seems like she has decided to be less soft on him. She seems to suggest that when he was younger it was more difficult to expect him to be responsible. I use this perspective to ask Drégan what he thinks the difference is between his responsibility then and now. He explains that in principle he agrees with his mother. She just seems to forget that he has been incarcerated for five years. When he went to prison he was a child and due to his incarceration he still is in many ways. The feeling of not being grown up and having missed out on something because of his prison stay comes back here.

I have seen Drégan interact with Neewal and other girls so I know what his mother means by being a 'smooth talker'. She seems to believe that being able to interact with girls with good manners is a kind of false performance when it is combined with not working, drinking at weekends and violating his parole. I come to the conclusion that Drégan might disappoint his mother but he is not false. He adapts to the people he interacts with and is able to change his behaviour depending on the contexts he becomes a part of. Guys who become involved in criminal activities are not only troublemakers like Drégan's mother seems to believe; they are also charismatic, charming and able to twist the minds of girls with 'good manners'.

Uncle

Drégan's uncle (not the drunken one just described) invites me to his house three times during my fieldwork: twice together with Drégan and once alone. He lives in a middle-class area which was defined as White during apartheid. His house is huge and full of expensive consumer goods. He works as a journalist for a well-known newspaper in Cape Town and has many times taken care of Drégan's mother when she had trouble with her partners. He behaves like a powerful man whenever I meet him and speak to me as if we are of the same kind: in his eyes we are the kind of people with successful lives; Drégan and his mother are different. He describes Drégan's situation in the following way:

> Drégan's mother came to my house whenever she was into trouble. Her life has not been easy because of those husbands of hers. It started going wrong with Drégan when she was with her second husband. He did not like Drégan and they got into a conflict. Drégan ran away and they did not even care enough to go and look for him in the street. He lived on the street for half a year. Then she was forced to come to court to deal with her parental responsibility because he had gotten himself into trouble. I went with her. Whenever there was trouble with Drégan I went with her. I guess I tried to be strict with him like I think his own father should have been but he was never there. Later on I got really tired of his games. I have sponsored computer courses, engineering courses and I have found jobs for him but he just screws up all the time. Last week I offered him to work in my garden but he never showed up.

From Drégan's uncle's perspective it is clear that Drégan is not the only one who 'screws up' things like his mother seemed to suggest. According to him it was the situation at home which got Drégan into trouble in the first place. When I speak to Drégan about his uncle he seems to agree that he has given him many chances; he also agrees that he has not always been grateful enough to him. He cannot really explain why his uncle's help has not prevented him from getting involved in criminal activities. Exchanging guns, hanging out with his friends in the neighbourhood, looking for a thrill and being independent are activities which cannot be replaced by stable jobs and education. Drégan's mother and uncle do not seem to understand why Drégan is compelled by those activities. Perhaps excitement and independence is less important to them or maybe they get those needs fulfilled in different ways. Their version of why Drégan got involved in criminal activities is different but they agree that his irresponsibility and tendency to lose focus on what they think is important (education and employment) is the core of his problem.

The perspectives of the warder, mother and uncle not only provided different views on why Drégan might have become involved in criminal activities, they also gave me the opportunity to discuss new perspectives with Drégan. By discussing I do not mean finding out if they are true or false but rather to figure out why they might be true or false to the one proposing the perspective. When Drégan explains his involvement in crime as getting a thrill and independence, it is not a perspective which contradicts his mother's and uncle's explanations. Not telling about his diploma as a teacher and the chances his uncle have given him seem to be a way to construct his problems with getting a job and staying away from crime as less related to him and more with the stigma of having been to prison. His mother therefore seems to be right when she talks about not taking responsibility. On the other hand, she also seems to lack understanding of why he got into trouble in the first place and what it meant for him to be incarcerated from such a young age. The perspective provided by the uncle emphasised those nuances in his story. The triangulation of actors helped to situate perspectives in relation to the actor providing them and in relation to other actors' perspectives, which when put together gives a better understanding of why Drégan got involved in criminal activities.

Contexts

The three types of contexts I will describe are: Pollsmoor prison, Mitchell's Plain and the Bossa Nova night club (see Figure 7.3). Drégan was incarcerated for five years in Pollsmoor prison, which houses 8,000 inmates and is the biggest prison in the Western Cape. Mitchell's Plain is the biggest Coloured residential area in Cape Town. People who were

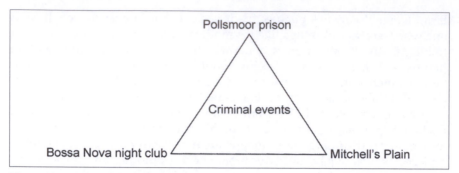

Figure 7.3   Triangulation of contexts

classified as Coloured (not Black, not White) during apartheid were forcefully moved to areas like Mitchell's Plain. Currently these areas are known for high concentrations of social problems such as crime, gangsterism, unemployment, alcoholism, drugs and AIDS (Erasmus 2001). I went to Mitchell's Plain with Drégan to visit Ralf, who was his best friend in prison. Bossa Nova is a hip night club situated in downtown Cape Town. When I went out with friends during my fieldwork I would usually go there. Coincidentally Drégan and his friends also went to this club when they were going out. The perspectives from these different contexts deal more with the question of *when* criminal events occur in Drégan's life than why and how they occur.

Pollsmoor prison

When I met Drégan the first time while working for an NGO, I went to the prison every day for a week to conduct group discussions with inmates and to try to figure out what crime meant in their lives. The narrative I got to hear from Drégan in this context is quite different from what I later understood from the criminal events he got himself into:

> During a group discussion the youngsters have tried to explain how they got involved in crime. Drégan is one of the most outspoken in those discussions. He comes across as tough, leans back on the chair while he talks and uses his hands to emphasise what he is saying. He does not say what he is sentenced for but it was a part of gangster activities. When he explains why he ended up in those activities peer-pressure, not taking responsibility for his life and making the wrong choices are dominant in his narrative. He explains that when he gets out of prison he is going to change his life; he is going to think before he acts and select his friends carefully. He is going to say sorry to his family and provide for them. These narratives come back again and again. I am not sure what his position is within the prison

hierarchy but he wears a watch like the youngster who is high in the gang hierarchy so he must have some kind of powerful position.

In the context of the prison Drégan describes his criminal activities as related to being a part of a gang. He explains why he became a part of a gang through a narrative of 'peer-pressure, not taking responsibility for his life and making the wrong choices'. When I start doing research in the prison later on I realise that this discourse of gangsterism and the explanations Drégan provides for why he became a part of a gang are dominant in the narratives of youngsters in prison. It seems like labelling their activities as gangsterism makes further elaboration unnecessary. Among South Africans who have little or no experiences with crime, gangsterism is generally perceived as something you need to be a part of in order to understand (Jensen 2006; Lindegaard 2009). Peer-pressure, not taking responsibility for one's life and making the wrong choices are explanations which could have been taken out of any NGO, bible study or restorative justice programme in prison. After having conducted interviews in prison I became aware of these discourses and tried to break them down by asking questions in different ways and positioning myself as different from those programmes (Lindegaard 2007).

When I get to know Drégan better after he has been released from prison, it becomes clear that he has never been a part of a gang. I once confront him with the fact that he claimed to be a gangster when he was still in prison, which makes him explain:

> It was just an easy way to describe the stuff I was doing. It is also a way to make other inmates afraid of you. In fact I was tougher than real gangsters because I operated alone but I am sure they would not have believed that.

Gangsterism means doing criminal stuff, being tough, standing up for oneself and proving willingness to be violent. In prison such willingness creates respect and makes it easier to be left alone by other inmates (Lindegaard 2007). Being a gangster means being certified for such activities; it provides authority to certain things inside prison. On the one hand, Drégan did not 'lie' when he claimed to be a gangster: the activities he was involved in and the way he reacted in dangerous situations were similar to gangsters; he had to be even tougher because he operated alone. On the other hand, he did not tell the full story about those activities. His story was adapted to the context of the prison and to the listener, me as representative for an NGO, who might not understand the complexity of these activities anyway. By applying the method of triangulation, however, it became clear that some perspectives were more probable than others: Drégan was never involved in a gang but he operated like a gangster.

Mitchell's Plain

When I conducted group discussions for the NGO in prison, Ralf was also a part of the discussions. At that time I did not know that Drégan and Ralf were best friends. During the last two years of Drégan's incarceration they stayed together in a room and they had a lot of privileges other prisoners only dreamt about: cooking stove, meat to cook, cell phone and cigarettes. When both of them were released they met at a few parties and kept in contact. Their contact depended on the possibility of getting transport to each other's residential areas. When I started doing research I provided that transport. Going with Drégan to Mitchell's Plain provided a perspective on him I had not yet encountered in my interaction with him outside prison. On one of the days we went to visit Ralf the following situation took place:

> I hang out with Ralf and Drégan in Ralf's house in Mitchell's Plain. I picked up Drégan in the afternoon and we drove together to Ralf's place. Ralf just got married to his girlfriend, who is on the way out of their house when we park the car. We walk to the back of the yard and get into their living room. I notice that Drégan changes his body language when we leave the car and enter the house. He starts walking like a gangster, looks cool and uses more slang than when I chat to him alone. After a while the conversation changes from being causal about the lack of jobs, last weekend's party and soccer, to become some kind of code language I cannot understand. I realise the code is about guns. Ralf and Drégan exchange guns; Ralf suggests he can get another one for Drégan if he wants. When we are back in the car again I ask Drégan what was going on with those guns. He explains people had been threatening him since he snapped and almost stabbed a guy to death recently so he needed a gun. Ralf had married the girl because he believed that getting married would be a way to get out of crime but as far as Drégan was concerned he was not too successful with that.

It is only after this visit that Drégan tells me about the situation where he almost stabbed a guy to death. The situation sounds similar to the one he got incarcerated for. The difference is that this time the audience manages to stop him from killing the guy he is busy stabbing with an axe. The situation takes place under similar circumstances to his murder: he is drunk, it is late in the evening, an argument breaks out, and Drégan feels the need to do something about it to prove he is not a fool you can treat like you want. It sounds like his whole dignity and self-respect is put on one plate and in those situations he allows the guy he fights with to take away the plate instead of defining him as not worth fighting with and just walking away. It is the first time he has reacted like that since he came out of prison and he is now afraid it will not be the last time. He is very disappointed in himself; he had expected he would be able to just walk away but somehow the tension made him 'snap', as he expresses it.

The description of this event confirms his explanation that his tendency to be violent and thereby to become a part of a criminal event is related to the context of what he referred to as gangsterism: guys who are busy with criminal stuff, who behave tough towards each other, stand up for themselves and prove their willingness to be violent when they get into arguments. He also mentions being drunk in both situations. When I later see Drégan reacting like that at home towards his drunken uncle, in a situation where he is sober, I realise that perhaps it is not so much the context of gangsterism, guys playing tough towards each other, and the condition of being drunk that brings Drégan into criminal events, but rather situations which become emotionally tense, situations which threaten his dignity and self-respect. In situations with his girlfriend, which I would imagine to be emotionally tense as well, I do not, however, see such reactions taking place.

Bossa Nova night club

After a few visits to Mitchell's Plain, Drégan, Ralf and I decided to go out dancing on a Saturday night. This experience confirms what Drégan's mother has said about him: he is able to talk 'smooth' to the girls; he can behave as if he is not someone who would ever get involved in criminal events; different forms of interaction bring about different aspects of him which I do not perceive as a sign that he manipulates people but rather that he adapts and changes his behaviour in order to fit in and feel comfortable:

> Drégan stands with his arms around Neewal leaning against a wall next to the dance floor. Ralf and the other friends are dancing, flirting and moving close to the girls around them. Neewal is smiling. I am thinking about what she just said in the car. Her parents do not like Drégan. He is not a guy for her. But she does not care. She is in love and as long as Drégan proves himself and does not get into trouble they will be fine. Neewal lives in Surrey Estate which is far away from Drégan and a much more posh area. Her father is a successful mechanic and she is in her last year of high school. They want her to continue studying afterwards. Drégan and his friends do not look like guys who have been to prison in this context. They are flirting, joking and dancing like everyone else.

It is not the first time I have heard Neewal challenging Drégan by telling about her trouble with being with him. Whenever I spend time with them she shares those doubts and I am every time surprised by Drégan's reaction. He does not try to convince her that she should not have reasons to doubt. He rather shows understanding and admits that he is not the dream of a boyfriend for a girl like her. I experience those conversations as extremely emotionally loaded and always wonder why they discuss it in my presence. In my experience a lot of emotional tension is hanging in the air during those talks but I never saw Drégan responding to that tension by becoming aggressive in any sense. It is therefore not all emotionally tense situations which make him violent. The criminal events he becomes a part of are characterised by interaction between men who are similar to himself, situations in which the relative hierarchy between these men becomes unclear; and emotional tension. The chance that such events occur within the framework of what Drégan described as gangsterism is big but nevertheless not as exclusive as he claimed.

Triangulation of contexts showed how Drégan's narrative about his involvement in criminal events changed depending on his audience. It also showed how his behaviour, whether he behaved like a gangster, spoke code language and moved like a gangster or talked smooth and remained in the background when a situation became tense, depended on the context of his interaction. The point of applying this triangulation was not to find out when he showed his 'true colours' but rather to find out when certain aspects of him became pronounced and expressed; this helped me to formulate a pattern for Drégan's involvement in criminal events.

Conclusion

An analysis, which aims at understanding what really happened during criminal events, requires the incorporation of various perspectives on the situation, and these perspectives cannot be achieved through interviews alone. I have suggested that triangulation of methods, actors and contexts is a way to increase the probability that the perspective collected both on what really happened during a criminal event and on the motivation of the offender are valid perspectives. Triangulation of methods, actors and contexts is a tool to systematise what is usually referred to as 'ethnographic research'. Too often ethnographic research is treated as a 'black box' for various kinds of qualitative data collection. In this chapter I have unpacked what this black box could consist of and shown how ethnographers can deal with the issue of validity.

In the case I analysed about Drégan, it became clear that the initial explanation of why he got himself involved in criminal acts was not the most probable. In the context of the prison he explained that gangsterism was the reason he ended up killing someone. During interviews outside it became clear that he had in fact never been a part of a gang but he had been busy with activities similar to gangsterism. According to his narratives, he would only react violently in interaction with men who also had experiences with criminal activities. Through observation it became clear that such reactions also occurred in other contexts of his life: they were related to emotional tension among males and relatively unclear social hierarchies between the interacting parties. Based on triangulation of methods and contexts, his explanation that such situations were about getting a thrill and being respected seemed probable. Looking for a thrill and wanting to be independent was, according to Drégan, his motivation for getting involved in criminal activities. This perspective was not contradictory but different from the perspectives of his mother, uncle and the warder. Through the uncle it became clear that Drégan's involvement in crime was not just about him not taking responsibility for his life as his mother suggested but also about her providing an unstable home environment for him.

The answers to the questions *how*, *why* and *when* Drégan became a part of criminal events were the following:

- *how* – by being captured by emotional tension, by blocking out the victim and focusing on his own emotions, by wanting to prove himself;

- *why* – because he was looking for a thrill and his independence, because he did not know what to do with his intelligence in the place he grew up, because he was not taking responsibility for his life and felt neglected through his upbringing;

- *when* – in interaction characterised by emotional tension and unclear social hierarchies between males. Interaction between men who were involved in criminal activities and being drunk both seemed to be facilitating factors for his violent behaviour but were not necessary factors as I saw him reacting violently towards his uncle who was not a gangster in a situation where he was sober. Nor was alcohol use a sufficient factor for violent behaviour since I saw him drunk many times without perpetrating violence.

During the period of my PhD research I used other kinds of triangulation than the types I have focused on in this chapter. When my dissertation was written I went back to discuss my chapters with the youngsters I had written about. They provided their perspectives on my findings and corrected things I had misunderstood or misinterpreted (Lindegaard 2009). I also exchanged letters with them during the period of writing where we discussed issues related to my research. Furthermore, I have become virtual 'friends' with eight of them on 'Facebook' where we continue to exchange information and I am able to follow what they are doing. These different forms of contact provide me with new perspectives on the questions of my research and have also given me the opportunity to follow how their narratives have changed over time.

The method of multiple forms of triangulation in the same project has the obvious disadvantage of being extremely time-consuming. It also requires personal investment – a willingness and ability to become embedded in people's lives – which in the case of working with offenders of severe crimes such as murder can be emotionally challenging. Developing relationships which are not easy to distinguish from friendships with people who have killed and hurt others raises various moral and ethical concerns and issues of safety which the researcher has to find ways of dealing with both during and after the research (Lindegaard 2007, 2009). Combining different kinds of triangulation is nevertheless an effective way to create validity of findings generated during ethnographic research, both when the aim is to know what really happened during a criminal event and when the focus is what motivated the offender to commit a crime. This method therefore brings criminologists closer to knowing what really happened during criminal events.

Acknowledgments

I thank Drégan and his friends and family for allowing me into their lives for a while.

Note

1   The programme was run by a South African NGO called Ukukania Kwameni, which cooperated with a Danish NGO called South Africa Contact. I was doing a pilot study for the Danish NGO. In 2006 we got funding from 'Operational One Day Work' for a five-year rehabilitation project for male youngsters who just got out of prison. (See: http://www.od.dk/english (accessed 23 July 2009).)

References

Bourdieu, P. (1984) *Distinction: A Social Critique of the Judgement of Taste*. London: Routledge.
Bourdieu, P. (1999) 'Field sites', in P. Bourdieu *et al.* (eds), *The Weight of the World: Social Suffering in Contemporary Society*. Stanford, CA: Stanford University Press, pp. 123–30.
Collins, R. (2008) *Violence: A Micro-Sociological Theory*. Princeton, NJ and Oxford: Princeton University Press.
Erasmus, Z. (2001) *Coloured by History, Shaped by Space: New Perspectives on Coloured Identities in Cape Town*. Cape Town: Kwela Books.
Ferrell, J. and Hamm, M. (eds) (1998) *Ethnography at the Edge: Crime, Deviance, and Field Research*. Boston, MA: Northeastern University Press.

Hammerley, M. and Atkinson, P. (1995) *Ethnography: Principles in Practice*. London and New York: Routledge.

Hannerz, U. (2003) 'Being there . . . and there . . . and there!', *Ethnography*, 4 (2): 201–16.

Hastrup, K. (1995) *A Passage to Anthropology: Between Experience and Theory*. London and New York: Routledge.

Jensen, S. (2006) 'Capetonian back streets: territorializing young men', *Ethnography*, 7 (3): 275–301.

Katz, J. (1988) *Seduction of Crime: Moral and Sensual Attraction in Doing Evil*. New York: Basic Books.

Kvale, S. (1996) *Interviews: An Introduction to Qualitative Research Interviewing*. Thousand Oaks, CA: Sage.

Lindegaard, M. R. (2007) 'Angels, prisoners and other human beings: doing research with boys who have killed', *Medische Antropologie*, 19 (1): 59–78.

Lindegaard, M. R. (2009) *Coconuts, Gangsters and Rainbow Fighters: How Male Youngsters Navigate Situations of Violence in Cape Town, South Africa*. PhD thesis, University of Amsterdam.

Lindegaard, M. R. (forthcoming) 'Moving to the "dark side": how male youngsters interpret emotions during the act of killing in Cape Town, South Africa', *Ethnofoor*.

Marcus, G. E. (1995) 'Ethnography in/of the World System: the emergence of multi-sited ethnography', *Annual Review of Anthropology*, 24: 95–117.

Schinkel, W. (2004) 'The will to violence', *Theoretical Criminology*, 8 (1): 5–31.

Spradley, J. P. (1979) *The Ethnographic Interview*. New York: Holt, Rinehart & Winston.

Tankink, M. (2007) 'My mind as a transitional space: intersubjectivity in the process of analysing emotionally disturbing data', *Medische Antropologie*, 19 (1): 135–45.

Vysma, M. and Tankink, M. (2006) 'The intersubjective as analytical tool in medical anthropology', *Medische Antropologie*, 18 (1): 249–65.

Chapter 8

Repeat, triangulate and reflect: ethnographic validity in a study on urban minority youth

Frank van Gemert

Abstract

The interview is not always a productive method to find out why and how offenders do what they do. In their quest for valid data scholars have pointed to ethnography, mainly stressing its advantages for finding respondents. This contribution does not address ethnography as a mere recruitment tool but as an approach using a variety of methods including participant observation to describe the 'world' in which offenders live that provides context and meaning to their behaviour. Using examples of ethnographic research on Moroccan boys in Rotterdam, it is claimed that ethnographic validity is built on repeated measurements, triangulation to various sources and continuous reflection by the researcher.

The interview is not always a productive method to find out why and how people do what they do. One can approach bakers, housewives or even members of parliament and ask them about their daily work. If they have the time, chances are they will be cooperative and answer, but obtaining reliable and valid answers from 'regular' populations can still offer methodological challenges. Now, when it comes criminological research, the interviewer can face frauds, carjackers or murderers, and this is where new obstacles loom. Even if he is able to make contact, these offenders may not talk to him, or give invalid answers because they cannot properly remember. Of more importance is that offenders have broken the law or they plan to do so. Talking about this bears obvious risks. Furthermore, feelings of shame or guilt can make people silent. So it is understandable that offenders don't want to talk to researchers, especially when they are (still) free. The success of interviewing offenders is certainly not guaranteed.

Still, most contributions to this volume are based on what offenders say. There is quite a bit of variety on when, where and how to talk to these offenders, but in essence the authors have interviewed them on past behaviour. They have found ways around the obstacles by using a number of strategies and techniques. These vary from recruitment in a detention setting, paying respondents for their cooperation, the use of complex sampling techniques or working with (semi-)experimental settings. Also, ethnography is mentioned. This can refer to researchers doing fieldwork, approaching deviant populations such as drug users, homeless people or prostitutes. Once they have made contact and reached a certain level of rapport, they will sit down and interview the respondent. Thus ethnographic *methods* are merely used as a recruitment tool.

In this contribution 'ethnography' has a different meaning. Here, ethnography is an *approach* to a phenomenon using a variety of methods, among which is (participant) observation that leads to a certain product. It is not so much the obstacles in recruitment of respondents that have urged researchers to lean over to ethnography, rather it is the scope of the research. Nowadays in a number of disciplines scholars claim to do ethnographic fieldwork, but originally it was connected to anthropology. Anthropologists seldom study isolated aspects, they prefer holistic approaches. This means that the product of ethnography usually would not focus, for example, on the decision-making of burglars but on the 'world' in which these offenders live that provides context and meaning to their behaviour. Following Malinowski (1922), ethnographers look for their population in its everyday habitat, using participant observation to gain an inside view on their lives, interpret it and write about it. It is this meaning of ethnography as an approach that I will use in this chapter.

Ethnography of this kind became more popular in the last decades of the past century. Anthropologists such as Geertz (1973) stressed the importance of extensive 'thick' descriptions. As a consequence of a shift towards literary influences in social sciences, its narrative descriptions made ethnography attractive. In this period, the positivistic goal of objectivity was under attack and it was more or less replaced by the ideal of representation (Marks and Wester 2008). Descriptions must do justice to subjects. They should be convincing and truthful, they must present the 'native's point of view' (Wolcott 2005: 15–24).

More recently, because of an urge to produce international comparisons and the growing involvement of policy in research, social science methods are getting standardised. This has also touched upon ethnography. Ethnographers argued that they cannot change reality as they find it, and that research must rather be adapted to the field than the other way around. Ethnographers claim flexibility, especially at the beginning of research when it is not possible for the researcher to make a distinction between the object he studies and context (Hammersley and Atkinson 1983: 185; Hammersley 1992). They resist strict standardisation, and believe that a constant process of fine-tuning works better than structuring too strictly in advance. As a consequence, every ethnographic research should have its own approach and form. There is no ideal type for ethnography (Agar 2006).

The key questions in this book *Offenders on Offending* are on validity. Ethnographers can also study offenders, and if possible they will interview them on past behaviour, but these interviews will not be the sole data source in their research. It seems only fair to also look at validity in relation to ethnographic research, as it has been dealt with in the other chapters of this book. Ethnography provides statements on (other) people, based on empirical research. What means and arguments can bring value to these statements? Value that goes beyond trivialities, presumptions or ethnocentric judgments (Marks and Wester 2008). In the following paragraphs I will use my PhD research on Moroccan boys (Van Gemert 1998) to bring across a number of these means and arguments.

Moroccan boys

Since the mid-1980s, in the Netherlands Moroccan boys have drawn attention because of high crime rates (Junger 1990). These figures have been confirmed repeatedly at national and local levels ever since (Blom *et al.* 2005; Van der Laan and Blom 2006). Ethnographic studies have documented social context, cultural elements, and group processes that help explain this phenomenon (Werdmölder 1990; Van Gemert 1998; De Jong 2007). Members of these groups often have criminal records and are known to the police. Throughout the Netherlands, Moroccan boys have become known for their involvement in conflicts within neighbourhoods (Van Gemert and Stuifbergen 2008). Slotervaart in Amsterdam-west was the scene of uproar in February 1998, and ever since the whole western part of the city has been associated with problems related to this ethnic group (De Jong 2007). The same applies to the neighbourhood of Kanaleneiland in the city of Utrecht, to a somewhat lesser extend to Schilderswijk in The Hague and to neighbourhoods in the city of Gouda (Bervoets 2006). Even though these conflicts account for an endless collection of newspaper articles, they are mainly about nuisance (Van Gemert and Fleisher 2005). Still, Dutch citizens have made it clear over and over again that they perceive youth groups like these in their neighbourhoods as a very serious problem that deserves police priority (Wittebrood 2006; Bervoets 2006). Currently, Moroccan boys are mentioned by Dutch politicians, both right and left, when it comes to youth crime. Their stigmatisation is massive (De Jong 2007; Van Gemert and Stuifbergen 2008).

When I started my research in the mid-1990s, the situation was different. Even though reports on their criminal activities had been filed, at that time stigmatisation was far less. My ethnographic research was part of a bigger study that focused on problems in a few neighbourhoods in Rotterdam-south. It was when I got there, that my attention was directed towards Moroccan boys. They were said to cause a significant part of crime and nuisance in that area.

Moroccan boys are not specialists in the sense that they are known to be involved in specific crimes. That is to say, over and again they have been the focus of attention because of their involvement in disturbing the order in swimming pools and in cinemas. On the other hand, they hang out on the streets where they gather in groups. Youth crime in the Netherlands is 75 per cent group crime, meaning that offenders as a rule don't act alone (Weerman 2001). It may well be that for Moroccan boys this number is even higher. Group process is very important when it comes to understanding their behaviour (Van Gemert 2002; De Jong 2007). Furthermore, this is a key element in their decision-making, one that is hard to capture in one-on-one interviews.

Finding them and getting them to talk

The fieldwork of my research among Moroccan boys lasted almost three years. The boys formed a more or less stable group. In the beginning my strategy was simple: I would go where I could expect to meet my research population. The boys lived in the neighbourhood and on a daily basis they visited a community centre. This was where I often met them. In the beginning I was a stranger, much older than they were, not from their neighbourhood and of different descent. 'You are the police' was a statement Moroccan boys routinely made, not only to me – other researchers conducting similar ethnographic research were met with the same suspicion (Werdmölder 1990; De Jong 2007). There was no such thing as a test or an initiation, and of course I never became 'one of them'. By simply being there, they got used to me, and after a while it was clear that my presence had no negative consequences. The boys found out that I did not report to youth workers on what I saw and heard, and there were no arrests or other police activity because of me.

It seemed only logical that I would try to interview the boys, but soon enough I found out that nobody was interested in a formal face-to-face conversation. The more general reasons for this have been mentioned above. In addition, the Moroccan boys said they did not wish to talk about their homes. For Moroccans it is a rule that what goes on in this domain is not shared with outsiders. This is a cultural aspect that has hindered researchers before (Van Gemert 1998: 211). Their willingness to participate in a formal interview did not really change over time. In the end only a limited number of interviews were held. If this had been the only method, my research would have been cut short.

Fortunately, other methods were available and observations in particular turned out to be productive. For example, when Moroccan boys hang out on the streets they easily get into conflict with citizens or shopkeepers, and the researcher can witness how futile frictions can grow into more serious clashes with threats and intimidations (Van Gemert and Fleisher 2005). I was interested in their point of view and I was trying to get at it. But, if the interview was not an option, how should I get them to talk?

The first conversations with Moroccan boys were about why I had come. In my answer, even though mostly in few words, I truthfully explained why I was in their vicinity. I told them I wanted to write a book. In order to do that I wanted to see, hear and experience what everyday life in this neighbourhood was like. This probably did not sound plausible, and in very little time all Moroccan boys were informed about my presence. Apparently, it was interesting news to them.

Simple facts like these offered me insight and made me think. They could also initiate conversation, but this was difficult to plan in advance. In starting my research I had all kinds of questions, but in practice I was seldom in a position to decide when certain issues were raised. On some occasions I took the initiative and tried to get the boys to give answers. I did this by asking questions that showed I was aware of what was going on. Sometimes I could sometimes see them frown, and in general this did not work well. Realising that I maybe knew too much, the conversation ended because the boys simply walked away. Partly because of this attitude, I have labelled 'distrust' as a cultural trait of Moroccan boys (Van Gemert 1998). In this research, I was not in charge during fieldwork. I could ask questions, and every now and then I would try to start a discussion, but in general I just had to comply with what happened.

Say, think, do

What people do, what they say and what they think is somehow related. For a researcher it would be good if these three would converge, but in practice they often do not. In my research I learned that things were not always said to correctly inform others. The boys also said things to impress others, to stay out of trouble or to make fun of someone. Repeatedly, harsh lies were told, and I was certainly not the last to hear them. On one occasion a boy I had not met before told me about a murder. I did not believe his story and felt he wanted to impress me. I checked some of the details with a policeman I knew and found out he had indeed told a lie.

Stories like this may seem strange to colleagues who work with cooperative respondents, but when it comes to Moroccan boys this attitude has been reported over and over again (Kaufman and Verbraeck

1986; Van Gelder and Sijtsma 1988; Werdmölder 1990; Van Gemert 1998; Van Gemert and Fleisher 2005; Bervoets 2006; De Jong 2007). One has to realise that not only can their stigma play a role, but that they are youngsters who like to play tricks on each other, and certainly on researchers. To effectively fool someone can mean a good laugh, it can even bring respect from others. Given this, it is not wise to rely only on what respondents say. On the other hand, if all goes well, talking is the fastest route to useful data. Things were told to me, I could observe what happened and every now and then I got a glance of what my respondents thought. How can one assess ethnographic validity in research like this?

In the neighbourhood where I did my research I was allowed to use a small apartment that, because of urban renewal, was going to be pulled down. This place was a kind of office where the boys could meet me. There were no things of value, except for a computer that I kept in an iron box, firmly attached to the wall. In spite of this, I had mixed feelings when several boys together came to visit me. They seemed to like coming to that place and having a chat with a cup of coffee, but I could not keep an eye on all the boys present. Some seemed to have other intentions, as I found out after one of those visits. Just when I was about to close the apartment door behind four of these visitors, Ali – one of them – took a few steps back and handed me an object. 'Sorry, I wasn't thinking', he said. It was my ashtray.

From this incident I learned that I was right to have taken measures. Some of these boys would take anything they could lay their hands on. However, I also learned how Ali regarded me: he did not want to steal from me. Moreover, he had come back and forced himself to a confession and a kind of penance. Even though Ali had a long criminal record and he later would leave the scene to do a long sentence, he and I got along well. I regularly lent him money. Small amounts, which he would always pay back to the last penny.

Another boy, Said, was a different case. I repeatedly lent him money too, in total an amount of about forty guilders. I never got it back. Still, this was not a bad 'investment', because again I learned from it. When I talked to his older brother about Said not paying me back, serious measures were taken. Because their parents were away, the brother was head of the household. Said was shut out, and for two nights he was forced to stay out on the streets. Even though I had not wanted this and the relation between Said and me was then ruined, I learned about the relations between brothers, about family honour and about a tendency to harsh punishment.

Triangulation

What people say, do and think results in a variety of data. The moment a researcher registers things, he is not always sure what they mean. Later, different aspects may fit together and reveal a bigger picture, like the pieces of a puzzle. Using a holistic perspective, anthropologists try to reveal connections to other structures.

When research starts, one cannot see the bigger picture. It is important to carefully register various data. Writing up recorded conversations and making fieldnotes from observations is a time-consuming activity, but its importance cannot be stressed enough. In the end, these are the data that the researcher will use to write an article or a book. In my research there was an extra obstacle: because I could not record the conversations, I could hardly take notes. That is to say, I invented a way to do it without disturbing what was going on. Among the Moroccan boys I allowed myself to make jottings on paper. These were just a few scribbled words that would later help me remember what had happened. Repeatedly, the boys would ask me what I wrote, and I would answer: 'Things I don't want to forget'. Because I did not constantly want to explain or account for what I was doing, my writing was hasty and obscure. When boys grabbed the paper from my hands, they weren't able to read it. The bad writing, for that matter, also gave me the obligation to work up my notes. Had I waited, then I would have trouble reading the jottings myself. When I was in the field, but also when I was working on the notes of conversations or observations, new questions arose.

Every week there would be indoor football, and on a regular basis this would end in a row. Turkish boys also used the gymnasium, without fuss. The Moroccans' game on the other hand, routinely resulted in a quarrel or even a fight. I tried to grasp why this happened. Talking to many of them, I noticed the boys took it for granted. 'That's just the way it goes'. An answer like that is of course not very satisfactory, so I had to dig deeper to get a grip on the phenomenon. Was it the gymnasium, the equipment, the referee, or was there maybe an earlier conflict that played a role? Conversations did not provide me with a suitable answer, but in the end I found a plausible explanation. The boys are very competitive, and their relations are egalitarian. A simple game of football becomes a difficult task if under no circumstances do players want to be inferior to each other. So, if it looks like one of them is coming off badly, as a last resort, with mad behaviour, he tries to prevent that from happening. Shouting out loud, he kicks the ball away and flings chairs around the gym. 'If I don't succeed, neither will you', that's the message.

On another occasion the boys were enthusiastically discussing the odds when the football team Ajax was going to play AC Milan in an important Champions League game. In my presence they made bets, but this seemed to take place in a chaotic way. Several boys made one-on-one bets, only saying who the winner would be. Used to Dutch customs, I suggested making a pool. This would mean that everybody who wanted to join could make a bet by putting down on a piece of paper what he thought would be the final score of the match. Along with this bet he would pay a small sum of money. In the end, the one person who gave the right prediction, could take 'the pot'. Even though this is common practice in Dutch circles, the boys acted as if they didn't hear me. Because I thought they were unfamiliar with this way of making bets, I tried to explain how it works. None of them was interested. I was puzzled – why did they decline? I asked Kareem to explain this to me. 'Betting must be easy. Yes or no, then both have the same chances'. Najib added 'If we do it your way, only one person can win. That's not good, that will lead to a fight'. In a discussion with the two boys I learned about the key issue. For them, it was unacceptable that one of the boys would take all the money. All the others would hate him for this, and he would feel ill at ease in the group. In betting according to their own rules, the number of winners equals that of the losers. This prevents too big financial shifts within the group. Again, egalitarian relations were the outcome.

Sometimes I could ask questions on the spot, but more often I brought them up on a different occasion. I got along well with a few boys that I met regularly. After a while I started using them as walking encyclo-paedias, not because they were experts on all subjects, but because they were available and, more importantly, because I could rely on them to answer me to the best of their ability. As said, this was certainly not what I would expect from most of the boys. The conversations I had with these special respondents often were about things that I wanted them to comment on. As a rule, I raised these in relation to something that had happened, often the same incident that had made me wonder about the matter. This can be considered a kind of member test. As much as possible I tried not to give them my own provisional interpretations or explana-tions; I wanted their perspective. Through this triangulation, I did not so much compare statements from different respondents but rather com-pared data coming from different sources: observations and conversa-tions. On certain issues I could also consult other sources, like police data or local newspapers. But, in general, the comparison between what I saw and what people told me was much more important than resemblances to or differences from data from official agencies. This combination of various data made me understand what was going on with the Moroccan boys in the neighbourhood. I could not always grasp the things I heard and saw right away, but through taking the time to reflect on and address them again, they began to make sense.

Ethnographic validity

Ethnography as I understand it is not just a method applied to gain access to deviant populations, but an approach to research using a variety of methods, among which is (participant) observation. This results in a unique description of the population. The research can focus on certain aspects, but as a rule findings are presented as part of the world of the population. Offending is not seen as an isolated event, but presented in its relation to everyday life. Because of the unique characteristics of each population, ethnography seems resistant to standardisation. There are, however, international initiatives, such as Eurogang (Klein *et al.* 2001; Decker and Weerman 2005; Van Gemert *et al.* 2008), that have formulated guidelines on what data researchers should (at least) gather to be able to come to international comparisons.

In this contribution I have written about a number of practical issues of my PhD research on Moroccan boys. The findings of this research were not presented, because the aim was to address the matter of validity. An ethnography like this provides statements on people, based on empirical research. What means and arguments can bring value to these statements?

The interview is not always a productive method to find out why and how people do what they do. Interviewing can be a direct route to useful data, but for me it was not wise to rely only on what the Moroccan boys said. Things were told to me, but more than once these were untrue. As an ethnographer I could also observe what happened and every now and then I got a glance of what my respondents thought. Still, what I witnessed was complex and unclear. The behaviour of Moroccan boys on the street, in part, was the outcome of group processes and cultural values. How this works may be self-evident for insiders, but as a newcomer in the field it was obscure to me. I had to find out.

There were few clear-cut explanations presented to me, rather the research was a process that, step by step, led to an understanding of the population. By the same token, the research did not begin with a set of questions that remained unchanged until the end. In the field, I was confronted with things I did not understand, or while working on the notes of conversations or observations new questions arose. In this process the researcher is the instrument, and his constant reflections lead to an ever so constant fine-tuning of this instrument. Various sources repeatedly produce data and allow events or things to be looked at from different perspectives. This triangulation gives the researcher the opportunity to contrast and compare data, and through critical reflection he is tempted to make sense of the outcome. The researcher's reflection is a key element – no wonder the recording of reflections is treated as an essential aspect of writing fieldnotes (Bogdan and Biklen 1992; Emmerson *et al.* 1995). It is this process of repeating, triangulating and reflecting that is the core of ethnographic validity. New discoveries, further interpretation and elaboration mark the findings of one phase, but they can be tested in the next phase. Of course, over time the researcher learns, but it is hard to say when saturation is reached. Is it when the researcher knows everybody in the population, or when he can make jokes that make his respondents laugh, when he knows about taboos, or when he can predict what will happen in certain situations?

References

Agar, M. (2006) 'An ethnography by any other name . . .', *Forum: Qualitative Research* [online journal], 7(4), art. 36. Available at: http://www.qualitativeresearch.net/index.php/fqs/arti cle/view/177 (retrieved on 23 December 2008).

Bervoets, E. (2006) *Tussen Respect en Doorpakken: Een Onderzoek naar de Politiële Aanpak van Marokkaanse Jongeren in Gouda, Utrecht en Amsterdam.* Den Haag: Elsevier.

Blom, M., Oudhof, J. and Bijl, R. V. (2005) *Verdacht van Criminaliteit; Allochtonen en autochtonen nader bekeken.* Den Haag: Ministerie van Justitie, WODC.

Bogdan, R. C. and Biklen, S. K. (1992) *Qualitative Research for Education: An Introduction to Theory and Methods.* Boston: Allyn & Bacon.

De Jong, J. D. A. (2007) *Kapot Moeilijk: Een Etnografisch Onderzoek naar Opvallend Delinquent Groepsgedrag van 'Marokkaanse' Jongens.* Amsterdam: Aksant.

Decker, S. H. and Weerman, F. (eds) (2005) *European Street Gangs and Troublesome Youth Groups: Findings from the Eurogang Research Program.* Walnut Creek, CA: AltaMira Press.

Emmerson, R. M., Fretz, R. I. and Shaw, L. L. (1995) *Writing Ethnographic Fieldnotes.* Chicago: University of Chicago Press.

Geertz, C. (1973) *The Interpretation of Cultures.* New York: Basic Books.

Hammersley, M. (1992) *What's Wrong with Ethnography?* London: Routledge.

Hammersley, M. and Atkinson, P. (1983) *Ethnography: Principles in Practice.* London: Tavistock.

Junger, M. (1990) *Delinquency and Ethnicity: An Investigation on Social Factors Relating to Delinquency among Moroccan, Turkish, Surinamese and Dutch Boys.* Deventer and Boston: Kluwer.

Kaufman, P. and Verbraeck, H. (1986) *Marokkaan en verslaafd. Een studie naar randgroepvorming, heroïnegebruik en criminalisering.* Utrecht: Gemeente Utrecht.

Klein, M. W., Kerner, H.-J., Maxson, C. L. and Weitekamp, E. G. M. (eds) (2001) *The Eurogang Paradox: Street Gangs and Youth Groups in the U.S. and Europe.* Boston and The Hague: Kluwer.

Malinowski, B. (1922) *Argonauts of the Western Pacific.* London: Routledge & Kegan Paul.

Marks, H. and Wester, F. (2008) 'Etnografie, geldigheid van de Baron van Münchhausen', *Kwalon*, 13 (1): 3–14.

Van der Laan, A. M. and Blom, M. (2006) *Jeugddelinquentie: risico's en bescherming. Bevindingen uit de WODC Monitor Zelfgerapporteerde Jeugdcriminaliteit 2005.* Den Haag: Boom Juridische uitgevers.

Van Gelder, P. and Sijtsma, J. (1988) *Horse, coke en kansen. Sociale risico's en kansen onder Marokkaanse harddruggebruikers in Amsterdam.* Amsterdam: Instituut voor Sociale Geografie, Universiteit van Amsterdam.

Van Gemert, F. (1998) *Ieder voor zich; Kansen, cultuur en criminaliteit van Marokkaanse jongens.* Amsterdam: Het Spinhuis.

Van Gemert, F. (2002) 'Botsen met de buurt; Overlast en de wisselwerking tussen jeugdgroepen en de buitenwereld', *Tijdschrift voor Criminologie*, 44 (2): 162–71.

Van Gemert, F. and Fleisher, M. (2005) 'In the grip of the group: ethnography of a Moroccan street gang in the Netherlands', in S. H. Decker and F. Weerman (eds), *European Street Gangs and Troublesome Youth Groups: Findings from the Eurogang Research Program*. Walnut Creek, CA: AltaMira Press, pp. 11–30.

Van Gemert, F. and Stuifbergen, J. (2008) 'Gangs, migration and conflict: Thrasher's theme in The Netherlands', in F. van Gemert, D. Peterson, and I.-L. Lien (eds), *Street Gangs, Migration and Ethnicity*. Cullompton: Willan, pp. 79–96.

Van Gemert, F., Peterson, D. and Lien, I.-L. (eds) (2008) *Street Gangs, Migration and Ethnicity*. Cullompton: Willan.

Weerman, F. (2001) *Samenplegen: Over criminele samenwerking en groepsvorming*. Nijmegen: Ars Aequi.

Werdmölder, H. (1990) *Een Generatie op Drift: De Geschiedenis van een Marokkaanse Randgroep*. Arnhem: Gouda Quint.

Wittebrood, K. (2006) *Slachtoffers van Criminaliteit: Feiten en Achtergronden*. Den Haag: Sociaal Cultureel Planbureau.

Wolcott, H. F. (2005) *The Art of Fieldwork*. Walnut Creek, CA: AltaMira Press.

Chapter 9

Getting good data from people that do bad things: effective methods and techniques for conducting research with hard-to-reach and hidden populations

Ric Curtis

Abstract

This chapter outlines several problems that are inherent in conducting research with hard-to-reach or hidden populations, including locating the population(s) of interest, recruiting them into research, eliciting accurate and credible information from them and assessing the veracity of their accounts. Each of these problems is examined using examples from research conducted by the author to discuss where our ideas about the nature and severity of the problem are accurate, and where they are not, and suggestions for addressing some of the problems based on previous experiences are offered. One conclusion that can be drawn from the various examples provided in the chapter is that social science has already developed many data collection tools that can be successfully employed, but many of the problems that researchers face in conducting research with these populations stem from our own preconceived ideas about what is possible.

Good data is often hard to find for social scientists that are concerned about crime and public health problems, and many are deeply sceptical about self-report data that is collected from stigmatised populations (especially if they are 'captive'), like criminals, drug addicts or people with AIDS. It is widely believed that people that engage in highly stigmatised behaviour do not want to talk about it, and if they do, they often talk about it in ways that minimise their stigma, perhaps even denying that they ever did it. Yet these people – usually deemed hard-to-reach or hidden populations – are precisely those that are the most likely to be able to provide answers to the questions that preoccupy social scientists and, as such, we need to find reliable ways to find them, convince them to participate in our (often intrusive) research, elicit accurate and credible information from them, and assess the accuracy and veracity of their accounts. This chapter examines each of these problems using examples from research conducted by the author to discuss where our ideas about the nature and severity of the problem are accurate and where they are not, and it will offer suggestions for addressing some of the problems based on these previous experiences.

What we can learn from stigmatised populations (that is not available elsewhere)

To appreciate what we can learn about crime or public health problems from stigmatised populations, it is useful to get an overview of existing data to see what we do not know. In most cases, relevant data is quite limited in scope and often highly compartmentalised. For example, police departments regularly collect data on crimes that have been committed and much of it is aggregated in ways that help us understand the demographics of criminals and victims or detect crime trends. They also collect data that focuses on solving individual crimes. But police data generally cannot tell us why people commit crimes or adequately frame the wider contexts of their actions. In a similar fashion, data from public health and other medical sources also tend to provide overviews of problems (such as the incidence rates of diseases) or it focuses on particular risk behaviours that lead to problems or it focuses on healing individual patients, but they generally do not probe far beyond the immediate health problem at hand. And when they do, the data that is collected is often impossible to access by researchers because it would violate patients' or prisoners' rights of privacy. Public health and criminal justice data that is heavily redacted to remove unique identifiers is often useful to researchers, but the removal of unique identifiers usually means that data sets cannot be linked in ways that would allow researchers to gain more insight into problems. Without this strict compartmentalisation of data, researchers might be able to cobble together a much richer picture of pressing crime and health problems, but because they usually cannot, there is an urgent need to collect reliable data directly from people at the heart of the problem.

How do we find hard-to-reach or hidden populations?

Finding and recruiting hard-to-reach or hidden populations to participate in research about crime or health problems can be daunting,
especially when compared with the ease of accessing them in places like
jails or hospitals where they can often be found in large numbers. But
captive populations are only a segment of a larger group and they limit
our ability to generalise. After all, only a fraction of the criminals get
locked up – maybe the stupid and/or unlucky ones – and not everyone
who gets sick goes to the hospital or sees a doctor, and some may not
even know that they are sick. The problem of representativeness is not
the only issue that limits the usefulness of data generated from captive
populations, and clearly, it is better to recruit a sample that is
representative of the population of interest than not. The gold standard
method for recruiting a representative sample is random probability
sampling, but most criminals or at-risk populations cannot be recruited
via random sampling methods primarily because we do not know the
parameters of the universe: there is, for example, no complete index of
drug dealers or inventory of AIDS victims that we can consult to
randomly recruit a representative sample. In addition, the practical
problems that one might imagine are involved in recruiting representative samples of criminals or at-risk people make it seem almost an
impossible task.

Yet it is possible to recruit reliable, if not representative, samples of
criminals and at-risk persons that are far superior in many ways to using
data collected from secondary sources or from captive populations. Many
studies that have sought to recruit hard-to-reach or hidden populations
have championed ethnographic methods as one of the most reliable ways
to find these kinds of research subjects. Among the primary strengths of
the ethnographic method is the actual presence of the researcher in the
field conducting participant observation over extended periods of time
that allow them to develop relationships within a community. As a result
of this presence, ethnography holds the promise of being able to find
people that might otherwise remain hidden, and through the careful
cultivation and management of relationships with them and others,
recruiting them as willing participants in research. An additional benefit
of ethnography is that it affords researchers the opportunity to validate
data by triangulating it in ways that other researchers cannot. For
example, ethnographers can ask research subjects about each other to
assess the accuracy and the veracity of their claims, or they can see
first-hand whether subjects engage (or not) in specific behaviours. But
ethnography is not a panacea and it has been criticised for a variety of
shortcomings (Fine 1993, though see Borman et al. 1986), including that it
is time-consuming and, given the small samples that it typically generates,

that it does not appear to be especially cost-effective. But aside from ethnographers that employ traditional ethnographic methods to successfully recruit hard-to-reach or hidden populations, there are few examples of social scientists employing other methods to systematically accomplish this task. Yet it is possible to recruit them via other methods, and below, two additional examples of successfully recruiting robust samples of hard-to-reach or hidden populations are described that defied our initial beliefs about what was possible.

Multi-stage probability sampling in a high-crime neighbourhood

The Social Factors in HIV Risk (SFHR) project conducted in the mid-1990s that examined HIV and other sexually transmitted infections among 18–21 year olds in a poor 'community of color' with high rates of drug abuse and HIV in Brooklyn recruited a probability sample of youth using a multi-stage sampling strategy that, essentially, involved screening every dwelling unit (some blocks had more than 700 dwelling units) on 12 randomly selected 'face blocks' (out of a total of about 300 city blocks) (Friedman *et al.* 1997). Many people initially believed that it would be very difficult to successfully recruit a representative sample of youth in a door-to-door fashion in a high-crime, heavily policed neighbourhood where many residents were illegal aliens. Many predicted that residents would simply not open their doors to strangers (especially a white man), but surprisingly, more than 95 per cent of the dwelling units were successfully screened, and of the 129 youths that were identified as eligible, 111 (86 per cent) of them were subsequently interviewed in depth about their sex and drug use attitudes and behaviours, and 104 (81 per cent) provided blood and urine specimens (that were used to test for HIV-I, hepatitis B and C, HTLV-I, HTLV-II, syphilis, herpes simplex virus type 2 and chlamydia, and for opiates, cocaine and marijuana metabolites). The demographics of the sample of youth closely mirrored that from the US Census for this neighbourhood (28 per cent black, 67 per cent Hispanic, 51 per cent female, versus 29 per cent black, 67 per cent Hispanic and 52 per cent female, respectively) and thus the researchers were confident that this modest sample was representative of the larger population of 18–21 year olds in the area.

The findings from the study showed that these youth that were thought to be hard-to-reach (because of neighbourhood conditions) were not so hard to reach, but they did constitute a hidden population: 50 per cent of them were infected with HSV-2 (64 per cent of the women, 37 per cent of the men) and 12 per cent were infected with chlamydia, and most of them did not know that they were infected. And it is significant to note that the infections were not evenly distributed but rather were clustered on particular blocks, a finding that has important implications for public health intervention strategies. In addition, subjects were quite forthcoming about their level of sexual risk: 89 per cent said that they had sex in the last year (45 per cent with two or more partners), but only 19 per cent reported that they 'always' used a condom. The findings also revealed that many subjects willingly reported illegal and stigmatised behaviours, though there was some evidence of underreporting: 18 per cent said that they had sold cocaine or heroin at some time in their lives, but while only 3 per cent reported ever using heroin and 9 per cent reported ever using cocaine, 2 'non-reporters' had opiate-positive urines, 2 'non-reporters' had cocaine-positive urine and 1 'non-reporter' had marijuana-positive urine. In summary, household survey methods like those employed in this project demonstrate that it is possible to recruit hard-to-reach and hidden populations using recruitment methods that are familiar to social scientists, and research subjects will divulge a wide range of information, but the issue of 'under-reporting' (or over-reporting) continues to present problems to researchers.

Respondent driven sampling

Another method of recruiting representative samples of hard-to-reach or hidden populations is through respondent driven sampling (RDS), a methodology that recruits subjects by taking advantage of intra-group social connections to build a sample (Heckathorn 1997, 2002; Abdul-Quader *et al.* 2006; Robinson *et al.* 2006). RDS is much like the well-known and often-used recruitment strategies of 'snowball sampling' (Goodman 1961) and 'chain-referral sampling' (Erickson 1979), but unlike these methods whose primary utility is generating a large number of research subjects, RDS also provides a powerful set of analytic/statistical tools for creating weighted population estimates which are at least as powerful and robust as those generated through more common probabilistic statistics (Salganik and Heckathorn 2004). An additional benefit is that RDS has been shown to improve upon previous chain referral and snowball sampling methods by employing a systematic recruiting scheme and mathematical modelling techniques during data analysis in order to mitigate, estimate and correct for biases, including those due to (1) the selection of the initial sample, (2) volunteerism (higher levels of participation from cooperative and interested participants), (3) problems related to the how chain referral takes place (e.g. problems with inaccurate contact information and differential recruitment), and (4) homophily (the tendency of seeds and subsequent referrals to recruit those like themselves). As recruitment chains go through many waves of referral, the biasing effects of initial seed selection are minimised. RDS, like similar recruitment strategies, has proved extremely useful in quickly recruiting large numbers of people from hidden populations, but it also allows researchers to describe the salient characteristics of the population and, in some instances, make population estimates. Instead of making estimations directly from the sample to the population, RDS outlines a methodology for making indirect estimates by way of the social networks connecting the population. Because of these advantages over other recruitment strategies, RDS has increasingly been used nationally and internationally in studies of hard-to-reach groups, including injection drug users, commercial sex workers and men who have sex with men.

The basic mechanics of RDS recruitment are fairly straightforward: a small number of initial research subjects (called 'seeds') are recruited, interviewed by the researchers and paid for their time and effort. Following their interviews, the seeds are given three sequentially numbered coupons and instructed to pass them along to friends or associates who are like themselves. If recruitment chains do not develop as expected, additional seeds may be recruited as replacements. The numbers on the coupons allow the researchers to prevent duplication, identify who recruited each participant and keep track of subsequent recruitment patterns using the RDS 'Coupon Manager' software that is downloadable for free at http://www.respondentdrivensampling.org. When coupons are redeemed by eligible research subjects, their recruiter is compensated for each coupon redeemed. The eligible subjects referred by the seeds comprise the first wave of the sample and they are each given three coupons to recruit the next wave of study participants. Study participants are recruited in this fashion until the desired sample size is reached (which, in general, needs to be about double the size that true random sampling methods would employ to achieve similar confidence intervals).

A variety of research projects carried out by a research team at John Jay College over the last three years has demonstrated the ability of RDS methods to recruit sizeable samples of hard-to-reach populations such as drug dealers (Kennedy *et al.* 2006), prostituted teenagers (Curtis *et al.* 2008a), adult sex workers (Curtis *et al.* 2008b) and undocumented immigrants that have been victims of violence.[1] Though RDS generates spectacular numbers of potential respondents, one concern regarding this method is that it also invites considerable scamming and researchers must carefully screen prospective candidates for eligibility and find ways to assess the veracity of the information provided by the respondents (see below).

These two methods of finding hard-to-reach or hidden populations do not exhaust the possibilities that exist for researchers in this regard and additional methods may exist that have the potential to accomplish this task. At the very least, the two examples described above point out that recruiting representative samples of these kinds of populations is not an impossible job and that many of our ideas about what can or cannot be done may not be correct.

How do we convince hard-to-reach or hidden populations to participate in research?

Finding hard-to-reach or hidden populations is often easier than convincing them to participate in research. The study of 18–21 year olds described, for example, asked them to participate in a 2–3 hour interview that asked many intrusive questions about their drug use and sexual behaviour, and they were also asked to provide blood and urine (Friedman *et al.* 1997). In other studies, the John Jay researchers have asked drug dealers (Kennedy *et al.* 2006) and sex workers (Curtis *et al.* 2008a, 2008b) to provide details about their businesses, or illegal immigrants to talk about their employment and living arrangements. In each of these cases, it is easy to imagine that some respondents would refuse to participate and some did refuse. But surprisingly, their numbers were few (RDS, for example, asks specific questions about the number and type of people that refuse to participate), and the overwhelming majority of those that did participate likely did it for a variety of reasons.

Money was one of the biggest incentives to participate in research, and paying money for interviews (typically $20) or recruitment fees (typically $10), or for blood or urine that was provided (typically $20), was an important acknowledgment of the respondents' value to the project. Researchers are compensated for their work, and research subjects must be paid too, regardless of the ethical qualms that institutional review boards (IRBs) (whose mission is to protect the rights and welfare of research subjects) may have about the coercive effect of money on prospective research participants or the 'enabling' effect that some believe it may have on particular types of respondents (like drug users).

The goals of a project can also entice prospective research subjects to participate, especially those who feel some degree of guilt about being part of the problem. For example, the 'Social Factors in HIV Risk' study (Friedman *et al.* 1999) recruited more than 750 drug injectors in Brooklyn to participate in HIV research, and the ethnographers found that prospective subjects offered little resistance to recruitment from the street. Even though subjects were paid for participating in the research, interviews with injectors (especially ethnographic interviews that offered the opportunity to digress) often had a 'confessional' quality to them, and many research subjects reported a cathartic experience from participating in the study. In an RDS study of drug dealers in Rochester, NY, in 2005, one of the goals of the study was to better understand drug-related violence, particularly the high rates of shootings in the inner city (Kennedy *et al.* 2006). Prospective research subjects were told that the study wanted to find out 'why you are all shooting each other' and over eight days, more than 100 of them subsequently described their involvement in buying and selling drugs and guns, and provided details about specific events of gun-related violence.

Feelings of guilt and the desire to atone for perceived wrongdoing are often motives for participating in research that examines stigmatised or criminalised behaviour. Many research subjects harbour deep feelings of guilt and shame about the trajectories that their lives have taken and the negative consequences that their behaviour has had on those closest to them, especially their mothers. These feelings and impulses often have no outlet and research projects that ask subjects to talk about stigmatised or criminalised behaviours often receive far more cooperation than researchers expect. Ethnographers on the SFHR project (Friedman *et al.* 1999), for example, were surprised by the number of street-hardened men (drug dealers and users) whose initial 'life history' interviews produced riveting, detailed accounts of incriminating, painful and shameful experiences, prompting the staff to keep extra boxes of Kleenex on the desk for the flood of tears that often flowed. Some subjects were so astonished by their emotional and cathartic responses to the interview they asked if they could come back and do a second interview for no payment. But while we may feel confident that these respondents were not purposively distorting their accounts, it is necessary to contextualise their confessional narratives of self-loathing, guilt and shame that almost invariably (though, perhaps, justifiably) pointed the finger of blame inward, and understand the partial view that they offered into the nature and scope of the larger problem.

How do we elicit accurate and credible information from research subjects?

People that engage in illegal or stigmatised behaviours may not want to divulge very much information to researchers, even if they can be convinced to participate in the research. Indeed, some subjects may purposefully undermine the interview process for reasons that are never apparent to researchers. Subjects that comply with a research protocol may answer all the questions that are asked of them, but researchers may be uncertain about the accuracy or the veracity of the information they provide, especially in response to questions that probe highly stigmatised behaviours (like sharing needles or having unprotected anal sex). One way that ethnographers have tried to overcome this problem is by maintaining a steady presence in a community so that research subjects may come to believe that they cannot provide a deceptive, incomplete or untruthful account without being discovered. But the belief that sufficient immersion into a community will discourage research subjects from providing inaccurate and self-serving narratives is self-delusional; indeed, if those closest to us – our family and loved ones – often engage in these behaviours, why should research subjects be any different? And experience in the field bears this out. For example, when asked about using sterile equipment to inject drugs, some subjects from the SFHR project insisted that they religiously practised safe injection techniques, even though they knew that the ethnographer asking the questions had previously observed them injecting drugs in an unsafe fashion in shooting galleries. The ethnographer could not elicit an accurate description of their injection practices, even though the subjects knew that the ethnographer had observed them injecting drugs on multiple occasions and that other injectors were very likely to provide highly contradictory accounts. The challenge for ethnographers when confronted with these kinds of discrepancies is to understand and explain how and why it happens.

While a deeply-rooted and long-standing presence in a community does not always produce more accurate information or narratives from respondents, the *unknown* nature of the researcher during initial interviews with research subjects often produces surprisingly frank and revealing information that subjects might otherwise not divulge. Interviews that are conducted in conditions that formalise the roles and the boundaries between researchers and subjects (for example, interviews conducted in an office with a standardised questionnaire on a clipboard) and that do not offer the opportunity for subjects to provide long, explanatory narratives are often thought to invite less open and truthful responses from research subjects than responses to questions asked by ethnographers that get to 'know' subjects over the course of conducting fieldwork. But experience shows that this is not always the case. Indeed, ethnographers sometimes have difficulty explaining their job in ways that are clear to research subjects (ethnographers can and do assume different identities, and each of these is problematic in some way (Fine 1993)), and because of this, research subjects sometimes remain suspicious of the 'real' intentions that motivate ethnographers and may remain aloof. The role of survey researcher, on the other hand, is almost universally understood by research subjects, and they generally do not question the researchers' motives for going about their business. But, of course, while subjects may be more willing to talk with survey researchers because of the well-defined and bounded nature of their relationship, survey researchers cannot stray from their script or triangulate the data they collect in ways that are available to ethnographers, and hence they are often uncertain about the degree to which research subjects provide complete and accurate responses to their questions.

One way to improve the odds of collecting data that is complete and reliable is to gain research subjects' 'buy-in' to the goals of the project. Ethnographers often accomplish this through immersion in the 'field' where they develop close relationships with a small number of research subjects to assist them in negotiating the local terrain, identifying and recruiting appropriate research subjects, and in vouching for the trustworthiness of the researcher to those that might otherwise be hesitant to participate in the study. This approach can be very rewarding, but finding research subjects that can perform this role and partnering with them is often challenging and time-consuming, and it depends heavily on the ethnographer's skill and commitment to the research. And even when ethnographers are successful in recruiting a small number of subjects to assist in the research, the baggage and biases that these research subjects bring to the research effort may skew the data that is collected in ways that are impossible to anticipate and difficult to overcome (Broadhead 2001).

It is often assumed that research subjects that assist researchers in gaining access to hard-to-reach or hidden populations can use their good name, status or prestige within a community to ensure that others buy into the goals of the project and participate in the research, but experience conducting research with stigmatised or criminalised populations suggests that some of the most effective advocates for researchers are those who exercise power or who are feared by members of a community (though this raises serious ethical issues that are not discussed here). For example, when conducting research on the Latin Kings gang in Brooklyn in the mid-1990s, one way to ensure that gang members participated in interviews was to recruit the head of the gang to act as the ethnographer's field assistant (a very time-consuming process) (Curtis and Hamid 1999). Not only did this ensure that all of the gang members under his control participated in the research, but other factions of the gang and rival gangs were envious of the attention that his group was receiving and they requested that the researcher 'write their story' too. Their interest in participating in 'research' resulted in the ethnographer being invited to speak at their 'universal' meeting, where all the local factions of the gang met – nearly 1,000 members (Curtis 2002).

If the example of the Latin Kings highlights the advantages of recruiting those with power to help in advancing the research, another project that was done at about the same time demonstrated the usefulness of fear and 'respect' as a way to recruit subjects, in this case 18–24 year olds in Brooklyn that were involved in the local drug scene (Friedman et al. 2003; Flom et al. 2001). One of the most effective recruiters for this project was a former 'enforcer' for local drug distribution organisations that had recently been released from Attica prison where he had served time for murder. His fearsome, scar-faced appearance and well-deserved reputation for killing people ensured that very few young drug sellers refused to participate in interviews, and because he was so familiar with their business, very few of them provided inaccurate responses to questions that were asked. But this route is dangerous in many respects and not recommended: several months later, a group of young men that he recruited into the project shot him dead in a dispute over stolen jewellery.

Yet many research projects, especially those on a tight schedule, cannot rely on building personal connections with research subjects to gain their buy-in to the goals of the project. For them, other methods of promoting it have been successful. The SFHR project appealed to a sense of altruism among the injecting drug users that they recruited to provide honest and accurate information, and they paid them for their time, but staff from the project also noted the importance of their 'neutral stance on drug use' and the 'complete separation of the study, both organisationally and philosophically, from law enforcement and drug treatment' as additional factors that were critical in ensuring the success of the project (Goldstein *et al.* 1995).

To fulfil the requirements of IRBs, researchers must typically review the potential 'benefits' of participating in research as a required part of the informed consent process, and many researchers use these potential benefits to appeal directly to a sense of altruism to encourage prospective research subjects to participate in the project. This method is often surprisingly effective, especially when researchers take care to explain to each research subject how their contribution to the project is valuable, and when the value of their contribution is acknowledged in non-verbal ways (e.g. paying them) that promote buy-in. In projects that use RDS to recruit subjects, some researchers have been tempted to offer more money for distributing coupons (to ensure the growth of robust recruitment trees) than for the actual interview that each respondent completes. But this strategy delivers an unspoken message to research subjects that they are valued more for their recruiting prowess than for the information that they provide to the researchers. The importance of research subjects to a study is validated by paying them money for *their* participation and it helps develop 'buy-in' to the goals of the research.

How do we assess the accuracy and veracity of self-report information?

One of the primary ways to check the accuracy and veracity of self-reports is to triangulate it with other sources of information. Ethnographers often use this technique: they observe subjects over time to see whether the subject's behaviour matches what was reported, they ask others that know the subject for additional perspectives, and they consult other sources, like official records, to confirm self-report information. But the ability to triangulate in this fashion presupposes that ethnographers are sufficiently embedded in a community to take advantage of these options, and it is not a skill that is easily transferrable to another site without a lengthy period of gaining acceptance into a new community. Here, we are concerned with additional methods that can be employed.

To provide insight into the degree that survey respondents provide inaccurate information to researchers who cannot check up on the veracity of their answers, the SFHR study (Friedman *et al.* 1999) asked each research subject to nominate up to 20 people that had been sex partners and 20 people that had been drug injection partners in the last 30 days, and they were asked a battery of questions about the two types of people that they nominated. The project staff used a variety of methods to link the respondents and they were eventually able to verify 521 unique pairs for which responses could be compared. None of the subjects were aware of nor expressed any concerns whether the project had the capacity to link their responses, so there was no coaching or coordinating of responses (often, respondents were interviewed weeks or months apart), and thus the project was able to assess the degree to which subjects provided accurate information about a range of self-reported behavioural data without this concern. The findings from the study were instructive: there was 100 per cent agreement between respondents on gender, 92 per cent agreement on race/ethnicity, 93 per cent agreement on ever having injected drugs with each other, 99 per cent agreement on ever having had sex with each other and 82 per cent agreement on condom use. Agreement on the most stigmatised behaviours was slightly less than non-stigmatised behaviours, but the results of the study showed that drug injectors 'are reliable reporters of their own HIV/AIDS risk behaviours as well as of other important information (years injecting, demographics)' (Goldstein *et al.* 1995). While the results from this study cannot be generalised to drug injectors elsewhere, or to other populations that engage in stigmatised or illegal behaviours, at the very least it suggests that it is possible to collect reliable self-report information from them and that, more often than not, they tell the truth. While the value of this research was its demonstration that researchers can elicit credible self-report data from stigmatised populations, the process by which they accomplished this – especially the 'linking' process (Ildefonso *et al.* 1993; Neaigus *et al.* 1993) – would be difficult for other researchers to replicate.

More recently, with the assistance of computer technology, new methods of linking respondents have become available. In a current study of methamphetamine users in New York City,[2] the research team is using RDS to recruit a sample that will be asked a battery of questions about their use and sale of methamphetamine, but we hope to link a subset of the respondents in a much more efficient manner than previously attempted, to compare and contrast their responses and to learn more about the overall topography of the network to which they belong. To accomplish this, each respondent will be asked to examine the phonebook on their cell phones and provide the last four digits of the phone numbers of people that are also involved with methamphetamine that begin with particular letters (which the researchers will choose at random for each respondent). This information will provide the researchers with a way to construct randomly selected networks for each research subject that is not biased by their own selection preferences. If any of the people that they name appear in the database (i.e. people with the same first initial and last four digits of their phone number), the researchers will be able to link the two respondents.

One problem with self-report data is the 'Rashomon' effect: people sometimes provide quite different yet credible accounts of the same event (a crime victim, for example, may provide an account that contrasts with that of a witness to the crime). When this is the case, it is very useful for researchers to be able to compare and contrast these various points of view. Researchers may never realise that two or more subjects have described the same event, but if they know which subjects are linked, it provides them with a methodical way of comparing subjects' accounts of events to determine whether this is the case. For example, a May 2008 study conducted in Hempstead, Long Island by a research team from John Jay College used RDS methods to recruit and interview a sample of 153 illegal immigrants (primarily, Central Americans) that had been 'victims of violence'.[3] Each respondent was asked to describe the various incidents in which they had been victimised, and many provided harrowing accounts of violent robberies, muggings and assaults. It is likely that some subjects described the same event, and the researchers wanted to know when that was the case, but RDS typically permits researchers to link only those research subjects that gave coupons to each other. In this case, the immigrant community seemed to be fairly small and, clearly, many more inter-group connections existed than those the RDS recruitment trees revealed. To permit the research team to link research subjects, each subject was asked to describe their friends or acquaintances that had also been victims of violence, and they were asked to provide their friends' nicknames, first and last initials, gender, height, weight, age, marital status, country of origin, region within a country, skin colour, occupation and tattoos. While the analysis of the data has not been completed, with this information, if any of the friends that they mentioned were interviewed by the project, the research team can calculate the odds that they were the same people and thereby allow the researchers to link their interviews to examine whether they described the same violent incidents and the degree to which their narratives about those incidents (which were audio-recorded on a digital recorder) produced similar or contrasting accounts. Preliminary analysis of the data suggests that the accounts provided by these victims of violence vary in some of the details, but not in the broader facts surrounding most of the incidents, and thus we expect to easily link many of the accounts of incidents. But there are other examples where markedly different accounts were provided by respondents.

A research project conducted in 2005 that focused on drug-dealing and gun violence in Rochester, NY, provides an example of contrasting accounts of the same phenomena given by different observers (Kennedy *et al.* 2006). In this project, police sources described Rochester as a city that was overrun with drug-dealing gangs whose members were the primary perpetrators of gun-related violence. They had developed an extensive database that included dozens of 'gangs' that existed in the area and it was updated on a daily basis using incident reports written by police officers on patrol. The database consisted of a map of Rochester that located each gang within the city and featured a detailed roster of its members, including their rap sheets. This database was used by the police to identify and focus on gangs that were especially problematic, to track the gangs' memberships and activities over time, and to monitor the police department's progress in addressing the issues associated with specific gangs.

But interviews with drug dealers in Rochester that were recruited via RDS provided a substantially different perspective on the issues of gangs, drugs and gun violence. For example, as the report noted, not a 'single research subject described their drug dealing activities as having been organised, directed or controlled by a gang that they *"repped"'* (i.e. were members of). The notion that gang leaders were somehow pulling the strings of the soldiers that they placed in the streets to sell drugs was consistently disputed by the descriptions that respondents gave about how they sold drugs. Many young people who claimed that they 'repped' a particular gang in Rochester also claimed that they were 'independent' drug dealers who made all of their own business decisions. And this was very likely the case: gangs did not generally appear to be organised around making money as a goal and gang members described organising themselves in an ad hoc fashion to conduct business on a daily basis. Yet it was clear that gang membership was beneficial to some independent operators (Kennedy *et al.* 2006). The police provided a substantially different portrait of the structure and organisation of gangs and drug dealing activities in Rochester than those provided by gang members and drug dealers, but the point here is that this does not mean that one view is uninformed or that another is deceptive and self-serving, but rather that they represent different perspectives on the same phenomena and any analysis of this data needs to account for those perspectives.

Truth, lies and digital recording

What if research subjects do not provide credible alternative perspectives but rather serve up self-serving narratives, overly embellish their accounts of events or simply tell bare-faced lies to researchers? Of course, researchers attempt to screen these subjects out of the research project and the database as soon as they are discovered, but often deceptive or dishonest subjects manage to evade detection and many prove quite adept at convincing researchers that they are providing legitimate information. For example, a 2006 study of 'commercially sexually exploited children' (CSEC) funded by the National Institute of Justice that was conducted in New York City used RDS methods to recruit a sample of 329 research subjects, 18 years old or younger, that were involved in commercial sex markets (Curtis *et al.* 2008a). Many potential subjects were screened out during intake as either too old (i.e. over 18) or not involved in commercial sex markets, but screening this population for eligibility was considerably more difficult than other populations (drug injectors, for example, can be checked for 'track marks' on their bodies) and a large number of ineligible subjects were admitted into the study despite these efforts. During the data analysis phase of the study, the eligibility of each research subject was closely scrutinised in a systematic review process, and ultimately 77 of the 329 were determined to be not eligible for inclusion in the database that was used to make generalisations about commercially sexually exploited youths. While the existence of non-credible research subjects was a clear indication of the degree of scamming that plagued the project, it is significant to note that non-credible subjects recruited eligible ones (see Table 9.1), and is evidence of the larger web of social relationships to which CSEC youth belonged that included more than simply other sexually exploited youth. The interconnectedness of eligible and non-eligible youth in this study suggests that, for some analyses, data from some of the non-eligible subjects might merit inclusion in the database.

Yet there were some ineligible subjects that were not involved in commercial sex markets that, nevertheless, provided elaborate accounts of their involvement. This was especially true of the boys in the sample; many of them could not or would not tell the far more believable story that they had sex with another man for money (there was a booming market in NYC for this), but rather, they provided fanciful accounts of their lives as male 'gigolos', handsomely paid by 'ugly women' that were desperate for sex. While it was fairly easy to flag these accounts and remove them from the database to include only eligible subjects, they formed a database of their own and will be subject to analysis in future publications. There were several themes that the various non-credible interviews appeared to share, and analysis of them may shed light on the

Table 9.1 The Commercial Sexual Exploitation of Children in New York City: recruitment by gender* and credibility of respondent

Person who recruited	Recruits				
	Credible male	Non-credible male	Credible female/TG	Non-credible female/TG	Total
Credible male	48	24	51	1	124
Non-credible male	21	23	18	2	64
Credible female/TG	37	20	38	5	100
Non-credible female/TG	2	2	1	0	5

*To run analyses on RDS, the female and transgender categories were merged.

normative ideas that youth in general have about sex, sex markets and their participation in them. The point here is that deceitful and dishonest research subjects can be useful regardless of these qualities, and they may provide data that can tell us much about topics that we struggle to understand.

Conclusion

Social scientists concerned with pressing issues related to crime and public health are often hampered by a lack of data that is directly relevant to their primary concerns and often proxy measures are used to make assumptions or draw conclusions about problems for which there is little data. For example, measurements of the 'crime rate' are extremely difficult to approximate (after all, not all crimes are reported) and so many criminologists use the rate of homicide (a crime that is very difficult to conceal or reclassify) as a barometer of crime in general, but clearly, there are limits to what this can tell us. This chapter has argued that collecting data directly from those that engage in the behaviours that lead to social problems can tell us far more than we currently know, and that it is possible to collect reliable data from them despite many sceptics that believe otherwise. Indeed, one of the surprising findings from research with these populations is the degree to which many of the standard methods of data collection in social science seem to work with them and it suggests that the biggest challenge for researchers might simply be selecting the right tool from the box and applying it in the appropriate manner.

Several challenges to the collection of such data were described in this chapter, including locating the populations of interest, recruiting them into research, eliciting accurate and credible information from them, and assessing the veracity of their accounts. Each of these issues may present serious obstacles to the collection of useful and reliable data, but in finding a variety of ways to overcome these problems, this chapter has argued that it is often our own preconceived ideas about what is possible that is the biggest impediment to the collection of these data.

Notes

1 This ongoing study is funded by the New York State Division of Criminal Justice Services.
2 This ongoing study at the National Development and Research Institutes, Inc. is funded by the National Institute on Drug Abuse.
3 This ongoing study is funded by the New York State Division of Criminal Justice Services.

References

Abdul-Quader, A., Heckathorn, D., McKnight, C., Bramson, H., Nemeth, C., Sabin, K., Gallagher, K. and Des Jarlais, D. C. (2006) 'Effectiveness of respondent driven sampling for recruiting drug users in New York City: findings from a pilot study', *Journal of Urban Health*, 83: 459–76.

Borman, K. M., Lecompte, M. D. and Goetz, J. P. (1986) 'Ethnographic and qualitative research design and why it doesn't work', *American Behavioral Scientist*, 30 (1): 42–57.

Broadhead, R. S. (2001) 'Hustlers in drug-related AIDS prevention: ethnographers, outreach workers, injection drug users', *Addiction Research and Theory*, 9 (6): 545–56.

Curtis, R. (2002) *Crime, Justice and the New York Miracle: Quality of Life Enforcement and the War on Drugs*. Invited paper presented at the annual meeting of the Associação Brasileira de Antropologia, Gramado, Brasil, 14–20 June.

Curtis, R. and Hamid, A. (1999) 'Neighborhood violence in New York City and indigenous attempts to contain it: the mediating role of the third crown of the Latin Kings', in P. L. Marshall, M. Singer and M. Clatts (eds), *Integrating Cultural, Observational, and Epidemiological Approaches in the Prevention of Drug Abuse and HIV/AIDS*. Washington, DC: National Institute on Drug Abuse, pp. 143–74.

Curtis, R., Terry, K., Dank, M., Khan, B. and Dombrowski, K. (2008a) *The Commercial Sexual Exploitation of Children in New York City, Volume One: Size, Characteristics and Needs*. Report submitted to the National Institute of Justice.

Curtis, R., Mack, R. and Dombrowski, K. (2008b) *Evaluation of the Philadelphia Community Court: A Study of Active Offenders' Attitudes, Orientations and Behaviors*. Report submitted to the National Center for State Courts, Williamsburg, VA.

Erickson, B. (1979) 'Some problems of inference from chain data', *Sociological Methodology*, 10: 276–302.

Fine, G. A. (1993) 'Ten lies of ethnography: moral dilemmas of field research', *Journal of Contemporary Ethnography*, 22 (3): 276–94.

Flom, P., Friedman, S. R., Jose, B. and Curtis, R. (2001) 'Peer norms regarding drug use and drug selling among household youth in a low-income "drug supermarket" urban neighborhood', *Drugs: Education, Policy, and Prevention*, 8: 219–32.

Friedman, S. R., Curtis, R., Neaigus, A., Jose, B. and Des Jarlais, D. C. (1999) *Social Networks, Drug Injectors' Lives and HIV/AIDS*. New York: Kluwer Academic, Plenum Publishers.

Friedman, S. R., Flom, P., Kottiri, B., Neaigus, A., Sandoval, M., Curtis, R., Johnson, B. D. and Des Jarlais, D. C. (2003) 'Drug dealing and attitudes and norms about drug dealing among young adults and their peers in a high-risk community', *International Journal of Drug Policy*, 14: 261–8.

Friedman, S. R., Curtis, R., Jose, B., Neaigus, A., Zenilman, J., Culpepper-Morgan, J., Borg, L., Kreek, M. J., Paone, D. and Des Jarlais, D. C. (1997) 'Sex, drugs, and infections among youth: parenterally- and sexually-transmitted diseases in a high-risk neighborhood', *Sexually Transmitted Diseases*, 24 (6): 322–6.

Goldstein, M. F., Friedman, S. R., Neaigus, A., Jose, B., Ildefonso, G. and Curtis, R. (1995) 'Self-reports of HIV risk behavior by injecting drug users: are they reliable?', *Addiction*, 90 (8): 1097–104.

Goodman, L. (1961) 'Snowball sampling', *Annals of Mathematical Statistics*, 32: 148–70.

Heckathorn, D. (1997) 'Respondent-driven sampling: a new approach to the study of hidden populations', *Social Problems*, 14 (2): 174–99.

Heckathorn, D. (2002) 'Respondent-driven sampling II: deriving valid population estimates from chain-referral samples of hidden populations', *Social Problems*, 49 (1): 11–34.

Ildefonso, G., Neaigus, A., Curtis, R. and Friedman, S. R. (1993) *Methods for Assigning Linkages in Studies of Drug Injector Networks*, NIDA Technical Review: Social Networks, Drug Abuse and HIV Transmission. Bethesda, MD, 19–20 August.

Kennedy, D., Curtis, R. and Wolf, T. (2006) *Controlling Drug Markets and Related Harms in Rochester, NY: An Ethnographic Study*. Report submitted to the Rochester City Council.

Neaigus, A., Friedman, S. R., Goldstein, M., Ildefonso, G. and Curtis, R. (1993) *Using Dyadic Data for a Network Analysis of HIV Infection and Risk Behaviors Among Injecting Drug Users*, NIDA Technical Review: Social Networks, Drug Abuse and HIV Transmission. Bethesda, MD, 19–20 August.

Robinson, W. T., Risser, J. and McGoy, S. (2006) 'Recruiting injection drug users: a three-site comparison of results and experiences with respondent-driven and targeted sampling procedures', *Journal of Urban Health*, 83 (1): 29–38.

Salganik, M. and Heckathorn, D. (2004) 'Sampling and estimation in hidden populations using respondent-driven sampling', *Sociological Methodology*, 34 (1): 193–239.

Part 4
Social categories of offenders and researchers

Chapter 10

The impact of gender when interviewing 'offenders on offending'

Jody Miller

Abstract

Drawing from representative examples from three qualitative interview studies with active offenders, this chapter addresses the following questions: What role does gender play in the interview process when talking with active offenders? How do social positions of race, class, and age shape this gendered process? In what ways do gendered interactions affect both what offenders tell us about their experiences and how they talk about the nature of their offending? To what extent are the validity and reliability of what we learn affected by the gender combinations of interviewers and interviewees, and how does this vary across setting and context? Finally, what can we learn from interviews in which gender becomes highly salient in the interview context? In discussing these complex issues, I will assess how researchers' consideration of these issues can optimise what we learn from offenders.

The interview is an unavoidably gendered interaction. It involves some combination of individuals, each of whom bring gendered identities, ideologies and performances to the exchange. To make this statement, though, is not particularly revealing. Social relations of gender are contingent, situational and historically shifting (see Connell 2002; Lorber 1994). They vary from place to place, from interaction to interaction, and, as intersectional feminist analyses reveal, cannot be divorced from their relationship to other features of identity and social structure – such as race, class and age – with which they combine to create a seemingly unending variety of social locations (Baca Zinn *et al.* 2002; Collins 1990).

The issues I grapple with here thus address the following questions: What role does gender play in the interview process when talking with active offenders? How do social positions of race, class and age shape this gendered process? In what ways do gendered interactions affect both *what* offenders tell us about their experiences and *how* they talk about the nature of their offending? To what extent are the validity and reliability of what we learn affected by the gender combinations of interviewers and interviewees, and how does this vary across setting and context? Finally, what can we learn from interviews in which gender becomes highly salient in the interview context?

To assess these issues, I begin with a brief review of the literature on the role of gender in interview research. In each of the three subsequent sections, I draw from one of my major studies to assess the questions raised above. Each employed both male and female interviewers, with additional variations across race, nationality, age and class background. Drawing on representative examples from each, I examine the role that gender (in combination with other variations) plays within the context of the interview process, assess how gender affects data quality and discuss how the researcher's consideration of these issues can optimise what we learn from offenders.

First, my study of young women's gang involvement (Miller 2001) provides an opportunity to examine the impact of gender and race when interviewing adolescent *female* offenders. Second, a study of violence among urban African American youth – focusing here on young men's participation in sexual exploitation (Miller 2008) – provides a similar opportunity to examine the role of masculinity, race and gender in the construction of *male* offenders' accounts. Finally, I move to a study of the commercial sex industry in Sri Lanka (Miller 2000, 2002). This allows me to raise further points about how gendered interactional dynamics are shaped across divergent settings. I conclude with a brief discussion of what my research suggests for how we can best go about conducting and utilising interviews about offending.

Gender and social research

Concerns about the role of gender in social research emanate from a variety of sources. Survey researchers, for example, have long concerned themselves with whether interviewer gender, among other characteristics, affects respondents' answers (Groves 1989). Debates concern the relative importance of a *social attribution model* in which 'interviewer characteristics alone are sufficient to influence the reporting behaviour of respondents' (Fendrich *et al.* 1999: 38), versus a *conditional social attribution model* in which respondents' 'perceptions and judgments about interviewer norms influence reporting behaviour' (Fendrich *et al.* 1999: 39). Results tend to be mixed, with some evidence that the *content* of the interview plays an important mediating role (see Axinn 1991; Heeb and Gmel 2001; Hutchinson and Wegge 1991; Johnson and Moore 1993; Johnstone *et al.* 1992; Wilson *et al.* 2002).

Moreover, Dijkstra (1983: 179) warns that 'a dramatic overestimation of the impact of ... interviewer characteristics (e.g. race or gender) on response variation can result without controlling for the individual interviewer per se.' Specifically, he suggests that interviewers' socio-emotional style, including whether they are more personable or formal in their approach, plays an important role in the accuracy and adequateness of survey responses (Dijkstra 1987). Such interactional styles may correlate with interviewer gender or race but are not wholly about them.

Among researchers who adopt qualitative methods, there is a fairly lengthy history of primarily feminist research that examines the impact of gender on ethnography (Hunt 1984; Kleinman 2007; Warren 1988; Whitehead and Conaway 1986; Wolf 1996). Much of this work examines how gender affects researchers' fieldwork roles, emphasising the unique challenges women fieldworkers face in negotiating gender and sexuality in the field. Of particular importance are problems related to perceptions of women's sexual availability, the negotiation of sexual 'come-ons', responses related to so-called chivalry or paternalism, and women's marital status and motherhood roles. Little research, however, has focused on *male* researchers' fieldwork roles or their impact on the field (Silverman 2006: 85). Instead, men's gender is taken for granted or normalised, rather than problematised as an aspect of social identity that likely shapes fieldwork roles and field research.[1]

Compared to analyses of survey research and ethnography, research on the impact of gender (as well as race/ethnicity, class, age) in the context of qualitative interviewing has a somewhat shorter history. As with ethnographic research, much of this work has emerged through the efforts of feminist social researchers. Early analyses were situated in women's standpoint theory (see DeVault 1999; Smith 1987). Grounded in goals of feminist methodology – most notably 'giving voice' to women – initially, there was a relatively uncritical assumption that when women interviewed women, their shared experiences *as women* would result in identification, rapport and, consequently, the authentic revelation of 'women's experiences'.

This resulted in two somewhat competing sets of arguments. First, assumptions about women's unique 'ethic of caring', empathy and listening abilities led to the assumption that women bring particular skills to the interview process, regardless of whether they are interviewing other women or interviewing men. There is, of course, evidence that 'gender structures ... conversational dynamics' (Eckert and McConnell-Ginet

2006: 6). Thus regardless of whether one assumes that women have unique ethical qualities *as women*, how gender affects the social construction of speech in the interview context remains an important consideration.[2]

On the other hand, others have posited that same sex interviews are the most appropriate or effective route to knowledge-building – e.g. women interviewing women, and men interviewing men. This argument is based both 'on the intuitive notion that rapport is more easily achieved in these contexts' (Williams and Heikes 1993: 281) and on evidence and beliefs that gender inequalities make it difficult for women to interview men. For instance, some feminist scholars have assumed that 'male interviewees are likely either to respond to [women] with aggression, or to be unforthcoming or repressed' (Gatrell 2006: 244). Others have reported that male interviewees are sometimes 'careful about how they present views which could be seen as "hostile and sexist"' in order to avoid offending female researchers (Gatrell 2006: 244).

These rather straightforward assumptions have been problematised in three ways of relevance to an analysis of the impact of gender on the study of offending. First, recent analyses of the role of gender in interviewing – including, especially, cross-gender interviewing – challenge the uncomplicated assumptions that same-gender interviewing produces the 'best' results, that women are especially or uniformly more comfortable being interviewed by other women, or that gendered power operates in clear-cut and unidirectional ways in the context of women interviewing men (Gatrell 2006; Grenz 2005; Lewis 2007; McDowell 2001; Ortiz 2005; Padfield and Procter 1996; Presser 2005; Seale *et al.* 2008; Williams and Heikes 1993).

Second, a number of recent studies point to the importance of additional facets of difference that come into play in the interview context – including race, ethnicity, cultural identity, nation, class and age (Bhopal 2001; Egharevba 2001; Fawcett and Hearn 2004; Garg 2005; Hall 2004; McDowell 2001; Song and Parker 1995; Veroff and DiStefano 2002). These intersect with gender to shape the nature of the interview exchange. For example, there is evidence that 'ethnicity enters into the woman-to-woman interview in complex and unpredictable ways' (Hall 2004: 128). Some argue that outsider status is a hindrance for establishing rapport, particularly when the interviewer is from a privileged racial group, as it creates distrust and suspicion among interviewees who may not be willing to share insider knowledge with outsiders. However, there is also evidence that outsider status can sometimes result in richer information, as social distance 'may elicit explanations that are assumed to be known by someone with insider status' (Taylor *et al.* 1995: 36). Sometimes both types of insider/outsider dynamics can exist within the same project, or even within the same interview, vis-à-vis different topics.

This leads to my final point concerning the problematisation of assumptions about how gender matters in conducting research: what to make of interview data. Given an abundance of evidence that our social locations *matter* in the production of interview conversations (including our locations *as researchers*), how do we treat interview accounts? This is particularly important given evidence that the more sensitive the topic, the more likely such effects will be heightened rather than taken for granted. Interviewing 'offenders on offending' certainly falls into this category – such research is inescapably about researching 'others,' as the offenders we interview occupy 'less powerful social locations and [are] significantly "different" from "us" as researchers' (Fawcett and Hearn 2004: 203). Yet there has been little reflection on how social positioning affects this particular type of interview exchange (but see Grenz 2005; Presser 2005).

I would argue that no matter how much we strive to improve the validity of our data when interviewing 'offenders on offending', ultimately the interview itself cannot provide authentic access to individuals' 'experiences.' Interviews are accounts. Such accounts offer a means of 'arriving at meanings or culturally embedded normative explanations [for behaviour, because they] represent the ways in which people organise views of themselves, of others, and of their social worlds' (Orbuch 1997: 455). Moreover, these are never unmediated by the context of the interview itself. Thus the narratives produced in interviews should be treated and analysed as 'instances of social action – as speech-acts or events with common properties, recurrent structures, cultural conventions, and recognisable genres' (Atkinson 2005: 6; see also Silverman 2005, 2006). We need to maintain some healthy scepticism about the extent to which interviews with 'offenders on offending' provide access to unmediated 'truth' about experiences, actions and motives. Nonetheless, we can obtain information about social worlds through in-depth interviewing. Indeed, 'what matters is to understand how and where the stories [we collect] are produced, which sort of stories they are, and how we can put them to honest and intelligent use in theorising about social life' (Miller and Glassner 2004: 138).

To this end, I argue here three essentially simple points. First, gender matters in the context of interviewing offenders on offending. Second, *how* gender matters is not simple or straightforward. It doesn't operate independently of other facets of interviewers' and interviewees' social positions, nor does it operate independently of interviewers' particular research styles or skills. Finally, paying attention to how gender matters can reveal a great deal about how individuals construct particular sorts of accounts of their offending, and about the contexts and meanings of offending (see Miller and Glassner 2004; Silverman 2006: 128–43).

Studying young women in street gangs

The first project I draw from is a comparative study of young women's participation in street gangs in two US cities. Three interviewers were involved in the project. I was, at the time, a young white woman interviewing primarily African American adolescent girls. In addition, I employed two graduate students to assist with data collection – an African American man who grew up in an urban neighbourhood in the same city as those of the study participants and a light-skinned African American young woman from a suburban, middle-class background.

Comparing our experiences conducting interviews with girls in gangs, we found that the way young women responded to us sometimes varied and appeared to be shaped in part by race and gender. For example, Rod faced some scepticism that I and Niquita did not. He was asked by several young women for assurances that he was not a police officer, and in one case a member of the secret service. No young women ever appeared to be suspicious of us on those grounds. On the other hand, perhaps because many of the girls we interviewed had had less than positive experiences with other adult men in their lives, they also responded to Rod – an older African American male who was empathetic and interested in their lives – as a paternal figure, and felt quite safe disclosing and talking at length with him (and without prompting) about their experiences of victimisation. One girl even asked him to adopt her; another tried to fix him up with her aunt. Conversely, while young women disclosed victimisation to Niquita and me, there was rarely an instance in which they appeared comfortable speaking to us about these experiences in detail.

While feminist researchers have sometimes assumed that women are more comfortable discussing victimisation with other women, Currie and MacLean (1997) suggest that this is not necessarily the case. In fact, in some instances women are more comfortable speaking with sympathetic males. Gender dynamics operate, not just in mixed-gender settings, but also in single-gender settings, so that 'regardless of how "sisterly" a feminist researcher may feel toward other women, there is no guarantee that respondents perceive other women as necessarily supportive' (1997: 178). Because women so often internalise ideologies that blame women for their victimisation, they may be particularly uncomfortable sharing their experiences with other women, whom they believe may judge them.

In my case, it may be that our perceived similarity in age, coupled with social distances created by race and class differences, were a source of uneasiness for some young women, hindering their willingness to open up to me about these issues. In Niquita's case even more, their similarities of race and age, in conjunction with their class differences, meant that she had the most difficulty getting girls to open up to her about aspects of their lives they felt could be scrutinised. Thus it appeared that Rod's position as a similarly situated African American *male* was best suited for examining issues of girls' victimisation, while Niquita's shared racial background but other social distances was least suited for pursuing such questions.[3]

On the other hand, we also found that my differences from respondents – particularly in relation to race – often were beneficial in eliciting information about girls' gangs. As noted earlier, one potential advantage of social distance is that it 'may elicit explanations that are assumed to be known by someone with insider status' (Taylor *et al.* 1995: 36). Reading Rod's transcripts against mine, we found instances in which girls assumed shared understandings with Rod, while they took more time to explain things to me. In addition, social distances facilitated young women's recognition of themselves as experts on their social worlds. Many of the girls were cognizant of the 'controlling images' (Collins 1990) used to describe aspects of their lives. Consequently, some responded to me in ways that purposely challenged common stereotypes about adolescents, inner-city youth, gangs and the place of young women within these groups. For instance, Tamika told me:

> Some people stereotype, they just stereotype gang members to be hardcore and to always be shootin' at somebody. They don't stereotype people that that could be a gang member but still they could go to school and get straight A's. That's stereotyping because I know, I know a few gang-bangers who go to school, get straight A's, hit the books but still when they on the street, you know, they take good care of theirs. They takin' care of theirs in school and they takin' care of theirs on the street and I don't think that's right to stereotype people.

Moreover, in their interviews with me, young women constructed 'collective stories' (Richardson 1990) about their place within youth gangs. In doing so, they did more than just challenge prevailing stereotypes in explaining their gang involvement (i.e. 'I was not sexed in', 'I have respect'). Instead, they also presented a collective story of the gang as a space of gender equality. Specifically, they were quite resistant to my attempts to elicit discussions of gender inequality, emphasising instead that everyone in the gang was 'all the same'. For example, Chantell was visibly frustrated with my line of questions and repeatedly cut me off, or talked back, in response:

> *Jody*: You said before that the gang was about half girls and half guys? Can you tell me more about that? Like you said you don't think there are any differences in terms of what –
> *Chantell*: There isn't!

Jody: OK, can you tell me more –

Chantell: Like what? There isn't, there isn't like, there's nothing – boy, girl, white, black, Mexican, Chinese.

Such construction of their place in gangs appeared, in part, a reaction to their perceptions of outsiders' stereotypes of girls' experiences in gangs, and thus was about positioning themselves relative to my presumed orientation to their experiences. But in addition, telling this collective story allowed them to position themselves, in their own understandings of life in the gang, as uniquely empowered vis-à-vis other girls. As Veronica told me:

A lot of girls get scared. Don't wanna break their nails and stuff like that. So, ain't no need for them to try to be in no gang. And the ones that's in it, most of the girls that's in act like boys. That's why they in, 'cause they like to fight and stuff. They know how to fight and they use guns and stuff.

According to this collective story, the gang is an arena in which they receive status and esteem from being strong and being willing to stand up for themselves, exhibiting traits that cultural stories commonly associate with males rather than females.

At the same time, other contradictory realities emerged in my analysis of girls' accounts. Despite their collective story of equality, without exception the young women interviewed for the project provided evidence to the contrary. For example, they described a distinct gender hierarchy within their gangs that included male leadership, a sexual double standard, the sexual exploitation of some young women and most girls' exclusion from serious gang crime – specifically those acts that build status and reputation within the group. By juxtaposing girls' collective stories with these incongruous facets of girls' interviews, I was able to build my theoretical discussion around the contradictory operation of gender within gangs (Miller 2001).

Thus the varying interactional contexts of the interview process – including the use of a diverse research team – helped reveal a variety of important facets of girls' social worlds within gangs. The context in which the interviews were completed, including who conducted them and how girls responded to our differences, allowed for particular sorts of important revelations. Specifically, this study suggests that same-sex interviewing cannot be assumed to be the 'best' route to the production of knowledge; moreover, social distances – particularly when they can effectively be put to use in recognising interviewees' expertise – can be useful for the research enterprise.

Gender, race, and the study of violence against adolescent girls

Next, I turn my attention to a recently completed study of violence against urban African American girls (Miller 2008). As with the gang study, the research team on this project was diverse with regard to race, class and gender, as well as nationality. Though we interviewed both young women and young men for this project, here I focus on young men's accounts of their participation in sexually exploitative behaviours towards girls. Specifically, I compare how they described such incidents to two members of the research team: an African American female PhD student who, like Rod, had grown up in an urban neighbourhood in close proximity to those of the interviewees; and a white male PhD student who was distanced further because he was European rather than American.

The most striking differences in young men's responses to the interviewers were found in their accounts of the phenomenon of 'running trains' on girls. Nearly half of the boys interviewed for the project described having engaged in 'trains', a sexual encounter that involved two or more young men engaging in penetrative sexual acts with a single young woman. Researchers routinely classify such incidents as gang rape because the individual girl is outnumbered by multiple male participants making consent difficult to establish (Ullman 1999). However, the young men interviewed in our project routinely defined girls' participation in trains as consensual.

Dennis, the European interviewer, did not attempt to clarify this interpretation, revealing his own (gendered) desensitisation to the problem. An especially striking feature of the accounts provided in his interviews was the adamancy with which boys claimed that girls were willing, even eager, participants. Moreover, their descriptions were quite graphic, focusing specific attention on the details of their sexual performances. Consider the following examples:

I mean, one be in front, one be in back. You know sometimes, you know like, say, you getting in her ass and she might be sucking the other dude dick. Then you probably get her, you probably get her to suck your dick while he get her in the ass. Or he probably, either I'll watch, and so she sucking your dick, or while you fuck her in the ass. It, I mean, it's a lot of ways you can do it.

There's this one girl, she a real, real freak . . . .She wanted me and my friend to run a train on her . . . [Beforehand], we was at the park, hopping and talking about it and everything. I was like, 'man, dawg, I ain't hitting her from the back.' Like, 'she gonna mess up my dick.' . . . He like, 'oh, I got her from the back dude.' So we went up there . . . [and] she like, 'which one you all hitting me from the back?' [I'm] like, 'there he go, right there. I got the front.' She's like, 'okay.' And then he took off her clothes, pulled his pants down. I didn't, just unzipped mine 'cause I was getting head. She got to slurping me. I'm like, my partner back there 'cause we was in the dark so I ain't see nuttin'. He was back, I just heard her [making noises]. I'm like, 'damn girl, what's wrong with you?' [More noises] [I'm like], 'you hitting her from the back?' He's like, 'yeah, I'm hitting it.'

Notice both accounts, which emerged in the interviews conducted by the white male interviewer, emphasised young men's performance. In fact, research suggests that group processes play a central role in gang rape. The enactment of such violence increases solidarity and cohesion among groups of young men, and the victim has symbolic status and is treated as an object (Franklin 2004; Sanday 1990). Just as performance played a central role in young men's accounts of these incidents, their accounts were themselves a particular sort of masculine performance in the context of their interview exchange (see also Presser 2005).

In contrast, when young men were interviewed about their participation in 'running trains' by Toya – the African American female PhD student – two different features emerged. First, they were much less sexually graphic in their accounts. Second, due in part to Toya's gendered sensitivity to issues of consent, she was able to follow up with questions that undermined young men's attempts to construct the events as consensual. The following conversation with Terence is illustrative:

Terence: It was some girl that my friend had knew for a minute, and he, I guess he just came to her and asked her, 'is you gon' do everybody?' or whatever and she said 'yeah'. So he went first and then, I think my other partna went, then I went, then it was like two other dudes behind me . . . It was at [my friend's] crib.
Toya: Were you all like there for a get together or party or something?
Terence: It was specifically for that for real, 'cause he had already let us know that she was gon' do that, so.
Toya: So it was five boys and just her?
Terence: Yeah.
Toya: And so he asked her first, and then he told you all to come over that day?
Terence: We had already came over. 'Cause I guess he knew she was already gon' say yeah or whatever. We was already there when she got there.
Toya: Did you know the girl?
Terence: Naw, I ain't know her, know her like for real know her. But I knew her name or whatever. I had seen her before. That was it though.
Toya: So when you all got there, she was in the room already?

Terence: Naw, when we got there, she hadn't even got there yet. And when she came, she went in the room with my friend, the one she had already knew. And then after they was in there for a minute, he came out and let us know that she was 'gon, you know, run a train or whatever. So after that, we just went one by one.

By Terence's own account – but emerging due to the sensitivity with which Toya probed – the girl arrived at a boy's house that she knew and may have been interested in. Waiting for her on arrival were four additional boys whom she did not know or know well. And they had come in advance specifically for the purpose of running a train on her. Terence apparently had not considered the possibility that the young woman may have felt threatened or that she hadn't freely consented. Instead, because his friend said 'she was down' for it, Terence took his turn and left.

Similar inconsistencies were revealed in Tyrell's account, again precisely because of Toya's sensitised probing:

This girl was just like, I ain't even know her, but like I knew her 'cause I had went to work [where she did] last year . . . Then my boy, when he started working there, he already had knew her, 'cause he said he had went to a party with her last year. And he was gonna have sex with her then, but . . . [her] grandmamma came home or something, so they ain't get to do it. So one day he was just like, we was all sitting watching this movie [at work] and it was real dark or whatever. And she had come in there or whatever, and he was just talking to her, and he was like, 'let's all go 'head and run a train on you.' She was like, 'what?' And she started like, 'you better go on.' Then, like, [he said], 'for real, let's go over to my house.' And then, you know what I'm saying, she was like, 'naw.'

Tyrell explained that later that day, he and his friend were leaving work and saw the girl 'walking over there to the bus stop'. His friend invited the girl over to his house and she agreed to go. Tyrell admitted, 'I think she liked him', and this was the reason she came over. However, because they had previously introduced the idea of running a train on her, Tyrell and his friend appear to have decided that her consent to go to his house was consent to have a train run on her. The discussion continued:

Toya: Do you think she really wanted to do it?
Tyrell: I can't really say. 'Cause at first she was like laughing and stuff, like, 'don't!' But we didn't pressure her. I didn't say nothing to her for the rest of the [work] day. I probably talked to her, but I say nothing about like that. And then she just came with us, so I mean, she had to want to.

171

Thus, in his account, Tyrell maintained his interpretation that the incident was consensual, offering evidence that the fact that he and his friend did not mention running a train on the girl again during the day they spent at work together meant they had not 'pressured' her. He did not appear to consider an alternative interpretation – that their silence on the issue allowed the girl to interpret the earlier comments as innocuous. Instead, he insisted that 'she knew' (see also King 2003; Willan and Pollard 2003).

Further, Tyrell's account of the young woman's behaviour afterwards – which, again, emerged as a result of Toya's continued questioning, also belied his insistence that she had engaged willingly. He explained that 'she missed like a week of work after that.' And while he believed the girl liked his friend before the incident, he said, 'I know she didn't like him after that ... .She don't even talk to him at all. Every time they see each other they'll argue.' In addition, Tyrell said 'she go to my cousin's school now, and she be talking all stuff like, "I hate your cousin!" But I don't care, I mean I don't even care. She shouldn't have did that.'

Given this evidence, Toya asked whether he thought she felt bad about what happened and the conversation continued:

> *Tyrell*: I can't even say. I don't even know her like that. I really can't say. She do that kinda stuff all the time.
> *Toya*: She does?
> *Tyrell*: No. I'm just saying. I don't know. If she don't she probably did feel bad, but if she do she probably wouldn't feel bad ... But if she didn't really wanna do it, she shouldn't have did it.

Notice how Tyrell slipped easily into noting that 'she do that kinda stuff all the time', but when questioned, conceded that he had no basis on which to draw such a conclusion.

It was not just Toya's gender, per se, that allowed these nuanced accounts to emerge. It had much to do with both her skills as an interviewer and her sensitisation to the topic (which was likely shaped by gender). Nonetheless, the role that gender (and race) played in producing these disparate accounts of the same phenomenon also cannot be discounted. Most importantly, both revealed important facets of the nature of 'running trains'. Dennis' interviews demonstrated its function as masculine performance. In fact, young men's acts of *telling* Dennis about the events were also masculine performances, constructed in response to *whom* they were doing the telling. In contrast, Toya's interviews revealed important evidence of the processes by which young men construct their interpretations of girls' consent, and reveal the various ways in which they do so by discounting the points of view of their female victims (see King 2003). Thus this example further reveals the benefits of utilising diverse research teams. Moreover, it suggests that it is necessary to pay close attention to how the interview context shapes accounts in order to identify those features of offending such disparate accounts can reveal.

Gender and the study of Sri Lanka's sex industry

Thus far, my discussion has focused on the role of gender in interview-based research conducted in the US. Adding a non-Western dimension to research on offending highlights additional considerations, as cultural and interactional dynamics pose distinct and situationally specific challenges. I draw from my research on Sri Lanka's commercial sex industry to illustrate. The study was based on interviews with a vast array of stakeholders and participants, and again employed a diverse research team. I focus here on the experiences of two researchers in two interview contexts: first, Manori, a Sri Lankan woman in her early 20s, interviewing police officers and clients; second, myself, a white American woman in my early 30s at the time, also interviewing clients.

Gender, but also markers of nationality and political orientation, often played an important role in our data collection, especially when inter-viewing men. Sinhala Buddhist nationalism in Sri Lanka is intensely gendered, with 'cultural preservation' tied explicitly to women's morality, which is understood both in terms of sexual behaviour but also 'being innocent of all foreign and modern corrupting influences' (Lynch 2007: 93). Though Manori was traditional in her personal behaviour, her appearance, comportment and attitudes were not those of a traditional Sri Lankan 'good girl'. She was university educated abroad. Moreover, she dressed in salwar kameez (an Indian, rather than Sri Lankan, clothing style), or even jeans and a T-shirt, and her shoulder length hair was typically worn loose. These were markers of both modernisation and Westernisation.

Manori was also a budding feminist and outspoken in her position that prostitution is legitimate work that should be decriminalised and destig-matised. This played an important role in getting some male police officers to reveal the nature of their gendered belief systems, and how these operated to shape both their official treatment of sex workers and their informal (and illegal) participation in prostitution as clients. The following focus group excerpts reveal how Manori's gender politics shaped her line of questioning, and how it produced an ensuing antagonism that was quite illuminating. She asked the officers how they typically intervened on street-level sex work, and they initially provided a by-the-books description. Officer A explained: 'Only if they misbehave in a popular place can you arrest them. When we catch somebody in the street, we have to list [that] it's misbehaviour. We have to make notes: it's like this, this number of buses went.'

Dissatisfied with how the label 'misbehaviour' was determined, Manori pressed them, and the officers' responses revealed important information about their attitudes and discretionary practices:

> *Manori*: So she was standing on the road, buses went, now let's say you arrested her. But that's not misbehaviour, she was just standing there, no?
>
> *Officer A*: We must get the sense that she was misbehaving, that is the thing.
>
> *Manori*: Explain that to me, what is actually there in the law? Explain that to me.
>
> *Officer B*: Miss, I will tell you. There is a woman in the road at one o'clock in the morning, alone in the road. Then as a police officer, is it suspicious or not miss?
>
> *Officer A*: Suspicious.
>
> *Officer B*: Miss, tell! A woman like that stays in the bus stand, one o'clock in the morning, with a bag. Nobody coming or going, then do you not feel, 'why is this?'
>
> *Officer A*: Not even that, walks up and down [a well known prostitution stroll] around ten, eleven, with a bag. True picture, is it suspicious or not? What do you say? [laughs sarcastically]

Rebuffing Manori's attempt to problematise their labelling process, the officers culled from the most blatant example of street prostitution – standing alone in a known stroll late at night – and attempted to box Manori into conceding the point. Undeterred, she pressed on.

> *Manori*: Now a woman who has previous convictions can be arrested if they just walk on the street, no?
>
> *Officers*: [indicate affirmative]
>
> *Officer A*: But it's like this, don't misunderstand. Even if she goes a hundred times and we arrest her, we file the cases according to the right procedure. That is, 'she stayed like this,' we have to make notes that she stayed like this at these times, she looked like this, the way she looked at people [e.g. documenting misbehaviour].
>
> *Manori*: But the writing is in your hands, no?
>
> *Officer A*: Writing is in our hands, that of course we have to do properly.
>
> *Officer B*: Otherwise problems. [But] there's nothing a police officer who can't write well can't do.
>
> *Manori*: What?
>
> *Officer B*: If he can write well, a police officer can do anything.
>
> *Officer A*: Can make Dayawansa[4] the owner and can make you [i.e. Manori] the prostitute. Or you can be made the owner and Dayawansa the prostitute.

Officer B: Miss, there's a saying, *gorakathe dhada mas kerenava*. Can do that also.
Officers: [laughter]

Directly translated, this phrase means *goraka*, a kind of vegetable, can be changed into *dhada mas*, a kind of meat, through a cooking process that gives *goraka* the appearance of meat. The officers were admitting that reports can be constructed to say whatever the officer wants, so long as he knows what to include. It was only through Manori's dogged persistence – tied to her feminist indignation – that she got the officers to inadvertently admit her point: 'misbehaviour' is a problematic social category that officers can utilise to write false but credible reports. Moreover, linked with sex workers' accounts of being pressured to provide the police with 'free' services, their revelation implicated the police in illegal practices.

The focus group concluded with even more insights into the gendered construction of Sinhala Buddhism and its impact on sex work. Asked their opinion on prostitution's criminalisation, Officer A said, 'it should be banned ... I don't like a pious country like Sri Lanka getting drawn to such a thing.' Officer B concurred that its criminalisation was necessary for 'preserving the culture'. Yet the officers had previously admitted being clients. Manori used this contradiction to push the officers further:

Manori: Now you say it's a pious country, the country shouldn't get drawn to it. But you are also a person who has gone to prostitutes, no?
Officer A: I don't deny that, no? Personal necessity of course is a different story. If it's illegal, what we want is to minimise it ... But if we legalise it, then you'll see what kind of situation arises. There will be open brothel houses on every street, they'll earn as much money as possible, they'll transact any person for money ... You know what would happen in the end? The family structure will break down ... Like what happened in Russia, women will get unruly. OK? It will lead to a point where it will totally destroy the society.

This exchange came about precisely because of the interactional dynamics between a young Sri Lankan feminist and socially conservative Sri Lankan men who were responding to both her gender and her feminist politics.[5] It illuminated how the organisation and control of the sex industry hinges on gender inequality: criminalisation functions to keep prostitution available for its male consumers while keeping women from 'get[ting] unruly'.

Adding a white woman to the mix: more on gender and nation

Given my limited command of Sinhala, I conducted interviews for the project only with those who were fluent in English. Initially we used snowball sampling to obtain client interviews and these were conducted by both Manori and me. One snowball chain proved to be particularly problematic (yet illuminating). It began with a young man who worked at Manori's gym. She conducted the interview, which took place at my flat. Manori was immediately struck by how Jagath dressed for the occasion – tight jeans with a shirt unbuttoned low on his chest revealing a sleeveless undershirt and gold necklace. She commented that he looked like a 'thug' that day. My initial plan was to sit in the living room while Manori conducted the interview at the dining room table across the room. Jagath, however, said he was uncomfortable with me being within earshot, so I moved instead to my bedroom. A short time later, under the guise of needing a new tape, Manori came back to my room. She was becoming afraid of the young man, and asked me to come into the room every now and then to remind him of my presence.

Jagath appeared to take pleasure in giving her graphic accounts of his sexual encounters, including the sexual abuse of a niece and nephew, other children, and young women and young men his age. Manori got the sense he was delighting in telling her these stories, and even asked whether she was frightened of him. She said yes, but that she could defend herself. When she attempted to shift the conversation away from his graphic accounts, he shifted back. My presence appeared to rein him in, but the problems didn't end there. Jagath subsequently began stalking Manori, threatening to sexually assault her.

In the meantime, Jagath called me to say he had another client lined up for me to speak to: an English-speaking attorney who came to his gym. Eager for the rare chance to participate in data collection myself, I agreed. Kushil worked in the Attorney General's office, and our interview began in a professional manner with a discussion of Sri Lankan laws regarding prostitution. However, as with Manori's experience with Jagath, our interview eventually became downright creepy. Asked how often he visited prostitutes, Kushil used the opportunity to become sexually graphic, describing a recent visit to a massage clinic:

It's good, only 500 or so rupees, and you get a healthy massage. As she was massaging my backside, I was fully naked, she put her hand beneath the anus, tickling my testicles. Gradually [gave] the massage, applied oil.

At this point, Kushil began stroking the ginger ale bottle I had given him to drink, indicating to me how the woman massaged his penis. I looked at the computer screen then, and at other times when his descriptions got particularly graphic, as a way of subtly discouraging his graphic accounts. Undeterred, he continued:

> It was a lot of fun, I was getting a lot of feeling. Obviously it was not possible to do anything with her there, I put my hand under her saree and touched her pussy and that area and touched her ass, and then she slowly like this [stroking the ginger ale bottle] gave the hand job, not very fast [but] very slow, and it was about to go out, the way she did was very fascinating.

I shifted topics by asking if he ever spoke with the women he hired. This began a new shift in his commentary, making specific reference to the distinctions between white Western women and those of Sri Lanka: 'You also can very plainly see these women in Sri Lanka – and I'm only comparing this with Triple X movies I've seen from West, I have seen in Triple X movies that they do it with a lot of feeling – here they do not do it with feeling.' He then began using this reference to continue his graphic sex talk: 'The techniques we use to gain and give satisfaction ... are hardly used in Sri Lanka. Maybe in the West. I'll tell you one of these techniques.' Subtlety hadn't worked, so I was blunt: 'I don't need to hear about the techniques.' He continued anyway, and so I told him I was finished with my questions. The interview itself had been an opportunity to engage in 'sex talk' with a white woman.[6]

So what do we make of my and Manori's experiences interviewing clients? In both cases, our participation in research on the sex industry gave the men – in her case, an acquaintance, in mine, a stranger – an assumption of sexual licence. Our talk about prostitution was equated with our perceived sexual availability. The incidents played out, however, in somewhat different ways. Jagath's threats to Manori were grounded in the place that female sexual purity holds in Sri Lankan culture. His threats had deep cultural meaning, as a sexual assault could have two potential outcomes: She could be 'ruined' – in colloquial Sinhala, *winasha karanna* (literally 'to destroy') is often used in reference to women's loss of virginity – or she could be coerced into marrying her rapist. Hussein's (2000) research on violence against women in Sri Lanka uncovered the basis of such tactics. Given the stigmatisation of 'impurity', rape cases involving unmarried women – particularly in rural areas – are sometimes referred to local mediation boards with the goal of resolving the case without criminal prosecution and maintaining the young women's honour by marrying the victim to her rapist.

On the other hand, Kushil's interactions with me were grounded in notions of white Western women's presumed hypersexuality. Analysing the use of the term *suddi* (colloquial for white women), Lynch (2007: 94) explains:

This [is] not simply a reference to a generic category of 'white' Europeans. This racial 'othering' of white women as sexually immoral continues in contemporary Sri Lanka. Most Sri Lankans never interact one-on-one with white women, so all they know of them are the images they see on television and in films, or the views they get from a distance in tourist areas. Pornographic films available in Sri Lanka often feature whites, and white women who frequent the country's southern beaches in skimpy bathing suits are the objects of much criticism.

Kushil brought these sexualised ideas of white womanhood to his meeting with me and was determined to turn the interview into a sexual encounter or conquest.

In both cases, gender – in combination with race/nationality, and most likely age – played a critical role in the interview process, in how the participants responded to us as interviewers. At the same time, these gendered interactions provided rich insights into the ways in which Sri Lanka's sex industry is embedded within cultural ideologies about gender, race and nation.[7] Thus, even when gender and race became highly salient in shaping the nature of the interview exchange, as happened in the stories recounted in this section and in Dennis' interviews with boys about 'running trains', these exchanges nonetheless reveal important 'truths' about the phenomena of interest to the researcher. Here, the combined insights that emerged from examining how research participants responded to us provide a rich theoretical layer to my analysis of Sri Lanka's commercial sex industry. As Archer (2002: 108) reports, 'comparative analysis of accounts produced with different interviewers can help reveal "hidden" structures of power within the texts.'

Conclusion

I began this chapter by suggesting that interviewing is an unavoidably gendered phenomenon. Making this claim, however, does not lead to a straightforward understanding of *how* gender matters in any given interview or any given interview-based project on the nature and meaning of offending. The answer to that question lies in our analysis of the interview as a socially constructed speech event, in which both parties enter the exchange from a particular stance, shaped by their own and one another's social location, including their gender, race/ethnicity, class, nationality and age. Moreover, it is not simply either or both parties' ascribed status that matters, but also the identity they bring to the exchange and their perceptions of the identity of the other party.

Recognition of this, I would argue, does not mean we can learn nothing about the social world of offenders beyond the speech event of the interview itself. Instead, attention to how gender and other facets of social location shape the nature and dynamics of the interview can function to provide deeper insights into the life worlds and meanings of those we are interviewing. For instance, because young women in gangs viewed me as an outsider, they used the opportunity to challenge the stereotypes they perceived outsiders to hold. Yet, their recognition of themselves as experts on a social world I wished to learn about also meant that they adopted the role of 'educator' and consequently provided rich narratives of their experiences in gangs that I was able to analyse in conjunction with the collective stories they told. Likewise, though Manori and I both had personally troubling encounters with clients, the interviews were terrifically revealing about the cultural underpinnings of Sri Lanka's sex industry.

Finally, my examples clearly suggest that interview-based research on offending is enhanced when such projects include diverse research teams and this diversity is taken into account when the data is analysed. Without noticing, for example, that how young men talked about 'running trains' varied considerably when they spoke to Dennis versus Toya, I might have looked upon all or some of the data as incongruous and perhaps not 'valid'. Instead, my recognition of the patterned ways in which boys spoke to the two interviewers provided evidence of two important facets of the phenomena – the role of masculine performance and the elision of victims' points of view. Here, the production of accounts across various combinations of interviewers and interviewees is itself particularly illuminating.

As a scholar of gender, obviously the relevance of gender in the interview process is specific to my particular theoretical goal of 'illuminat[ing] gender as central to our understanding of social life' (Lewis 2007: 274). Nonetheless, this chapter has import to a broader audience: paying attention to our social locations, and our positioning vis-à-vis those we interview, offers a vital window through which to better understand the life worlds and experiences of those we study.

Notes

1   One recent example has certainly problematised this issue: Goode's (2002) account of his routine practice of having sexual intercourse with women during his research on the National Association to Aid Fat Americans. Ironically, his own account was thoroughly absent an analysis of gender and power, though the firestorm of responses that followed certainly made the exploitative nature of his behaviour abundantly clear (see, especially, Bell 2002; Saguy 2002).

2   Kosygina (2005), for example, reports that her interviews with men and women on forced migration in Russia resulted in longer interviews with women, the greater likelihood of monologues with women as compared to questions and

answers with men and greater reflexivity in interviews with women. Importantly, she suggests that these differences were partly the result of her own gendered strategies in the field. She allowed herself greater informality in her interactions with women, while she remained more formal in her exchanges with men, both out of concern that she could diminish her authority as a researcher and thus 'lose control over the conversation' (2005: 90) and because she feared informality could be conflated with 'flirting', which would raise additional challenges for the research.

3 Again, it is important to caution that firm conclusions cannot be drawn about the extent to which social distances – as opposed to or in addition to interviewing and rapport-building skills – were behind these differences. For instance, Niquita was also a new mother at the time of the interviews and occasionally asked somewhat pointed questions about the responsibilities of motherhood that seemed to make a handful of girls defensive.

4 Dayawansa was an older male research assistant who had driven Manori to the interview.

5 Several of the focus group participants had previously participated in client interviews. It is also important to note that the participants were her age contemporaries; it is unlikely she would have been as confrontational had they been her elders.

6 This was not the only instance in which I faced such experiences but after several similar encounters it appeared to be a pattern.

7 On a practical level, however, these incidents revealed that our research strategy was too dangerous. I subsequently utilised a male researcher for interviews with clients.

References

Archer, L. (2002) '"It's easier that you're a girl and that you're Asian": interactions of race and gender between researchers and participants', *Feminist Review*, 72: 108–32.

Atkinson, P. (2005) 'Qualitative research – unity and diversity', *Forum: Qualitative Social Research*, 6: Article 26 (http://www.qualitative-research.net/fqs/).

Axinn, W. G. (1991) 'The influence of interviewer sex on responses to sensitive questions in Nepal', *Social Science Research*, 20: 303–18.

Baca Zinn, M., Hongdoneu-Sotelo, P. and Messner, M. A. (eds) (2000) *Gender Through the Prism of Difference* (2nd edn). Boston: Allyn & Bacon.

Bell, S. E. (2002) 'Sexualizing research: response to Erich Goode', *Qualitative Sociology*, 25: 535–9.

Bhopal, K. (2001) 'Researching South Asian women: issues of sameness and difference in the research process', *Journal of Gender Studies*, 10: 279–86.

Collins, P. H. (1990) *Black Feminist Thought*. Boston: Unwin Hyman.

Connell, R. W. (2002) *Gender*. Cambridge: Polity Press.

Currie, D. H. and MacLean, B. D. (1997) 'Measuring violence against women: the interview as a gendered social encounter', in M. D. Schwartz (ed.), *Researching Sexual Violence Against Women: Methodological and Personal Perspectives*. Thousand Oaks, CA: Sage, pp. 157–78.

DeVault, M. L. (1999) *Liberating Method: Feminism and Social Research*. Philadelphia, PA: Temple University Press.

Dijkstra, W. (1983) 'How interviewer variance can bias the results of research on interviewer effects', *Quality and Quantity*, 17: 179–87.

Dijkstra, W. (1987) 'Interviewing style and respondent behavior: an experimental study of the survey-interview', *Sociological Methods and Research*, 16: 309–34.

Eckert, P. and McConnell-Ginet, S. (2006) *Language and Gender*. Cambridge: Cambridge University Press.

Egharevba, I. (2001) 'Researching an-"other" minority ethnic community: reflections of a black female researcher on the intersections of race, gender, and other power positions on the research process', *International Journal of Social Research Methodology*, 4: 225–41.

Fawcett, B. and Hearn, J. (2004) 'Researching others: epistemology, experience, standpoints, and participation', *International Journal of Social Research Methodology*, 7: 201–18.

Fendrich, M., Johnson, T., Shaligram, C. and Wislar, J. S. (1999) 'The impact of interviewer characteristics on drug use reporting by male juvenile arrestees', *Journal of Drug Issues*, 29: 37–58.

Franklin, K. (2004) 'Enacting masculinity: antigay violence and group rape as participatory theater', *Sexuality Research and Social Policy*, 1: 25–40.

Garg, A. (2005) 'Interview reflections: a first generation migrant Indian woman researcher interviewing a first generation migrant Indian man', *Journal of Gender Studies*, 14: 147–57.

Gatrell, C. (2006) 'Interviewing fathers: feminist dilemmas in fieldwork', *Journal of Gender Studies*, 15: 237–51.

Goode, E. (2002) 'Sexual involvement and social research in a fat civil rights organization', *Qualitative Sociology*, 25: 501–34.

Grenz, S. (2005) 'Intersections of sex and power in research on prostitution: a female researcher interviewing male heterosexual clients', *Signs*, 30: 2092–113.

Groves, R. M. (1989) *Survey Errors and Survey Costs*. New York: John Wiley & Sons.

Hall, R. A. (2004) 'Inside out: some notes on carrying out feminist research in cross-cultural interviews with South Asian women immigration applicants', *International Journal of Social Research Methodology*, 7: 127–41.

Heeb, J.-L. and Gmel, G. (2001) 'Interviewers' and respondents' effects on self-reported alcohol consumption in a Swiss health survey', *Journal of Studies on Alcohol*, 62: 434–42.

Hunt, J. (1984) 'The development of rapport through the negotiation of gender in field work among the police', *Human Organizations*, 43: 283–96.

Hussein, A. (2000) *Sometimes There Is No Blood: Domestic Violence and Rape in Rural Sri Lanka*. Colombo: International Centre for Ethnic Studies.

Hutchinson, K. L. and Wegge, D. G. (1991) 'The effects of interviewer gender upon response in telephone survey research', *Journal of Social Behavior and Personality*, 6: 573–84.

Johnson, T. P. and Moore, R. W. (1993) 'Gender interactions between interviewer and survey respondents: issues of pornography and community standards', *Sex Roles*, 28: 243–61.

Johnstone, B., Ferrara, K. and Mattson Bean, J. (1992) 'Gender, politeness, and discourse management in same-sex and cross-sex opinion-poll interviews', *Journal of Pragmatics*, 18: 405–30.

King, N. (2003) 'Knowing women: straight men and sexual certainty', *Gender and Society*, 17: 861–77.

Kleinman, S. (2007) *Feminist Fieldwork Analysis*. Thousand Oaks, CA: Sage.

Kosygina, L. V. (2005) 'Doing gender in research: reflection on experience in field', *Qualitative Report*, 10: 87–95.

Lewis, L. (2007) 'Epistemic authority and the gender lens', *Sociological Review*, 55: 273–92.

Lorber, J. (1994) *Paradoxes of Gender*. New Haven, CT: Yale University Press.

Lynch, C. (2007) *Juki Girls, Good Girls: Gender and Cultural Politics in Sri Lanka's Garment Industry*. Ithaca, NY: Cornell University Press.

McDowell, L. (2001) '"It's that Linda again": ethical, practical, and political issues involved in longitudinal research with young men', *Ethics, Place, and Environment*, 4: 87–100.

Maher, L. (1997) *Sexed Work: Gender, Race and Resistance in a Brooklyn Drug Market*. Oxford: Clarendon Press.

Miller, J. (2000) 'The protection of "human subjects" in street ethnography: ethical and practical considerations from a field study in Sri Lanka', *Focaal*, 36: 53–68.

Miller, J. (2001) *One of the Guys: Girls, Gangs and Gender*. New York: Oxford University Press.

Miller, J. (2002) 'Violence and coercion in Sri Lanka's commercial sex industry: intersections of gender, sexuality, culture and the law', *Violence Against Women*, 8 (9): 1045–74.

Miller, J. (2008) *Getting Played: African American Girls, Urban Inequality, and Gendered Violence*. New York: New York University Press.

Miller, J. and Glassner, B. (2004) 'The "inside" and the "outside": finding realities in interviews', in D. Silverman (ed.), *Qualitative Research* (2nd edn). London: Sage, pp. 125–39.

Orbuch, T. L. (1997) 'People's accounts count: the sociology of accounts', *Annual Review of Sociology*, 23: 455–78.

Ortiz, S. M. (2005) 'The ethnographic process of gender management: doing the "right" masculinity with wives of professional athletes', *Qualitative Inquiry*, 11: 265–90.

Padfield, M. and Procter, I. (1996) 'The effect of interviewer's gender on the interviewing process: a comparative enquiry', *Sociology*, 30: 355–66.

Presser, L. (2005) 'Negotiating power and narrative in research: implications for feminist methodology', *Signs*, 30: 2067–90.

Richardson, L. (1990) *Writing Strategies: Reaching Diverse Audiences*. Newbury Park, CA: Sage.

Saguy, A. C. (2002) 'Sex, inequality, and ethnography: response to Erich Goode', *Qualitative Sociology*, 25: 549–56.

Sanday, P. R. (1990) *Fraternity Gang Rape: Sex, Brotherhood, and Privilege on Campus*. New York: New York University Press.

Seale, C., Charteris-Black, J., Dumelow, C., Locock, L. and Ziebland, S. (2008) 'The effect of joint interviewing on the performance of gender', *Field Methods*, 20: 107–28.

Silverman, D. (2005) 'Instances or sequences? Improving the state of the art of qualitative research', *Forum: Qualitative Social Research*, 6: Article 30 (http://www.qualitativeresearch.net/fqs/).

Silverman, D. (2006) *Interpreting Qualitative Data* (3rd edn). London: Sage.

Smith, D. E. (1987) *The Everyday World as Problematic: A Feminist Sociology*. Boston: Northeastern University Press.

Song, M. and Parker, D. (1995) 'Commonality, difference and the dynamics of disclosure in in-depth interviewing', *Sociology*, 29: 241–56.

Swart, W. J. (1991) 'Female gang delinquency: a search for "acceptably deviant behavior"', *Mid-American Review of Sociology*, 15: 43–52.

Taylor, J. M., Gilligan, C. and Sullivan, A. M. (1995) *Between Voice and Silence: Women and Girls, Race and Relationship*. Cambridge, MA: Harvard University Press.

Ullman, S. E. (1999) 'A comparison of gang and individual rape incidents', *Violence and Victims*, 14: 123–33.

Veroff, J. and DiStefano, A. (2002) 'Researching across difference: a reprise', *American Behavioral Scientist*, 45: 1297–307.

Warren, C. A. B. (1988) *Gender Issues in Field Research*. Thousand Oaks, CA: Sage.

Whitehead, T. L. and Conaway, M. E. (1986) *Self, Sex, and Gender in Cross-Cultural Fieldwork*. Urbana, IL: University of Illinois Press.

Willan, V. J. and Pollard, P. (2003) 'Likelihood of acquaintance rape as a function of males' sexual expectations, disappointment, and adherence to rape-conducive attitudes', *Journal of Social and Personal Relationships*, 20: 637–61.

Williams, C. L. and Heikes, E. J. (1993) 'The importance of researcher's gender in the in-depth interview: evidence from two case studies of male nurses', *Gender and Society*, 7: 280–91.

Wilson, S. R., Brown, N. L., Mejia, C. and Lavori, Ph.W. (2002) 'Effects of interviewer characteristics on reported sexual behavior of California Latino couples', *Hispanic Journal of Behavioral Sciences*, 24: 38–62.

Wolf, D. L. (ed.) (1996) *Feminist Dilemmas in Fieldwork*. Boulder, CO: Westview Press.

Talking to snakeheads: methodological considerations for research on Chinese human smuggling

Sheldon X. Zhang

Abstract

This chapter discusses field strategies used to gain access to the secretive world of Chinese human smuggling groups, and reflects on what seemed to have worked well over the years by the author. One key element that seemed to have worked well is expanding one's informal social networks to include those of others for data-gathering purposes. The concept of guanxi *(personal contacts) has been extensively applied in my field activities as an important venue to develop and reinforce research-relevant social contacts because they offer the quickest entry into a target population. After all, human smuggling is a business built upon a myriad of personal connections. By tapping into a common cultural practice, I have been able to gain the trust and confidence of many subjects. This myriad of social networks in turn also validate data gathered from different sources.*

Ethnographic studies that rely on interviews and observations are often used to deal with subject matters that cannot be handled through traditional surveys or other quantitatively oriented designs. This is particularly true for topics involving criminal activities, in which the most knowledgeable people are also least likely to be found or, even if found, to divulge. Organised crime is one such topic.

Organised crime is a loose term referring to a long list of illicit enterprises in which groups of individuals pool together resources to engage in organised and clandestine activities for profits. These include illegal numbers games, drug trafficking, currency counterfeiting, credit card fraud, human smuggling and labour racketeering. Most literature on criminal organisations is based on data that are relative easy to obtain, such as police investigations, news stories, crime statistics, victim accounts and interviews with law enforcement officials. The least studied is the perspective of those who are involved in these enterprising activities – the entrepreneurs themselves. To understand these criminal activities, it is important to learn from those who are actually 'doing it'. For logistical reasons, empirical research in this respect has remained rare. Detailed accounts, even when available, are mostly from incarcerated offenders who may have reformulated their stories and life experiences for the inquiries of the judicial process.

Field research is not for everyone, and it is even more challenging if the subject matter involves populations who have nothing to gain from telling their stories. Although subject payment has been widely used in American social science to encourage participation, when it comes to organised crime, such incentives are often ineffective. In my research on Chinese human smuggling, paying smugglers was downright awkward. In this chapter, I will discuss the strategies I used in my fieldwork and the experience I have gained from studying Chinese human smugglers (or snakeheads).

Before I dive into more detailed descriptions of my fieldwork, a few clarifications are provided here to orient the readers. The first is how the term 'snakehead' came about. Fuelled by strong desires among many Chinese nationals to improve their economic opportunities overseas, Chinese human smuggling has gone global in the past two decades. The list of destination countries has stretched to include most industrialised nations in the West. The smugglers who facilitate this irregular migration process are collectively called 'snakeheads' both in China and in the overseas Chinese communities. The term was first used among Chinese migrants and smugglers of Fujianese decent – a province along China's southeast coast facing Taiwan. The exact origin of 'snakehead', however, remains unclear, although it has been widely since the late 1980s to brand anyone involved in organising or coordinating the transportation of people into another country without going through legal immigration channels. Illegal Chinese migrants and their smugglers alike know little about how the terminology first came about. Those who wrote about Chinese smuggling understood the term mostly as a figurative description of the clandestine process of human smuggling, which resembles the movement of a snake (Burdman 1993; Chin 1999). The earliest documented use of this term appeared in a United Press International story about Hong Kong-based mobsters involved in smuggling illegal immigrants from mainland China into the British colony (UPI 1981).

The second clarification is on where human smuggling fits in the realm of organised crime. Human smuggling involves enterprising agents who pool their resources in a coordinated manner to provide essentially travel services for people to circumvent regular immigration control by any host nation. Although all criminal organisations share some common attributes such as secrecy and conspiracy to profit from providing illicit goods and services, divergent opinions exist on how to clarify the differences between organised crime and crime that is organised.

In mainstream criminology, there are two traditional perspectives on criminal organisations. One, shared by many scholars and law enforcement agencies and perhaps articulated best by Donald Cressey (1969), describes an organised crime groups as a hierarchical, centralised and bureaucratic structure similar to that of a modern corporate, such as the Italian Mafia (Cressey 1969; Abadinsky 1990). These criminal organisations are operated like a normal corporation where there is a clear division of labour and chain of command. Rules and regulations govern members' activities, and membership is restricted. Much of the literature on Chinese organised crime follows this school of thought in their descriptions of the triads in Hong Kong and the gangsters in Taiwan (Zhang 2008). Although contemporary triad societies are said to be far more fragmented than their forebears, they still possess well-defined organisational structures with multiple levels of hierarchy and clearly assigned roles and responsibilities at each level (see Chu 2000: 27–8). To join these groups, potential recruits pass through a certain period of probation and then are inducted through ritualised procedures.

On the opposite side of this corporate perspective is the enterprise model. Researchers in favour of this model argue that the traditional concept of organised crime should be abandoned (Passas and Nelken 1993; Block and Chambliss 1981; Van Duyne 1997). The enterprise model suggests that organised crime is made up of mostly flexible and adaptive networks of enterprising individuals who can easily expand and contract to deal with the uncertainties of the illicit market. These entrepreneurs are organised only to the extent that they can effectively carry out profit-generating activities, which is a rather utilitarian or rational behaviour as some economists have advocated (Reuter 1983; Savona 1990). Reuter (1983), based on principles of industrial organisation and market economy, argued that illegal enterprises are relatively small and short-lived. Apart from a relatively small group of core members, most associates are brought in as required to provide needed services. Human smuggling, as an illicit enterprise, fits the enterprise model nicely. Human smugglers form temporary business alliances and the organisation lasts as long as smuggling opportunities exist. A smuggling group may dissolve after one operation is completed if there are no new opportunities on the horizon. Although social interactions may continue among smuggling partners, the smuggling business itself lies dormant.

As an alternative to these two different perspectives on the structure of organised crime, Dwight Smith (1975, 1980) provided the continuum perspective and argued that 'entrepreneurial transactions can be ranked on a scale that reflects levels of legitimacy within a specific marketplace' (p. 336). Illegitimate markets exist beyond the boundaries of legitimate markets and should be examined in their specific industries to understand the 'spectrum of legitimacy' (Smith 1975). Such a spectrum perspective offers alternatives to the dichotomous views to classify criminal enterprises either as formal organisations or as informal entities. Kenny and Finckenauer (1995: 25) argued that organised crime is sufficiently varied and complex that one explanation or one theory cannot cover all the bases. Criminal organisations respond to varying market demands by contracting or expanding in size; they assume a variety of organisational structures shaped passively by external social-legal factors rather than by design. However, different ways of conceptualisation lead to different understandings of criminal organisations, describe different trajectories in their activities and may well produce different policy recommendations.

My coincidental adventure into research on Chinese human smuggling

My research entry into Chinese human smuggling was rather accidental, largely due to a combination of the prominence of the topic and biographical coincidence. For about two decades since the mid-1980s, the vast majority of illegal Chinese immigrants who arrived in America came from a geographically concentrated region in three townships (Changle, Tingjiang and Mawei) – or the greater Fuzhou area, the capital city of Fujian Province in southeast China region. Fuzhou and its adjacent counties have long been considered the epicentre of Chinese human smuggling activities. There have been various explanations as to why such large number of Chinese immigrants would leave from such a small geographical area (see Zhang 2008). The phenomenon was unprecedented in US immigration history. I happened to have grown up in the Fuzhou area and spent most of my formative years in the region. Frankly, many of my acquaintances in Fuzhou, including childhood friends, were directly involved in the smuggling business. With my extensive social networks in a region where most illegal Chinese human smuggling activities originated, it was impossible for me not to take advantage of my unique but somewhat fortuitous biographical background.

Organised Chinese human smuggling activities to the United States began around the mid-1980s. Other than occasional news stories, human smuggling by Chinese nationals went largely unnoticed by the larger society until the *Golden Venture*, a Honduras-registered freight boat with 286 illegal Chinese immigrants on board, ran aground on New York's

Long Island in November 1993 (Fritsch 1993). It was a watershed event in American politics on illegal immigration and created tremendous anxieties among the public and policy-makers alike about a possible onslaught of illegal immigrants from a country with one-fifth of the world's population. Federal law enforcement agencies immediately took the complex smuggling routes and daring methods as signs of involvement of well organised criminal groups.

Jobs, sneezed at by US citizens but sought by illegal migrants, were indeed plentiful in the 1980s and 1990s. A drive through migrant-sending townships in China's Fujian Province can provide a glimpse of the growing demand for cheap labour to work in the kitchens of the ever expanding Chinese restaurants in the US. Only a handful of scholars have taken an interest in illegal migration from China back in those years. Relevant scholarly literature only began to emerge within the past decade (Liang and Ye 2001). This is largely because human smuggling is not a traditional racket of choice for criminal organisations. More importantly, illegal Chinese immigrants have for many years remained 'invisible' because of linguistic and cultural barriers erected by the ethnic enclaves in the US.

A few scholars ventured into the illegal Chinese migration business. Chin (1999) conducted the largest survey of illegal Chinese immigrants in New York and produced probably the most authoritative account of the smuggling process based on immigrants' experiences. Peter Kwong (1997) wrote a book, based on personal interviews in New York City and a trip to China, about the illegal workforce in an underground economy and argued that the increase in Chinese illegal immigration was tied to unfair American labour practices. A few other researchers also produced scholarly work on Chinese human smuggling (see Bolz 1995; Wang 1996). Empirical studies on human smuggling and illegal immigration by Chinese nationals have remained rare in the US.

A systematic study of Chinese human smugglers

From the mid-1990s, I began exploring the topic by approaching a few of my friends who were apparently snakeheads. As I spent time with these people, I became intrigued by their social interactions and the various business arrangements. Strangely enough it was not difficult to find snakeheads in Fuzhou and its adjacent counties in the 1990s despite the criminal nature of the business. In those days, everyone in my social networks in Fuzhou seemed to know someone who was involved in the smuggling business. Snakeheads, big and small, were often known in their respective social circles and discussed their businesses with few reservations.

The most concentrated field work on Chinese human smuggling activities took place betwen 1999 and 2001, when Ko-lin Chin of Rutgers University (in Newark, New Jersey) and I received a grant from the

National Institute of Justice (NIJ), US Department of Justice. In the three-year span, Professor Chin and I used a variety of strategies to gather data that included face-to-face interviews, social conversations and field observations, and secondary sources such as government documents and news media stories. We also enlisted assistance from local researchers in Fuzhou and research assistants in Los Angeles and New York areas.

We interviewed a total of 129 snakeheads in the United States and China. These were people directly involved in recruiting, organising and transporting Chinese nationals illegally into the United States or other countries. We conducted additional interviews with key informants who were familiar with the smuggling business or whose close friends or relatives were snakeheads, and with law enforcement officials in anti-smuggling details both in China and the United States.

The study took place in three primary locations: New York City, Los Angeles and Fuzhou. New York City has long been the primary settlement destination for undocumented Fujianese in the US (US Senate 1992; Myers 1994). The Fujianese community is well-established in the city's Chinatown, a social and commercial centre for newly arrived Chinese immigrants (Kwong 1987).

Los Angeles is a major port of entry and gathering point for illegal Chinese immigrants (Chin 1999). It has become a major final destination, especially for non-Fujianese immigrants. Chinese communities in Los Angeles are located east of downtown Los Angeles along the I-10 freeway corridor that extends twenty miles and spreads across such cities as Monterey Park, Alhambra, West Covina, Roland Heights and Diamond Bar.

For smuggled Chinese who fly to the United States, the Los Angeles International Airport is a popular entry point. Illegal Chinese smuggled across the Mexico–US border usually arrive in Los Angeles before they are transported to New York or other parts of the country. Those who come by sea usually arrive in Los Angeles. Its many container yards are often used for unloading illegal human cargoes.

Fuzhou, with a population of more than 5.4 million, is located in the northern coastal area of Fujian Province, which directly faces Taiwan across the Taiwan Strait. The city consists of five districts and eight counties. The communities sending the most illegal immigrants are the villages of Mawei, Changle, Tingjiang, Lianjiang and Fuqing, all along the coast within a forty-mile radius of Fuzhou. US law enforcement agencies once estimated that up to 90 per cent of all illegal Chinese immigrants in America were from this region (Hood 1994).

Finding snakeheads

Professor Chin and I decided to define human smugglers as anyone who helped fee-paying clients to leave China through fraudulent means, as opposed to going through the legal emigration process. Because little was known about the smuggler population and random sampling was not feasible, we had to rely on chain referrals (or the snowball technique) to reach and expand our pool of prospective subjects.

The snakeheads we interviewed for the NIJ study and later met in other situations were all self-identified human smugglers residing in either China or the United States. All subjects were somehow connected serially through our own social networks or the networks of our research associates. Therefore all subjects were somehow socially related to me and Professor Chin, usually by two or three degrees of separation (i.e. friend of a friend).

Both Professor Chin and I already had extensive social contacts (separately from one another) in Fuzhou, which provided an easy platform for us to initiate field activities. We made ourselves known to our friends in the US and China and what we were studying and asked for help for referrals. When we were in town, we called our friends and went out to dinners or lunches with them. We maintained busy social schedules, meeting and talking to people whenever they became available. Our friends knew why we were in town and we never stopped asking for referrals. It was not clear whether such a loud-mouthed approach helped us recruit or scared away potential subjects. At least we were sure that those who stayed (or did not run away from us) were aware of why we were there.

We made frequent trips to conduct field observations in the Chinese communities in New York and Los Angeles. We also made several trips to the sending communities in the villages outside Fuzhou where most households had either immediate family members or close relatives overseas, mainly in the United States. We stayed in these sending communities and talked to villagers about their family members overseas. We also visited local English language schools that were preparing the children of those already in the United States for their eventual trip to America, and we observed daily events and interactions on the street.

Despite our familiarity with the local culture and population, the study was no easy ride. We often found ourselves snowballing up the hill as opposed to down, and we tried to start snowballing simultaneously at different locations and in different directions. Because human smuggling is a criminal activity and snakeheads face constant threats from law enforcement, we encountered many difficulties in finding subjects who would agree to be interviewed. During the course of data collection, Professor Chin and I made numerous time-consuming and costly efforts to cultivate personal relationships, either directly or through our field contacts, with prospective subjects. We often spent days in Fuzhou waiting for prospective subjects to meet with us for a few brief hours. Many of these conversations produced little useful information. Others occurred in locations where it was impossible for us to probe sensitive topics. We made frequent trips to Los Angeles and New York to meet with interviewers who assisted us with field activities. We often felt that we were collecting more receipts than data.

Despite many no-shows and refusals by our prospective subjects, we did get to talk to many snakeheads. I even got to hang out with associates from the inner circle of the infamous Sister Ping, who was considered the mother of all snakeheads by the US law enforcement (Barnes 2000). At one point, one of Sister Ping's associates agreed to arrange a place for me to meet with her. A phone call was made to Sister Ping's home. Her family told us that Sister Ping was in Beijing negotiating some business. I waited a few more days and she did not return home. Not sure when she would return, I had to leave China but planned to meet Sister Ping in the following trip. A few months later, I saw her name in the news. She was arrested in Hong Kong. She spent the next three years fighting her extradition to the US but lost her case. In 2006, Sister Ping was sentenced in a federal court in New York to 35 years on charges of conspiring to commit alien smuggling, hostage taking, money laundering, and laundering ransom money (US Immigration and Customs Enforcement 2006).

Interviewing snakeheads

Most of my research questions over the years on Chinese snakeheads revolved around two key issues: (1) operational characteristics by groups of enterprising agents; and (2) the organisational features of these smuggling groups. For the smuggling operations, I am interested in finding out how individuals discover, develop and deploy their resources such as knowing someone at the passport issuing office of the local government or having a relative who works at the security checkpoint at an airport. I want to learn about how people enter the smuggling business, negotiate their positions and acquire additional services. The business transactions and arrangements are always of great interest to me.

As for organisational features, I am interested in learning about smugglers as a social group. As with all social groups, there are rules and customs. Because all members of a smuggling group are aware of the illicit nature of their business activities, I want to learn how snakeheads manage their risk exposure and protect themselves. To understand how social groups function, I am also interested in the hierarchical arrangement of these organisations – that is, who is in control or who has more influence in the directions or pace of various group activities. How does power or authority emerge through these social interactions, either implied or clearly understood? What are the consequences if members of a smuggling group choose not to play by the rules or attempt to cut out other members to maximise their own profits? To what extent do cultural expectations play a role in the conduct of a smuggling organisation? In short, as a sociologist, I am interested in the social organisation of Chinese human smugglers. This is not much different from sociologists who study other clandestine social groups such as gamblers, the mafia or drug users.

Following traditional ethnographic research, I typically have only broad guidelines for my questions. They usually take the form of a semi-structured interview questionnaire, consisting of mostly broad questions without any fixed responses. In fact, except for a few demographic variables (such as age and education), all my questions have been open-ended. My goal is to learn about the perceptions and experiences of my subjects and try to see the enterprise from their perspective.

Most of my interviews have been of two types: formal and informal. In all formal interviews, I get to ask questions very much in the same order as they are constructed in the guideline. I personally prefer these formal interviews when all relevant questions are asked and additional questions can be generated that pertain to specific issues for clarifications. Formal interviews are an efficient way to gather data in a concentrated period of time. Such interviews can also be dissected systematically to produce common themes suitable for statistical analysis such as common tasks in the different smuggling operations and certain financial aspects of the business.

Informal interviews usually take place in restaurants or other social gathering places, where formal inquiries are neither feasible nor socially acceptable. Over the years, I have encountered many subjects who were not comfortable to a formal sit-down interview. However, they had no problem going out to social gatherings or lunches and dinners with me where relevant conversations would take place. These were essentially 'natural' conversations that allowed me discretion over how and when to probe sensitive questions while maintaining the atmosphere befitting the larger social environment. Some of these 'interviews' took place in hotel lobbies, restaurants or subjects' living rooms. At these occasions, research questions were mixed with social conversations. Informal interviews are often necessary and oftentimes unavoidable in field research, but they are not efficient for data-gathering purposes. Oftentimes a long conversation produces little useful information, while at other times conversations are interrupted by other people or the surrounding activities. In these informal interviews, questions are often asked out of sequence, which makes it hard for probing and expanding.

Different interview settings call for different logistical arrangements. For formal interviews, I would take a notepad and several pens. I typically brought with me a few copies of the interview guideline and gave my subjects a copy should they desire it. I have never used any taping devices during my interviews with human smugglers for obvious reasons. The last thing any of my subjects wanted was evidence of their illegal activities. No identifying information was ever recorded on these note-pads, so that even if confiscated by police they would be of little use.

In comparison, informal interviews (or natural conversations) have been far more challenging. Over the years, I found that human smugglers in informal interviews were typically not comfortable with me taking notes or writing anything down on a piece of paper. I would have to recall the answers as soon as I returned from the interviews. It is a skill that can be sharpened through practice. One rule that I have developed and followed for many years of fieldwork is that as soon as an informal interview takes place I will write down my field notes before I go to bed no matter how late it may be. I also try to avoid scheduling more than one interview a day. Otherwise the stories of different individuals may begin to converge.

Strategies to improve validity and reliability of field data

Ethnographic studies are often challenged for their validity and reliability. In my work on Chinese human smuggling, it was particularly challenging. My subjects had little to gain by telling me about their business and much to lose if the information they provided wound up in the hands of the police. For instance, one snakehead invited his passport counterfeit artist to lunch with me. When he arrived, he quickly pulled out his cell phone and called his friend outside to inform him about his location and who else was present in the room. Once we entered a private dining room, he again placed a call to his friends somewhere informing them which room he was in. Judging from his nervous look, I gathered that he was taking precautions and informed his people about his whereabouts and whom he was with. The conversation started slow and it took a long time for him to believe that I was just a nosey professor and was not there to get him in trouble.

Although I would never know for sure how many of my subjects had lied to me or deliberately misconstrued their stories, I have learned over the years several steps to increase the validity and reliability of my field data. The primary strategy is to build adequate rapport, thus increasing the trust and confidence in these subjects. For the study on Chinese smugglers, I spent many months in the field, meeting and talking to the people who claimed to have done a thing or two in the business. Sceptical at first, many eventually were convinced that my guarantee of anonymity and confidentiality was sincere. Being a college professor also helped me gain respect in the Chinese context. Many of my subjects were delighted to impart their expertise to me once their suspicion subsided.

Another factor that helped me earn the trust of potential subjects was that I had cultivated many personal contacts (or *guanxi*) in my other research projects in Chinese communities. Using my social resources and native language ability to help study subjects deal with mainstream society (e.g. to explain how the school system works in the United States or to help non-English speaking migrants fill out official forms) earned several friends who later provided valuable information about smuggling operations. To build and reinforce *guanxi*, I would also take them to nice restaurants where they were treated well. I offered to help them write English letters or inquire about social services. In response to my favours, they referred me to their friends and shared personal stories with me. Needless to say, I took every opportunity to help. By raising the level of personal social debt (or obligations), these subjects were often willing to trust me with their stories. After all, human smuggling is essentially a business built upon a myriad of *guanxi*. By tapping into this common cultural practice, I was able to gain the trust and confidence of many subjects.

Another method is to recruit research assistants from the communities where prospective subjects are found. For the NIJ study, Professor Chin and I hired interviewers in New York City and Los Angeles who also provided vital access to a wider smuggler population through their networks in the Chinese communities. The interviewers recruited for this project were themselves involved in smuggling activities at one time. They were able to reach a much larger population through their connections. Because they knew the subjects personally, spoke their dialects and lived in the same communities, it took them less time than it would have taken me to build enough trust to allow interviews to take place.

Internal validity of field data can be further strengthened by cross-checking answers obtained from other sources, such as formal interviews against informal interviews or interview data against existing literature. For the NIJ study, most questions in the questionnaire were designed to reflect the knowledge of human smuggling activities Professor Chin and I had accumulated in our previous fieldwork. Unlike studies in other empirical settings (such as street drug dealers), where easy cash in the form of subject payment may have motivated respondents to answer questions in an anticipated manner consistent with the goal of the project (Jacobs *et al.* 2000), in this study few of our subjects took money from me and my interviewers. There was little financial incentive to lie. Furthermore, because all of the formal interviews and most of the informal interviews were conducted in private settings, it would be all but impossible for our subjects to conspire to mislead me.

Although I can never rule out the possibility that some of the subjects had distorted their stories, I felt confident that the methods employed in this study (semi-structured interviews, informal conversations and field observations) were probably the most viable on the topic of transnational human smuggling.

Reliability in ethnographic data, however, is more problematic. In most cases, much of the information gathered from informal or formal interviews with subjects is based solely on confidential interviews or conversations. Holding repeated interviews or conversations over time with the same subject is not only unrealistic, but also prohibitively expensive. It is simply impractical to validate the reliability of the interview protocol or instrument in a study such as my NIJ study, thus leaving open the question whether the subjects can provide the same answers if they are interviewed the second time. In this aspect, I can only rely on the fact that responses from our subjects (based on both formal interviews and informal conversations) became repetitive and patterned, which can be interpreted as a measure of confidence.

There are several limitations in the use of personal contacts and the snowball-sampling technique vis-à-vis external validity (Biernacki and Waldorf 1981). Professor Chin and I used a quasi-quota sampling method to generate the sample of human traffickers. To make the study sample more representative, we strove (1) to interview smugglers that specialised in different stages of the smuggling operation (e.g. recruiters, transporters and debt collectors); (2) to recruit subjects at multiple sites (i.e. New York, Los Angeles and Fuzhou); (3) to include smugglers who specialised in different trafficking schemes (e.g. fraudulent marriages, business delegations and passport substitution); and (4) to solicit information from both active and retired smugglers.

Methodological limitations

As with all field activities, the methods I employed carry inherent problems that may affect the interpretation of the findings. The major limitation is access to the target population through one's social network. Despite extensive, deliberate efforts to locate a wide variety of smugglers, I was limited in the selection of the subjects and their referral networks for the most part to the initial contacts in our own personal networks, and therefore the findings could very well be systematically biased. For instance, it is possible that any social networks I relied on led me to smuggling networks that were composed of smugglers who were mostly non-violent and ordinary business people. In this case, the lack of evidence to substantiate the link between traditional Chinese criminal organisations and the human smuggling trade could be an artifact of this limited access – the fact that only part-time, moonlighting 'non-criminals' were located, and not serious, well-organised professionals. Therefore it is impossible to rule out the role of traditional criminal organisations in smuggling activities.

Another limitation that I have come to realise in later writings is the fragmented nature of the descriptions based on individual snakeheads affiliated with diverse groups of other snakeheads. Organisational features had to be inferred from data provided by individuals who in their smuggling affiliations were unrelated to one another. No researchers, to my knowledge, have made attempts to infiltrate a smuggling group and to follow an entire smuggling operation from start to finish. Therefore, the so-called 'smuggling organization' was pieced together from fragmented descriptions provided by unrelated individuals. Although some distinctive 'roles' were derived from the information provided by the subjects, it is not possible to get an in-depth look at the components of one complete organisation. The lack of hierarchical relations and of evidence of well-organised smuggling organisations in our data may be a result of the sampling technique rather than an actual finding.

Finally, regardless of what strategies I chose to gain confidence or how successful I was in convincing my subjects, I cannot be certain of the extent to which these snakeheads gave me honest answers. As all researchers of sensitive topics must do, I relied on my intuitive understanding of the information gathered from multiple sources.

Despite the many drawbacks in using chain referrals as a recruiting method, there are few other alternatives to reach the prospective subject populations. It is through the cumulative efforts by many researchers that can we move closer to a true understanding of the research topic at hand.

In recent years, social scientists have developed respondent driven sampling (RDS), which modifies the traditional chain-referral method. There are two basic elements in RDS: (1) a dual-incentive system whereby subjects are rewarded for both participation and for recruiting others into the study; and (2) subjects do not have to identify referrals to a researcher but actually recruits them into the study (Heckathorn 1997). Although many qualitative researchers use a dual incentive system anyway (paying subjects for participation in the interviews and paying for their referrals), RDS is a significant improvement because, if carried out properly, it can overcome problems associated with the traditional snowball technique and provide parametric estimates about the 'hidden' population. First, limiting the recruitment opportunities of the initial seeds ensures diversity within the sample. This diversity can be empirically verified. Second, volunteerism bias is minimised due to the dual-incentive system in which subjects are both incentivised to participate and to recruit others. Third, 'masking' is minimised since researchers are not pointed in the direction of group members but rather recruited by group members themselves. Fourth, homophily bias is minimised since recruitment is limited to three subjects per participant, and theories of Markov chains indicate that equilibrium (the point at which initial samples no longer mirror later samples) can be achieved through a relatively small number of waves. Fifth, this also minimises biases which result from later samples coming only from those with larger personal networks. In essence, if the procedure is rigorously followed, even a biased starting point (such as from the researcher's own social network) can lead to a representative sample of the target population (Heckathorn 1997, 2002).

The hazards of doing prolonged fieldwork

Many situations can occur that endanger the continuity of prolonged fieldwork. Below I describe how historical events may disturb fieldwork and how researchers can accidentally become involved in the illegal activities they study.

After the Dover incident in England, in which dozens of illegal Chinese immigrants from Fujian Province suffocated to death inside a locked lorry (McAllister 2000), the Chinese government launched a massive manhunt in Fujian Province to round up any identified snakeheads, whether or not they were connected to the Dover incident. Many of my subjects and their referrals with whom I had ongoing relationships went into hiding or declined to talk. Scheduled interviews were cancelled, pager numbers were suddenly out of service and phone calls went unanswered. Once I drove more than two hours to meet a snakehead north of Los Angeles for a scheduled interview. Upon arrival and after the exchange of a few niceties, I began what I thought we had previously agreed – a formal interview for my study. She suddenly became ignorant of what we both knew about her business. When I inquired about clients and their travel directions, she said it would be unethical to reveal any information about her clients. Her sudden refusal to talk and playing dumb were jarring. After about 15 minutes of futile persuasion, I left empty-handed. A few years later, well after I finished the project, during an accidental social run-in, I inquired about that incident she revealed that it was because of the Dover incident and that several of her smuggling partners in China had been arrested.

There is an old Chinese saying: 'If you walk alongside a river bank often enough, you are bound to get your shoes wet.' It means it is hard not to get involved in something if one gets too close. There have been times where getting to know my subjects too well created ethical dilemmas. During one informal interview, one of my subjects (who specialised in marriage fraud and claimed to move anywhere between 30 to 40 clients into the US each year) was struggling with her limited English to communicate her expectations to her partner. Her English-speaking partner was supposed to send an eligible bachelorette to Fuzhou for a 'marriage ceremony' on a certain date. But this partner of hers changed the plan without notifying her. He then disappeared for a few days without giving her any advance warning. He later resurfaced and claimed that he had been sick. After the initial delivery date was missed, this subject of mine set another date and urged her partner to carry out his part of the deal as soon as possible because her contact in China had already made all the arrangements with the 'groom's family'. A few days later, her partner missed the appointment again and claimed he had been on a vacation. Then a national holiday came, which became yet another excuse to miss another deadline. Throughout this period, my subject made numerous attempts to obtain updates from her partner while informing her contacts in Fuzhou of the changes and delays. Throughout this period of repeated delays and confusion over dates, my subject frequently asked me to translate certain words for her while she was on the phone. Her limited English was hampering her communication with her partner and she turned to me repeatedly for help.

While this was happening, one of her eligible bachelorettes in another case changed her mind and decided to quit the 'marriage' arrangement. One day when I arrived for a lunch appointment, she asked me to get into her car to meet someone. She said she needed me to translate for her for a quick meeting. It happened so fast that I had no time to think of excuses to back out. Her insistence certainly made me feel I had no choice. On the other hand, although I had never planned to get personally involved in any smuggling activities, the opportunity to observe directly how a smuggler was doing her business was simply too tempting to miss.

While we were riding in her car, she told me about this Vietnamese girl who was quitting in the middle of a case. The Vietnamese girl had agreed to act as the bride-to-be and gone to China to meet her 'fiancé' and his family. She was showered with lavish gifts while in China and given $5,000 as down payment for her part. Although the actual financial terms were not disclosed to me, a 'bride-to-be' was typically paid about $30,000 when the entire deal was completed. But this American-born Vietnamese woman became scared.

We arrived at a convenience store in Little Saigon in Orange County, California. The Vietnamese woman, in her late teens or early 20s, was seemingly worried about her continued involvement in a criminal activity. But the snakehead was persistent and reminded the Vietnamese girl how well she had been treated while she was visiting China – the lavish gifts and banquets and sightseeing tours. The snakehead was pleading with the Vietnamese girl not to quit because she had invested a lot of time and money in the case. I rapidly exchanged translations between the two for about half an hour. Finally, the Vietnamese woman said she had to think it over. We parted. A few days later, I called to follow up on this case. She said the Vietnamese woman decided not to go through the deal. When I asked what about the down payment of $5,000, my snakehead subject calmly responded,

I have hired a gangster to pay her a visit. The guy is from a Vietnamese crime group. He has worked out a payment plan for her to pay back the original deposit I gave her, plus more. I am now charging her double for the money she took from me. Because my debt collector takes half of whatever is collected. To cover my loss, I have to charge her twice the amount she owed me, and all the middlemen who referred her to me also had to return the fees I paid out. That's the rule.

Human subject protection issues

To my knowledge, subjecting social scientists to human subject safety reviews is an American practice. With all ethnographic work comes the daunting challenge of convincing the university human subject protection committee (or the institutional review board – IRB) that what we are about to do does no harm to anyone physically or psychologically.

Originating in the medical field more than half a century ago, in which some researchers deliberately withheld from or subjected human subjects to certain treatment protocols that posed clear risks to their health, human subject safety review committees have become a standard fixture in all American higher education institutions. To engage in any type of research (broadly defined) that involves another human being as a subject, a researcher must submit for approval a detailed document of research protocol, describing the research questions, relevant literature, research methodology, confidentiality and anonymity procedures and data safeguarding procedures, among other things.

Since these review committees consist of individuals from diverse backgrounds at a university, ranging from administrators to professors with little or no field research experience, reactions to IRB applications vary tremendously and often become infuriating to the researchers. 'Concerns' over the well-being of human subjects that are found in these review committees have become legendary and often border on absurdity. One oft-cited example is that to ask a consenting adult any embarrassing or private questions, a researcher must be prepared to hand out a list of psychological counselling services available free of charge in the event the interview triggers an emotional breakdown. Almost every field researcher in the field of criminology and criminal justice in the US has horror stories to tell about their experiences in dealing with these human subject review committees. But one still has to obtain the committee's blessing or the researcher is not permitted to engage in the proposed study.

Over the years, I have gone through many of these reviews, explaining to the university community what I am about to do in the field. Since fieldwork is inherently unpredictable in its execution, in most cases I could only provide my planned activities. There have been times when I ran into serious problems with the review committee and even had my project suspended in the name of protecting my subjects from 'potential harm'.

For my NIJ study on Chinese human smuggling, when a potential subject was willing to be interviewed, he or she would be invited to meet a member of the research team in person. At the informal meeting, an interviewer would explain the study to the potential subject. Several measures were taken to ensure the cooperation and comfort of the prospective respondents:

- Potential smugglers were screened to ensure that only willing and candid participants were recruited.

- The questionnaire was pilot-tested beforehand to make sure subjects would be comfortable providing answers to most of the questions.

- A nominal fee was offered as an incentive to our subjects for their participation.

- The interviews were conducted in the subject's own dialect (e.g. Mandarin, Cantonese or Fujianese).

- The subjects were assured repeatedly that their participation in the study would not lead to investigation by any authorities. In addition, the data collected in this study were not accessible to persons other than members of this research team.

In all cases, the subjects were informed of the intention and identity of the research staff. No deception was used in any interviews. All project staff, including my Chinese research collaborators, were told that deception, trickery or manipulation of any kind was not an acceptable method of obtaining field data. I was very serious about the informed consent process, although I was not rigid about the manner or sequence of how the consent procedure was to be carried out. I made it clear that all snakeheads knew who we were and could receive a copy of the questionnaire should they desire it. By being frank and open about my intent and sincerity in protecting identifying information, I wanted to make sure my subjects would tell the 'truth' about their business activities. These procedures worked well in the field.

About the only procedure that did not work well was the subject payment issue. In my interactions with my snakehead friends, it was clear that most would either tell me their stories regardless of the payment or would not tell a thing no matter how much I offered. In these cases, subject payment was either irrelevant or downright awkward. Our budgeted payment of $75.00 in 1999 was significantly higher than any of my previous projects involving human subjects. However, the amount turned out to be far from sufficient to entice potential subjects to come forward. Those who did talk to me mostly refused to accept the payment. Those who declined said the money was not worth the risk or their time. Many of the snakeheads could make $10,000 per client. One subject bragged that in the heyday of his smuggling business in the late 1980s, he and his partners used to weigh cash in sacks because so many clients were paying them about $20,000 a piece at the same time. He noted:

When people arrived in New York in their hundreds, their families rushed to us to pay up the smuggling fees. We had to rent a hotel room to handle the transactions. We had to weigh the money in sacks using vending scales instead of counting the notes, because it would take too long.

Discussion

In the years of my fieldwork on illegal Chinese migration, I have come to rely heavily on my informal social networks and those of others to reach snakeheads. I have developed extensive social networks. I have applied the Chinese cultural practice of *guanxi* to carry out field activities and to seek assistance and information from trusted sources while reciprocating with favours. These social networks are continuously developed and maintained. They existed before any of the studies and will continue long after. There are many culturally sanctioned strategies to build social contacts. Friends and relatives can offer the quickest entry into a study population, but relational closeness offers no guarantee.

I have learned to provide favours that are seemingly simple but can be highly valued in an immigrant community, such as filling out government forms, explaining how the US school system works, finding out information from social service agencies or checking out local schools. By tapping into a common cultural practice, I have been able to gain the trust and confidence of my subjects.

One factor that has worked in my favour is the fact that transnational human smuggling, while illegal, does not carry the stigma typically associated with street crimes. Most ordinary people do not perceive snakeheads as 'real' criminals. Instead, they are most often viewed simply as risk takers who just want to make money.

My cultural and linguistic familiarity has certainly provided me unusual access to Chinese human smugglers. However, I have also wondered if my critical faculties are clouded by my close relationships with many smugglers in China and the US. I have thus far interpreted Chinese human smuggling mostly as an illicit enterprise in most of my writings and described their activities mostly from a socio-economic perspective.

Although I have occasional doubts about the potential impact of my relations with my research subjects, I have realised that without these close relationships I would not have had the access to the inner workings of their smuggling activities and to understand these individuals through authentic cultural lenses. I have developed greater appreciation of the 'culture of migration' in Fujian, which is a crucial element in understanding the motivation and pattern of the outward migration among Fujianese.

My local contacts have allowed me to develop a nuanced understanding of the regional culture. I have realised that more than anything else the 'culture of migration' is probably more influential in pushing people outward than the economic reform, political uncertainty or some other socio-economic factors reported in the news or government reports. As the smuggling prices indicate, the ability to raise tens of thousands of dollars for the journey to the United States is not something impoverished peasants from the interior of China can afford. In fact, most illegal immigrants from China are not destitute by any Chinese standard.

Over the past ten years I have published a fair amount of work on illegal Chinese migration, its enterprising characteristics and its players. I have come to believe that people in general want to share their stories, provided they feel safe and confident of the benign intent of the listener. People also feel good about themselves when they perceive themselves in a favourable knowledge differential (i.e. that they know more than their listeners). People do tell lies, but to lie consistently and continuously is difficult.

Although field researchers all develop their own bags of tricks, we are all in a constant search for more effective field strategies and techniques. After years of fieldwork dealing with Chinese nationals who participate in transnational migrant smuggling and recently drug-trafficking activities, I still find myself learning how to approach these individuals. Whatever leverage I think I have perfected may not always work. As a field researcher, I am forever confronted with worries of not being able to collect good data. Fieldwork is labour-intensive and time-consuming, and the funding is never adequate. But the intrigue of the subject matters has kept me hooked.

References

Abadinksy, H. (1990) *Organized Crime* (3rd edn). Chicago: Nelson-Hall.
Barnes, E. (2000) 'Two-faced woman', *Time*, 31 July, pp. 48–50.
Biernacki, P. and Waldorf, D. (1981) 'Snowball sampling', *Sociological Methods and Research*, 10: 141–63.
Block, A. A. and Chambliss, W. J. (1981) *Organized Crime*. New York: Elsevier.
Bolz, J. (1995) 'Chinese organized crime and illegal alien trafficking: humans as a commodity', *Asian Affairs*, 22: 147–58.
Burdman, P. (1993) 'Huge boom in human smuggling: inside story of flight from China', *San Francisco Chronicle*, 27 April, p. A1.
Chin, K. (1999) *Smuggled Chinese: Clandestine Immigration to the United States*. Philadelphia: Temple University Press.
Chin, K. (2007) 'Into the thick of it: methodological issues in studying the drug trade in the Golden Triangle', *Asian Criminology*, 2 (2): 85–109.
Chu, Y. (2000) *Triads as Business*. London: Routledge.
Cressey, D. R. (1969) *Theft of the Nation: The Structure and Operations of Organized Crime in America*. New York: Harper & Row.
Fritsch, J. (1993) 'One failed voyage illustrates flow of Chinese immigration', *New York Times*, 7 June, p. A1.

Heckathorn, D. (1997) Respondent-driven sampling: a new approach to the study of hidden populations', *Social Problems*, 44 (2): 174–99.

Heckathorn, D. (2002) 'Respondent-driven sampling II: deriving valid population estimates from chain-referral sample of hidden populations', *Social Problems*, 49 (1): 11–34.

Hood, M. (1994) 'The Taiwan connection', *Los Angeles Times Magazine*, 9 October, p. 20.

Jacobs, B. A. (1996) 'Crack dealers and restrictive deterrence', *Criminology*, 34 (3): 409–31.

Jacobs, B. A. and Wright, R. (1999) 'Stick-up, street culture, and offender motivation', *Criminology*, 37 (1): 149–73.

Jacobs, B. A., Topalli, V. and Wright, R. (2000) 'Managing retaliation: drug robbery and informal sanction threats', *Criminology*, 38 (1): 171–98.

Kenney, D. J. and Finckenauer, J. O. (1995) *Organized Crime in America*. San Francisco: Wadsworth.

Kwong, P. (1987) *The New Chinatown*. New York: Hill & Wang.

Kwong, P. (1997) *Forbidden Workers: Illegal Chinese Immigrants and American Labor*. New York: New Press.

Liang, Z. and Ye, W. (2001) 'From Fujian to New York: understanding the new Chinese immigration', in D. Kyle and R. Koslowski (eds), *Global Human Smuggling: Comparative Perspectives*. Baltimore, MD: Johns Hopkins University Press, pp. 187–215.

McAllister, J. F. O. (2000) 'Snaking toward death', *Time*, 3 July (online at: http://www.time.com/time/europe/magazine/2000/0703/snaking.html).

Myers, W. (1994) *Transnational Ethnic Chinese Organized Crime: A Global Challenge to the Security of the United States, Analysis and Recommendations*. Testimony of Willard Myers, Senate Committee on Foreign Affairs, Subcommittee on Terrorism, Narcotics and International Operations, 21 April.

Passas, N. and Nelken, D. (1993) 'The thin line between legitimate and criminal enterprises: subsidy frauds in the European community', *Crime, Law and Social Change*, 19 (3): 223–43.

Reuter, P. (1983) *Disorganized Crime: The Economics of the Visible Hand*. Cambridge, MA: MIT Press.

Savona, E. U. (1990) 'A neglected sector: the economic analysis of criminality, penal law and the criminal justice system', *Sociologia del Diritto*, 17 (1–2): 255–77.

Smith, D. C. Jr (1975) *The Mafia Mystique*. New York: Basic Books.

Smith, D. C. Jr (1980) 'Paragons, pariahs and pirates: a spectrum-based theory of enterprise', *Crime and Delinquency*, 26 (3): 358–86.

United Press International (UPI) (1981) *Mobsters Smuggle Immigrants from China*, 7 September (online at: http://www.wordspy.com/words/snakehead.asp).

US Immigration and Customs Enforcement (ICE) (2006) *Sister Ping Sentenced to 35 Years in Prison for Alien Smuggling, Hostage Taking, Money Laundering and Ransom Proceeds Conspiracy*, news release, 16 March (online at: http://www.ice.gov/graphics/news/newsreleases/).

US Senate (1992) *Asian Organized Crime*, Hearings before the Permanent Subcommittee on Investigations of the Committee on Governmental Affairs, 3 October to 6 November 1991. Washington, DC: US Government Printing Office.

Van Duyne, P. C. (1997) 'Organized crime, corruption and power', *Crime, Law and Social Change*, 26 (3): 201–38.

Wang, Z. (1996) 'Ocean-going smuggling of illegal Chinese immigrants: operation, causation, and policy implications', *Transnational Organized Crime*, 2 (1): 49–65.

Zhang, S. X. (2008) *Chinese Human Smuggling Organizations – Families, Social Networks, and Cultural Imperatives*. Palo Alto, CA: Stanford University Press.

Chapter 12

Blue-collar, white-collar: crimes and mistakes

Neal Shover and Ben W. Hunter

Abstract

A rising tide of white-collar crime throughout much of the world signals unambiguously that those who commit these offences merit increased scrutiny from investigators and policy-makers. This chapter begins by documenting briefly the growing importance of white-collar offences in Western nations as well as the financial toll they exact. Descriptive comparison of the demographic characteristics of and explanations for their crimes provided by convicted white-collar criminals and street offenders shows pronounced differences. Their sources lie in the different class origins and cultural capital of white-collar and common offenders. Class-based cultural capital affects the way each construes their criminal acts, their treatment at the hands of the criminal justice apparatus and research participation. Their middle-class and upper-middle-class backgrounds inevitably constrain the conduct of investigations in which white-collar criminals are informants or subjects. It also points to ways potentially of enhancing the validity and utility of ethnographic data collected from them.

Writing at the dawn of the twentieth century, E. A. Ross (1907: 3) was among the first sociologists to note that 'crime changes its quality as society develops'. Ross highlighted increasing social and economic interdependence and emergent forms of criminal opportunity that permit both exploitation of trust and the commission of crime at a distance from victims. The transformative developments he described continued in the years that followed, but the pace accelerated rapidly after the Second World War. Throughout the world, nations witnessed the expansion of state-funded welfare programmes of various kinds, the growth of insurance, a financial services revolution and the explosion of consumer credit, widespread adoption of the computer and other technologies for information sharing and financial transactions, the historically unprecedented globalisation of economic markets and relationships and, most recently, the attenuation of regulatory oversight. Spurred by these developments, the supply of white-collar criminal opportunity has increased to unprecedented levels across much of the globe (Shover and Hochstetler 2006).

The lives, decision-making and crimes of burglars, robbers and other street criminals have been the foci of ethnographic research for decades. An impressive variety of techniques and materials have been employed to examine these matters, and a remarkably consistent picture has emerged (Nee 2010; Shover and Copes 2009). White-collar offenders have received much less attention. What has been learned about them suggests, however, that they differ from their street-crime cousins in several ways that may be significant for data collection and data quality. Given the increasing importance of white-collar crime, we believe it may be useful to draw these differences into sharper relief and to examine their implications for the research enterprise and for data quality. That is our objective in the pages that follow.

The chapter begins by noting the increasing prevalence of white-collar crime in Western nations and the financial toll it exacts from victims. This is followed by comments on the demographic characteristics of convicted white-collar and common criminals. Next the presentation shifts to a description of the materials analysis of which undergirds the observations in the remainder of the chapter. Following this, note is made of differences in the descriptions of their crimes given by street criminals and white-collar criminals before we compare the class backgrounds and cultural capital of offenders reared in middle-class and working-class circumstances. The implications of middle-class cultural capital for the conduct of ethnographic research on white-collar criminals are presented next. The chapter concludes with suggestions for enhancing the quality and utility of data provided by white-collar criminals.

Background

As the concept is employed here, *white-collar crime* is crime committed by offenders whose lives are distinguished by material privilege and respectability (Shover and Hochstetler 2006). This means that preoccupation with meeting basic material needs, fiscal precariousness and unceasing concern about it are alien to them and their worlds; white-collar criminals are free from the 'daily struggle to keep themselves from falling over the cliff' into insolvency (Shipler 2004: 300). In stark contrast to their privileged backgrounds and circumstances, 'the necessity of paid labor and the fear of losing it dominate the lives of working-class individuals' (Dunk 1991: 41). White-collar criminals generally do not live in families where injury to the breadwinner can plunge all into material desperation in a matter of days. Instead, their automobiles start on command; their refrigerators and wine racks are adequately, if not amply, stocked; their homes are commodious, comfortable and secure; and their children are well-clothed and well-fed. Material privilege is important because it shapes every aspect of life, from options available at critical junctures in the life course to the availability of leisure to evaluate them carefully.

The offences committed by materially privileged offenders are an increasingly significant part of the overall crime problem around the globe. Victimisation surveys conducted primarily in Western nations make clear that white-collar crime is commonplace in occurrence, becoming more so, and that rates are substantially higher than comparable rates for burglary, robbery and other street crimes of acquisition (van Dijk *et al.* 2007; Flatley 2007; Gordon *et al.* 2007; Kane and Wall 2006; Nicholas *et al.* 2007; US Department of Justice 2007). Monetary losses to white-collar crime also dwarf losses to street crime. Few white-collar crimes are as costly as the crimes of Bernie Madoff, investment bankers, the Enron corporation and other transnational corporations in the past decade, but what they lack in newsworthiness is more than made up for by their large numbers and aggregate victim losses. The increasing prevalence of white-collar crime and the resulting harm to victims leave little doubt that it merits increased attention from policy-makers and investigators (Association of Certified Fraud Examiners 2008; Bussmann 2006; Levi *et al.* 2007; Levi and Burrows 2008; PriceWaterhouseCoopers 2007; US Department of Justice 2006, 2007).

Materials

Diverse materials were examined as the basis for description of differences between street offenders and white-collar criminals and an interpretation of their potential significance for research. In addition to ethnographic studies of criminal offenders, they include ethnographies of working class worlds and lives and autobiographical books and essays written by socially mobile citizens. The majority of the latter were penned by academicians who began life in the working-class but later experienced upward mobility (e.g. Dews and Law 1995). Others were written by socially mobile academicians who by contrast experienced *downward* movement in the class structure (e.g. Snyder 1997), although the setback for some was short lived (e.g. Seider 1993). In addition to these materials we draw from comparative studies of child rearing and family dynamics in middle-class and working-class worlds (e.g. Newman 1999) and sociological research conducted on academicians with origins in the working-class (e.g. Grimes and Morris 1997). Last, the analysis draws from autobiographies penned by 40 convicted white-collar criminals, a number of whom subsequently wrote multiple books on their lives and experiences. A total of 52 books were examined for what they reveal about the lives, decision-making, crimes and criminal justice experiences of their white-collar-criminal authors. A complete list of autobiographical sources is included as an appendix to this paper.

The autobiographical materials were examined to identify common themes in the authors' accounts and experience of crime and punishment. Plummer terms this 'thematic analysis', where 'the subject is more or less allowed to speak for him or herself but where the sociologist slowly accumulates a series of themes – partly derived from the subject's account and partly derived from sociological theory' (1983: 113–14). The autobiographies vary markedly on several dimensions; for example, some cover a much greater expanse of time than others. The account provided by some authors is restricted to their crimes or their period of imprisonment while others also describe aspects of their earlier lives and careers. The extraordinary nature of their criminal conviction means, however, that it is given more than cursory attention by most authors, thus providing much material for comparison. Some topical themes are suggested by the authors themselves, as when they make mention of or highlight specific experiences. Where we have chosen to quote or cite specific works they are by no means unusual when set against the writings of white-collar offenders generally.

Common and white-collar offenders

The social background and demographic characteristics of white-collar offenders differ conspicuously from what is typical for street-level thieves and other common criminals. The contrast varies by offence type, however; for crimes of international banking it is immense, but for white-collar crimes that do not require advanced education, hierarchical or complex organisational arrangements or arcane criminal skills it can be nearly imperceptible. In addition to a substantial proportion of offenders with middle-class backgrounds, the ranks of identity thieves, for example, include appreciable numbers of offenders with prior involvement in street crimes (Copes and Vieraitis 2007; Duffin et al. 2006; Jackson 1994). The reasons are clear: unlike insider trading by executives of Wall Street investment firms, these crimes require of perpetrators 'not much more than the ability to read, write, and fill out forms, along with some minimum level of presentation of a respectable self' (Weisburd et al. 1991: 182–3). In contrast to identify thieves, however, telemarketing fraudsters typically carry out their criminal pursuits in organisations that in outward appearances resemble legitimate direct marketing firms. This is one reason why nearly all telemarketing fraudsters have middle-class backgrounds (Shover et al. 2003).

Still, the social origins and social worlds of criminal telemarketers and identity thieves are far distant from what is typical of elite white-collar criminals, whether they be executives of transnational corporations or national political leaders. These upperworld white-collar criminals are much wealthier and generally older. Most also are white, married and own homes. By contrast, those who commit less complex and remunerative white-collar offences are noticeably younger, and their ranks include more minority citizens, women, poor or borderline-poor individuals, single or divorced individuals and renters (Alalehto 2003; Benson 2002; Benson and Kerley 2001; Benson and Moore 1992; Daly 1989; Doocy et al. 2001; Forst and Rhodes 1980; Mason 1999; Shover et al. 2004; Shover and Hochstetler 2006; Weisburd et al. 1991).

Proportionately few white-collar criminals have repeated contact with the criminal justice process, albeit the numbers are not insignificant; in some studies more than four in ten convicted white-collar offenders had previous criminal convictions (Shover and Hochstetler 2006). The highest rates are found among those convicted of the least sophisticated white-collar crimes. Forty-six per cent of credit fraud violators, for example, had previous criminal convictions, but only 8 per cent of antitrust offenders did (Weisburd et al. 1991: table 3.1). Regardless of how it is defined, however, a substantial majority of those who commit white-collar crime do not have previous criminal convictions, which cannot be said about common criminals.

Descriptions of criminal participation

The crime-commission and target-selection decisions of burglars, robbers and other street criminals have been the foci of ethnographic research for decades. A great deal has been learned about their criminal participation, and there is remarkable consistency in reports by investigators using a variety of methodological procedures (Nee 2010; Shover and Copes 2010). Studies of white-collar criminals are much smaller in number than investigations of street criminals, and they also show substantially less methodological and topical diversity. Still, the picture that emerges is clear and consistent. Interviews with 24 white-collar offenders imprisoned in the UK, for example, caused the investigator to observe that '[a]ll rationalized their behaviour in one way or another' (Spencer 1965: 260). Investigators since report similar findings. Simply put, white-collar criminals are doggedly resistive to admitting culpability; they acknowledge making 'mistakes' or describe in the third person tragedies that befell them. Likewise they assiduously avoid calling their acts 'crime' (Benson 1984, 1985; Cressey 1953; Daly 1989; Mason 1999; Shover et al. 2004; Zeitz 1981). Typical are the remarks of a former high-level elected public official:

I am writing this book because I am innocent of the [criminal] allegations against me which compelled me to resign from the vice-presidency of the United States ... This is not to say I have not made mistakes, or failed to do things I ought to have done, or done things I ought not to have done. I am human, and my conduct has been no better and no worse than that of other officeholders in these United States. (Agnew 1980: 9)

What is true of reluctance to acknowledge guilt by individual white-collar offenders is true of them in the aggregate also. Prison observations caused a white-collar criminal to highlight a difference between the inmate populations of federal prison camps and federal correctional institutions (FCIs):

At a low-security camp, you have the first offenders and white-collar criminals, the 'short-timers' ... [At an FCI] you have many repeat offenders; some are hardened criminals doing hard time ... At a camp, many inmates tell you they feel themselves to be innocent; at an FCI ... for the most part, they ... freely admit their guilt. (Wachtler 1997: 78)

For an understanding of why this is the case the analysis now turns to comparative examination of the class backgrounds of street offenders and white-collar criminals and the consequences of this for their cultural capital.

Privilege and its consequences

Their lives of material privilege mean that one of the most significant variables on which the backgrounds of street criminals and white-collar criminals differ is social class. The latter overwhelmingly are products of the middle and upper classes. They are privileged also by the respectable work they do and their position in the corresponding moral hierarchy. As Skeggs remarks (1997: 1), '[r]espectability is one of the most ubiquitous signifiers of class.' White-collar criminals hale from worlds where people do not do 'dirty work'. Dirty work is jobs or tasks that most people understand must be carried out albeit they are undesirable to many and morally 'dirty'. Dirty workers hang drywall, collect and process household trash, clean the bodies and beds of nursing home residents or guard prisoners. Dirty workers punch time clocks and their pay is provided in the form of wages rather than salaries. Increasingly many are required to submit to urine testing as a condition of employmentm, and their location while on the clock may be tracked and recorded by global positioning systems. Their use of computer facilities while at work may be monitored by employers to ensure they do not 'steal time' or indulge in unproductive pursuits.

The advantages conferred by respectability are ubiquitous. When they confront officialdom or mid-level bureaucrats, for example, respectable citizens receive a polite and often sympathetic hearing, and they are not subjected to sanctimonious or classist comments about their 'inappropriate' behaviour. Their verbal skills, which include the ability to speak capably and confidently in *formal register*, permit use of presentational and interactional tactics that increase the odds of prevailing (Payne 2005). Working-class citizens, whose appearance, demeanour, and spoken use of *casual register* suggest they fall short of being respectable, generally do not meet with the same reception as privileged citizens. This gives to many a sense of personal insignificance that is only strengthened by awareness that their views are not solicited and usually are not considered by people who count (Sennett and Cobb 1972). Although they make up a majority of the population, working-class citizens and families are largely invisible to respectable people (Ehrenreich 2002; Shipler 2004; Zweig 2002). After falling to a position as construction labourer, a former faculty member at an elite university, remarks that 'up until [that time] ... I had really always thought I was a little better than these guys' (Snyder 1997: 247–8).

It would be foolish to presume that privilege and respectability are dichotomous variables, because they are not. The population of large and demographically heterogeneous nation states can be arrayed on a continuum from those who have an adequate if precarious income and at least a modicum of respectability to citizens with multi-million dollar annual compensation packages and both access to and deference from elites. It includes those who cling precariously to being and to being counted as middle-class and also citizens who live in opulence and move in high social circles. The privileged includes those whose material conditions of life place them comfortably above the threat of penury and who routinely are treated with respect by others. It also includes clerks, bank tellers and similar low-level organisational functionaries whose lives are far removed from the elite envisioned by many lay citizens when they imagine 'white-collar criminals'.

Cultural capital

The different class backgrounds and lives of street criminals and white-collar criminals is the source of variation in countless other matters. Simply put, class

is script, map and guide. [It] tells us how to talk, how to dress, how to hold ourselves, how to eat, and how to socialise. It affects who we marry; where we live; the friends we choose; the jobs we have; the vacations we take; the books we read; the movies we see; the

211

restaurants we pick; how we decide to buy houses, carpets, furniture, and cars; where our kids are educated; what we tell our children at the dinner table (conversations about the Middle East, for example, versus the continuing sagas of the broken vacuum cleaner or the half-wit neighbour). (Lubrano 2004: 5)

Class intersects and interacts with gender and race, but its distinct effects persist and can be disentangled analytically (McCall 2001).

The importance of class as an irreducible source of variation in *cultural capital* has been recognised for decades (Bordieu 1977; Bordieu and Passeron 1977; Croteau 1995). As it is used in sociological analysis, cultural capital designates the 'general cultural background, knowledge, disposition, and skills that are passed from one generation to the next' (MacLeod 1996: 12). Among its components are commonly held understandings, perspectives and skills. For working-class citizens, cultural capital may include knowledge of 'what problems to look for in a used car', 'how to get someone out of jail', 'how to fight and defend [oneself] physically' and 'where the free medical clinics are'. The cultural capital of middle-class adults is likely to include knowledge of 'how to properly set a table', 'how to get one of the best interest rates on [a] new-car loan', 'which stores are most likely to carry the clothing brands [one's] family wears', and 'how to order in a nice restaurant' (Payne 2005: 38–9).

Class background affects the cultural capital acquired by children and adults in large measure because child-rearing practices vary conspicuously by class (Aries and Seider 2005; Farkas 2003; Heath 1983; Lareau 2003; Nelson and Schutz 2007). Lareau (2002: 773) describes child rearing by middle-class parents as 'concerted cultivation'. Unlike working-class parents, who see the lives of their children 'unfolding', middle-class parents make a 'deliberate and sustained effort to stimulate children's development and to cultivate their cognitive and social skills'. They try to foster children's talents through organised recreational activities to the point that for many their free time leaves little opportunity for spontaneous play and peer-organised activities. Middle-class children likewise have limited experience of inter-class relationships; they 'move from nannies at home to private nurseries to private school, privileged and "secure sites" . . . insulated from the frissons of social mix and social diversity' (Vincent and Ball 2006: 68). An assured and adequate family income makes it possible to pay for these pursuits, some of which are expensive.

Working-class parents are less likely than their middle-class counterparts to approach child rearing as a full-time and calculated process. 'Natural growth' describes their approach (Lareau 2002: 747). By this is meant that 'parents [view] children's development as spontaneously unfolding, as long as they [are] provided with comfort, food, shelter and other basic support' (Lareau 2002: 773). Working-class parents have neither the fiscal nor cultural resources to provide what is commonplace in middle-class households. They try instead to provide 'the conditions under which children can grow but [leave] leisure activities to children themselves.' Poor and working-class parents generally believe that 'love and firm discipline should produce a "good kid"' (LeMasters 1975: 116).

Conversation and discussion are important in the dynamics of middle-class households; children are both encouraged verbally and included in conversation with adults. Everything is fair game for discussion or contest, and negotiation is commonplace. One result is that middle-class children develop 'ways with words' (Heath 1983). This prepares them far better than less-privileged citizens to produce carefully reasoned and meticulously documented if not florid justifications for their criminal decision-making as circumstances require.

Communication in middle-class child rearing is explicit, and much of it is devoted to unraveling the intentions behind puzzling or deviant actions. Children learn to look for and consider what motivates untoward conduct and to pay less attention to its formal status. In contrast to working-class citizens, norms are viewed not as absolutes but as situationally applicable. Infraction, which is seen as a product of internal dynamics that explain if not justify it, is a matter for discussion. The reasons for punishment or correction must be explained defensibly, and it can be a protracted process. Middle-class children learn early that arguable lack of intent mitigates an array of misconduct.

Working-class parents typically use directives rather than reasoning in efforts to influence the behaviour of their children. Communication tends toward the implicit; much is understood but goes unsaid. Children do not engage in conversation with adults so much as receive opinions or edicts. Children reared in these families likely do not belong to high-school forensic or debate clubs nor do they take classes that encourage search for arcane meanings and complex interpretations.

Working-class citizens are attuned and pay attention to external qualities of behaviour. Offenders reared in the working class generally have available and employ a narrow range of acceptable explanations for their crimes. Street thieves, for example, typically refer to their activities as 'stealing' or 'doin' wrong', and the circumstances of their crimes leave little room for denial or creative explanations in any case. Twenty-year-old males arrested on the street carrying electronics products and a pry bar only blocks from where residents were burglarised readily invite the label 'perp'. Add to this the fact that working-class citizens typically discourage public exploration of motives or interpret it as weakness, deception or whining.

The higher levels of education, verbal acuity and competitiveness characteristic of middle-class families make for a willingness to intervene with institutions and to challenge decisions that work to their disadvantage. In conferences or meetings with school officials, for example, the former are far more likely than working-class parents to pose questions and to request detailed information about their children's performance (Lareau 2003). On their own initiative they intervene to gather information from professionals, organisational representatives or from the Internet. They actively explore options. Children witness willingness by their parents to accommodate their needs, which may include permitting them as adults to move home in order to secure better schooling (Vincent and Ball 2006). Likewise, middle-class children are encouraged to question and request clarification from authority figures and organisations. This willingness to question and intervene fosters a sense of efficacy, which is 'perhaps more important than any other cultural resource'. In contrast to children of the middle class, working-class citizens are 'unlikely to have [a] ... vision of achievable change' (Croteau 1995: 139). Believing that in all likelihood it would be unsuccessful and therefore pointless, they are less likely than middle-class citizens to challenge institutional officials and their actions.

Narratives of white-collar criminals

Patterns in the narratives and data provided by white-collar criminals distinguish them from what is typical of street criminals. Recall that investigations consistently have shown that white-collar criminals are unrepentant and disinclined to accept responsibility for their crimes. Typical are the comments of 42 New York and California physicians charged with acts of fraud against publicly funded medical programmes. Investigators who interviewed the subjects remarked:

> To hear them tell it, they were innocent sacrificial lambs led to the slaughter because of perfidy, stupid laws, bureaucratic nonsense, and incompetent bookkeepers. At worst, they had been a bit careless in their record keeping; but mostly they had been more interested in the welfare of their patients than in deciphering the arcane requirements of benefit programmes ... [W]e were surprised by the number of rationalizations that these doctors offered, by the intensity of their defenses of their misconduct, and by their consummate skill in identifying the villains who, out of malevolence or ineptitude, had caused their downfall. (Jesilow et al. 1993: 148)

We examined the autobiographical sources for what they reveal about these matters. Investigations of street criminals have shown that materials of this kind can be revealing and exceedingly useful sources of data about offenders, their crimes and their criminal careers (Cotterhill and Letherby 1993; Maruna 1997; Shover 1996, 2010). The 52 autobiographical sources we examined for this chapter shows this is no less true of the life histories of white-collar offenders (Hunter 2009; Smith and Watson 2002). More importantly, the patterns and tendencies revealed in these autobiographical narratives are remarkably consistent with reports from studies in which interview methods were employed.

Their cultural capital means that most white-collar criminals have a level of verbal creativity and adroitness that enables them to argue self-interested interpretations of their fall from grace (Benson 1984). Typically, authors deny they were guilty of crime or 'real' wrongdoing and focus instead on what 'really' occurred with promises to 'set the record straight' (Jett 1999; Leeson 1996). Rarely do they push outright denial of specific actions that occurred but instead deny criminal intent or that the acts were harmful. Stories told by white-collar criminals make clear why they could not possibly have offended, why the accounts of others are born of malice or other unworthy motives and why the evidence that convicted them was false or misunderstood. Alternatively, they outline why they are only 'technically' guilty or were hamstrung by circumstances that caused them to make mistakes that later would be labeled 'crime'. Appeals to higher loyalty are a common refrain. Where offences are admitted, autobiographies become stories of changes that have taken place in their authors; past lives are renounced as 'wrong' in some manner followed by descriptions of how authors now are different. Personal stories of change by religious conversion, for example, are featured prominently (Aitken 2000, 2005). Recounted stories of transformation and redemption make clear that despite mistakes in the past their authors have returned to the ranks of the respectable. Evidence to the contrary can count for little in these respectability projects. In their distinctiveness the autobiographies of white-collar criminals are decidedly different from similar narratives penned by street criminals. Overwhelmingly, the latter acknowledge guilt and cast their narratives as a warning to readers not to repeat their mistakes.

Many common criminals have repeated experience with arrest, jail confinement and judicial processing. Over a period of years authorities perhaps have built revealing and morally damaging dossiers on them, other family members and perhaps their families. The subjects of these reports and rulings have had little choice but to accommodate, and by the time they reach adulthood they are well aware of their low moral standing in and beyond the world of officialdom. Street offenders rarely take overt offence to bureaucratically impersonal, incompetent or inefficient processing by criminal justice personnel or other state functionaries.

For white-collar criminals, however, criminal justice processing poses a harsh and unavoidable threat to their sense of respectability. Few have faced or been reconciled with its inextricable moral degradation, and all but the most ordinary among them are unprepared for it. For the first time in their lives they are in the realm of and cannot escape from those they regard as social inferiors. The sanctimonious tone of their descriptions of encounters with subordinate classes is clear in their autobiographical narratives: 'I realized over and over, the longer I was there, that I had absolutely nothing in common with anyone else in the jail. All the conversation – the entire atmosphere – was filled with vulgarity, filth, despair' (Laite 1972: 111). Classism and racism are veneered but thinly in these tales, and *unclean* is how they and their families will feel after close contact with the police, jail and the courts (e.g. Berger 2003). Those sent to confinement quickly learn the value of keeping quiet. They may be big talkers in the free world, but in jail and prison most become part of the background, and their fear of the unknown and the uncontrollable soon gives way to a condescending distaste for institutions, their routines and many staff. White-collar criminals view the criminal process and imprisonment specifically as entirely inappropriate for people like themselves (e.g. Timilty 1997).

In recounting their experience of punishment, much is made of the difference between the orderly, civilised and sane world that offenders were part of and the environment in which they find themselves:

> I couldn't . . . adjust to the language . . . Everybody swore. It was vile and filthy. I was horrified by the whole experience. It seemed like another age. It's so Dickensian. It really is unreasonable, the whole thing . . . It is ghastly, filthy. There is rubbish lying about. Cells are inches thick in cigarette ash. And to top it all you are thrown in with all sorts of people. (Breed 1979: 52)

White-collar criminals are not above exaggerating the unfairness and inhumanity of what they experience or witness while confined. Evidence is anecdotal, but descriptions of rapes committed by inmates against other inmates are recounted by formerly imprisoned white-collar offenders with a frequency that would seem to leave prisoners time for little else. In light of the fact that generally they are confined in minimum security institutions where inmates are older, have learned to be compliant and display less of the predatory conduct more common in high-security penitentiaries, the veracity of these stories is highly suspect.

Unlike street criminals, who characteristically see the media and functionaries of criminal justice abstractly as persons 'doing a job', white-collar offenders personalise their treatment by both and cast themselves as victims. They may, for example, seize upon the smallest of inaccuracies in press reporting as evidence of this. Told how his prison stay accommodations were described in newspapers, a former British MP recounts:

> [The prison officer] tells us that [North Sea Camp Prison] has now been dubbed 'the cushiest prison in England' (*Sun*) . . . 'The best food in any prison' (*Daily Star*); 'I have "the biggest room in the quietest block"' (*Daily Mail*); and 'he's the only one allowed to wear his own clothes' (*Daily Mirror*). Not one fact correct. (Archer 2004: 17)

These experiences reinforce belief in the minds of white-collar offenders that imprisonment is undeserved and cruel punishment for them.

Implications for inquiry

The contrasting cultural capital of street offenders and white-collar criminals and the constructed narratives of their offending and criminal justice experiences are the background to understanding how they affect the conduct of research, data collection and data interpretation.

Research participation

The proportion of criminal offenders who will for this reason ever be contacted by researchers or will be research subjects is infinitesimally small. But for those who are asked to participate in a research project, there are clear differences in the responses of common criminals and white-collar criminals. Generally, investigators report few intractable problems approaching and securing cooperation from the former. With few exceptions, they are forthcoming in acknowledging their culpability and criminal participation (Bageant 2007). Imprisoned by the United States government for crimes of extortion, the former chief judge of the New York court system observes of his fellow institutional travellers: 'Conventional wisdom tells us that most convicts claim to be innocent. That is not true' (Wachtler 1997: 88). In the types of institutions in which primarily poor and minority offenders are confined, '[c]ontrary to popular myth you don't find the halls ringing with cries of "I was framed"' (Harris 1986: 235). Further, when interviewed by investigators, they readily provide detailed descriptions of their lifestyles, criminal decision-making and factors that caused them to select crime from their available options. In short, few, if any, of the challenges many would expect to meet in ethnographic research on street criminals are born out by experience. There are exceptions, however, and sex offenders stand as the most notable example (e.g. Scully and Marolla 1984).

With street offenders the research process typically proceeds without complications, albeit they generally seem alternately confused, puzzled or unconcerned by explanations of research objectives and the informed consent process. Most seem trusting of investigators, and they rarely dispute the investigator's use of a tape recorder. Few ask questions or show reluctance to sign documents affirming consent to participate. There are few reported significant problems of truthfulness in accounts and information provided by common criminals. Many readily admit to a record of criminal participation that is considerably lengthier than arrest records reveal. Most common offenders see little reason to misrepresent themselves or their pasts and readily grant access to their records.

217

White-collar offenders who are asked to participate in research will bring to the experience a patchy but crude understanding of what 'research' entails. Many are aware of its ubiquity in contemporary life and the uses that are made of it. They may ask questions about the investigator's long-term objectives, whether or not a report will be written and whether it will be available to the public. Some may be parties in other legal proceedings of one kind or another that would cause them to fear that information divulged in research interviews could jeopardise their interests in these matters. Some may have a rudimentary awareness of the informed consent process and the strictures it places on investigators. When these matters and their options are explained they are attentive and typically ask questions. White-collar criminals also show a willingness to decline outright or to attempt negotiated participation in research.

How is cultural capital manifested in ethnographic research with offenders? An investigator who has interviewed both street criminals and ordinary white-collar offenders notes that '[n]one of the 70+ auto thieves and carjackers [I interviewed] refused to sign the [informed consent] form or prohibit me from recording them. However, four identity thieves would not sign the form, and nine of the 62 identity thieves refused to be recorded' (Copes 2008). Of 105 physicians contacted by Jesilow *et al.* as potential interview subjects in their study of Medicaid fraud, 60 per cent indicated in one way or another that they were unwilling to be interviewed (1993: 150). Of 67 imprisoned telemarketing offenders contacted by Shover *et al.* (2003), 42 per cent either failed to acknowledge receipt of the letter outlining the study or declined to participate after research objectives were explained to them. There is little question that the mortality rate in samples of white-collar offenders is higher than the comparable rate for studies of street criminals.

Investigators who have studied the latter are well aware of how difficult it can be to locate and maintain contact with them when they are in the free world. White-collar offenders may be less likely to disappear from the radar screen in comparable circumstances, but a surprisingly high proportion prove difficult to locate once they leave prison. This was true of 15 per cent of physicians in the sample of fraud offenders constructed by Jesilow *et al.* (1993: 150). In light of the fact that most of these offenders formerly were high-profile and presumably respected members of their communities, this surprises. It may attest to a desire by some convicted white-collar criminals to break off contact with their former lives and livelihood; those who are tracked down and approached may have made swift returns to employment and want nothing more than to put the past behind them. Unlike street criminals, many of whom have spoiled identities from past involuntary processing by officials, much about the backgrounds and previous conduct of white-collar criminals is inaccessible to researchers. They have little reason to change this by exposing to scrutiny themselves and their past lives. Investigators who call at the house may reopen wounds and be difficult to explain to the neighbours.

Investigator strategies

Apart from distinctiveness in the way white-collar criminals describe and explain their offences, little is known about the truthfulness of their narratives and the data they provide. The accessibility, extensiveness and validity of information generated in social histories and background checks is clear, however, whether conducting research on white-collar offenders or their street brethren. Offence histories and other external facts generally are verifiable and can be used if necessary to challenge factually incorrect assertions by offenders. Awareness and understanding of the cultural capital of white-collar criminals and the tendentious qualities of their stories are the context for considering how ethnographic investigators might improve the quality of data elicited from them. In addition, respectability and being seen as respectable anchor the self-concepts of white-collar criminals, and both data collection and interpretation should be approached with this awareness.

Consider the matter of their criminal decision-making, which is a largely neglected area of inquiry; simply put, '[w]e have little evidence about [their] beliefs or knowledge of [possible criminal penalties] *at the time they contemplated their offences*' (Levi 2006: 3; emphasis in original). Investigators who study decision-making by street criminals have learned that they can focus narrowly and in a matter-of-fact manner on discrete steps in the decision-making process. Subjects can be asked to respond to questions exemplified by 'Tell me when you initially decided to commit this crime?' Likewise the question 'How old were you when you started stealing?' meets with no umbrage from street criminals. 'Tell me how you decided to do this crime' evokes no reactions of puzzlement or disputed meanings from them. White-collar offenders are more likely to baulk at being asked questions predicated on their criminality, which complicates efforts by investigators to secure succinct descriptions of their decision-making and actions. More general queries (e.g. 'Can you tell me what happened?') generally elicit a less contentious and more expansive response. This approach was employed and worked satisfactorily for Jesilow *et al.* (1993) in research on physicians who committed Medicaid fraud and also in interviews with 15 imprisoned white-collar offenders in the UK (Hunter 2008).

Paradoxically, their tendency to deny culpability or to label their acts as crime may reduce error and wilful deception by white-collar criminals. Because they believe themselves guilty of nothing more serious than mistakes and see themselves as victims of official incompetence or persecution, data provided by them may contain little systematic bias. In the same way that the belief one is telling the truth, regardless of the reasons for it, can cause individuals not to appear deceptive in polygraph examinations, data provided by white-collar criminals may be reliable, because belief in their own innocence gives them little reason to prevaricate or mislead; with little disreputable lurking as background there is no reason to adjust the past as explanation. Still, given their need to be seen as successful with a perfect life ruined by prosecutors it may be important to examine closely claims made by white-collar criminals about their prior accomplishments. The worlds in which most are reared and work value formal education and credentials as both prerequisites for and markers of success. Periodic media reports of false or exaggerated claims of credentials and research breakthroughs by renowned scientists (e.g. BBC 2006) suggest that investigators should scrutinise carefully claims about legitimate achievements.

Historically, the study of criminal offenders has been focused almost entirely on individuals. The corpus of published criminological theory and empirical work, therefore, is replete with efforts to account for why some individuals are more prone to criminal participation than others and why the severity of criminal punishment varies across individuals and categories of offenders. But a substantial majority of the costliest and most destructive white-collar crimes are committed by individuals or groups in their employment roles. In the industrialised and post-industrialised world, overwhelmingly these are situated in organisations. The designation *organizational crime* is applied to violations of criminal statutes committed in the context of or in pursuit of the goals of legitimate organisations, organisational sub-units or work groups.

A variety of evidence shows that organisational properties and dynamics affect significantly decision-making by organisational white-collar criminals. There is no challenge faced by investigators interested in explaining and predicting variation in white-collar crime greater than examining these matters close up. Creative responses almost certainly are required. Clinard (1983), for example, conducted ethnographic interviews with *retired* former mid-level managers of large corporations. White-collar offenders are skilled at attributing their crimes to contextual conditions before which they were powerless. Still, there may be few better ways of getting at criminogenic organisational conditions and dynamics than to explore these matters with convicted white-collar criminals. There is the bonus perhaps of enlisting as partners in a collaborative cause respondents who would be less forthcoming and truthful if the spotlight is turned brightly or exclusively on them and their criminal decision-making. Investigators are cautioned, however, to be wary of descriptions they provide.

Upper-world white-collar criminals are the least studied and least interpreted subjects of criminological interest, and they present a formidable set of problems for investigators. Unlike ordinary offenders, whether working-class or middle-class, it is next to impossible to gain access to them; they are shielded by gatekeepers of one kind of another, and on the rare occasion when investigators talk with them face-to-face or by telephone few will consent to be interviewed. Alternatively, entreaties to them are met with the suggestion that questions should be taken up with legal counsel or that the matter is so complex as to defy description and understanding by lay persons. Almost certainly, intermediaries could be used to good effect by investigators interested in the lives and crimes of elite offenders.

Conclusion

Ethnographic studies of street offenders and white-collar offenders are markedly different kinds of enterprises. Their cultural capital gives white-collar offenders a perspective on criminal culpability, research and punishment that is uncommon among their less salubrious criminal peers. The class-based social worlds in which the former are reared and move before criminal conviction are an important reason for this. Investigators are advised to understand something about the background of individual white-collar offenders to appreciate the bearing these may have upon research and analysis. Research that has a regard for the ways in which offenders' backgrounds mediate their perception of their convictions and punishment can only contribute to what is an underdeveloped field of inquiry. The worldwide growth of white-collar crime leaves little doubt that its importance increases daily.

Appendix: Autobiographical sources

Note: Where books have more than one author cited, the first author is the offender.

Agnew, S. T. (1980) *Go Quietly . . . Or Else*. New York: Morrow.

Aitken, J. (2000) *Pride and Perjury*. London: Continuum.

Aitken, J. (2004) *Prayers for People Under Pressure*. London: Continuum.

Aitken, J. (2004) *Psalms for People Under Pressure*. London: Continuum.

Aitken, J. (2005) *Porridge and Passion*. London: Continuum.

Archer, J. (2004) *A Prison Diary Volume 1: Hell*. London: Pan Books.

Archer, J. (2004) *A Prison Diary Volume 2: Purgatory*. London: Pan Books.

Archer, J. (2004) *A Prison Diary Volume 3: Heaven*. London: Pan Books.

Bakker, J. (2005) *I Was Wrong*. Nashville, TN: Thomas Nelson.

Belfort, J. (2007) *The Wolf of Wall Street*. London: Hodder & Stoughton.

Berger, R. L. (2003) *From the Inside: A Prison Memoir*. New York: iUniverse.

Blundell, W. E. (1976) 'Equity funding: I did it for the jollies', in D. Moffitt (ed.), *Swindled: Classic Business Frauds of the Seventies*. Princeton, NJ: Dow Jones Books, pp. 42–89.

Bond, A. and Mundle, R. (2003) *Bond*. London: Harper Collins.

Breed, B. (1979) *White-Collar Bird*. London: John Clare Books.

Bullen, D. (2004) *Fake: My Life as a Rogue Trader*. Sydney: John Wiley & Sons.

Christensen, N. (2005) *Five Years of Bad Coffee: A White-Collar Criminal Does Blue Collar-Time*. New York: iUniverse.

Colson, C. (1976) *Born Again*. Royal Oak, MI: Chosen Books.

Colson, C. (1979) *Life Sentence*. London: Hodder & Stoughton.

Colson, C. (2005) *The Good Life*. Carol Stream, IL: Tyndale House.

Cruver, B. (2002) *Anatomy of Greed: The Unshredded Truth from an Enron Insider*. New York: Carroll & Graf.

Dean, J. (1976) *Blind Ambition*. New York: Pocket Books.

Dean, J. (1982) *Lost Honor*. Los Angeles: Stratford Press.

Earley, P. (1997) *Confessions of a Spy: The Real Story of Aldrich Ames*. New York: G. P. Putnam & Sons.

Ellsberg, D. (2002) *Secrets: A Memoir of Vietnam and the Pentagon Papers*. New York: Viking.

Friedrich, J. and Flanagan, R. (1991) *Codename Iago: The Story of John Friedrich*. Port Melbourne, Vic.: William Heinemann.

Guppy, D. and Davies, N. (1996) *Roll the Dice*. London: Blake Publishing.

Harris, J. (1986) *Stranger in Two Worlds*. New York: Macmillan.

Harrris, J. (1988) *They Always Call Us Ladies: Stories from Prison*. New York: Scribner's.

Hoffa, J. R. (1970) *The Trials of Jimmy Hoffa* (as told to D. I. Rogers). Chicago: Henry Regnery.

Hubbell, W. (1997) *Friends in High Places: Our Journey from Little Rock to Washington, D.C.* New York: William Morrow.

Jett, J. and Chartrand, S. (1999) *Black and White on Wall Street: The Untold Story of the Man Wrongly Accused of Bringing Down Kidder Peabody*. New York: William Morrow.

Laite, W. (1972) *The United States v. William Laite*. Washington, DC: Acropolis Books.

Lance, B. (1991) *The Truth of the Matter: My Life In and Out of Politics*. New York: Summit Books.

Lawson, S. (1992) *Daddy, Why Are You Going to Jail?* Colorado Springs, CO: Harold Shaw.

Leeson, N. and Tyrrell, I. (2005) *Back from the Brink: Coping with Stress*. London: Virgin Books.

Leeson, N. and Whitley, E. (1996) *Rogue Trader*. London: Little, Brown.

Leopold, N. F. (1958) *Life Plus 99 Years*. Garden City, NY: Doubleday.

Levine, D. and Hoffer, W. (1991) *Inside Out: An Insider's Account of Wall Street*. New York: Berkley Books.

Magruder, J. (1978) *From Power to Peace*. Waco, TX: Word Books.

Minkow, B. (1995) *Clean Sweep: The Inside Story of the ZZZZ Best Scam ... One of Wall Street's Biggest Frauds*. Nashville, TN: Thomas Nelson.

Minkow, B. (2005) *Cleaning Up: One Man's Redemptive Journey Through the Seductive World of Corporate Crime*. Nashville, TN: Nelson Current.

Moll, H. (with Leapman, M.) (1988) *Broker of Death: An Insider's Story of the Iranian Arms Deals*. London: Macmillan.

Pavlo, W. and Weinberg, N. (2007) *Stolen Without a Gun: Confessions from Inside History's Biggest Accounting Fraud – the Collapse of MCI WorldCom*. Tampa, FL: Etika Books.

Rose, P. and Hill, R. (2004) *My Prison Without Bars*. New York: Rodale.

Stonehouse, J. (1975) *Death of an Idealist*. London: W. H. Allen.

Stonehouse, J. (1976) *My Trial*. London: Wyndham Publications.

Swartz, M. (with Watkins, S.) (2003) *Power Failure: The Inside Story of the Collapse of Enron*. New York: Doubleday.

Timilty, J. (1997) *Prison Journal*. Boston: Northeastern University Press.

Tosches, N. (1986) *Power on Earth: Michele Sindona's Explosive Story*. New York: Arbor House.

Vandivier, K. (1972) 'Why should my conscience bother me?', in R. L. Heilbroner (ed.), *In the Name of Profit*. New York: Warner Paperback Library, pp. 11–33.

Volpe, T. (2002) *Framed: Tales of the Art Underworld*. Edinburgh: Cutting Edge Press.

Wachtler, S. (1997) *After the Madness: A Judge's Own Prison Memoir*. New York: Random House.

References

Agnew, S. T. (1980) *Go Quietly . . . Or Else*. New York: Morrow.

Aitken, J. (2000) *Pride and Perjury*. London: Continuum.

Aitken, J. (2005) *Porridge and Passion*. London: Continuum.

Alalehto, T. (2003) 'Economic crime: does personality matter?', *International Journal of Offender Therapy and Comparative Criminology*, 20: 1–22.

Aries, E. and Seider, M. (2005) 'The interactive relationship between class identity and the college experience: the case of lower income students', *Qualitative Sociology*, 28: 419–43.

Association of Certified Fraud Examiners (2008) *2008 Report to the Nation on Occupational Fraud and Abuse*. Austin, TX: Association of Certified Fraud Examiners.

Bageant, J. (2007) *Deer Hunting with Jesus: Dispatches from America's Class War*. New York: Crown.

Benson, M. L. (1984) 'The fall from grace: loss of occupational status as a consequence of conviction for a white collar crime', *Criminology*, 22: 573–94.

Benson, M. L. (1985) 'Denying the guilty mind: accounting for involvement in a white-collar crime', *Criminology*, 23: 583–608.

Benson, M. L. (2002) *Crime and the Life Course: An Introduction*. Los Angeles: Roxbury.

Benson, M. L. and Kerley, K. R. (2001) 'Life course theory and white-collar crime', in H. N. Pontell and D. Shichor (eds), *Contemporary Issues in Crime and Criminal Justice: Essays in Honor of Gilbert Geis*. Upper Saddle River, NJ: Prentice Hall, pp. 121–36.

Benson, M. L. and Moore, E. (1992) 'Are white-collar and common criminals the same?', *Journal of Research in Crime and Delinquency*, 29: 251–72.

Berger, R. L. (2003) *From the Inside: A Prison Memoir*. New York: inverse.

Bordieu, P. (1977) *Outline of a Theory of Practice*. Cambridge: Cambridge University Press.

Bordieu, P. and Passeron, J.-C. (1977) *Reproduction in Education, Society and Culture*. Newbury Park, CA: Sage.

Breed, B. (1979) *White Collar Bird*. London: John Clare Books.

British Broadcasting Corporation (BBC) (2006) 'South Korea scientist on fraud charge', 12 May. Online at: http://news.bbc.co.uk/1/hi/world/asia-pacific/4763973.stm.

Bussmann, K.-D. (2006) 'Addressing crime in companies: first findings from a global survey of economic crime', *British Journal of Criminology*, 46: 1–17.

Clinard, M. B. (1983) *Corporate Ethics and Crime: The Role of Middle Management*. Beverly Hills, CA: Sage.

Copes, H. (2008) Personal communication, 19 May.

Copes, H. and Vieraitis, L. (2007) *Identity Theft: Assessing Offenders' Strategies and Perceptions of Risk*, Research report prepared for the National Institute of Justice. Birmingham, AL: University of Alabama, Birmingham, Department of Justice Sciences.

Cotterhill, P. and Letherby, G. (1993) 'Weaving stories: personal auto/biographies in feminist research', *Sociology*, 27: 67–79.

Cressey, D. R. (1953) *Other People's Money*. Glencoe, IL: Free Press.

Croteau, D. (1995) *Politics and the Class Divide: Working People and the Middle-Class Left*. Philadelphia: Temple University Press.

Daly, K. (1989) 'Gender and varieties of white-collar crime', *Criminology*, 27: 769–94.

Dews, C. F. B. and Law, C. L. (eds) (1995) *This Fine Place So Far from Home: Voices of Academics from the Working Class*. Philadelphia: Temple University Press.

Doocy, J. H., Shichor, D., Sechrest, D. K. and Geis, G. (2001) 'Telemarketing fraud: who are the tricksters and what makes them trick?', *Security Journal*, 14: 7–26.

Duffin, M., Keats, G. and Gill, M. (2006) *Identity Theft in the UK: The Offender and Victim Perspective*. Leicester: Perpetuity Research.

Dunk, T. W. (1991) *It's a Working Man's Town: Male Working-Class Culture in Northwestern Ontario*. Montreal: McGill-Queen's University Press.

Ehrenreich, B. (2002) *Nickel and Dimed: On (Not) Getting by in America*. New York: Henry Holt.

Ernst & Young (2008) *Corruption or Compliance – Weighing the Costs: 10th Global Fraud Survey*. Online at: http://www.ey.com/Global/assets.nsf/International/FIDS_Corruption_or_compliance_weighing_the_costs/$file/Corruption_or_compliance_weighing_the_costs.pdf.

Farkas, G. (2003) 'Cognitive skills and noncognitive traits and behaviors in stratification processes', *Annual Review of Sociology*, 29: 541–62.

Flatley, J. (2007) *Mobile Phone Theft, Plastic Card and Identity Fraud: Findings from the 2005/06 British Crime Survey*. Online at: http://www.homeoffice.gov.uk/rds/pdfs07/hosb1007.pdf.

Forst, B. and Rhodes, W. (1980) *Sentencing in Eight United States District Courts, 1973–1978*. Ann Arbor, MI: Inter-University Consortium for Political and Social Research.

Gordon, G. R., Rebovich, D. J., Choo, K.-S. and Gordon, J. B. (2007) *Identity Fraud Trends and Patterns: Building a Data-Based Foundation for Proactive Enforcement*. Utica, NY: Utica College, Center for Identity Management and Information Protection.

Grimes, M. D. and Morris, J. M. (1997) *Caught in the Middle: Contradictions in the Lives of Sociologists from Working-Class Backgrounds*. New York: Praeger.

Harris, J. (1986) *Stranger in Two Worlds*. New York: Macmillan.

Heath, S. B. (1983) *Ways with Words: Language, Life, and Work in Communities and Classrooms*. New York: Cambridge University Press.

Hunter, B. (2008) Personal communication with N. Shover, 10 August.

Hunter, B. (2009) 'White-collar offenders after the fall from grace: stigma, blocked paths and resettlement', in R. Lippens and D. Crewe (eds), *Criminology and Existentialism*. London: Routledge, pp. 145–68.

Jackson, J. (1994) 'Fraud masters: professional credit offenders and crime', *Criminal Justice Review*, 19: 24–55.

Jesilow, P., Pontell, H. N. and Geis, G. (1993) *Prescription for Profit – How Doctors Defraud Medicaid*. Berkeley, CA: University of California Press.

Jett, J. (with Chartrand, S.) (1999) *Black and White on Wall Street: The Untold Story of the Man Wrongly Accused of Bringing Down Kidder Peabody*. New York: William Morrow.

Kane, J. and Wall, A. D. (2006) *The 2005 National Survey on White Collar Crime*. Fairmont, WV: National White Collar Crime Center.

Laite, W. E. Jr (1972) *The United States v. William Laite*. Washington, DC: Acropolis.

Lareau, A. (2002) 'Invisible inequality: social class and child rearing in black families and white families', *American Sociological Review*, 67: 747–76.

Lareau, A. (2003) *Unequal Childhoods: Class, Race, and Family Life*. Berkeley, CA: University of California Press.

Leeson, N. (with Whitley, E.) (1996) *Rogue Trader*. Boston: Little, Brown.

LeMasters, E. E. (1975) *Blue-Collar Aristocrats: Life-Styles at a Working-Class Tavern*. Madison, WI: University of Wisconsin Press.

Levi, M. (2006) *Sentencing Frauds: A Review*. Cardiff: Cardiff University, Department of Social Sciences.

Levi, M. and Burrows, J. (2008) 'Measuring the impact of fraud in the UK: a conceptual and empirical journey', *British Journal of Criminology*, 48: 293–318.

Levi, M., Burrows, J., Fleming, M. H. and Hopkins, M. (with the assistance of Matthews, K.) (2007) *The Nature, Extent and Economic Impact of Fraud in the UK*. London: Association of Chief Police Officers.

Lubrano, A. (2004) *Limbo: Blue-Collar Roots, White-Collar Dreams*. Hoboken, NJ: John Wiley & Sons.

McCall, L. (2001) *Complex Inequality: Gender, Class, and Race in the New Economy*. New York: Routledge.

MacLeod, J. (1996) *Ain't No Makin' It* (rev. edn). Boulder, CO: Westview.

Maruna, S. (1997) 'Going straight: desistance from crime and life narratives of reform', in A. Lieblich and R. Josselson (eds), *The Narrative Study of Lives*, Vol. 5. London: Sage, pp. 59–93.

Mason, K. A. (1999) 'Middle-Class, White-Collar Offenders: Needy Women – Greedy Men?' Unpublished doctoral thesis, Sociology, University of Tennessee, Knoxville, TN.

Nee, C. (2010) Research on residential burglary: ways of improving validity and participants' recall when gathering data, in W. Bernasco (ed.), *Offenders on Offending: Learning about Crime from Criminals*. Cullompton: Willan.

Nelson, M. K. and Schutz, R. (2007) 'Day care differences and the reproduction of social class', *Journal of Contemporary Ethnography*, 36: 281–317.

Newman, K. S. (1999) *No Shame in My Game: The Working Poor in the Inner City*. New York: Alfred A. Knopf.

Nicholas, S., Kershaw, C. and Walker, A. (2007) *Crime in England and Wales 2006/2007*, Home Office Statistical Bulletin 11/07. London: Home Office.

Payne, R. K. (2005) *Framework for Understanding Poverty* (4th rev. edn). Highlands, TX: AHA! Process.

Plummer, K. (1983) *Documents of Life: An Introduction to the Problems and Literature of a Humanistic Method*. London: George Allen & Unwin.

PriceWaterhouseCoopers (2007) *Economic Crime: People, Culture and Controls: The 4th Biennial Global Economic Crime Survey*. Online at: http://www.lecercle.biz/Portals/3/ECONOM~1.pdf.

Ross, E. A. (1907) *Sin and Society*. Boston: Houghton Mifflin.

Scully, D. and Marolla, J. (1984) 'Convicted rapists' vocabulary of motive: excuses and justifications', *Social Problems*, 31: 530–44.

Seider, M. (1993) *Year in the Life of a Factory*. New York: Charles H. Kerr.

Sennett, R. and Cobb, J. (1972) *The Hidden Injuries of Class*. New York: Alfred A. Knopf.

Shipler, D. K. (2004) *The Working Poor: Invisible in America*. New York: Alfred A. Knopf.

Shover, N. (1996) *Great Pretenders: Pursuits and Careers of Persistent Thieves*. Boulder, CO: Westview.

Shover, N. (2007) 'Generative worlds of white-collar crime', in H. N. Pontell and G. Geis (eds), *International Handbook of White-Collar and Corporate Crime*. New York: Springer, pp. 81–97.

Shover, N. (2010) 'Life histories and autobiographies as ethnographic data', in D. Gadd, S. Karstedt and S. Messner (eds.). *Sage Handbook of Criminological Research Methods*. London: Sage.

Shover, N. and Copes, H. (2009) 'Decision making by persistent thieves and crime control policy', in H. Barlow and S. Decker (eds), *Criminology and Public Policy: Putting Theory to Work*. Philadelphia: Temple University Press.

Shover, N. and Hochstetler, A. (2006) *Choosing White-Collar Crime*. New York: Cambridge University Press.

Shover, N., Coffey, G. S. and Hobbs, D. (2003) 'Crime on the line: telemarketing and the changing nature of professional crime', *British Journal of Criminology*, 43: 489–505.

Shover, N., Coffey, G. S. and Sanders, C. R. (2004) 'Dialing for dollars: opportunities, justifications, and telemarketing fraud', *Qualitative Sociology*, 27: 59–75.

Skeggs, B. (1997) *Formations of Class and Gender: Becoming Respectable*. London: Sage.

Smith, S. and Watson, J. (2002) *Reading Autobiography: A Guide for Interpreting Life Narratives*. Minneapolis, MN: University of Minnesota Press.

Snyder, D. J. (1997) *The Cliff Walk: A Memoir of a Job Lost and a Life Found*. Boston: Little, Brown.

Spencer, J. C. (1965) 'White-collar crime', in E. Glover, H. Mannheim and E. Miller (eds), *Criminology in Transition*. London: Tavistock, pp. 233–66.

Timilty, J. (with Thomas, J.) (1997) *Prison Journal*. Boston: Northeastern University Press.

US Department of Justice (2006) *Crime in the United States, 2005*. Online at: http://www.fbi.gov/ucr/05cius/index.html.

US Department of Justice (2007) *Identity Theft, 2005*. Washington, DC: Bureau of Justice Statistics.

van Dijk, J., Manchin, R., van Kesteren, J., Nevala, S. and Hideg, G. (2007) *The Burden of Crime in the EU*. Online at: http://www.gallup-europe.be/euics/Xz38/downloads/EUICS%20-%20The%20Burden%20of%20Crime%20in%20the%20EU.pdf.

Vincent, C. and Ball, S. J. (2006) *Childcare, Choices and Class Practices*. New York: Routledge.

Wachtler, S. (1997) *After the Madness: A Judge's Own Prison Memoir*. New York: Random House.

Weisburd, D., Wheeler, S., Waring, E. and Bode, N. (1991) *Crimes of the Middle Classes*. New Haven, CT: Yale University Press.

Zietz, D. (1981) *Women Who Embezzle or Defraud: A Study of Convicted Felons*. New York: Praeger.

Zweig, M. (2002) *The Working Class Majority: America's Best Kept Secret*. Ithaca, NY: Cornell University Press.

Part 5
Learning about the act

Chapter 13

Research on residential burglary: ways of improving validity and participants' recall when gathering data

Claire Nee

Abstract

This chapter reviews the grounded approach to undertaking offender-based research which has been utilised effectively in research on residential burglary. It looks at the worth of triangulating methods as a way of increasing the validity and hopefully the outcome of that research. It discusses the relative value of reports gleaned from both active (non-apprehended) and imprisoned offenders. It reviews developments in our understanding of autobiographical memory and how this can help us in our quest for more reliable data from offenders. It ends with some innovative ideas about how we can take offender-based research forward.

The emphasis of our current debate is on the extent to which we can increase the veracity of what offenders tell us. I would argue that offenders are human beings, subject to the same limitations of memory as any individual, but equally influenced by the methods we have learnt to enhance memory. The grounded approach to research on residential burglary that has prevailed in the last 30 years has encouraged a triangulation of various methodologies and has certainly aided us in incorporating existing memory-enhancing techniques and discovering new ones. This will be the focus of this chapter. I will begin with a brief overview of grounded approaches to offender-based work and review the research on residential burglary within that paradigm. I will look at the debate surrounding the relative value of data gleaned from convicted offenders in comparison to active offenders and I will point to the remarkable consistency in the findings gleaned from a whole variety of samples and methodologies in the residential burglary field. I will then turn to an examination of the parameters of autobiographical memory and how techniques which have emerged in our offender-based research can complement these strictures well. I will describe some memory-enhancing techniques developed over the last two decades and how all of these can help us in our quest for more accurate data, including life-events calendars and lessons learnt from the cognitive interview (Fisher and Geiselman 1992). I will end with a description of some planned new work which will bring together expertise in context-reinstatement using laptop simulations and may resolve the long-standing discussion over the use of active versus incarcerated offenders in research.

An overview of a 'grounded' approach to offender-based data collection

In the late 1960s, Glaser and Strauss (1967) put forward their description of 'grounded theory' as a method for conducting social research in which the emphasis is strongly placed on the 'actor' or 'agent' of the behaviour in question. Instead of generating hypotheses in isolation, away from the environment in which the behaviour of interest happens, they encourage the researcher to embroil themselves in that environment and allow the 'expert' in that behaviour to set the research agenda. In this way, they argue that the inquiry remains grounded in the reality of the expert and allows us much greater insight into the perceptions, understandings and decision-making of that agent. As work progresses, stages of increased methodological sophistication occur resulting in greater and greater theoretical elaboration and insight into the reality of the social cognition and behaviour of that agent.

In the grounded approach to data collection where crime is the focus of attention, importance should be placed on the offender's involvement in the formulation of the basic research questions. They should be involved in every subsequent stage of methodological refinement until 'theoretical elaboration' is reached (Glaser and Strauss 1967). In this way, the researcher can be confident that the inquiry begins and remains as relevant, valid and reliable as possible. In the preliminary, exploratory stages of research one should fully involve the 'experts' in the behaviour under scrutiny. Pilot work (e.g. focus groups) can be undertaken with basic topic guides so that terminology and other cultural parameters relevant to the group involved are identified and research questions are developed by participants. Hypotheses should be judged as pertinent to the offenders as they are to the research team. Once this stage is complete, researchers can begin preliminary data collection with a broader sample of offenders, be they active or incarcerated. Ideally, a loosely structured approach is still advisable at these early stages of the investigation. This might involve semi-structured or qualitative interviews. Prudence at this stage will allow the offender and not the researcher to sharpen the focus of the inquiry.

At this stage the researcher should be reasonably confident about the validity and focus of their inquiry, having had feedback and endorsement from a reasonably large group of offenders. They can now embark on refining the sophistication of their methodology, perhaps testing out the reliability of offenders' verbal reports by observing behaviour, though the latter is rarely possible in the area of offending behaviour. 'Proxy' observational methods, however, have been successfully undertaken in a variety of ways in offender-based research. These have included simulations using maps, slides, photographs, videos and point light displays (Bennett and Wright 1984; Rengert and Wasilchick 1986; Nee and Taylor 2000; Topalli 2005) and quasi-participant observation at scenes of recent crimes (Carroll and Weaver 1986, Cromwell *et al.* 1991; Wright and Decker 1994, 1997).

As well as evaluating hypotheses, each investigation typically results in new puzzles generated by the offender who will judge issues and environments differently from the researcher (as we will see below in the discussion of expertise). A triangulation of different research methods can be used to ascertain the validity of our findings (Brewer and Hunter 1989), all the while allowing us to get closer and closer to the 'truth' of our inquiry, understanding the actual behaviour of the offender at work. This is Glaser and Strauss's (1967) final stage, that of 'theoretical elaboration'. In a perfect world, researchers should aim to go through these stages many times within one programme of research. Realistically though, it is more often the case that separate studies build on and extend previous pieces of work in the same vein.

Nowhere can this be seen more clearly than in research on residential burglary since the 1970s (Nee 2003). One of the most thoroughly investigated types of offending behaviour at the scene of the crime, each study has employed the offender as the expert in creating the next set of hypotheses. Each subsequent research study has built on the previous findings and has in turn, using increasingly sophisticated methodologies, allowed the offender to extend the line of inquiry, contributing to clear theoretical elaboration in our understanding of this criminal activity.

This research has been reviewed many times before (e.g. Nee and Meenaghan 2006; Nee 2003, 2004; Nee and Taylor 2000). Suffice it to say here that previously I have aimed to show how tranches of work can be characterised by Glaser and Strauss's stages of grounded research. Early North American work (Scarr 1973; Shover 1973; Repetto 1974; Waller and Okihiro 1978) could be seen as the exploratory, 'pilot' stage that set the agenda from which the more focused, crime-prevention work grew on both sides of the Atlantic: interview studies (Maguire and Bennett 1982) and quasi-experimental work using videos, maps and slides (Bennett and Wright 1984; Rengert and Wasilchick 1986; Nee and Taylor 1988). We can already see the development in methodology from semi-structured to more focused interviews and the beginnings of the use of visual stimuli such as videos, photographs, maps and slides. We know that asking questions in interview – even the most open-ended – may result in a cued response reflecting the interviewer's pre-conceptions (Oppenheim 2001). Ideally we should be observing the offender's actual offending behaviour in order to move away from researcher-led interpretations, but this has obvious ethical and safety issues. In our context, the use of visual stimuli in a free-responding paradigm is a significant move towards observing something closer to actual behaviour that has not been cued verbally.

Taylor and Nee (1988) and Nee and Taylor (2000) moved the research forward by comparing the responses of burglars to householders in relation to their simulated residential neighbourhood, finding burglars to be considerably more systematic in their approach to the task. Work continued to grow in this new direction (extended, of course, by the offenders) which aimed to explore more closely the cognitive mechanisms underlying the decisions made by offenders. It involved experiments using recognition memory (Logie et al. 1992) and daring ethnographic interviews at the scenes of recent crimes (Cromwell et al. 1991; Wright and Decker 1994). The sophistication of our methods of inquiry clearly increased over time and continues to increase (see later). With this has come a remarkable insight into the workings of the burglar's decision-making processes, and theoretical elaboration. However, as Glaser and Strauss (1967) would agree, burglars, like all human beings, are adaptable and cognitively dynamic, and further work will always need to be done. It is important to remember, too, that as well as the exciting new methods that have been employed over recent years, excellent data has been gained using traditional interviewing methods and I will argue that the triangulation of methods used has proved in fact that each method, if done effectively, is a valid means of data collection.

Incarcerated versus active offenders

The ethnographers working more recently in the field (Wright and Decker 1994; Cromwell et al. 1991) have cast doubt on the validity of prison-based work indicating that the latter is based on the reports of 'failed' criminals, who are reconstructing criminal events from at least months to possibly years ago, probably in a biased manner, under the limits of autobiographical memory (see below), and in a barren and hostile environment (the prison). While these arguments are justifiable, I would contest that most offenders are acquisitive offenders, who indulge in a high-rate mix of property-oriented crime (Tarling 1993) and are therefore likely to serve some time in prison at some point in their careers. Therefore, realistically it is only a matter of time before the active criminals with limited experience of the criminal justice system who have taken part in the ethnographic interviewing studies might become the prison-based offenders of other studies. Further, many prison-based studies (including all the research I have undertaken) do not rely only on offenders *convicted* of residential burglary to participate in their studies. Over half of the burglars used in the Nee and Taylor studies were serving prison sentences for other crimes and were recommended as experienced burglars by prison personnel and other offenders. In this case then, they are not 'failed' burglars.

Linked to this, it could be argued that the snowball samples typical of ethnographic interview studies are not representative of 'average' residential burglars but reflect burglars typical of the geographical area and culture from which they were drawn. Their views on their behaviour are nonetheless a valuable and interesting reflection of that culture, and it is important to note that sentencing bias affects which classes and cultures are sent to prison (e.g. Phillips and Bowling 2003). Still, it could be said that participants found in prisons will represent a more generalisable profile of behaviour, drawn from a much broader range of cultures, behaviours and environments than those of a snowball sample.

Other authors (e.g. Jacques and Wright this volume) argue that active offenders (unlike those in custody) typically receive payment for their participation in research and that this inherently guarantees better quality data. I do not accept the latter argument. Firstly, the payment is merely a token – a fraction of what they would 'earn' in the same amount of time spent on a criminal activity, so this is unlikely to be a strong motivation to participate and more to do with a gesture of respect from the researchers. Secondly, active offenders are more likely to be irritated by the amount of time the research process is keeping them away from their more lucrative criminal activities. In comparison, prison-based offenders have plenty of time at their disposal, are often bored and have less to lose (and possibly something to gain morally) by engaging in the research. Thirdly, active offenders are more likely to have an acute drug dependence than an offender in prison – another reason why they may be less cooperative during the data-gathering process than their incarcerated counterparts. I would suggest then that there are compromises associated with both types of samples. What is gained through the superior environment in research with active offenders may be more than equalled by the greater patience and commitment of the offender in custody, especially if memory-enhancing techniques are utilised in the custodial context.

Finally, it is certainly worth pointing out that, while interviewing offenders at recent scenes of crimes is significantly more ecologically valid (with its wealth of real visual cues relevant to the decision to burgle) than interviewing in prison, it is still *interviewing*. Ethnographic interviewing of the type employed in burglary studies does not observe real behaviour and, as such, is still subject to the limitations of memory described below. One could suggest that a sophisticated simulation (undertaken in prison or otherwise), in which the participant responds freely to a realistic environment, may be closer to observing actual behaviour and therefore of equal ecological validity than simply interviewing an individual about their earlier behaviour at the scene of the crime.

Consistency as a measure of reliability and validity in research

It is difficult, if we have no 'ground truth' – no concrete documentation or evidence of what really happened – to ever prove which study, which sample or which methodology allows us to get closest in our understanding of the actual behaviour of the offender. Thus it is important that we employ as much as we can in terms of memory enhancing strategies and environments as resources allow when we set about our studies. However, there is one striking feature about the findings regarding all of the research that has been done on residential burglars which points to the underlying reliability and validity of the data collected. That is the remarkable consistency of response gained from the many and diverse samples of burglars that have been studied, no matter what research method has been used (Nee and Taylor 2000). Three areas of consistency can be highlighted by research to date.

Firstly, there has been great concurrence among burglars regarding the sequential nature of the decision-making that leads to the commission of burglary at the scene of the crime for most burglars. 'Searchers', a term coined by Bennett and Wright (1984) and adopted by Nee and Taylor (1988), Taylor and Nee (1988) and Nee and Meenaghan (2006), or 'journeymen' as described by Cromwell *et al.* (1991), characterise the vast majority of samples studied regarding the chain of decisions that results in offending. Burglars decide to commit the burglary away from the scene of the crime when funds are likely to run out in the not-too-distant future. They will find their way to a vulnerable geographical area spotted during daily routine activities or previously victimised, and tend to pick their targets at this point, based on the array of cues available at potential scenes of crimes. Most burglars, be they British, Irish or American, black, white or mixed-race, drug-dependent or not, exercise skill and experience in choosing targets and do not respond to opportunities completely indiscriminately (Bennett and Wright 1984; Wright and Decker 1994; Nee and Meenaghan 2006).

Secondly, remarkably similar findings have been found in relation to the environmental cues burglars use to select targets at or near the scene of the eventual crime. Relative gain is one of the foremost considerations in the offender's mind, with cues such as decor, size of property and cars parked outside reflecting the relative reward inside. These cues are usually mediated by cues signifying the ease of access into the property, such as position on street, cover, access to rear, etc. Burglars prefer properties to be empty, though this will be contingent upon the level of choice in the neighbourhood (i.e. if the only worthwhile house in the locality has sleeping occupants, this will not deter the burglar). Low visibility is important to the vast majority of burglars; alarms and dogs are conditional deterrents; and levels of security always afford the least amount of consideration (as they are usually surmountable and house-holders are consistently lax in their approach to security (Nee and Meenaghan 2006)). These findings have been similar across many, many studies of residential burglars. They discount notions of the burglar as an opportunistic, indiscriminate, unskilled individual. In contrast, we see an offender who (at least in relation to the crime he commits) demonstrates a practised expertise in selecting targets commensurate with the bounded rationality Cornish and Clarke (1982) described in *The Reasoning Criminal*.

If results are so consistent, with hindsight should we now bother with increasing the sophistication of our inquiries, embarking on expensive simulations or dangerous ethnographic interviews, when we could simply interview burglars in prison? Indeed we must as each subsequent study and change in methodology has thrown further light and given greater detail regarding the knowledge that has gone before. In true 'grounded' fashion, the expert agent (the offender) has enriched and extended the inquiry with each piece of research and revealed other paths of inquiry to explore and triangulate using contrasting methodologies. As well as complementing and consolidating the prison-based work, the later ethno-graphic work importantly extended our knowledge by revealing data on drug use patterns in burglars (Cromwell *et al.* 1991) and the habitual behaviour of burglars once inside the property (Wright and Decker 1994).

This leads to the third area of consistency that is currently emerging: that of burglars' cognitive processing and resulting behaviour once inside the target they have chosen. Wright and Decker (1994) were the first to explore the decision-making and behaviour of the burglar once inside his target, a neglected area which clearly has significant crime-prevention spin-offs. As part of an ethnographic interview study involving 105 active burglars at the scenes of recent crimes, Wright and Decker (1994) shed new light on the sophisticated cognitive mechanisms employed by burglars undertaking a burglary. Similar to the virtually habitual pro-cesses drawn on to select a target, burglars reported using tried and tested navigational strategies in order to execute the burglary with maximum gain and minimum time, effort, anxiety and risk. The authors termed these processes 'cognitive scripts' similar to the obligatory mental pro-cesses described by Logan (1988) in his discussion of the automatic

237

perception and decision-making in experts. We discovered from this study that the vast majority of these burglars generally used one habitual route, going straight to the main bedroom to locate cash, jewellery, guns and other small valuable items and then engaging in a short, superficial search of the downstairs rooms, exiting the property within minutes of entering.

Though groundbreaking, this research needed replicating, and preferably in a different country and culture. Nee and Meenaghan (2006) employed a simple interview study with 50 convicted, experienced burglars and a focus on behaviour inside the property from a UK perspective. Using a dramatically different methodology involving a simple semi-structured interview and despite a prison-based, largely white and less drug-dependent sample, they found remarkably similar findings. Participants clearly described the use of habitual, automatic scripts which were used to help navigate the burglar around the property in the fastest time and with the maximum reward. Work to further illuminate the cognitive mechanisms used inside the burglar's target will be described at the end of this chapter. But suffice it to say here that prison-based work should plainly not be discounted as less reliable, if conducted sensitively and with an understanding of the limits of autobiographical recall. Indeed there is no alternative to prison-based research in cases of less usual or less accessible types of crime (e.g. sex offending, domestic violence) in which active offenders would simply be too difficult (and possibly too risky for the researcher) to track down and engage in research.

In terms of theoretical elaboration, Nee and Meenaghan (2006) made strong links between burglars' decision-making and the concept of perceptual expertise as described extensively in the mainstream cognitive psychology literature. According to their research, burglars, like experts in many other domains, employ cognitive processing that appears removed from explicit deliberation when undertaking their specialist behaviour, in this case a crime. In comparison to novices (e.g. householders, students, etc.) information processing is speedy and methodical, recognises relevant stimuli virtually instantaneously and allows enough spare processing space to afford multi-tasking. Extending our understanding of explicit (and in this case criminal) behaviours through generic and mainstream theory in this way not only affords us a richer and more versatile explanation of offending behaviour, but also increases our chances of finding more effective prevention, intervention and rehabilitation techniques. The triangulation of many different methods of research has led us to these findings over a number of years.

I suggest that all of these findings accumulate into clear evidence of a routine, bounded rationality in relation to the commission of crime, which Cornish and Clarke (1986) spoke of in the mid-1980s. Adopting an econometric model of human behaviour, Rational Choice Theory in their iteration explains behaviour at the scene of the crime not as a cold, cost-benefit analysis of pros and cons, but as driven by the kind of habitual, previously successful decision-making that guides the majority of all human behaviour. Further, the automatic, instantaneous recognition of cues exhibited by the practised, seasoned burglars in Nee and Meenaghan's (2006) study fit well with this overall explanation of offending behaviour at the scene of the crime.

All of the methods described above, however, except perhaps conducting research in simulated environments, are subject to the limits of autobiographical memory and it is wise to revisit what we know from mainstream cognitive psychology once more and bear these findings in mind when designing research.

The limits of autobiographical (or 'episodic') memory: seven important facts to remember when studying offending behaviour

In 1987, Bradburn *et al.* published their excellent review of research evidence on the effects of memory in remembering autobiographical sequences, still considered the cornerstone work in this field. Some of the salient findings emanating from this review are as follows. When asked a question about the *incidence* of particular events over a protracted period of time, individuals rely on fragmented memories about the past and make inferences and approximations based on this. They do not utilise a clear, quantitative strategy of recall to answer the question. There is greater room for *overestimation* when numerous very similar incidents (e.g. persistent offences) are recalled – multiple occurrences are likely to be 'telescoped' into greater numbers of events and telescoped forwards in time to have happened nearer the present time. Further, some *types* of information are remembered far more readily than others. For instance, memories about the critical details of meaningful daily events can be accessed more easily than, for instance, street names in a familiar area. Offence-related data is likely to fall into the meaningful event category and indeed there is evidence that it can be readily accessed when contextual cues are put in place. We group autobiographical events into overarching *autobiographical sequences* (such as 'the Christmas period' or 'last semester'). *Over 70 per cent* of a whole range of life's details can be remembered accurately for up to two years if cued correctly (in their case, asking the right context-enhancing questions). *Proxy reporting* (e.g. a parent for a child) can be highly correlated with self-reporting if carried with knowledge of the limits of recall.

Work generated from this review (e.g. Sudman *et al.* 1996) on improving autobiographical memory indicates that researchers should try to involve *retrieval cues* compatible with memory whenever possible. Visual stimuli is particularly useful, and the slides and maps used in the residential simulations of Nee and Taylor (2000), the videos employed by Bennett and Wright (1984) and the naturalistic visual cues of the 'in-situ' ethnographic interviews (e.g. Wright and Decker 1994) fit neatly into this model of memory. These methods readily invoke the images, contexts and emotions that draw out the instantaneous 'exemplar' memories (Logan 1988; Waagenar 1986) that all experienced agents rely on in decision-making – in our case, burglars. If feasible to incorporate, any of the methods in this array of possibilities will result in a clear pay-off in terms of the quality of the data we can yield and, therefore, what we learn from the offender.

Two further important areas of contribution associated with these findings and memory-enhancing techniques in general are life-events calendars and the cognitive interview.

The life-events calendar (LEC) was developed for collecting retrospective psychiatric (Freedman *et al.* 1988) and other data, and has been used with offenders most notably by Julie Horney and her colleagues (Roberts *et al.* 2005; Horney 2001). All of these studies have shown it to be a robust and effective tool for collecting detailed data about events and sequences of events and superior in collecting accurate information to simple questioning. One study, comparing the LEC with weekly interviews (Roberts *et al.* 2005) found the LEC to be less efficient in accurately identifying violent incidents over a three-year period. One could predict, however, that this would be the case given such a stringent test. If one had the resources to undertake weekly interviews with large samples of offenders then these would be likely to result in superior data due to their far lighter demand on retrospective memory. If, alternatively, one has to limit data collection to one or two sessions per participant, one could predict much more reliable and valid data from the use of an LEC than straightforward interviewing.

The technique involves the following stages. First, the basic contextual features of an individual's life are recorded on the calendar such as living circumstances, employment, custody, etc. Other significant life events (gleaned during pilot work) are then plotted beneath this, such as illnesses, sports fixtures, etc. Once the basic context of recent life has been plotted, participants then find it easier to more accurately locate in time periods of criminal activity, alcohol and drug use, problems with relationships, etc. The 'mnemonics' or memory-enhancing features of the life-events calendar helps to provide a much richer picture of an individual's circumstances and offending than free recall alone. Lewis and Mhlanga (2001) compared free recall with data collected on a life-events calendar for the same period with 2,000 UK prisoners. The use of the calendar significantly reduced the overestimation and telescoping forward of criminal events characteristic of the free-recall phase which Bradburn *et al.* (1987) would have predicted. Like many of the methods described here, however, it is difficult to fully test the effectiveness of the LEC with the offenders in the absence of 'ground truth'. It is worth remembering though that in its original form the responses gleaned using the LEC correlated very highly with official psychiatric data and one can only deduce from this that it is very likely to enhance memory to some extent. Both Julie Horney and I are convinced, after years of interviewing offenders using different methods, that introducing a cognitively complex task which thoroughly engages and distracts the offender (such as a calendar or an experiment) increases the veracity of what is reported. The offender forgets to exaggerate or produce an overly negative or positive story. He becomes engrossed in the task and often changes his story, as Lewis and Mhlanga (2001) found.

Other lessons can be learned about interview technique from the major field of research on witness testimony, in particular that of 'cognitive' interviewing (Fisher and Geiselman 1992). A wealth of evidence indicates that four mnemonic techniques employed during interviewing significantly improve the recall of witnessed events (see Dando *et al.* 2008 for a review) and there is no reason why these should not work when interviewing compliant offenders. These include: an initial free recall phase listing most recent events first and working backwards; context reinstatement – describing the whole environment – physical, emotional and situational; encouraging and reinforcing the recall of isolated pieces of information, even if they seem irrelevant to the interviewee; and finally working backwards and forwards from well-remembered sequences of events.

Future research

I would like to end the chapter by describing some planned research which will arguably raise the level of offender-based methodology to its most sophisticated level yet. Richard Wright, Amy Meenaghan and myself, together with colleagues in the creative technologies field, are designing a virtual environment – a laptop simulation – of an array of terraced houses which can be 'entered' and explored inside as if undertaking a burglary. This will allow us to empirically test what burglars on both sides of the Atlantic have said regarding their behaviour once inside a property during interviews. It will also afford a further empirical test of expertise and spatial navigation between burglars and other populations as follows. The first phase will be based in the UK. The research will involve the comparison of prison-based male burglars with matched prisoners who have little or no experience of burglary and with a further group of males in the general population with no history of offending, matched on educational and socio-economic background. The non-burgling prisoners will represent a more stringent test of expertise than comparison with non-offenders alone, in common with Logie *et al.*'s

(1992) groundbreaking work on expertise in young burglars. We predict that burglars will explore the simulated environment with greater ease, speed and efficiency than others. We expect their navigation strategies and patterns to be different, resulting in speedier response and greater 'reward' than comparison groups. We expect the non-burglary-experienced offenders to be more proficient on all of these factors than the non-offending controls, and less proficient than the experienced burglars. In phase 2 we plan to repeat the study with active offenders in the United States and include female burglars. The latter are rare and very difficult to access in the prison population but should be more accessible in the 'active-offending' arena. This will allow us to look at any differences (or otherwise!) emerging from the data of active offenders in comparison to imprisoned offenders and also allow us insight into the approach taken by females in terms of their expertise and spatial navigation.

Developing simulations of scenes of crimes may change the way we think about and undertake offender-based research in the future. We must, however, proceed with caution for a variety of reasons. The considerable advantage of a simulated crime is that it will allow us as researchers to observe the behaviour and verbalised decision-making of the offender. However, to what extent is the offender aware, or able to articulate his thought processes and cognitions as he undertakes his task? While the free-responding nature of the procedure should remove the subtle coercion of false explanations of actions that interviewing may produce (Elffers this volume), the latter author highlights the fact that the offender, engaged in fairly habitual behaviour, may not normally have access to the underlying reasons that drive his behaviour. Indeed, if 'automaticity' characterises the thought processes of the expert burglar (Nee and Meenghan 2006), how far will the research participant be able to access these unconscious processes?

How can cognitive psychology help us with these serious questions? In their development of a protocol to analyse human verbalisations about the tasks we undertake, Ericsson and Simon (1996) have undertaken and reviewed copious amounts of research in which participants have been asked to 'think aloud' while undertaking a huge variety of tasks. To support Elffers and others, they purport that verbalisations in our research contexts do *not* describe the underlying cognitive process, but the information that comes into consciousness at the end of the thought process. By comparing 'think-aloud' techniques with silent procedures and retrospective verbalisations, they conclude that think-aloud procedures produce meaningful information of at least a subset of thoughts attended to when asked to verbalise what you are doing. That is 'the end products of perception and retrieval from long-term memory that reach attention' (p. xxxv). Importantly, performance on a task does not change, whether one verbalises what one is doing or one is silent about it. It does, not surprisingly, slow down our performance a little, however.

Straighforward, 'think-aloud' verbalisations *will not* tell you how and why the information in that thought was attended to enough to be verbalised. Further, if you ask someone to explain their verbalisations, another set of cognitive processes are put into play which *do* interfere with performance and take us another step away from naturalistic behaviour. Therefore, to keep methods as ecologically valid as possible, explanations for actions should not be sought until after the free-responding exploration of an environment is complete.

It seems then we can legitimately illuminate some of the more conscious cognitive processes involved in the undertaking of a burglary by asking participants to think aloud during a simulated burglary. It would be naïve and erroneous though to suggest that responses to simulated criminogenic environments could uncover the unconscious thoughts and motivations of the offender that even he is unlikely to have access to. Information we will glean from these proposed studies will help us to solve more of the puzzle by allowing us access to the more conscious, spontaneous verbalisations, appraisals and decisions at the scene of the crime. As humans, we must accept that we are all limited in our ability to describe our performance in the world at large, but nevertheless comparisons of the burglars' verbalisations with other offenders and non-offenders will be compelling.

To sum up, in this chapter I have looked at the value of employing a grounded approach to research, and supplied evidence that a whole range of research methods are valid and reliable especially if conducted with integrity and an acknowledgment of how our memories work. As a result of this I would hope that the chapter has two strong 'take-home' messages. Firstly, there is doubtlessly room and valuable information to be gleaned by using as many different methods as possible when designing research and that this should be encouraged in order to assess the veracity and consistency of what the offender is telling us. Secondly, I hope I have thoroughly discounted the argument that 'active' offenders are indisputably superior in terms of the insight they give us as researchers to prison-based offenders. I would argue that both are equally compromised by a variety of confounding factors, but both are also equally valuable regarding what they can tell us. To continue with this distinction is illogical and anti-research.

References

Bennett, T. and Wright, R. (1984) *Burglars on Burglary*. Aldershot: Gower.

Bradburn, N. M., Rips, L. J. and Shevell, S. K. (1987) 'Answering autobiographical questions: the impact of memory and inference on surveys', *Science*, 236: 157–61.

Brewer, J. and Hunter, A. (1989) *Multimethod Research: A Synthesis of Styles*. Newbury Park, CA: Sage.

Carroll, F. and Weaver, J. (1986) 'Shoplifters' perceptions of crime opportunities: process-tracing study', in D. Cornish and R. V. G. Clarke (eds), *The Reasoning Criminal*. New York: Springer-Verlag, pp. 19–31.

Cornish, D. and Clarke, R. V. G. (eds) (1986) *The Reasoning Criminal*. New York: Springer-Verlag.

Cromwell, P., Olson, J. and Avary, D. (1991) *Breaking and Entering: An Ethnographic Analysis of Burglary*. Newbury Park, CA: Sage.

Dando, C., Wilcock, R. and Milne, R. (2008) 'The cognitive interview: the efficacy of a modified mental reinstatement of context procedure for frontline police investigators', *Applied Cognitive Psychology*, 23: 138–47.

Ericsson, K. and Simon, H. (1996) *Protocol Analysis: Verbal Reports as Data*. Cambridge, MA: Massachusetts Institute of Technology.

Fisher, R. F. and Geiselman, R. E. (1992) *Memory-Enhancing Techniques for Investigative Interviewing*. Springfield, IL: Charles Thomas.

Freedman, D., Thornton, A., Camburn, D., Alwin, D. and Young-DeMarco, L. (1988) 'The life history calendar: a technique for collecting retrospective data', *Sociological Methodology*, 18: 37–68.

Glaser, B. and Strauss, A. L. (1967) *The Discovery of Grounded Theory*. Chicago: Aldine.

Horney, J. (2001) 'Criminal events and criminal careers', in R. Meier, L. Kennedy and V. Sacco (eds), *The Process and Structure of Crime: Criminal Events and Crime Analysis*. New Brunswick, NJ: Transaction Publishers.

Lewis, D. and Mhlanga, B. (2001) 'A life of crime: the hidden truth behind criminal activity', *International Journal of Market Research*, 43 (2): 217–40.

Logan, G. (1988) 'Toward an instance theory of automatization', *Psychological Review*, 95: 492–527.

Logie, R. H., Wright, R. and Decker, S. (1992) 'Recognition memory performance and residential burglary', *Applied Cognitive Psychology*, 6: 109–23.

Maguire, E. M. W. and Bennett, T. (1982) *Burglary in a Dwelling: The Offence, the Offender and the Victim*. London: Heinneman Educational.

Nee, C. (2003) 'Burglary research at the end of the millennium: an example of grounded theory?', *Security Journal*, 16 (3): 37–44.

Nee, C. (2004) 'The offender's perspective on crime: methods and principles in data collection', in A. Needs and G. Towl (eds), *Applying Psychology to Forensic Practice*. London: BPS Blackwell.

Nee, C. and Meenaghan, A. (2006) 'Expert decision-making in burglars', *British Journal of Criminology*, 46: 935–49.

Nee, C. and Taylor, M. (1988) 'Residential burglary in the Republic of Ireland: a situational perspective', *Howard Journal*, 27 (2): 105–16.

Nee, C. and Taylor, M. (2000) 'Examining burglars' target selection: interview, experiment, or ethnomethodology?', *Psychology, Crime and Law*, 6 (1): 45–59.

Oppenheim, A. N. (2001) *Questionnaire Design, Interviewing and Attitude Measurement*. New York: Continuum.

Phillips, C. and Bowling, B. (2003) 'Racism, ethnicity and criminology: developing minority perspectives', *British Journal of Criminology*, 43: 269–90.

Rengert, G. and Wasilchick, J. (1986) *Suburban Burglary: A Time and a Place for Everything*. Chicago: Springfield.

Repetto, T. A. (1974) *Residential Crime*. Cambridge, MA: Ballinger.

Roberts, J., Mulvey, E., Horney, J., Lewis, J. and Arter, M. (2005) 'A test of two methods of recall for violent events', *Journal of Quantitative Criminology*, 21: 175–93.

Scarr, H. A. (1973) *Patterns of Burglary*. Washington, DC: Government Printing Office.

Shover, N. (1973) 'The social organisation of burglary', *Social Problems*, 20: 499–514.

Sudman, S., Bradburn, N. M. and Schwarz, N. (eds) (1996) *Thinking About Answers: The Application of Cognitive Processes to Survey Methodology*. San Francisco: Jossey-Bass.

Tarling, R. (1993) *Analysing Offending: Data, Models and Interpretations*. London: HMSO.

Taylor, M. and Nee, C. (1988) 'The role of cues in simulated residential burglary', *British Journal of Criminology*, 28 (3): 396–401.

Topalli, V. (2005) 'Criminal expertise and offender decision-making: an experimental analysis of how offenders and non-offenders differentially perceive social stimuli', *British Journal of Criminology*, 45: 269–95.

Wagenaar, W. A. (1986) 'My memory: a study of autobiographical memory over six years', *Cognitive Psychology*, 18: 225–52.

Waller, I. and Okihiro, N. (1978) *Burglary: The Victim and the Public*. Toronto: University of Toronto Press.

Wright, R. T. and Decker, S. (1994) *Burglars on the Job: Streetlife and Residential Break-ins*. Boston: Northeastern University Press.

Wright, R. T. and Decker, S. (1997) *Armed Robbers in Action*. Boston: Northeastern University Press.

Chapter 14

The use of maps in offender interviewing

Lucía Summers, Shane D. Johnson and George F. Rengert

Abstract

This chapter provides a discussion of the use of two different types of mapping tasks in offender interviews, namely sketch and cartographic maps. The methodological issues associated with their use are discussed and examples of their application in previous studies presented. To provide a more concrete example of how they may be used together to examine a specific research hypothesis, illustrative findings from a recent study concerned with the spatial decision-making of property offenders are presented. The use of maps in offender interviews is associated with a number of problems, but we argue that they are beneficial and help to elicit information that otherwise might not be revealed.

Introduction

Different approaches to data collection and analysis offer different insights into phenomena under investigation. In the case of offender decision-making, the use of offender interviews has provided understanding that could not be uncovered through other means (e.g. see Rengert and Wasilchick 2000; Wright and Decker 1994). In addition to simply asking offenders about their decision-making, researchers have used a variety of tasks to better understand offender cognition. For example, to explore offenders' attention to and the use of perceptual cues, Logie *et al.* (1992) showed offenders and non-offenders a series of photographs of possible burglary targets. Both groups were asked to identify the characteristics of the houses that would be attractive to a burglar, after which they were asked to complete an unexpected recognition test. For the recognition test, they were shown the same photos but for half of the original photos some of the physical features of the homes had been changed. Not only did the offenders show greater awareness of the cues presented in the first half of the task, they were also better at identifying those cues that had been altered (also see Cromwell *et al.* 1991; Nee 2003; Nee and Meenaghan 2006; Nee and Taylor 2000; Taylor and Nee 1988).

Of course, the particular task used should be informed by the hypotheses under investigation or the cognitive process(es) of interest. In this chapter we examine offender spatial targeting decisions for property offences and describe two mapping tasks that were used – in concert with semi-structured interviews – to examine this.

The chapter proceeds as follows. We start by briefly reviewing the existing literature in relation to the elements of spatial cognition and decision-making of interest and the options for their measurement, with an emphasis on sketch and cartographic maps. In the second part of the chapter, these issues are illustrated with findings from a recent study. Finally, we discuss the relative usefulness of sketch and cartographic maps as instruments for examining spatial cognition and decision-making, referring to the existing literature and our own research experience.

Maps as data-gathering instruments

During the last few decades, researchers have repeatedly employed map-related tasks to assess participants' geographical knowledge. The measurement of such knowledge is important in that it guides decisions people make about whether to stay or go, where to go, which route to take (Cadwallader 1976) and how to get there (Garling *et al.* 1985). *Cognitive mapping* describes the processes by which 'an individual acquires, stores, recalls, and decodes information about the relative locations and attributes of the phenomena in his everyday spatial environment' (Downs and Stea 1973: 9). Cognitive maps, therefore, influence our exposure to the environment, which in turn further develops the cognitive maps, making this a dynamic, iterative process. Analyses of representations of people's 'cognitive maps' can provide insight into spatial decision-making and the behaviour that follows from these decisions.

Sketch maps are free-hand drawn maps that are assumed to represent a person's knowledge of his/her physical environment. Kevin Lynch (1960) pioneered this procedure when he asked participants to create drawings of the city they lived in. He classified the elements of these maps into five separate categories, namely nodes, paths, edges, districts and landmarks. Nodes refer to any specific point locations in a map; examples are the home, school, workplaces, recreation sites such as shopping centres and, in the case of offenders, crime locations. Paths are the routes between these nodes and usually take the form of streets, railway lines, etc. Edges

247

are the boundaries that separate areas which differ in relation to factors such as ethnic composition or land use (e.g. commercial vs residential, rural vs urban). Districts are areas of considerable size within a map that have a unique set of characteristics. Finally, landmarks are special types of nodes that are used as reference or navigational points.

In contrast to sketch maps, *cartographic maps* are actual maps of a specific geographical area. The level and type of detail provided in the map (e.g. outlines of streets, physical barriers such as rivers, landmarks such as hospitals and so on) will vary according to the scale of resolution used (i.e. maps with a small scale should provide the most detail of local features), but with the availability of geographical information systems (GIS) and good map data the cartographer can also easily choose which features to show and which to omit. When presented with such a map, participants are invited to draw on it to indicate (for example) the areas with which they are familiar, their movement patterns and the features of the environment that influence their spatial decisions.

Something of an analogy may be drawn between these two mapping tasks and the type of questions being asked in an a more typical interview, with sketch maps being the equivalent of open-ended questions and cartographic maps analogous to closed-ended ones. Cartographic maps have been used much less frequently than sketch maps, and this will be reflected in the review of the literature that follows, but as we will later discuss, they offer considerable advantages over sketch maps in the investigation of offender spatial awareness.

The measurement of spatial cognition and decision-making

Within the domain of spatial cognition and decision-making, at least three phenomena can be studied, namely the participants' levels of awareness of specific geographical areas, their movements (e.g. distances and routes travelled) and their activity patterns (e.g. distribution of offence locations). These three phenomena, as well as how they can be measured, are examined in detail in the next section.

Spatial awareness

As described above, it is the amount and quality of knowledge stored in individuals' cognitive maps that determine their level of awareness or familiarity with specific geographical areas and, in turn, influence spatial decision-making. Therefore the first step in trying to understand these decision-making processes is to identify offenders' awareness spaces, that is the areas they are familiar with.

According to crime pattern theory (e.g. Brantingham and Brantingham 2008), offenders tend to identify crime opportunities within their awareness spaces. Evidence for this is provided by ethnographic and interview research which has shown that offenders prefer to operate in those areas with which they are the most familiar and do so even when they are aware of alternative targets in other neighbourhoods (Potchak *et al.* 2002; Rengert and Wasilchick 2000; Rengert *et al.* 1999; Repetto 1974).

Offenders can define and expand their awareness spaces in different ways, either through routine activities of the offender's day-to-day life (Cohen and Felson 1979), the active spatial exploration of unknown areas (i.e. in preparation for future offending in such an area), or through secondary sources (e.g. media, other offenders). Past research has suggested that spatial exploration is rare for criminals; instead, they prefer to operate in familiar territory defined by their routine activities (Rengert and Wasilchick 2000).

Levels of spatial awareness can be inferred by the drawing style and the range and elaboration of a sketch map. According to Lynch (1960), two types of drawing styles may be observed: sequential (or linear) and spatial (or planar). In sequential maps, it is the paths between various elements in the map (e.g. nodes, landmarks) that are emphasised. In the spatial maps, emphasis is given to the nodes instead. Appleyard (1970) took this classification further and subdivided these two types of maps into additional categories, depending on the quantity and positioning of the map elements. The general assumption is that sequential maps, and particularly those where both paths and nodes are emphasised, are indicative of more extensive awareness of the area portrayed. The range and elaboration of a sketch map can also provide an indication of the level of familiarity an individual has for a particular geographical area (see Lynch 1960). For example, a sketch map which covers a large area would be interpreted as indicating that the offender has an awareness of a large geographical area. An elaborate sketch map with plenty of detail is usually taken as an indication of increased familiarity with the area being portrayed.

One problem with using sketch maps in this way lies in the assumption that elements that are omitted (or not drawn in sufficient detail) are unknown to the offender. However, there are other reasons why an offender may omit information from a sketch map (also see Elffers's chapter in this volume for a discussion of this topic in relation to self-report in general). For instance, offenders may simply not recall the information during completion of the task, despite being aware of the features, or choose not to include such information for one reason or another. Where the reason for details being excluded is unknown, this can make sketch maps difficult to study or classify (Blades 1990; Bryant 1984). This methodological difficulty is also linked to the fact that sketch maps assume a degree of drawing ability. Where this is limited, it may reduce the reliability of inferences made from the maps produced (Golledge 1976; Tobler 1976).

Other factors which may affect how well a sketch map reflects offender spatial awareness include the task instructions, materials used (e.g. paper size) and the participant's starting point on the map, which, in combination with the size of the paper provided, may limit how much information can be provided in various directions. To take a simple case, a participant could have detailed awareness of a large area but only have sufficient space on the paper provided to draw a map of a small neighbourhood.

The use of cartographic maps offers an alternative way of examining awareness that is not affected in the way described. For example, in their study of prolific residential burglars, Rengert and Wasilchick (2000) used cartographic maps to assess the offenders' awareness and perceived opportunity spaces. Participants were given a map of Delaware County, Pennsylvania, which showed the geographical boundaries of the 50 districts within the county (which was 495 km^2). The maps were blank with the only information available being the boundaries (and names) of the districts (i.e. no landmarks or street names were provided). Using an eleven-point rating scale (from 0 to 10), each burglar was asked to rate each district in terms of how familiar they were with it, and in which areas they would be most likely to commit offences.

By taking this approach, participants were required to focus both on areas they would target and those they would *not* (and the reasoning behind such decisions), how familiarity related to targeting decisions and whether consensus could be reached across offenders as to the 'best' districts for the commission of burglary offences (see Figure 14.1). Rengert and Wasilchick (2000) showed that offenders were most familiar with areas close to their home, as well as a further two neighbourhoods where the Common Pleas court and the local prison were located. The areas chosen for the commission of burglaries were those with mid-price residences just outside the offenders' home areas, which led them to conclude that distance and familiarity were important factors. It is the examination of distance travelled by offenders to commit crime that we turn to next.

Distances travelled

Analyses of crimes detected (i.e. solved) by the police generally indicate that property offenders tend not to travel far from their home location to commit crimes (Costello and Wiles 2001; Snook 2004). However, in isolation the empirical analysis of such data has limited value. One reason for this is that this type of analysis is based only on those crimes solved by the police. These may reflect a fraction of the crimes committed by offenders known to the police and may represent a biased sample of data; for example, being those easiest to detect or those within the geographical area for which the researchers have access to data.

Nearly all research exploring journey to crime patterns has used the home of the offender as the anchor point of crime journeys. The reasoning is that this is the location that the offender starts off from in the morning

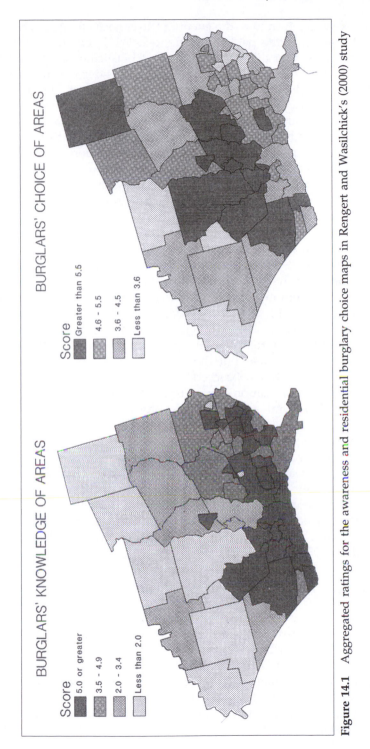

Figure 14.1 Aggregated ratings for the awareness and residential burglary choice maps in Rengert and Wasilchick's (2000) study

and is likely to return to in the evening (Rossmo 2000). As such, it is most likely to influence the pattern of offences. While ethnographic research provides support for this (e.g. Rengert and Wasilchick 2000; Rengert *et al.* 1999; Repetto 1974), it also indicates that an offender's crime sites may be clustered around alternative anchor points. For instance, the crime sites of the drug-dependent property offenders in Rengert's (1996) study tended to be clustered around the location where they purchased their drugs rather than their home locations. Information on alternative or additional anchor points can only be obtained from the offenders themselves (i.e. it is not readily available from police recorded crime data). Both sketch and cartographic maps enable offenders to provide information on these unexpected anchor points, which may be drawn on a sketch map or marked on a cartographic one.

In addition to exploring the distances offenders travel to commit crime and where their journeys actually start, researchers have also considered the accuracy of offender's perceived distances as drawn on a sketch map. For example, the relative distances between elements of a map can be examined to determine how accurate a person's spatial knowledge is (by comparing these with the actual distances) and to examine those factors that might influence distortions identified. It is assumed that routes which are perceived as shorter than the actual distances are those that are favoured by an offender, but the question of interest is what is it that generates the distortions observed?

The subjective evaluation (perception) of distance has been determined to vary with several aspects of the physical and social environment referred to as the 'backcloth' (Brantingham and Brantingham 1991). Concerning the physical environment, distances tend to be perceived as longer than they actually are if the journey involves several turns rather than being a linear path (Sadalla and Magel 1980). Distances toward the centre of the city tend to be perceived as further than the same distance toward the suburbs (Briggs 1973; Golledge and Zannaras 1973). Finally, paths that include obstacles such as traffic lights are perceived as farther than the same distance without these interruptions (Cohen *et al.* 1978; Thorndyke 1981).

Spatial distribution of offences

So far, we have considered the distances travelled by offenders to commit crimes and the possible anchor points that could be used as starting points for these journeys. Also of substantial interest is the actual positioning of offences in relation to these anchor points. To illustrate how serial burglars' cognitive maps might influence their spatial decision-making, Rengert (1991) devised the following classification: (1) a uniform pattern around the anchor point with no evidence of distance decay – up to a certain distance offenders are likely to offend at all locations with equal

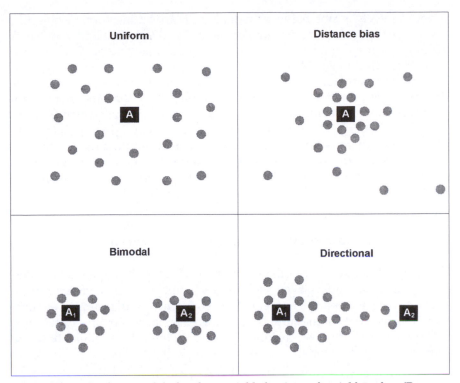

Figure 14.2 The four models for the spatial behaviour of serial burglars (Rengert 1991). The black squares represent the location of the offender's anchor points while the grey circles represent the offences he/she has committed

likelihood; (2) a cluster of offences around the offender's anchor point – exhibiting a pattern of distance decay; (3) a bimodal distribution where the offences are clustered around two separate anchor points; and (4) a teardrop pattern with a cluster around one anchor point that displays a directional bias towards a second (see Figure 14.2). Of course, offenders may have more than two anchor points.

Directional bias has rarely been studied in the criminological literature (for exceptions, see Costanzo *et al*. 1986; Kocsis *et al*. 2002; Lenz 1986; Rengert and Wasilchick 2000). For this type of analysis, the aim is to determine if crime site locations are placed so as to suggest a directional bias (or gravity) relative to the offender's most important subjective anchor points, with the aim of uncovering factors other than distance that might influence offender spatial decision-making.

Where offenders have a range of salient nodes of activity, the question arises as to which anchor points should be used to measure any (relative) angular deviation. The home of the criminal is generally used as one anchor point, the centre of the city as the other (Rengert 1996). However, if the research is not based in a major urban setting, other subjective anchor points such as the workplace can be used (Rengert and Wasilchick 2000) or even more objective anchor points such as true north (Costanzo *et al.* 1986; McConnell 2009).

A prerequisite for the analysis of directional bias – and cognitive distortions in relation to distance of travel – is that the participant provides enough detail for the locations portrayed in the sketch map for them to be identified (and related to an actual map of the area). In the case of offenders, there is the risk that, due to fear of incrimination, offenders may choose to omit undetected crime locations from a map or the details of such locations (e.g. street name), making it impossible to relate the sketch map to an actual map of the same area.

The context and rationale of the present research

To further illustrate how both sketch and cartographic maps may be used during offender interviews, we discuss some of our recent research findings. This was part of a larger study concerned with acquisitive crime, which aimed to examine how offenders choose targets in space *and* time, the sequence of decision-making (if there is one), and if and how the outcome of prior experience shapes future choices.

Recent research has suggested and tentatively tested the existence of specific offender foraging strategies (Bernasco 2008; Johnson and Bowers 2004; Johnson *et al.* 2007; Johnson *et al.* 2009). According to this hypothesis, when a burglar (for example) targets a particular home he learns about that property, including the internal structure of the home, the security features of the house, the types of goods to be found inside, neighbour vigilance and so on. Through direct observation or inference, he also learns about proximate homes. Where he is successful in committing an offence and the conditions are judged to be favourable, the offender is likely to return, either to the same home (i.e. repeat victimisation; see Pease 1998), or those homes nearby (i.e. 'near repeats'; Johnson and Bowers 2004; Townsley *et al.* 2003). Over time memory fades, victims respond to their experience and repeated victimisation of the same street is likely to lead to the exhaustion of opportunities and attract police attention. Thus, according to the foraging hypothesis, at some point the foraging offender would be expected to move on.

The aims of the larger research project were fourfold: (1) to see if the basic finding that crime clusters in space and time is evident in our study area for both burglary and vehicle crime; (2) to examine patterns in crimes detected by the police to determine if they supported either of the above hypotheses (e.g. are crimes which occur close in time and space committed by the same offenders?); (3) to use computer simulation to examine these questions using theoretical models; and (4) to complement these quantitative approaches and to gain a deeper insight into offender decision-making through the analysis of qualitative data.

The qualitative data were obtained through semi-structured interviews during which offenders were asked a range of questions about their offending history, routine activities and their spatial decision-making. Offenders were also asked to perform two mapping tasks and to narrate their responses while completing them. As stated above, the data collection methods must be informed by the hypotheses or cognitive process(es) under investigation. It was hoped that the mapping tasks would facilitate the communication of information that, by its inherent spatial nature, may have been difficult to articulate otherwise.

As stated earlier, sketch maps have been more widely used than cartographic maps but we do not believe this is due to a superiority of the former. By including both types of task in our research, we aimed to evaluate their relative contributions, advantages and disadvantages.

The specific issues we hoped would be illuminated during the interviews and particularly as a consequence of using the maps were: (1) the geographical range of the offenders; (2) how their awareness of spaces informed their self-reported targeting decisions; (3) the identification of common navigational anchor points and lacunae of awareness; and (4) any foraging-like behaviour described by the offenders and their reasons for using such strategies.

Methodology

A total of 28 offenders from Dorset (UK) were interviewed. Of these, seven were convicted for only residential burglaries, six vehicle crime and 15 for both crime types. Part of our inclusion criteria was that participants should have committed a minimum of 10 offences (of any combination of the two offence types). All police data analysed in the other elements of the larger project were for the county of Dorset. Thus, to facilitate comparisons across analyses, the offenders interviewed were those who had been active in the same area. Participants were aged between 16 and 48, with a mean age of 27.54 (SD 10.4). Most participants were male ($N_M = 24$). They were recruited either from local prisons ($N_P = 17$), the community (through a service working with drug-using prolific offenders, $N_{C1} = 6$), or a supported housing project ($N_{C2} = 5$).

In addition, a group of non-offenders was asked to complete one of the mapping tasks. The reason for interviewing this particular group was to see if the offenders exhibited expertise regarding the spatial distribution of opportunities or if the two groups of people, who lived in the same area, would have the same perceptions of good places to commit crime. A second reason for interviewing the non-offenders was to see if they expressed the same considerations when selecting areas. This second group comprised a total of 13 participants who had never committed a property offence and were recruited through a local council neighbourhood office, in an area where many of the offenders themselves lived. All non-offender participants were male and aged between 20 and 40, with a mean age of 31.1 (SD 7.5). None of the participants (in either group) had ever attended university.

While undertaking the two mapping tasks, offenders were asked about their criminal histories (detected or undetected), any factors they perceived as affecting their decision-making when choosing offending areas and/or individual targets, their routine activities, repeat victimisation and co-offending. The interview questions were mostly open-ended, although two multiple-choice questions were also included to systematically examine repeat offending and to help categorise any searching behaviour they engaged in. In the first question, offenders were asked about their most recent burglary and asked to indicate whether they (or anyone they knew) had previously broken into the same residence. In the second question, offenders were asked to choose the statement that best described their target searching behaviour, from three possible options: (1) 'I'd burgle the first house I come across'; (2) 'I'd burgle the first house I come across that meets some sort of criteria' (e.g. in relation to the type of house); and (3) 'I'd check all the houses in an area and, after this was done, I'd choose the best one'.

For the first mapping task, offenders were given a blank A3 piece of paper (297 × 420 mm) and asked to draw a sketch map that illustrated the routine activities which best represented their typical daily activity, along with the locations of crimes committed (where possible). The aim of the exercise was to gain an appreciation of the types of area with which they were familiar, anchor points that they might use to navigate or delineate space, the geographic scale of their routine activity spaces, and to reveal lacunae of awareness. In an attempt to achieve consistency and minimise bias, we asked all participants to draw their home location (or whichever was their starting location) at the centre of the paper.

For the second task, offenders were given an A2 (420 × 594 mm) Ordnance Survey map (at a scale of 1:50,000 resolution which showed details of roads, train lines, landmarks, fields, bodies of water, points of interest and so on) of the study area. To complete the task they were asked to draw the boundaries (of any shape or size) of the areas for which they had some awareness, and for each of these to indicate how well they knew them using a rating scale from 0 (I don't know this area at all) through to 10 (I know this area like my own neighbourhood). They were then asked to consider the areas that they had not identified and to rate how well they knew them. Generally offenders would rate such areas as those for which they had no awareness, but it was possible that they might simply have forgotten to identify some areas and so this served as a useful checking procedure.

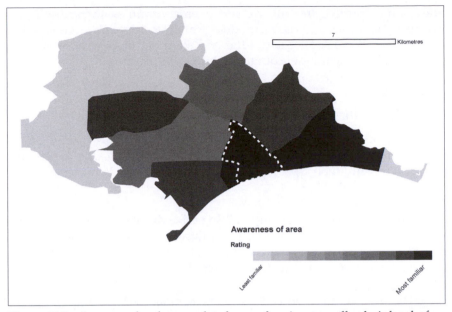

Figure 14.3 An example of a completed map showing one offender's level of awareness and the area offended in (dash boundary)

Figure 14.3 shows an example of a (digitised) completed map. Participants were instructed to draw the boundaries of the areas identified free hand. In addition to identifying the areas they knew the best (least), they were asked to identify those areas that they felt were the best (worst) possible areas for *them* to commit offences in. They were asked to do this separately for the crimes of burglary and vehicle crime. For all tasks, participants were asked to narrate their responses so that insight could be gained into any neighbourhood characteristics that influenced offender targeting decisions and any physical or social barriers to offender movement (see Rengert and Wasilchick 2000). A particular advantage of this method compared to simply asking offenders about where they choose to offend is that it requires them to consider *all* of the areas that are within a reasonable distance of their home locations and to discuss not only the areas for which they express a preference but also those that they would avoid. In terms of hypothesis testing and generation, determining what environmental factors deter offenders is just as interesting as what attracts them.

Findings

As discussed, in keeping with the scope of this book, the aim of the chapter is not to present the final analyses of the qualitative element of the research project. Instead, we aim to concentrate on the utility of the two mapping tasks and the methodological difficulties encountered when using them. We discuss each of the two mapping tasks in turn, starting with general difficulties encountered with each method.

Sketch maps

General difficulties

The offenders varied in their ability to produce maps. Many of the offenders were (initially) reluctant to carry out this task due to anxieties associated with their spelling and drawing ability. For instance, one stated:

> I'm not very good at drawing ... I don't like drawing, I've got a thing ... it'll sound funny, but I've got a thing with pencils and pens, I don't ... I just ... don't like it, I honestly don't, it makes me feel at school like and I hated that. (Offender RC01)

In such instances, the researcher had to encourage the offenders and even draw a quick sketch map to illustrate what the exercise entailed, reassuring them that it was the information contained in the maps rather than their aesthetic value that we were interested in. While most of the offenders went on to produce the sketch maps, two refused altogether, a decision that was respected by the researcher. An additional four participants drew the maps but were reluctant to provide enough detail which made them impossible to analyse. An example of such a map was one which included just a few lines and no identifiable nodes. A further five were unable to grasp the objective of the exercise and hence did not produce useable maps. This meant sketch maps were available for 17 of the offenders. A total of 21 maps were produced as some of the offenders drew more than one map (one drawing three and a further two offenders drawing two maps each).

In addition, many found it difficult to remember the names of places drawn, which made it difficult to relate the sketch maps to actual maps of the same area:

> ... like I say don't ask what the area's called because I haven't got a clue, I really haven't. (Offender P02)

We were unable to assess the accuracy of the offenders' sketch maps as insufficient information was available to relate them to actual maps of the same area. When asked if they could provide further details, offenders either admitted to being reluctant to provide detailed locations for their undetected offences or they stated they were unable to remember such information. Unfortunately, no access could be gained to the criminal histories of the offenders being interviewed, so it was impossible to obtain relevant information this way either (even for detected offences).

Spatial awareness and distances travelled

Approximately half of the offenders in our study tended to draw maps at the neighbourhood level (e.g. see Figure 14.4) and reported that their offending was generally local in nature, while others reported that they travelled longer distances (e.g. see Offender RC08's map in Figure 14.5). The smallest distance was reported by an offender who burgled his next door neighbour (see Figure 14.4). The longest distance was estimated to be 35 miles. This was reported by Offender RP06 who reported travelling along a train route to identify potential burglary sites. As described in the quote to follow, he would purchase a ticket for a particular destination which was approximately 35 miles away from his home. In some cases, however, he would fail to reach this destination and instead offend in areas surrounding intervening stations. This type of strategy was unusual for our sample of offenders and more generally is rare within the research literature (for an exception, see Polišenská 2008).

Factors that emerged as influencing the journey to crime included the offender's age (with older offenders travelling further), the type of residence targeted (with more remote, rural areas requiring longer travelling distances) and the means of transport available. Examples of

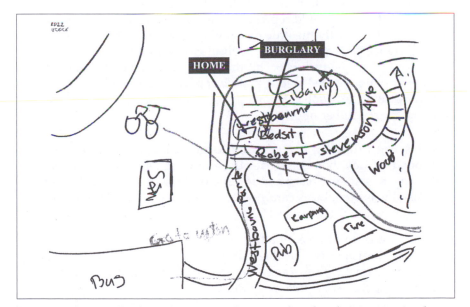

Figure 14.4 An offender's sketch map showing a burglary being committed next door to his home

how offenders articulated these issues while drawing the maps are presented below:

> When I was younger I used to be very much like round my area where I'd commit all the crimes and stuff like that. But as I got older ... (Offender P01)

> I didn't have means of transport so I couldn't really go very far. (Offender RP22)

Movement and activity patterns

The most prevalent pattern that emerged from the sketch maps was a (semi-)radial structure exhibiting distance decay, with a buffer around the offender's home (see Figure 14.5). One of the offenders explained his targeting behaviour in the following way:

> I suppose I can tell you as any burglar that it'll be a mile that way, a mile that way, a mile that way, a mile that way in a circle ... the police actually had a map of all my burglaries and it was just like that, a circle getting closer to the house. (Offender RC02)

In some cases, the offenders also explained how they alternated between the areas targeted – which were fairly equidistant from their home – in an attempt to avoid detection. In the behavioural ecology literature this type of spatial behaviour would represent a patch departure strategy (see Pyke 1984). It is also exactly the type of foraging behaviour that would lead to the occurrence of near repeats. A good illustration of this type of strategy is illustrated in Figure 14.6. In this case, the offender illustrated a sequential pattern of behaviour that he reported commonly adopting. As illustrated by the quotes below, this type of spatial behaviour was reported by a number of offenders:

> If this area I didn't get caught in, I earned enough money to see me through the day then I'd go back the following day to the same place. If I was in, say, that place and it came on top, and by it came on top I mean I was seen, I was confronted, I didn't feel right, I'd move areas straight away ... (Offender P02)

> The police certainly see a pattern, don't they, so even a week's a bit too long. Basically two or three days is ideal, you just smash it and then move on ... find somewhere else and then just repeat it, and then the next area ... (Offender RC02)

> I'll stay away from the areas what I've hit, and I'll go to the other areas what I haven't hit, you see. (Offender RP06)

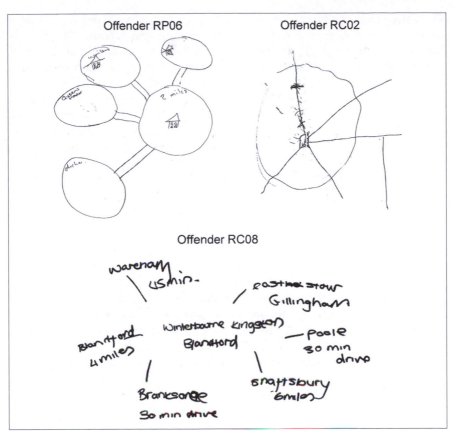

Figure 14.5 Examples of offender sketch maps showing (semi-)radial distributions around the home

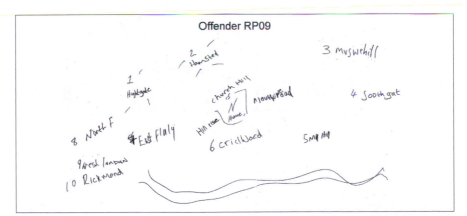

Figure 14.6 An offender sketch map showing the sequence of targeting of areas for residential burglary, which are alternated in an attempt to avoid detection

The effect that physical barriers (such as a river) can have on offender awareness and targeting decisions are also apparent from Figure 14.6. Despite the ample availability of residential properties south of the river, the offender chose to offend north of the river where he resided suggesting a directional bias generated by a physical barrier.

The spatial behaviour of other offenders was more consistent with a linear, rather than a radial, structure. For instance, one offender reported that he would walk down a main street and target vehicles that were parked on the side streets. When he had too many items to carry, he would stash them and then collect them all later on the way back (see Figure 14.7). Another offender explained how he committed various burglaries along a train route, which also illustrates how the public transport network can affect the distribution of crime:

> Well I'll buy a ticket for X, but it doesn't necessarily mean I'm going to X, I could be going, getting off at any one of them ... as far as I see it, buy a ticket, that's a whole day ticket, you see, so you can get off at any stop on the way up ... if you hop on a train and think 'Oh, that's a nice area, near this station ... Oh, I'll try this one', do you know what I mean? ... Yeah, and I'd pick it up at that station, go up again, get off at that station and then when I come back, get off, jump back on, get off, jump back on, because I've got stolen property

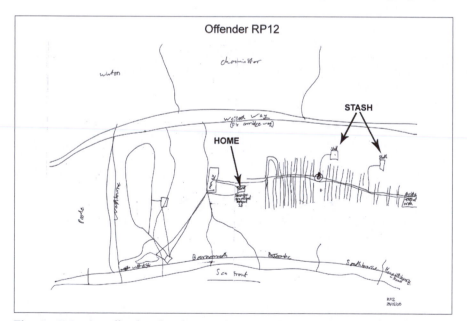

Figure 14.7 An offender sketch map showing a linear pattern for theft from motor vehicles

around the area you see, do you know what I mean, so . . . it can be a long working day. (Offender RP06)

Cartographic maps

Offenders were asked about their awareness and perceptions of the areas likely to be most suitable for the two types of offences (vehicle crime and burglary) separately to help uncover any variation in influences across crime types. In the interest of simplicity, only the maps for residential burglary are discussed here. The maps generated, and the accompanying narratives, were analysed to explore those factors that the offenders identified as influencing their targeting decisions to see how their awareness of the area and other factors affected their thinking.

General difficulties

One difficulty experienced with this task was that the maps had to be produced at a scale that made the map readable while still covering a large enough geographical area. In our study, the scale employed was 1:45,000 (1:50,000 resolution) and the maps were 420×594 mm, to cover an area of approximately 12,000 hectares. Although this was suitable for most of the offenders interviewed, some explained their targeting range covered an area larger than that displayed in the map (e.g. county wide, the county being 265,000 hectares).

Unfortunately, five of the burglars interviewed in the prisons were unable to complete the map concerning their perceptions of burglary opportunities. This was because they had very limited knowledge of the study area. The reason for this only became apparent during the interviews when they revealed that, despite serving their custodial sentence in the study area, they had not committed offences in the area. They were only at the prison concerned because those in their home area(s) were full. Thus 17 burglars (out of the 22 in our sample) completed the awareness and burglary opportunities maps.

The final sample of offenders who completed the relevant mapping tasks had a lower mean age than the non-offenders. As this might have implications for their awareness of the study area and their routine activities, we decided to perform the analyses using a sub-sample of 11 offenders and non-offenders matched on age. This produced the same pattern of results as for the full sample.

On a methodological note, caution should be exercised when this type of task is used with ex-offenders who have not committed crime for considerable periods of time. In such cases, the possibility exists that their awareness of an area may be more recent than their perceptions of which places provide good opportunities for crime, with implications for the reliability of any inferences drawn.

Spatial awareness, perceived crime opportunities and distribution of offences

To examine the relationship between offender awareness spaces and their perceptions of the spatial distribution of crime opportunities, the maps were digitised using a geographical information system (GIS). Having done so, it was possible to generate maps to show the collective awareness and perceptions of opportunity for the two groups. To do this, a lattice of 100 m × 100 m cells was added to the map and a 'spatial join' used to intersect the digitised maps for each offender with the lattice. The patterns were then aggregated for each group (offender and non-offender). These are shown in Figure 14.8, together with kernel density hotspot maps of the actual distribution of residential burglary (both those detected and those not) in the area for 2001–5.

Visual inspection of the maps suggested that the two groups shared similar collective awareness of spaces and showed higher degrees of awareness around their home locations. However, they had different collective perceptions of where the best places would be to offend. It appears that the non-offenders rated many more areas as representing good places to commit burglary. Relative to the offenders, it also appears that they tended to be less discriminatory. Moreover, the spatial distribution for the locations the offenders collectively identified as the best places to commit burglary appear to more closely align with the actual hotspots of detected and undetected burglaries as shown in the right-most panel of Figure 14.8.

The visual inspection of maps can generate illusory patterns and so further analyses were conducted to verify whether our impressions were valid. Using the grid cells of the lattice as the unit of analysis (N = 12,845), descriptive statistics and Spearman rank correlations were performed to examine the relationships discussed. The results shown in Table 14.1 are consistent with the above observations, indicating that the two groups reported having similar levels of awareness across the area considered, and that the non-offenders rated more areas as offering good opportunities for offending.

The correlations shown in Table 14.2 also confirm the patterns suggested above. For example, it is clear that offenders and non-offenders had awareness of very similar areas (r = 0.92), but rank ordered the areas differently in terms of their suitability for burglary (r = 0.31). It is also clear that the collective perceptions of the offenders were much more in line with the actual distribution of where burglaries took place than were those of the non-offenders. This validation suggests two things to us. First, that the offenders demonstrated expertise regarding those areas that were actually exploited by burglars. And second, that the maps they drew were likely to represent reliable approximations of what their perceptions actually were rather than being unreliable or resulting from the offenders trying to deceive us. The use of the recorded crime data and a GIS thereby

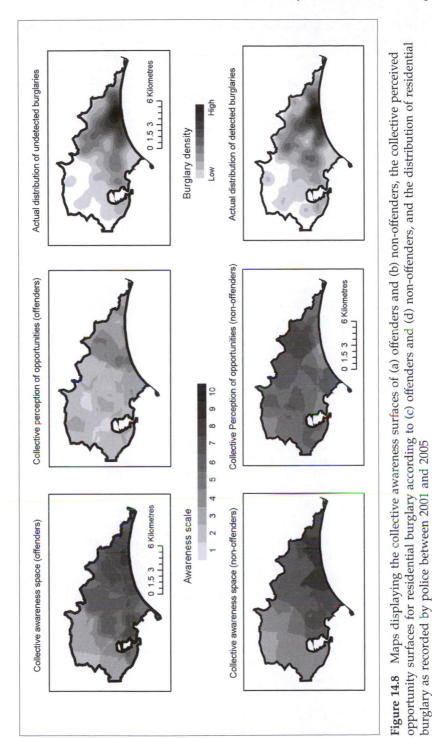

Figure 14.8 Maps displaying the collective awareness surfaces of (a) offenders and (b) non-offenders, the collective perceived opportunity surfaces for residential burglary according to (c) offenders and (d) non-offenders, and the distribution of residential burglary as recorded by police between 2001 and 2005

Table 14.1 Descriptive statistics for ratings (range 0–10) of awareness and perceived opportunities for residential burglary at the area level

	Awareness		Burglary	
	Offenders	Non-offenders	Offenders	Non-offenders
Mean	5.37	4.73	2.28	4.54
Standard deviation	2.22	1.66	1.22	0.84
Minimum	1.55	2.45	0.27	2.56
Maximum	9.64	8.36	6.05	6.86

Table 14.2 Spearman's rank correlations for ratings (range 0–10) of awareness and perceived opportunities for residential burglary at the area level

	A	B	C	D	E
A Offenders – Familiarity					
B Offenders – Opportunities Res Burglary	0.66				
C Non-offenders – Familiarity	0.92				
D Non-offenders – Opportunities Res Burglary		0.31	0.22		
E Actual Undetected Res Burglary (2001–5)		0.47		0.28	
F Actual Detected Res Burglary (2001–5)		0.51		0.28	0.97

NB: All correlations are significant at the $p < 0.001$ level.

provided an opportunity to extend our understanding of what the maps suggested and to easily cross reference what the offenders had drawn with patterns in crimes recorded by the police.

Considering what the participants said during the completion of the tasks, both offenders and non-offenders (although not in every case) made reference to the importance of familiarity when selecting target areas:

Years ago we used to, we used to drive off and go anywhere, but you tend to stick to the areas that you know well. (Offender RP07)

I don't really know the area so I just don't know it very well so I wouldn't go and burgle it myself because I don't know it. (Non-offender N04)

Four of the offenders even stated they would actively seek to become familiar with an area before committing burglaries there, showing some evidence of 'spatial exploration':

Obviously if you go into an area you want to know the best routes to get out quick and, you know, so you trawled it for a couple of days and then you'll go back and then if the police come you know you can go over how many fences to get to four streets away and you're off on the dual carriageway. (Offender RC02)

I know all the short-cuts, I know ... and basically when I move into a new area, the first thing I do I go out, I spend a week on a mountain bike finding all these back alleys, all the, you know, easy routes to get in and out of certain places, and anything like that I'll find, know what I mean? So I spend a week doing that. I certainly find everything what I need to find and then I start hitting what I need to hit, because I've already plotted up certain dwellings ready to be hit, before I've done it, if you understand that sort of thing. (Offender RP06)

The cartographic maps were useful in that it encouraged participants to evaluate all the individual areas within the geographical boundaries of the study area, which meant that reasons were given for why particular areas would be avoided, rather than them simply discussing those areas that would be targeted and the reasons for their preference. This led to the confirmation of the existence of various social barriers that affected offender decision-making including area-level affluence and community cohesion:

That, again that's, you know, pretty rich people, and if you go there, a stranger dressed like I'm dressed, they know you're a ... (Offender RC02)

That bit's the worst place in X, everyone knows each other. (Offender RC08)

A further social barrier identified concerned the composition of the resident population, with a preference stated for avoiding those areas with traveller communities:

There's no point robbing a house down X, because you're just going to get shot or something ... There's no point in going round there because they've got loads of traveller boys down there, gypsies, and if you go and rob one of their houses well you're going to be in the woods all stringed up and killed or something. So there's no point in messing with them ... It's people you don't want to mess around with really ... There's a whole load of them and, like I said, if you mess with one of them you mess with all of them. You don't want all of them to come round your house. (Offender RP21)

Yeah, this is all gypsies all round here so there's no point in going over there because they'll take your trainers off you ... it's not just that they haven't got anything, they're the type of people, gypsies are like me, thieves, basically. But if you thieve one of their houses you get a hundred people at your door and, you know, agro. (Offender RC02)

Discussion

Despite their shortcomings, the authors contend that the use of the mapping tasks helped further our understanding of the issues being explored in the current research. Not only was useful information elicited from the analysis of the maps themselves, the completion of the mapping tasks enhanced the participants' ability to articulate their spatial decision-making in at least two different ways. First, the tasks provided them with the opportunity to convey spatial information in spatial form rather than trying to verbalise what they meant alone. Second, it has been suggested that the requirement to complete complex and/or unexpected tasks during the course of an interview can increase the validity of findings, as the increased cognitive load makes it difficult to provide dishonest answers (Vrij *et al.* 2008a; Vrij *et al.* 2008b).

Both tasks presented us with various methodological difficulties at different stages of the data collection and analysis process. As stated earlier, not all offenders were able (or willing) to complete the mapping tasks. When presented with the sketch mapping task, some stated they did not like drawing and doubted their drawing ability. Following reassurances by the researcher, most proceeded with the task and produced sketch maps that did not differ in quality from the rest of the sample. Unfortunately a small number of offenders refused to draw the sketch maps altogether. For this sub-group, an alternative means of drawing (e.g. using a stylus and computer tablet) may have encouraged them to take part and so alternative methods of data capture are worth pursuing in future research. The cartographic mapping task did not seem to instil such negative feelings and offenders seemed confident in using the maps and identifying various areas within these. The data collection problems associated with the cartographic maps related to whether offenders were familiar with (or had offended in) the area portrayed by the map, which led to some degree of participant attrition.

Once completed, the cartographic maps appeared to be easier to analyse than the sketch maps. Part of the reason for this was that the data could be quantified in a systematic way which facilitated a range of analyses. For instance, we were able to easily compare the offender and the non-offender data and relate their maps to actual distributions of crime. The analysis of the sketch maps was problematic as some of the offenders failed to provide sufficient detail which made the identification of cognitive distortions impossible. In some cases, the information provided was so limited that no form of analysis was viable. This was the result of offenders being either unable to recall the relevant details, unwilling to provide them (due to fear of incrimination, for example) or offenders failing to understand the task altogether (despite examples and explanations being offered by the researcher). Although it is possible that simply attempting to complete the sketch mapping task facilitated and encouraged the offender narratives, it is suggested that the data obtained from the cartographic maps were much more complete and easier to process.

A further advantage of the cartographic maps (in relation to the sketch maps) was that they ensured that offenders considered both the areas they would target *and* those that they would not. Where a more complete understanding of decision-making is sought, this is of considerable value.

A difficulty that impacted on both mapping tasks was our inability to obtain access to the official criminal histories of the offenders interviewed, which prevented us from cross-referencing this information with that provided during the interviews (see Decker 2005). These data are (at least in the UK) protected by the Data Protection Act 1998 and informed consent forms need to be signed by the relevant offenders before they can be accessed. In our particular case, this was not ascertained until after the interviews had been carried out, by which time it was not possible to obtain all the signed forms. Other methods of determining validity were employed during the interviews (e.g. identifying inconsistencies in the accounts and challenging offenders accordingly) and it is our impression that, where lies were detected, these were by omission rather than by commission (e.g. offenders would state they did not want to provide details when questioned about a specific event). In any case, future researchers should organise access to police records if possible, as this gives an opportunity to triangulate the interview findings.

Further analyses could easily be conducted by relating the cartographic maps to other datasets. For example, the impact of social cohesion, or other influences that might affect offender decision-making, could be explored by comparing the maps with geo-demographic profiles generated using census data (for a suggestion as to how social cohesion can be estimated using these data, see Hirschfield and Bowers 1997).

The accuracy of spatial information is rapidly improving and methods of displaying such data commonplace – to the extent that most Internet users have probably used applications such as Google Earth. The increasing availability of good – and different types of – spatial data presents new opportunities for research methods. For example, both sketch and cartographic maps may be improved by the use of specific prompts such as photographs, video and even interactive maps such as those available through Google Earth. The use of such methods may, however, present new technical issues, either in terms of the technology used or in offenders' ability to interact with it.

Conclusion

The aim of this chapter was to evaluate the relative utility of sketch and cartographic maps in research concerned with offender spatial decision-making. Despite both types of task providing useful and interesting data, the cartographic maps were certainly the most useful for our research, being associated with fewer difficulties both in terms of data collection and analysis. This may not apply to all research concerned with spatial cognition but may be particularly true for studies involving offender populations, who, as discussed above, may be unable or reluctant to provide the information required. Consequently, we suggest that future researchers should further explore the use of cartographic maps (whose use in offender spatial decision-making research has, to date, been very limited), both in isolation and in combination with other approaches, in an attempt to further exploit this approach.

Acknowledgments

We would like to thank all those who took part in this study and the staff at various organisations who helped arrange the interviews. The current research was funded by British Academy Grant LRG 45507.

References

Appleyard, D. (1970) 'Styles and methods of structuring a city', *Environment and Behavior*, 2: 100–17.
Bernasco, W. (2008) 'Them again? Same-offender involvement in repeat and near repeat burglaries', *European Journal of Criminology*, 5 (4): 411–31.
Blades, M. (1990) 'The reliability of data collected from sketch maps', *Journal of Environmental Psychology*, 100: 327–39.
Brantingham, P. and Brantingham, P. (1991) 'Environment, routine and situation: toward a pattern theory of crime', in R. Clarke and M. Felson (eds), *Routine Activities and Rational Choice*. New Brunswick, NJ: Transaction Publishers.
Brantingham, P. and Brantingham, P. (2008) 'Crime pattern theory', in R. Wortley and L. Mazerolle (eds), *Environmental Criminology and Crime Analysis*. Portland, OR: Willan.
Briggs, R. (1973) 'Urban cognitive distance', in R. M. Downs and D. Stea (eds), *Image and Environment*. Chicago: Aldine.
Bryant, K. J. (1984) 'Methodological coverage as an issue within environmental cognition research', *Journal of Environmental Psychology*, 4: 43–60.
Cadwallader, M. T. (1976) 'Cognitive distance in intraurban space', in G. T. Moore and R. G. Golledge (eds), *Environmental Knowing*. Stroudsberg, PA: Dowden, Hutchinson & Ross.
Cohen, L. and M. Felson (1979) 'Social change and crime rate trends: a routine activity approach', *American Sociological Review*, 44: 588–608.

Cohen, R., Baldwin, L. and Sherman, R. (1978) 'Cognitive maps in naturalistic settings', *Child Development*, 49: 1216–18.

Costanzo, C., Halperin, W. and Gale, N. (1986) 'Criminal mobility and the directional component in journeys to crime', in R. Figlio, S. Hakim and G. Rengert (eds), *Metropolitan Crime Patterns*. Monsey, NY: Criminal Justice Press.

Costello, A. and Wiles, P. (2001) 'GIS and the journey to crime: an analysis of patterns in South Yorkshire', in A. Hirschfield and K. J. Bowers (eds), *Mapping and Analyzing Crime Data: Lessons from Research and Practice*. London: Taylor & Francis.

Cromwell, P. F., Olson, J. N. and Avary, D. A. W. (1991) *Breaking and Entering: An Ethnographic Analysis of Burglary*. London: Sage.

Decker, S. H. (2005) *Using Offender Interviews to Inform Police Problem Solving*. Washington, DC: US Department of Justice.

Downs, R. M. and Stea, D. (1973) 'Theory', in R. M. Downs and D. Stea (eds), *Image and Environment*. Chicago: Aldine.

Garling, T., Book, A. and Lindberg, E. (1985) 'Adults' memory representations of the spatial properties of their everyday physical environment', in R. Cohen (ed.), *The Development of Spatial Cognition*. Hillsdale, NJ: Erlbaum Lawrence.

Golledge, R. (1976) 'Methods and methodological issues in environmental cognition research', in R. G. Golledge and G. T. Moore (eds), *Environmental Knowing*. Pennsylvania: Dowden, Hutchinson & Ross.

Golledge, R. and Zannaras, G. (1973) 'Cognitive approaches to the analysis of human spatial behavior', in W. Ittelson (ed.), *Environment and Cognition*. New York: Seminar Press.

Hirschfield, A. and Bowers, K. J. (1997) 'The effect of social cohesion on levels of recorded crime in disadvantaged areas', *Urban Studies*, 34 (8): 1275–95.

Johnson, S. D. and Bowers, K. J. (2004) 'The stability of space-time clusters of burglary', *British Journal of Criminology*, 44: 55–65.

Johnson, S. D., Bowers, K. J., Birks, D. and Pease, K. (2009) 'Predictive mapping of crime by ProMap: accuracy, units of analysis and the environmental backcloth', in D. Weisburd, W. Bernasco and G. Bruinsma (eds), *Putting Crime in Its Place: Units of Analysis in Spatial Crime Research*. New York: Springer.

Johnson, S. D., Bernasco, W., Bowers, K. J., Elffers, H., Ratcliffe, J., Rengert, G. and Townsley, M. T. (2007) 'Near repeats: a cross national assessment of residential burglary', *Journal of Quantitative Criminology*, 23 (3): 201–19.

Kocsis, R. N., Cooksey, R. W., Irwin, H. J. and Allen, G. (2002) 'A further assessment of "circle theory" for geographic psychological profiling', *Australian and New Zealand Journal of Criminology*, 35 (1): 43–62.

Lenz, R. (1986) 'Geographical and temporal changes among robberies in Milwaukee', in R. Figlio, S. Hakim and G. Rengert (eds), *Metropolitan Crime Patterns*. Monsey, NY: Criminal Justice Press.

Logie, R. H., Wright, R. T. and Decker, S. (1992) 'Recognition memory performance and residential burglary', *Applied Cognitive Psychology*, 6: 109–23.

Lynch, K. (1960) *The Image of the City*. Cambridge, MA: MIT Press.

McConnell, P. (2009) 'Toward a Holistic Vectored Geography of Homicide'. Unpublished dissertation submitted to the Department of Criminal Justice, Temple University.

Nee, C. (2003) 'Burglary research at the end of the millennium: an example of grounded theory?', *Security Journal*, 16: 37–44.

Nee, C. and Meenaghan, A. (2006) 'Expert decision making in burglars', *British Journal of Criminology*, 46: 935–49.

Nee, C. and Taylor, M. (2000) 'Examining burglars' target selection: interview, experiment or ethnomethodology?', *Psychology, Crime and Law*, 6 (1): 45–59.

Pease, K. (1998) *Repeat Victimisation: Taking Stock*, Home Office Police Research Group, Crime Detection and Prevention Series, Paper 90. London: Home Office.

Polišenská, V. (2008) 'A qualitative approach to the criminal mobility of burglars: questioning the 'near home' hypothesis', *Crime Patterns and Analysis*, 1: 47–59.

Potchak, M., McGloin, J. and Zgoba, K. (2002) 'A spatial analysis of criminal effort: auto theft in Newark, New Jersey', *Criminal Justice Policy Review*, 13: 257–85.

Pyke, G. H. (1984) 'Optimal foraging theory: a critical review', *Annual Review of Ecolological Systems*, 15: 523–75.

Rengert, G. (1991) *The Spatial Clustering of Residential Burglaries About Anchor Points of Routine Activities*, American Society of Criminology Conference, San Francisco, CA, November 1991.

Rengert, G. (1996) *The Geography of Illegal Drugs*. Boulder, CO: Westview Press.

Rengert, G. F. and Wasilchick, J. (2000) *Suburban Burglary: A Tale of Two Suburbs* (2nd edn). Springfield, IL: Charles C. Thomas.

Rengert, G. F., Piquero, A. R and Jones, P. R. (1999) 'Distance decay reexamined', *Criminology*, 37: 427–45.

Repetto, T. (1974) *Residential Crime*. Cambridge, MA: Ballinger.

Rossmo, K. (2000) *Geographic Profiling*. Boca Raton, FL: CRC Press.

Sadalla, E. and Magel, S. (1980) 'The perception of traversed distance', *Environment and Behavior*, 12 (1): 65–79.

Snook, B. (2004) 'Individual differences in distance traveled by serial burglars', *Journal of Investigative Psychology and Offender Profiling*, 1: 53–66.

Taylor, M. and Nee, C. (1988) 'The role of cues in simulated residential burglary: a preliminary investigation', *British Journal of Criminology*, 28: 396–401.

Thorndyke, P. (1981) 'Distance estimates from cognitive maps', *Cognitive Psychology*, 13: 526–50.

Tobler, W. R. (1976) 'The geometry of mental maps', in R. G. Golledge and G. Rushton (eds), *Spatial Choice and Spatial Behavior*. Columbus, OH: Ohio University Press.

Townsley, M., Homel, R. and Chaseling, J. (2003) 'Infectious burglaries: a test of the near repeat hypothesis', *British Journal of Criminology*, 43: 615–33.

Vrij, A., Leal, S., Granhag, P. A., Mann, S. A., Fisher, R. P., Hillman, J. and Sperry, K. (2008a) 'Outsmarting the liars: the benefit of asking unanticipated questions', *Law and Human Behavior*, 32 (3).

Vrij, A., Mann, S. A., Fisher, R. P., Leal, S., Milne, R. and Bull, R. (2008b) 'Increasing cognitive load to facilitate lie detection: the benefit of recalling an event in reverse order', *Law and Human Behavior*, 32: 253–65.

Wright, R. T. and Decker, S. H. (1994) *Burglars on the Job: Streetlife and Residential Break-ins*. Boston: Northeastern University Press.

Chapter 15

Interviewing offenders in a penitentiary environment and the use of mental maps during interviews

Veronika A. Polišenská

Abstract

This chapter discusses the dynamics of conducting interviews in a penitentiary environment. The issues discussed mainly concentrate on the conditions of the research, how to motivate offenders to participate in the research and concerns regarding validation of data. The last part of the chapter concentrates upon the use of mental maps as a means to gain new information from the offenders which cannot be accessed from prison files, questionnaires or interviews. The use of mental maps as a research method will be put into the context of criminal mobility and aims to point out different ways to classify mental maps, issues regarding their limitations and how they can be used in specific research designs.

Despite the extensive research literature (for example, Patton 2002; Smith 2004; Silverman 2004), the uniqueness of a prison environment and its influence upon conducting research is rarely considered (Cieurzo and Keitel 1999; Noaks and Wincup 2004; Patenaude 2004).

The goal of offender-based research, which often takes place in prison settings, is to gain information from the offender that cannot be gained from police files. Such information can give insight into the processes of motivation, attitudes toward offending, external influences of crime, strategies, etc. Thus the use of various research methods such as interviewing, tests, questionnaires and others while conducting research in prison is the most advantageous as the offenders have different means to express themselves (Čermák 2002).

Due to the fact that research in prison environment is very specific, this chapter will examine the different characteristics of this environment in the Czech Republic. Specifically, the chapter will discuss the conditions of offender observation, motivating offenders to participate in the research and validation of information. The last part of the chapter will concentrate on the research technique of mental maps as a means to access a new type of information that has seldom been collected from offenders.

The first section of this contribution describes the conditions of offender observation. It focuses on the time regime of the prisons, legal limitations on conducting research in prisons, the interaction of the interviewer with the offender and the abilities of the interviewer as influencing factors. The section discusses various methods that can help to motivate offenders to participate in the research. It includes an examination of the role of the penitentiary psychologist. To consider ways of validating information given by the offenders, the third section discusses safety and security issues and the (im)possibility of recording in Czech prisons, as well as the use of semi-structured interviews. The last section examines one specific substantive issue of the interviews in this research: the use of mental maps as a means to access new information from offenders. Thus information on criminal mobility and a theoretical overview of mental maps will be given, followed by more detailed discussions on the classification of mental maps, the limitations and distortions of mental maps and their further use in research.

Each of the sections will first present a general description of the central issue, illustrate it with examples, mostly from the author's own experience in such a situation, and conclude with reflections on how it influences the validity of the data and how it can be dealt with.

The research upon which this chapter is based was conducted from 2007 to 2009 and its aim was to understand how the experience of offenders and the perceptions of their environment influence the behaviour of the offenders, their choice of target and strategy of burgling. The research took place in 19 prisons in the Czech Republic. The offenders were selected according to strict criteria (currently incarcerated for burglary, at least the second incarceration for burglary, identified as prolific burglar). The offenders were interviewed by psychology students (79 students). Overall the sample included 166 offenders (12 female, 154 male).

The battery of tests given to the offenders included a criminal and family history questionnaire, Cloninger's Temperament and Character Inventory – revised (personality test), Raven's Progressive Matrices (intelligence test), a Hand test (aggression test) and a place-attachment questionnaire. The session with the offender also included a semi-structured interview and the drawing of the mental map of a certain environment. The students who gathered the data visited the prisons in pairs. The reasons for this are explained later in this chapter.

The analysis of the data is now in process. However, the issues regarding the mobility of offenders, including the distance travelled and the relationship to the offenders' personality, have already been explored (Polišenská 2004, 2005, 2008). Other issues are still awaiting detailed analysis and will become available later.

Conditions of offender observation

When deciding to conduct research in a prison environment, the researcher must be aware of the conditions under which the research will take place and also how to entice offenders into joining the research. The conditions influencing the research in prisons and, therefore, the observation of the offender include the time regime of the prison, the legal limitations imposed on the researcher, the abilities of the researcher and the dynamics of interviewing the offender.

Safety of the researcher

Before going to prison, the researcher needs to be fully informed about the safety regulations (Payne 2000). In every country there are different regulations ensuring the safety of the researcher. In the Czech Republic, prison regulations state that no external person can be alone with a prisoner. Therefore, during the data gathering process, a guard, penitentiary psychologist or social worker were present. If they could not be present physically, they were next door and the room was controlled by a camera, and the prisoner knew they were. In a majority of the interviews, however, there was a third person present in the room with the researcher and the offender.

The presence of another person in the room influenced the interviews depending upon the behaviour and involvement of that person during the interviews. If the person took a neutral position and did not interfere with the process of interview, the offenders were not bothered by him/her and communicated quite spontaneously. If, however, the third person became active during the interviews and took part in the conversation the interview had lost its spontaneity, the offenders censored themselves and the researcher (student) had to control both the offender as well as the third person to achieve a certain response rate.

The presence of the third person, of course, influences the validity of the answers gained during the interview. The offenders checked their answers and very rarely volunteered information that was not generally known. They also slipped into the rehearsed mode of explaining their crimes. On the other hand, as the students or the researcher were denied access to the criminal records of the offenders and there were no means to verify the answers of the offenders, the presence of the third person prevented the offenders from exaggerating and trying to impress the interviewer. The best situation was when the interviewer and the offender were alone in the room and the third person was in the room adjacent to it or monitored the situation on camera.

Time regime of the prison

The inner prison regulations also determine the hourly schedule of the prison, such as the timing of the wake-up call, roll call, time to go to work, lunch, etc. The time regime of the prison is very strict and the researcher has to find means to fit into it. In the Czech Republic, the optimum time to conduct research was between 9:00 (10:00)–(15:30) 16:00 at the latest. Thus, when research, which includes more time-demanding methods or too many of them (as was the instance in this research), is taking place, what needs to be taken into account is that the researcher might interview one offender on two occasions. This, however, should be avoided, if possible. Between the first and the second interview, the offender can change his mind, be transferred, go into employment or be reprimanded, thus not allowing him to participate in the second part of the interview. It is then advisable to interview fewer offenders in one day, but complete them entirely. This will lower the chances of half-incomplete interviews.

In the case of this research, in order to use the time available in the best possible way, the students went into the prison in pairs. In the morning, they administered the methods that could be given in groups, so all offenders filled them out at the same time. These methods were: a consent form, a demographic and criminal history questionnaire, the TCI-r, an attachment questionnaire and an intelligence test. In the afternoon, each student worked with the offenders separately, interviewing them individually. This individual part also included the drawing of the mental map and the Hand test. Thus 4–6 offenders completed all the materials in one day. This has greatly decreased the numbers of incomplete interviews and it was in the accordance with the prison officials as the students were allowed in the prison for only one day.

The advantage of working in pairs in prison with regard to validity had both positive and negative aspects. The positive aspect was apparent in the 'group' session. As the offenders were all together in one room and filled the questionnaires at the same time, the students were available to answer any questions or misunderstandings the offenders might have. Also, by being present, the students prevented the offenders from 'cheating' their way out of the questionnaires and answering only randomly without actually reading the questions. This has happened on couple of occasions when a student left the offenders in the room alone without supervision and then simply collected the questionnaires.

The disadvantage of working in pairs was more evident in the 'individual' section of data collection. The prisons did not always have the capacity to put the students into separate rooms for the interviews (that would also require additional person to ensure the safety of both students). Thus often the two interviews were conducted in one room, which could have influenced the answers of the offenders present.

Legal limitations (in the Czech Republic) of the research

The researcher should be also aware of any laws that pertain to research in the prison environment. For example, in the Czech Republic one should be aware of the following laws:

- The law regarding the protection of personal data, which enforces anonymity of the participants of the research. This law is enforced throughout the research. Thus the researcher is prohibited to look into the personal file of the interviewed prisoners. Further, the researcher must enforce the anonymity of the participants by not publishing any information by which one could identify a specific person.

- The law regarding free access to information also prohibits the researcher to look into the files of the offenders.

- The law regarding unauthorised uses of personal information, as well as not reporting or not stopping a crime, relates to situations in which the offender might tell a researcher about a crime which he committed but was not sentenced for. In such a case, the researcher has a duty to report it to the authorities.

All these laws must be considered when preparing the research design. The researcher must be aware of the laws pertaining to the disclosure of personal data and to what type of information he/she will have access. For example, in the Czech Republic, the offenders could sign the consent form with their name, but they might not write their names on any of the questionnaires. Moreover, the researcher was prohibited from viewing the offenders' files to recheck the information given by the offenders.

Further, the researcher was prohibited to ask whether the offender was a gypsy (Roma) or not. The original aim was to have half of the offenders 'Roma' and then compare the two groups. However, the penitentiary officials informed the researcher that questions regarding ethnicity cannot be asked and further, despite the offender clearly being a 'Roma', the researcher cannot record that into his/her notes. Thus the demographic questionnaire asked for nationality in general and if a 'Roma' offender wrote 'Czech' then he was classified as Czech not Roma.

With regard to the duty of reporting a crime, the offenders were informed before the interview started that if the researcher learns of a violent crime against a person that has not been reported then he/she has the duty to report such a crime. The offenders accepted the conditions of the interview and there were no problems with regard to this fact. Of course, the disclosure of unknown crimes was also hindered by the presence of the third person, who was there to assure the researcher's safety.

Interaction of the researcher with the offender

The interaction between the researcher and the offender needs to be considered very carefully. As the relationship is not symmetrical (Payne 2000), the researcher needs to maintain authority during the research. At the same time, it is important that the offenders know that they can leave the research anytime they wish (Cieurzo and Keitel 1999).

The researcher needs to clarify with the prison officials that participation in the research is voluntary. It must be clear that the offenders will not get paid to participate or that they will not receive any benefits. The offer to participate in their research should be presented to all offenders that fit the selection demands and then it is up to them whether they choose to participate or not. Usually the offenders are eager to participate in the research as it is a break from their routine, the day is passed differently and also they get a chance to talk to a new person. Further, as they are put in a position of the 'expert' who gives information to the 'unknowing' interviewer, their self-esteem improves.

Due to the fact that the offender thinks of himself as 'the expert' he tries to use the participation for his own purposes as well. The first purpose is the hope of certain advantages (Polišenská 2005). Second, the offender may try to manipulate the interview (Polišenská 2008).

This manipulation takes different forms. The offenders can answer what they believe the researcher wants to hear. Thus the respondents may exaggerate their answers in terms of level of committed criminal activity or may not report the full extent of it (Breakwell 2000). Further, the offenders try to justify their behaviour and may not pay attention to the questions asked. Or due to sensitive or inappropriate behaviour, such as rape, or stealing from a family member, offenders may give inaccurate reports or not share the information at all (Fife-Shaw 2000).

All these factors can greatly influence the research outcomes and the researcher should stay neutral toward the offender's answers and not reinforce attempts at manipulation. It is important to realise, however, that the assumption of privileges and the feeling of monotony resulting from the prison routine can influence the research positively as well, as the respondents may be more open to participate.

Another aspect of the interview is not so dominant but should be taken into account. It is necessary to be aware of the fact that each interview has a slight therapeutic mode for the offender. Therefore the researcher needs to be careful about any signs of stress or nervousness from the offender and be prepared for different reactions. The entire interview should be based upon listening to the offender. The researcher should not evaluate the offender's behaviour or criticise; instead he/she should support any plans not to commit crime in the future (Cieurzo and Keitel 1999). The researcher should also make sure that the offender is not agitated at the end of the interview (Noaks and Wincup 2004).

With regard to the validity of the answers given by the offender during the interview, certain factors should be considered. The first is the possibility that long-term or repeated imprisonment can result in feelings of resignation, emotional flatness and living one day at a time, thus changing the personality of the offender (Heidlerová and Klik 1999).

The result of these changes can be such that the answers during the interview greatly differ from real experiences. The researcher needs to mind this change and possibly add questions during the interview about such changes.

Another aspect is the possibility that offenders can simply lie or exaggerate to make their answers more interesting. The interviewer should be neutral so as not to encourage such exaggerations. Repeat questions also serve as a validity check.

From personal experience, the offenders were very willing to participate in the research and once they committed to it they rarely stopped in the middle of it, despite the fact that it was quiet a lengthy process. The use of students to conduct the interviews has proven as a good strategy to 'melt the ice' between the offender and the interviewer. The students were informed not to over-encourage the offenders and not to support any signs of exaggeration.

Motivating offenders to participate in the research

The motivation of offenders to participate in the research has already been touched upon in the previous section. The offenders are motivated by the break of the routine in the prison, the opportunity to talk to someone new and to play the role of the expert in the interview. All these aspects play for the offenders such a role that it is not necessary to pay the offenders for their participation. Payment is, under Czech law, prohibited in any case and thus did not come into consideration when designing the research.

However, another aspect in motivating the offenders, which is often overlooked, is the role of the penitentiary psychologist.

Involvement of the penitentiary psychologist

The penitentiary psychologist is involved in the research from the beginning. When the researcher is granted access to the prison by the prison director, the psychologist is usually put in charge of the researcher. Thus the psychologist ensures that access to the prison determines the schedule of the visit and sets up all the safety precautions necessary.

However, the most important role of the psychologist is the pre-selection of the offenders participating in the research. The psychologist receives the criteria of selection before the interviewer enters the prison. The psychologist then pre-selects the offenders from the files and determines whether they fit the criteria and whether they will be available for the day (i.e. not in employment or in court).

The researcher then can leave the entire recruitment to the psychologist, which involves the psychologist choosing all the offenders. A more personal approach involves the psychologist choosing a 'pool' of possible offenders, which the researcher then meets, personally explains to them the goal of the research, answers any questions and lets the offenders choose for themselves whether they would like to participate in the research or not.

Both approaches are possible. However, the first completely depends on the psychologist's interest in the research. If he/she is not interested in the research and does not convey this interest to the offenders, then a situation may arise in which researcher enters the prison only to find that there are no participants.

The second approach is more under the control of the researcher. However, one should be mindful of the different influences among offenders. It has happened several times that when offenders are all in a group and one offender states that he will not participate in the research the others follow his suit and also decline participation. Thus it is necessary when presenting the research to present it to a moderate size group in which these forces are not so strong. Also, if this happens it is advisable not to simply give up and 'go home' but to give the offenders some time to think about the offer and then approach them individually.

Validation of information given by the offenders

The issue of the validity of the data has already been touched upon in the previous sections. However, with regard to checking and validating the information that offenders provide it must be remembered that under Czech law the researcher does not have access to the offender's file and therefore cannot check the information given from official sources. There were, however, other ways which the researcher could influence the veracity of the sample and answers.

Variability of the sample

Communication with the prison officials is firstly aimed at gaining access to the prison. Gaining access to prison for research purposes has always been difficult (Davies and Francis 2000).

In the presented research, access was granted through the highest level possible, the General Directorate of Prison Service of the Czech Republic. After the agreement of the General Director, communication was set up with a member of the Department of Arrest and Punishment, who relayed the information to the penitentiary psychologist, who then confirmed with the researcher whether they would participate in the research or not. Not all prisons had the necessary sample as specified by the research design, thus out of 25 prisons 19 agreed to participate.

The fact that most prisons agreed to take part in the research solved the problem of the sampling site. It needs to be borne in mind that the level of security, the geographic area and the size of the prison can influence the prison population. Thus, if research is conducted in one or two prisons, the research may be influenced by having only particular types of offenders present (Ingham *et al.* 1999). By having 19 prisons take part in the study spread across the entire Czech Republic, the variability of the sample was guaranteed. Thus the validity of the sample was solved by having a majority of the prisons involved in the research.

Choosing individual offenders

The previous issue regarding the involvement of the penitentiary psychologist in the research, especially in the selection of the offenders, directly relates to how valid is the choice of the offenders by the psychologist. It must be remembered that the researcher should ultimately be in charge of the selection of the offenders. If the researcher leaves too much freedom to the psychologist it could influence the selection of offenders in two ways. The first has already been mentioned, when the psychologist fails to interest the offenders and none decide to participate in the research. The second way is when the psychologist is overzealous and too interested in the research and thus selects for the researcher only the 'interesting' cases. Thus the researcher should always ask the offenders whether they fulfill the criteria of the research design and also make sure that the psychologist understands these criteria as well.

In the present research, the offenders were selected by both ways already described. In some prisons the psychologist selected the offenders ahead of the researcher, in other prisons the researcher was presented with a pool of offenders and then the offenders decided whether they would like to participate. Interestingly, in several prisons the researcher interviewed all the offenders present that fulfilled the criteria.

Another issue which must be remembered is that the research only included offenders with certain literacy skills and also knowledge of the Czech language. Thus foreigners, despite their having committed a crime in the Czech Republic, were not included in the sample.

Research design

The research design should be constructed according to what is possible in the specific setting. As has been said, in the prison environment in the Czech Republic, the researcher cannot be alone with the offender, cannot check information in the files and, most importantly, cannot record the interviews. Due to these restrictions, the design of the research must be adjusted accordingly.

Recording is the preferred method for interviews as it enables a word-for-word, permanent record of the interaction (Payne 2000). It offers richer material, spontaneity in the offender and a variety of analyses. When recording is not possible, note-taking is the only choice. In note-taking, some detail of the interview and its spontaneity is lost and recall is not complete. In Czech prisons, recording is strictly prohibited. To solve the problem, the open-ended questions, asked by the researcher were printed on a paper with possible answers (which were based on previous research). Thus the researcher asked a question, the offender responded, the researcher ticked off the appropriate answer and wrote one or two sentences of the offenders' answers as a commentary. This way, the spontaneity of the interview was ensured. However, only the most relevant information (for the researcher) was recorded. This type of note-taking is fast and efficient, but certain analyses cannot be executed on this type of data.

Because recording is prohibited and the pace of the interview can sometimes cause the researcher to loose certain information, it is important to first of all ask the questions precisely and in detail but also include some of the more factual information in the demographic questionnaire. That way certain information is reported both in the questionnaire and in the interview, which enables the offender to compare them and carry out a validity check. Thus it is advisable to set up the research in such a way that interview is not 'the main method' but 'one of the methods' used.

Mental maps as a means to access new information

Criminal mobility – brief introduction

This chapter is based upon research that explores burglars and one of the main issues studied in the research design is the criminal mobility of these offenders. For the study of mobility, the crime of burglary was chosen specifically as it is crime in which environmental influences play a significant role (Nee and Taylor 1988; Newman 1972).

It is known that the structure of the environment influences criminal activity patterns (Boggs 1965; Cohen and Felson 1979) as well that burglars follow a spatially structured decision-process when selecting

282

their targets (Brantingham and Brantingham 1978; Cornish and Clarke 1986).

Many studies have determined that offenders commit crime close to home (Brantingham and Brantingham 1981; Stephenson 1974; Baldwin and Bottoms 1976; Barker 1999; Wiles and Costello 2000; Ratcliffe 2003; Bernasco and Luykx 2003). However, recently a few studies have also introduced the possibility that this may not be true for all offenders (Morselli and Royer 2008). It is already known that there are differences between the distances to crime of offenders of different ages, gender and types of crime (Baldwin and Bottoms 1976; Nichols 1980; Repetto 1974; Snook 2004), thus it may be possible that many offenders do not commit crimes close to home (van Koppen and de Keijser 1997). The differences in distances travelled to target have already been supported by research regarding suburb boundaries (Ratcliffe 2001). Importantly, Eck and Weisburd (1995) also mention that the differences in distances travelled by offenders may be due to the research design itself, thus other approaches need to be explored. One such alternative is the use of mental maps of the offenders' environment.

Mental maps – theory overview

Mental maps represent how people understand and relate to the environment, thus making spatial decisions based upon the information they store. Information in the map is also used to solve problems, form opinions and attitudes, and direct actions. Mental maps offer information regarding the behaviour of offenders in space (Gärling 1989), the process of decision-making regarding behaviour in a certain environment (MacEachren 1992) and the following of strategies (Downs and Stea 1973).

The spatial behaviour, choices in space and the process of decision-making, finding a route and orientation in the environment, all of these aspects can be portrayed on the sketch of a mental map. A mental map is a unique process of portraying the network of known objects and routes which are important to an individual. Knowledge of the given environment is represented on the mental maps and creates or limits the behaviour (Polišenská 2006, 2007).

During the interview offenders were asked to draw a sketch map of places where they committed the offences and where they live. For this purpose, they were given A4 format paper and a black marker. The drawing can take several forms.

Classification of mental maps

There have been several studies concerning the classification of mental maps. Some classifications are concerned with the complexity represented by the number of structural variables (Lynch 1960) whereas other classifications look at the manner in which the mental map was drawn, such as a sketch being schematic or resembling a map (Ladd 1970) or whether the city is portrayed as sequential with lines between given points or spatial where the points are not connected (Appleyard 1970).

In accordance with this basic research, it is possible to classify mental maps according to certain criteria. One such classification is whether the drawn map is either very *general* or very *detailed* in information. This classification is mainly based on Lynch's (1960) analysis of mental maps, which includes the counting of components such as paths, edges, districts, nodes and landmarks.

Another way of classifying maps is whether they include directional bias which is represented by a *linear* representation of the route between two points or whether the points are *spread* in all directions, which is loosely based upon Appleyard's (1970) research. He divided maps according to whether they are sequential, with lines between given points, or spatial, having an object without lines.

The third way of classifying mental maps upon their structure is according to which region they portray. Thus they can portray a *large* or a *specific* region. The classification of what constitutes 'large' or 'specific' depends upon the researcher. In the current research a large region was defined as a county or the entire Czech Republic whereas a specific region was one village or city.

It must, however, be realised that this type of research is aimed only at the analysis of the structure of the maps.

There are, of course, other ways in which to analyse mental maps. One such analysis can be executed in conjunction with the content analysis of the interviews with regard to spatial mobility. Thus mental maps can be divided into two types – a *detailed local sketch* or a *schematic travel map*. This division is based upon Appleyard's characteristics of mental maps together with the content of the map, that is what locality the map represents, what specific places the offender has drawn and why.

A detailed map represents a specific locality which has a specific meaning to the offender. Such a map can represent one village or a certain part of a city. The map can include street names, specific buildings, etc. Such sketches are maps of places through which the offender moves quite regularly.

A schematic map can be rather general and incomplete, for example depicting specific cities only as crosses. The towns do not have to be connected by roads. Such a sketch does not represent a specific space; it is more of a travel plan from one city to the next. Offenders who drew such a map spent more time travelling between the cities.

Other types of analysis can concentrate upon a *comparison of the mental map with a real map or real situation*. The researcher can either concentrate on the way the real environment is misrepresented on a mental map (the distortions are discussed below) or what non-existent components the offender added to a map and why (in conjunction with the content analysis of the interviews).

In the present research, one such analysis included a comparison between the distances stated during the interview and the distances drawn on the mental map. The number of kilometres travelled to the target were determined by plotting the home town (from the demographics questionnaire) and the different cities onto a planning route server. The content analysis of the interviews served to better describe the individual categories. The distances mentioned during the interview were then corroborated with the sketches of maps (that is whether the offender estimated the distance correctly in relation to the sketch). Further, the information was used to compare the estimated distances in the interviews with the distances depicted on the real maps. This analysis enabled us to see the specificity of the Czech data (Polišenská 2008). The conclusion of the research was that in relation to the distance travelled a major factor to be considered is whether the offenders commit crime in the area surrounding their homes, in other areas which are known to them or in completely unknown areas.

This conclusion leads us to other possible ways in which mental maps can be incorporated into other research regarding the criminal mobility of offenders and other factors contributing to it such as place-attachment, the personality of offenders, the aggression of offenders, etc.

Limitations and distortions of mental maps

It has been noted that mental maps are an important tool for research (Golledge and Stimson 1997). However, it is also important to consider the limitations of this tool. The sketch does not represent everything the individual remembers or the important aspects of the environment. A mental map is only a crude conceptualisation and thus includes many distortions (Vybíral 1999):

- Mental maps tend to be incomplete – not only can they leave out minor details or paths, they can also miss large districts and important landmarks. Also, features not included may reflect lack of knowledge or deliberate selectivity.

- Mental maps can also include the error of augmentation, where a non-existing feature is added to a map – such an addition may be based upon a logical prediction of certain connections from personal experience, but they do not appear in the real world.

- The spatial proportions may not be correct – some places may be drawn closer or further away from each other. The maps can represent the spatial relation of two places in a more simplified way than in reality (Tversky 1981). The spatial relation in terms of geographical axis may also be misremembered. For example, one might draw the relation between two places as from south to north, when in reality they are oriented southeast to northwest (Moar and Bower 1983).

• The sketches may also show a preference for closer places over those that are further away – and represent places that are known as larger than those that are unknown (Canter and Hodge 2000). For example, Byrne (1979) found that subjects estimated that distances on routes with many turns were longer than equally long routes with fewer turns. Byrne hypothesised that the more locations that are remembered along a route, the longer the route is portrayed.

Consistency of mental maps

Overall, Stevens and Coupe (1978) discovered that false memories do not necessarily mean that cognitive maps are spatially inconsistent. Yet Moar and Bower (1983) in their research suggested that information judged on sketches of cognitive maps may be spatially inconsistent in terms of angular and directional properties.

Kirasic et al. (1984), in their study of configurational knowledge of large-scale environments, found that the length of residence may not have an influence on the accuracy or consistency of estimates of distance and direction. The estimates generated by older residents are likely to have more systematic errors than those of newer residents, as their knowledge of the area is more accurate and holistic. Gärling et al. (1982) also found that accuracy increased with the amount of experience and through that increased accuracy the mental map also more resembles a cartographic map.

With regard to the validity of using mental maps, most studies have assumed that the methods used to elicit knowledge would be reliable, as Blades (1990) concluded, in relation to a short period of time.

Conclusion

Research in a penitentiary environment is filled with problems and obstacles which the researcher needs to be prepared to solve and overcome. It also holds many advantages which cannot be gained from police-data research. Although research in prison is more difficult in terms of preparation, the analyses offer more deep and insightful views of the offender and his behaviour.

This chapter has focused on the practical side of research in a prison environment. It has discussed issues with regard to the conditions of offender observation, the motivation of offenders to participate in the research, the validation of information and the research technique of mental maps as a means to access new information from the offenders. Overall, this chapter has focused on the practicality of prison research.

The author hopes that the information offered will help future researchers in their preparation of their projects.

Acknowledgment

The chapter was supported by the grant 406/07/0261 'The Experience of Offenders and Its Influence on Behaviour and Prevention' of the Czech Science Foundation.

References

Appleyard, D. (1970) 'Styles and methods of structuring a city', *Environment and Behavior*, 2: 100–18.

Baldwin, J. and Bottoms, A. E. (1976) *The Urban Criminal: A Study in Sheffield*. London: Tavistock.

Barker, M. (1999) 'The criminal range of house burglars', in D. V. Canter and L. J. Alison (eds), *Offender Profiling Series, Volume 2: Profiling in Policy and Practice*. Aldershot: Ashgate.

Bernasco, W. and Luykx, F. (2003) 'Effects of attractiveness, opportunity and accessibility to burglars on residential burglary rates of urban neighborhoods', *Criminology*, 41 (3): 981–1002.

Blades, M. (1990) 'The reliability of data collected from sketch maps', *Journal of Environmental Psychology*, 10: 327–39.

Boggs, S. (1965) 'Urban crime patterns', *American Sociological Review*, 30: 899–908.

Brantingham, P. and Brantingham, P. (1978) 'A theoretical model of crime site selection', in M. D. Krohn and R. L. Akers (eds), *Crime, Law and Sanctions: Theoretical Perspectives*. Beverly Hills, CA: Sage.

Brantingham, P. J. and Brantingham, P. L. (1981) *Environmental Criminology*. Beverley Hills, CA: Sage.

Breakwell, G. M. (2000) 'Interviewing', in G. M. Breakwell, S. Hammond, C. Fyfe-Shaw (eds), *Research Methods in Psychology*. London: Sage.

Byrne, R. (1979) 'Memory for urban geography', *Quarterly Journal of Experimental Psychology*, 31: 147–54.

Canter D. V. and Hodge, S. (2000) 'Criminals' mental maps', in L. S. Turnbull, E. H. Hendrix and B. D. Dent (eds), *Atlas of Crime: Mapping the Criminal Landscape*. Phoenix, AZ: Oryx Press, pp. 184–91.

Čermák, I. (2002) 'Myslet narativně: kvalitativní výzkum „on the road"' ('To think narratively: qualitative research "on the road"'), in I. Čermák and M. Miovský (eds), *Kvalitativní výzkum ve vědách o člověku na prahu třetího tisíciletí* (*Qualitative Research in Human Sciences in the Beginning of the Third Millennium*), Sborník z konference. Tišnov: SCAN.

Cieurzo, C. and Keitel, M. A. (1999) 'Ethics in qualitative research', in L. A. Suzuki and M. Kopala (eds), *Using Qualitative Methods in Psychology*. Thousand Oaks, CA: Sage, pp. 63–75.

Cohen, L. E. and Felson, M. (1979) 'Social change and crime rate trends: a routine activity approach', *American Sociological Review*, 44: 588–608.

Cornish, D. B. and Clarke, R. V. (eds) (1986) *The Reasoning Criminal: Rational Choice Perspectives on Offending*. New York and Berlin: Springer-Verlag.

Davies, P. and Francis, P. (eds) (2000) *Doing Criminological Research*. London: Sage, pp. 215–33.

Downs, R. M. and Stea, D. (1973) 'Theory', in R. M. Downs and D. Stea (eds), *Image and Environment*. Chicago: Aldine, pp. 1–7.

Eck, J. and Weisburd, D. (eds) (1995) *Crime and Place: Crime Prevention Studies*, Vol. 4. Monsey, NY: Criminal Justice Press.

Fife-Shaw, C. (2000) 'Questionnaire design', in G. M. Breakwell, S. Hammond and C. Fife-Shaw (eds), *Research Methods in Psychology*. London: Sage.

Gärling, T. (1989) 'The role of cognitive maps in spatial decisions', *Journal of Environmental Psychology*, 9: 269–78.

Gärling, T., Böök, A. and Ergezen, N. (1982) 'Memory for the spatial layout of the everyday physical environment differential rates of acquisition of different types of information', *Scandinavian Journal of Psychology*, 23: 23–35.

Golledge, R. G. and Stimson, R. J. (1997) *Spatial Behavior: A Geographic Perspective*. London: Guildford Press.

Heidlerová, J. and Klik, J. (1999) 'Poznámky k současné práci psychiatra ve vězeňském zařízení' ('Notes on the correct work of psychiatrist in prison environment'), Československá Psychiatrie (*Czechoslovak Psychiatry*), 8: 524–8.

Ingham, R., Vanwesenbeeck, I. and Kirkland, D. (1999) 'Interviewing on sensitive topics', in A. Memon and R. Bull (eds), *Handbook of the Psychology of Interviewing*. Chichester: Wiley.

Kirasic, K. C., Allen, G. L. and Siegel, A. W. (1984) 'Expression of configurational knowledge of large-scale environments: students' performance of cognitive tasks', *Environment and Behavior*, 16: 687–712.

Ladd, F. C. (1970) 'Black youths view their environment: neighborhood maps', *Environmental Behavior*, 2: 64–79.

Lynch, K. (1960) *The Image of the City*. Cambridge, MA: Massachusetts Institute of Technology.

MacEachren, A. M. (1992) 'Application of environmental learning theory to spatial knowledge acquisition', *Cartographic Journal*, 28: 152–62.

Moar, I. and Bower, G. H. (1983) 'Inconsistency in spatial knowledge', *Memory and Cognition*, 11: 107–13.

Morselli, C. and Royer, M. (2008) 'Criminal mobility and criminal achievement', *Journal of Research in Crime and Delinquency*, 45: 4–21.

Nee, C. and Taylor, M. (1988) 'Residential burglary in the Republic of Ireland: a situational perspective', *Howard Journal*, 2: 105–15.

Newman, O. (1972) *Defensible Space: Crime Prevention Through Environmental Design*. New York: Macmillan.

Nichols, W. W. Jr (1980) 'Mental maps, social characteristics and crime mobility', in D. E. Georges-Abeyie and K. D. Harries (eds), *Crime: A Spatial Perspective*. New York: Columbia University Press.

Noaks, L. and Wincup, E. (2004) *Criminological Research. Understanding Qualitative Methods*. London: Sage.

Patenaude, A. (2004) 'No promises, but I'm willing to listen and tell what I hear: conducting qualitative research among prison inmates and staff', *Prison Journal*, 84 (4): 698–918.

Patton, M. Q. (2002) *Qualitative Research and Evaluation Methods* (3rd edn). London: Sage.

Payne, S. (2000) 'Interview in qualitative research', in M. Memon and R. Bull (eds), *Handbook of the Psychology of Interviewing*. Chichester: Wiley, pp. 89–102.

Polišenská, V. A. (2004) 'Burglars: territory and strategy', in A. Czerederecka *et al.* (eds), *Forensic Psychology and Law: Facing the Challenges of a Changing World*. Krakow: Institute of Forensic Research.

Polišenská, V. A. (2005) 'Kvalitativní výzkum ve vězeňském prostředí a ovlivňující faktory' ('Qualitative research in prison environment and influencing factors'), in M. Miovský, I. Čermák and V. Chrz (eds), *Kvalitativní přístup a metody ve vědách o člověku IV: Vybrané aspekty teorie a praxe* (*Qualitative Approach and Methods in Human Sciences IV: Selected Aspects of Theory and Practice*). Olomouc: Univerzita Palackého, pp. 109–14.

Polišenská, V. A. (2006) 'Mentální mapy: definice, výzkum a otázka prostorového rozhodování', ('Mental maps: definition, research and spatial decision-making'), *Československá psychologie* (*Czechoslovak Psychology*), 50 (1): 64–70.

Polišenská, V. A. (2007) 'Analýza chování v prostoru: využití mentálních map' ('Analysis of spatial behaviour: using mental maps'), in V. Řehan and M. Šucha (eds), *Kvalitativní přístup a metody ve vědách o člověku IV.: Vybrané aspekty teorie a praxe* (*Qualitative Research and Methods in Human Sciences IV: Selected Aspects of Theory and Practice*). Olomouc: Univerzita Palackého, pp. 185–98.

Polišenská, V. A. (2008) 'A qualitative approach to criminal mobility: questioning the near-home hypothesis', *Crime Patterns and Analysis*, 1: 47–59; online at: http://www.eccajournal.org/.

Ratcliffe, J. H. (2001) *Residential Burglars and Urban Barriers: A Quantitative Spatial Study of the Impact of Canberra's Unique Geography on Residential Burglary Offenders*. Canberra: Criminology Research Council.

Ratcliffe, J. H. (2003) 'Suburb boundaries and residential burglars', in *Trends and Issues in Criminal Justice*, Paper No. 246. Canberra: Australian Institute of Criminology.

Repetto, T. (1974) *Residential Crime*. Cambridge, MA: Ballinger.

Silverman, D. (ed.) (2004) *Qualitative Research: Theory, Method and Practice* (2nd edn). London: Sage.

Smith, J. A. (ed.) (2004) *Qualitative Psychology: A Practical Guide to Research Methods*. London: Sage.

Snook, B. (2004) 'Individual differences in distance travelled by serial burglars', *Journal of Investigative Psychology and Offender Profiling*, 1: 53–66.

Stephenson, L. K. (1974) 'Spatial dispersion of intra-urban juvenile delinquency', *Journal of Geography*, 73: 20–6.

Stevens, A. and Coupe, P. (1978) 'Distortions in judged spatial relations', *Cognitive Psychology*, 10: 422–37.

Tversky, B. (1981) 'Distortions in memory for maps', *Cognitive Psychology*, 13: 407–33.

van Koppen, P. J. and de Keijser, J. W. (1997) 'Desisting distance decay: on the aggregation of individual crime trips', *Criminology*, 35: 505–15.

Vězeňská služba České republiky (Prison Service of the Czech Republic) – online at: http://www.vscr.cz.

Vybíral, Z. (1999) 'Chyby v našich vnitřních mapách' (Mistakes in our internal maps'), *Psychologie Dnes* (*Psychology Today*), 10: 18–19.

Wiles, P. and Costello, A. (2000) *The Road to Nowhere: The Evidence for Travelling Criminals*, Home Office Research Study No. 207. London: Home Office.

Chapter 16

Validating offenders' accounts: learning from offender interviews with bank robbers in Austrian prisons

Birgit Zetinigg and Matthias Gaderer

Abstract

In this chapter we want to assess the possibilities and borders of validating offender interviews. The basis of our reflection upon how data validity can be assured or evaluated is a study about bank robbery in Austria, conducted in 2007. How can a researcher ensure a good quality interview and how can offenders' accounts be validated? Setting out the boundaries for validity starts when defining the research question and subsequently choosing adequate methods. We reflect upon the influence of the interview setting and the role of impression management. Prison files may help to detect 'flat lies' and are a valuable form of validation. Another method could be looking at the crime scenes. In some cases it is possible to compare the findings of the interviews and the stories of the offenders with the actual crime scenes, in this case the victimised bank branches.

Doing qualitative research by interviewing offenders, one is often confronted with biased opinions regarding the validity of the results, especially among those in the scientific community working mainly with quantitative methods. How can we be sure to capture substantial and valid information? How can validity in offender interviews be assured? What kind of data is generated? And finally: is it really worth listening to the offenders 'in their own words'?

These questions are not just part of a philosophical disquisition but are an integral part of doing research. Questions like these are substantial points every researcher conducting offender interviews has to take seriously as they are a fundamental part of the qualitative research paradigm in social sciences. Thus the research questions, the design of the study and methodological decisions are influenced by these issues.

This chapter discusses the problems of conducting offender interviews regarding a research project on bank robbers' patterns of decision-making and possibilities of validation. We want to show that the perspective of the offender is an integral and worthwhile part of researching crime patterns. In the first part of the chapter we try to show that the process of gaining valid data starts even before the interview. Deciding to perform interviews with incarcerated offenders is a research strategy that demands certain pathways. In the second part we want to introduce concepts of how validation of the offender's account is possible. Our goal is to stress that triangulation through the prison files and particularly through the crime scenes themselves are very promising methods of validating offender interviews.

The offender interviews were originally conducted in German. All interview passages cited in this paper are translations by the authors.

The situation in Austria

In recent years the offence of bank robbery became a major problem for banks and the police in Austria. In 2007 this development reached a peak. From an international perspective, Vienna became one of the world's leading 'bank robbery capitals'. Vienna experienced 68 robberies in the year 2006 and ranked fourth of the major European cities with more than one million inhabitants, behind Rome (206 offences), Milan and Prague.

Due to the rise of incidents in recent years and the fact that bank robbery has not as yet been the subject of extensive criminological research in Austria, the need for scientific data was obvious. Our research was co-funded by five financial institutions which were concerned at that time about the increase in bank robberies and wanted to find out about the robbers' motivation as well as their target selection. The main request of the co-funding financial institutions was to evaluate already existing crime prevention measures, but additionally to develop new strategies that covered situational, technical and organisational aspects. Our own research interest was to shed some light on the reasoning of the offenders and to develop offender types.

Therefore our main focus centred on specific and very narrow aspects of the offence. Thus we formulated our research questions as follows: 'Why do offenders choose a certain bank branch sometimes in an area with a high concentration of different branches? Are there some characteristics that make a robber inclined to choose a particular bank branch?

And finally: how is the decision embedded in the daily routine and other processes of sense-making?'

These questions require certain methodological pathways and research designs that focus on the genesis and structure of decision-making patterns. Because our research questions focused on the target selection and decision-making of the offenders, the biographical context was secondary to our study.

Overall research design

As a first step, a quantitative multi-level spatial analysis of 200 branches was carried out. The bank branches were selected via a quota sample, of which half of the branches had been victimised while the other half had not been a target up to the time of our study. A standardised question-naire was sent out to the bank managers in order to gain data about architecture, location, size, surroundings, and other characteristics of the bank, as well as data concerning the incidence of robbery.

As a second step we selected 41 offenders imprisoned in Austrian penitentiaries for qualitative interviews. This sample contains some 40 per cent of all bank robbers being detained who were in a penitentiary at the time of our interview process between May and July of 2007. While it was essential for us to consider the gender issue, unfortunately the two female offenders (the whole population of incarcerated female bank robbers at that time) we had selected refused cooperation.

As a third step we conducted a qualitative space-analysis of nine urban bank branches and nine non-urban branches. Sixty-six per cent of those bank branches had been victimised in our research period between 2002 and 2007. At the crime scenes we took photos of the surroundings and insides of the banks and we interviewed the bank manager and the staff, in some cases the victims of the robbery.

During the process of data aggregation we concentrated on the concept of 'theoretical sampling' introduced by Glaser and Strauss (1967). Theor-etical sampling does not follow the same aim as probabilistic sampling. The goal of the researcher is not to capture a representative sample, but rather to facilitate the development of an analytic frame. Data collection, coding and analysis are carried out at the same time. We continued with data aggregation until a theoretical saturation was reached and we were able to construct types of offenders with a sufficient number of interviews (Glaser and Strauss 1967: 37).

It might be argued that this process of selection of respondents means the research is not representative or objective. However, since not only the existing population of bank robbers is completely unknown, but also the prison population itself is pre-selected, the objective can never be to reach a perfectly representative sample (Matthews 2002: 12).

The main selection criterion was that the interviewee had been convicted for committing at least one bank robbery. Another criterion was that the offender was able to speak and understand German sufficiently well. Since we had to rely on the judgment of the prison staff concerning the language proficiency of our selected interviewees, we experienced that this was not the case with some offenders. We later had to exclude those offenders from our sample.

The overall response rate was 42 per cent and ranged from 10 to 66 per cent. The prison facility with the highest response rate was the penitentiary Simmering (6 out of 9 were interviewed), the prison with the lowest response rate was Krems-Stein (3 out of 30). While Simmering is a facility for first-time offenders, Krems-Stein specialises in multiple offenders and those who demand a high level of security. To avoid a possible under-representation of 'professional' offenders we also included the high-level security facilities Graz-Karlau and Garsten in our sample, where the coverage rate was 47 and 25 per cent respectively. However, as Blumstein *et al.* (1986) argue, high-rate, serious offenders are disproportionately more likely to be incarcerated and therefore the often expressed criticism of prisons being full of unsuccessful criminals is not a strong argument against doing interviews in prisons. Overall, 60 per cent of the offenders had a previous conviction; for the remaining 40 per cent the bank robbery was the first crime for which they had been convicted.

Fundamental preconditions for interviewing the offenders were that the interview had to be based on voluntary cooperation and that the interview data were treated in the strictest confidence. We also ensured a respectful attitude towards the interviewees. The instrument we used to interview the offenders was a semi-structured questionnaire consisting of three parts. We began the offender interviews with a narrative opening phase, followed by a more focused part on such topics as planning the robbery, committing the offence and the phase after the offence until imprisonment. The last part of the interview consisted of a short quantitative questionnaire, where the offender was asked to rate prevention measurements such as CCTV cameras, private security or police patrols. This gave us the possibility to quantify some answers of the offenders in terms of the effect of situational crime prevention measures.

Based on our interview material and following Matthews (2002) and Katz (1988) we constructed a set of offender types. We adapted Matthews' threefold division of offenders, namely the amateurs, the group of intermediate offenders and the professionals, which we then divided into more differentiated sub-categories (Matthews 2002: 22–30). Furthermore, we included Katz's concept of 'sneaky thrills' into our categorisation (Katz 1988: 52–79).

The defining criteria of our characterisation were the following: number of robberies, number of accomplices, selection of targets, previous engagement in criminal acts, level of planning, use of weapon, emotional state during the offence and use of violence during the offence. The 'amateur' is generally characterised by having no previous criminal record, a low level of planning and organisation, the selection of an accessible and often already known target and using imitation firearms or no weapon at all. He tends to operate alone and experiences an emotionally excited state before and during the robbery.

The 'intermediate' robber is more experienced, planned and organised than the 'amateur' robber. The 'intermediate' already has a criminal record, tends to engage in multiple forms of property crime or violent behaviour and operates with accomplices as well.

The typical characteristics of a 'professional' robber are the high level of planning and organisation, the selection of a possibly lucrative target and the readiness to use firearms and violence if necessary. The 'professional' is a persistent robber who carries out the offence in an emotionally concentrated and calm state. Among other things, he perceives the robbery as a 'sneaky thrill' – the robber 'appreciates the reverberating significance of his accomplishment in a euphoric thrill' (Katz 1988: 53).

Strategies to encourage offenders to tell the 'truth'

Interviewing in prison

Our decision to conduct interviews with imprisoned offenders was based on pragmatic as well as rational decisions. The pragmatic reasons included the availability of the interview partners and the limited time budget, whereas the rational decisions centred around the fact that it is hardly possible to observe a robber in action for legal and moral reasons. The characteristics of the offence, such as the seriousness of the crime, the lack of a criminal network within most offender types (at least within the group of 'amateurs') and the relatively high clear-up rate (49 per cent in the year 2006) influenced our decision to conduct the interviews within prison facilities and not in a 'natural' setting. Furthermore, one needs to question the concept of 'natural', free or unbiased settings for an interview in the social sciences. Following the criticism of Copes and Hochstetler in this volume there is 'no empirical evidence that active offenders reveal different aspects about their lives and crimes than do incarcerated ones' (Copes and Hochstetler this volume).

Another aspect that remained completely overlooked in the criminological discourse is the question of whether the offender type (underlying different personality structure) rather than the setting is influential on the validity of the interview. From that perspective we wanted to include in the discussion whether offenders of the same category produce similar accounts, regardless of the setting. Research is needed to evaluate the influence of the setting by comparing offenders of the same category (burglar, robber, ...) and type (amateur, professional, ...) inside and outside prison regarding their statements and accounts. Are the accounts of those interviewed in prison really different and thus is the setting really the key influential factor as claimed by some researchers (Wright and Decker 1994)? Furthermore, it is often argued that imprisoned offenders reconstruct their offences in a more rational way, as they have enough time to reflect upon their crimes (Cromwell *et al.* 1991). The results of our research have shown that this argument cannot be generalised. While we could find the rational reconstruction of the crimes especially within the category of the 'professional' robbers, we did not find this rational argumentation strategy within the 'amateurs'.

In order to gain access to the prison premises, conduct the interviews and record them, we had to apply for the general permission of the Ministry of Justice. Although we received a general permission for our research work, we were still dependent and had to rely on the goodwill of each prison director. Because of that, we were faced with different 'positions' concerning our research project among the prison directors: some were more cooperative, while some showed signs of resentment and perceived our research project as an extra workload.

We also experienced different procedures within the prison organisation, e.g. in a high-level-security prison the inmates were not exactly encouraged to participate in the interviews. All of the pre-selected robbers of this facility were asked by the prison management to fill out a written consent form weeks before the interviews even started. In other prisons we had the opportunity to interview almost every pre-selected offender and had almost zero drop-out rate, because the prison director had assigned social workers to ask offenders to take part in our research. We assume that this successful coverage rate of the sample is a result of the different approach and relationship between social workers and inmates compared to the prison guards.

Finally, it has to be mentioned that we had no access to dangerous or mentally deranged offenders, who may have posed a risk to interviewers. This restricted access is governed by a regulation of the administrative agency within the penitentiary system.

Conducting offender interviews in prison may have disadvantages that can be of a procedural nature, such as organisational and bureaucratic restrictions that lie within the prison system itself. As interviewers we could not influence the way the inmates were approached and asked to participate in the interviews. Similarly conducting interviews in prison involves disadvantages of a spatial nature. We had limited influence over the rooms that were provided to us to conduct the interviews.

The prison system in Austria consists of various facilities that differ by region and level of security. Some facilities specialise in inmates with mental disorders. Due to the fact that the offenders in our sample were widely spread over eight prison facilities in the eastern part of Austria we faced different interview settings. In most cases we were able to conduct the interviews in a 'social room' which had a comfortable and not intimidating atmosphere. However, in some cases we were forced to interview the offenders in a 'cell-like' atmosphere, constantly monitored (but not overheard) by the prison staff via CCTV cameras. Concerning the three interviews which we conducted in the latter setting we could witness several unfavourable outcomes. Not only were these interviews considerably short, but it was also difficult to establish rapport. The following passage from an interview shows how difficult it was to establish a trustful atmosphere in this setting:

> *Otto (O):* To be honest . . .
> *Interviewer (I):* Mhm.
> *O:* I mean, I'm not talking 'bout certain things. I'm open to doing things together in the future. But I mean, I'm not tellin' you everything. Cause I've learned to be careful.
> *I:* 'Cause you don't trust us, do you?
> *O:* Well . . . that would be quite understandable, wouldn't it?
> *I:* Of course.
> *O:* 'Cause, come on, what's the place we're in here?
> *I:* Certainly not a coffee house.
> *O:* Yeah, it's different.

Establishing rapport

Establishing rapport plays an integral role in every form of social interaction, independent of being non-verbal or verbal, namely in conversations. We were aware of the fact that establishing rapport consists of and is influenced by many factors. Most of them cannot be measured or even controlled by the interviewer, e.g. ethnicity, gender, age and social class. At the same time the interviewer may resort to his or her interpersonal skills, but cannot influence the sympathy that is shown to him or her by the interviewee. In our view, a key element for successful interaction, for example in an interview situation, is the authenticity of the interviewer. In our interviews we tried not to adopt a social role that deviates extensively from our everyday set of roles.

Social distance, be it through class, gender or other factors, may be more visible in a setting where bars divide the incarcerated from the 'free' (the researcher). However, this does not mean that social distance does not exist outside prison bars as well.

Key features of participatory interviewing are: drawing on interpersonal skills of being approachable, sympathetic and responsive; not trying to control the interview process; and promoting equality by presenting oneself as one is with study participants (Neuman 2003: 252).

Our strategy was to start the interview with a narrative opening phase to enable the interviewee to tell his story in an 'undirected way'. By listening carefully to the personal 'story' of the offender we could establish an atmosphere of trust. In other words, we exchanged our full attention to the interviewee without profiting directly from his story in order to gain the information we were interested in later.

A good interview is a fair exchange. For an interview to go well, an interviewer has to enter into mutually agreeable relations with his subject. No research participant will be comfortable in an interview situation unless he feels that the interviewer is listening with sincere interest and concentration. 'Concentration' means not asking the same interview questions repeatedly, as it then becomes obvious that the interviewer did not listen properly to the interviewee. These features demanded by the interviewer could be summarised by the term 'respect'. Thus respect towards the interviewee must be a key feature for each researcher.

Different languages and cultural backgrounds can hinder the establishment of trust between the researcher and the interview partner. Research shows that migrant offenders and offenders from ethnic minorities tend to have a higher level of distrust in the criminal justice system than the majority (Bauer 1999: 25; Phillips and Bowling 2002: 579–619). This barrier and the atmosphere of distrust may even extend to the social setting of the interview.

In our research we experienced that interviews with robbers belonging to ethnic minorities tended to be shorter and less detailed compared to interviews with Austrian robbers. Whether this is a result of the language barrier or distrust towards the interviewers was not evaluated by us but would be of interest for further research.

Motivations to take part in the interview

Jacobs and Wright (2006) claim that 'prisoners often bring an agenda to the interview setting that can compromise the validity and reliability of any information they provide to researchers.' According to them the critical point is that offenders 'tell researchers what they think they want to hear in the hope of receiving a reward or avoiding a penalty' (Jacobs and Wright 2006: 10). However, offenders interviewed in prison do not receive a monetary reward, as it is commonly used in ethnographic research to motivate offenders in a 'natural environment' to take part in an interview. Bruce Jacobs points out that the motivation for offenders recruited on the street is always related to money (Jacobs 1999). The fact that offenders are paid a reward when taking part in an interview can hardly mean that they are free of any agenda. We have to be aware of the fact that interview partners are never free of any agenda, be it in the prison or the 'outside world'. Likewise the interviewee as well is aware that the interviewer has their own agenda that is brought into the interview.

Before conducting the interviews we explicitly explained the context of our research project: who we were, what the overall goal of our research was and that we were not affiliated with the authorities. We emphasised the fact that taking-part in the interviews would not include incentives, that data would be treated in the strictest confidence and furthermore the interview would not have consequences either in a negative or in a positive way. Furthermore, before starting the interview, we thoroughly explained the rights of the interviewee and the confidentiality rules.

Contrary to Matthews (2002: 6) we decided not to emphasise the fact that our research was co-funded by financial institutions. By doing so we hoped to raise the willingness to participate in our research. Furthermore, we wanted to ensure a 'neutral' basis for the interview by emphasising our scientific curiosity. The term 'scientific curiosity' has had a positive connotation ever since Blumenberg (1966) reflected upon the concept. Both methodological decisions (to reveal the funding by the banks or not) led to good results. However, it is up to every researcher to take this method-ological decision and by doing so set out ethical boundaries.

In the context of prison interviews it is obvious that both sides (the researcher and the inmate) have their own agenda: the researcher wants to shed some light onto the nature of crime and develop strategies against it, the inmate wants to deal with the situation of being incarcerated (show remorse, fight boredom, gain benefits). Both sides are aware that the other part has a certain agenda, be it openly revealed or not.

Although we did not evaluate the motives of the offenders to take part in our research we found several tendencies. A prominent reason is a therapeutic one, especially among the 'amateurs'. We assume that 'amateurs' have not yet internalised a 'criminal identity' and are therefore more open to reflect upon their criminal acts in a way that later enables them to reintegrate themselves into society. An offender, whose motives are of a therapeutic nature uses the interview situation as a platform where he can come to terms with his criminal act and hope for absolution. By showing remorse and reflection upon past events the offender almost confirms his will to depart from the criminal path in front of himself rather than in front of the researcher. Albert, who had committed multiple robberies, described his imprisonment as an act of deep relief:

It worked for some time, but in the end I was happy about being arrested. I was happy to get out of my past life. Even if I had to pay a big price – eight years in prison. But I just couldn't have gone on with it. The pressure was so intense, I was glad that it was over. Of course I could have tried to keep up that facade for some time, but after all I'm happy with the way things ended.

Another reason to take part in an interview was that the offenders expected to gain advice or consultation about legal issues. Due to the fact that our research institute is based in an organisation well known for its legal expertise in the field of road and traffic safety some interviewees hoped to get advice. A conviction according to the Austrian penal code §§142 and 143 (robbery, serious robbery) involves the loss of the driving licence for several months after being released from prison. However, we did not expect this traffic-related issue would become a subject of discussion in our interviews. Only after two offenders asked for our legal advice after the taped interview did we become aware that this could be a possible reason for motivation. Since we are a research institute and not a legal authority, we could only advise our interview partners to seek help from a social worker or their probation officer.

Boredom or the chance to escape everyday life in prison (routine tasks, work) and to have contact with the 'outside world' was another notable motivation among our interview partners. Especially for long-term prisoners a sense of isolation is common. 'Making a connection with someone new outside helps a person feel a little bit closer to home, a bit more like a human being and a bit less like a prisoner' (Bosworth *et al.* 2005: 257). Nazif was a young offender imprisoned in the juvenile prison Gerasdorf, who seemed to show signs of regret that the interview was coming to an end.

I: Thanks for the interview. That's it, then.

N: Um, is it already finished? Don't you have some other questions for me?

I: No, we have everything . . .

N: Ah, OK, what a shame, it was really good to get out of there [work] for a while.

Strategies for validating offender accounts

Prison files as a method of validation

The validation process before conducting the qualitative interviews included a review of the prison file of the offender. The prison files we analysed contained various pieces of information, such as biographical data, the criminal history, the sentence and data of the evidence process during the trial, the medical condition (including drug addiction and substance abuse), police protocols and psychiatric data, etc. The information on the offender files was registered in a protocol and thoroughly discussed before the interview. Our motivation for examining the prison files was to get insights into and an overview of each individual case. We wanted to be prepared for each interview situation and were able to monitor deviations from the 'official' story. Prison files play an important role in creating an identity (or the 'moral career') for life inside the prison system since they are the only official and socially respected sources.

Offenders deal with this fact in different ways: they can either uncondi-
tionally accept the official story, partly accept the attributions if they
please or totally deny the 'story'.

One example of accepting an attributed identity could be witnessed
with our interview partner Mirko. During our offender interviews we
were confronted with an offender who lived the role of a 'celebrity'
robber. By 'celebrity robber' we understand a robber whose story was
printed several times in the newspapers and who is 'known' by the public
at large because of that fact. According to the file the modus operandi of
Mirko was spontaneous and rather clumsy. When committing the robbery
he was highly intoxicated and did not use any form of disguise. He not
only robbed the bank branch where he was customer, but also left his
ATM card at the counter. Because of these extraordinary circumstances his
story was a headline in various tabloid articles. When we wanted to start
the interview he came up with a set of articles he brought along to the
interview and expected us to already know him and his story from the
papers. When he told his story, it was mainly a summary of the story in
the article he had shown us. Mirko was able to use the newspaper article
as a form of self-reference to construct his identity as a 'sad' robber who
became a criminal because of romantic reasons rather than monetary. This
interview showed us that prison files are not the only source that matters
for the identity-construction of the offenders. Also the media can play an
important part in offering the offender a 'story' he can identify with. The
'official story' of the media provided him with an opportunity to justify
his offence as a technique of neutralisation.

Some robbers use parts of the files or newspaper articles to support the
statement they want to make in front of the interviewer. One offender,
Stefan, whom we defined as a 'professional robber' tried to portray
himself in a rather friendly, more gentleman-like way than one could
assume judging by the degree of penalty and the protocols. To prove his
point he referred to certain statements from witnesses at his trial
describing him (in his conception, as we could not find any of his claims
in the file) as a 'robber with proper manners'.

> There was this young girl, a trainee, in the branch, she was from
> Turkey. I went to her and said: 'Cool down, nothing's going to
> happen to you. We'll just take the money. It's much worse in Turkey
> with the war going on.' Then she calmed herself, because I tapped on
> her shoulder. It's not her fault she is so faint-hearted. But they didn't
> take this into credit at the court. They wrote in the newspapers: 'The
> friendliest bank robber ever!' It was a huge story in the newspapers.
> You can still read it today in the archives.

According to Stefan's selective form of perception he only picked out
passages that were suitable to show himself in a more favourable light.

From this perspective the prison file can be used by the offender to raise his own credibility in the interview.

In some cases the offenders did not accept their identity as a deviant person and denied their engagement in a bank robbery at all. One example is Bojan, who did not see himself as a robber and stated that he only 'knew' about the robbery and was not at all involved in the crime from his point of view.

> He told me 'I am going to do this bank' and I said 'you are crazy, you're going directly to prison!' And he said 'I don't care.' Later he came again with his friend and they organised this whole thing. And I only *knew* about it! It was *him* who did this crime. I wasn't inside the bank, I am not a bank robber. No, no, not at all.'

However, Bojan's prison file revealed that he provided the other two offenders with a weapon and an escape vehicle. From his perception he did not see himself as a 'bank robber', because he did not enter the bank.

One offender, Christoph, pretended to be less prone to violence than he actually was when he committed the robbery. This offender carried a gun in his jacket, and lied about the fact that he had carried a weapon, as he stated that he was only 'just an amateur'. 'I could never set any person in danger, or something like that. Because I went in there without a weapon, so I didn't carry a weapon, . . .'

By knowing the details of the offence through the sentence file, we could confront Christoph with this contradiction during the interview. We caught him telling a so-called 'open', 'flat' or 'barefaced lie', because of the unquestionable evidence that the person telling knew he lied and wilfully did so. Those caught telling a 'flat lie' during an interaction not only lose face, but risk their face being destroyed. For it is felt by many audiences that if an individual can once bring himself to tell such a lie he ought never again to be fully trusted (Goffman 1959). It is an interesting fact that he tried to integrate this new situation (our knowledge about the gas pistol because we had examined the prison file before the interview) into the story he told us. He could no longer deny it, but he also had to go on telling his story at that time.

> *Interviewer* (I): We were looking through your sentence and it said there that you carried a weapon with you.
> *Christoph* (C): It was a gas pistol.
> I: Yes.
> C: But it was inside my jacket.
> I: Okay.
> C: It was closed.
> I: Yes. Why did you carry it with you?

C: To feel more secure. I thought of it as my jackpot. I did not plan to use it, just to feel a little bit stronger.

The use of prison files enables researchers to detect 'open' or 'flat lies' as a form of validation and to identify exaggerations or understatements and especially contradictions in general throughout the interview situation. However, a confrontation with regard to the contradictions in the 'storyline' of the interviewee has to be handled with care.

The question is how to deal with such flat lies when they are detected? From our point of view, to confront the interview partner in a very harsh way and to reveal him as a liar is not advisable and constructive, because then the whole interview would be jeopardised. When 'flat lies' are detected repeatedly or the offender lies about serious passages or if the offender completely denies his involvement in the crime, the researcher should consider excluding the interview from his sample. In our study this was the case with three interviews that we found implausible in fundamental parts compared to the information we had from the prison files.

Prison files may contain psychiatric evaluations, which we experienced especially in the cases of offenders we later classified as 'professionals'. In our interview sample we found a small group of professional robbers (about 13 per cent of the sample), which represented an interesting but also challenging group of offenders. Those psychiatric reports described the 'professional' offenders as highly intelligent, self-centred, manipulative and narcissistic personalities. We assumed that there is a link between a 'narcissistic personality' and the tendency to exaggerate in an interview. We witnessed this tendency particularly in passages that allowed the 'professional' to stage himself as an expert. To prove an actual exaggeration in an interview situation is a difficult task because they work in a subtle way. Thus we had to critically question the authenticity and credibility of some passages in those interviews. However, we came to the conclusion that those interviews were able to open the framework of a very complex way of thinking. This means that perhaps we did not get 'the whole truth', but we got an insight into the way professional offenders think, what they consider and what they even could put into action in the future. Professional offenders can be seen as 'experts' in their field and in this role they reveal what is considered to be relevant for the execution of this criminal offence.

Psychiatric reports can help the researcher to prepare for a challenging and very complex interview situation. To sum up prison files allow the interviewer to get a broader picture about each individual case and at least enable to detect 'flat lies'.

Impression management

Impression management theory states that any individual or organisation must establish and maintain impressions that are congruent with the perceptions they want to convey to their publics. Impression management is accomplished by 'a strategic combination of enhancement, embellishment, suppression, ostentation or misrepresentation concerning the self' (Pogrebin 2002: 339). A researcher conducting qualitative interviews has to be aware of the fact that impression management plays a vital role not only in everyday-life interaction, but also during an interview situation.

In the field of offender interviews, inside or outside prison, impression management is used by both the researcher and the interview partner. Researchers use impression management to present themselves as trustworthy and sympathetic conversational partners, while offenders use impression management to present themselves as 'good' or 'bad' criminals, innocent or guilty, amateurish or professional, emotionally unstable or calm.

In the interview situation, the offender uses impression management, be it consciously or unconsciously, to convince the researcher and himself of a certain image and to act out emotional and rational accounts.

Stefan, a 'professional robber', favoured picturing himself as a sophisticated professional robber by portraying his modus operandi as extensively complex.

> *Stefan (S)*: [. . .] no subways if it's possible there is video surveillance . . . but I put make-up on anyway. I did this make-up artist course in Munich . . .
> *Interviewer (I)*: Really?
> S: Yes, yes. It is called make-up artist or how they call it. I did this course five times with that lady, in private. I told her I wanna do it cos I wanna do movies.
> I: Yes, yes, yes.
> S: So I bought this equipment. It was worth about $2,000. It had lots of stuff in it like they have it in Hollywood.
> I: Really?
> S: Then I put everything on and changed myself completely. Even my own mum wouldn't have recognised me.
> I: Really? That's what you did?
> S: Ya . . . silicon insoles, changed myself completely. Eyes, I even had contact lenses with different colours.
> I: Okay.
> S: I used a kajal on my eyes, a special kajal. And then we had this liquid we used – like a special ampulla. I drank it and my voice changed completely.

'Professional' robbers use various accounts to present themselves as rational actors, who commit their crime in a very calm or almost cold-blooded way. One example of a professional robber, who presented himself as a cold-blooded, intelligent planner with highly narcissistic tendencies, was Martin. He emphasised the natural ease of committing a robbery and finding a creative way to escape the police.

> *Martin (M)*: I even went inside a police station after a bank robbery.
> *Interviewer (M)*: What do you mean, inside?
> *M*: It counted as a negative factor when I was convicted. I did some things in a cold-blooded way. Yes, I went there after the bank robbery – you know, for me it's a completely logical thing to do. What is the perfect place the police won't look for me? A police station! Yeah, for sure! For me it's very clear.
> *I*: That's true.
> *M*: OK, and I did it this way. I robbed this bank in the tenth district [of Vienna] and then I went right into the police station. Reported my passport missing. There was this young officer – a young lady – and said: 'Please, take a seat, we're just having a bank robbery.' For me it's the most logical thing in the world. 'Cause they won't look for me there.
> *I*: It should be the most secure place to be at that moment.
> *M*: That's what they say – in the sentence they wrote about the 'cold-blooded way' I did the robberies ... Yeah, that's why I got this harsh sentence. That's what they meant.

'Amateurs' on the other hand often use emotional accounts to present themselves as offenders, who 'slid' into crime in a rather clumsy way. They often emphasise that their offence was everything other than planned and carried out in a rather unskilful way.

> Until the very end, when I was standing at the door ... I didn't know whether I should do it or not. But once the door was open, I knew there was no turning back ... (Hilmar, Sonnberg)

> Well, I was fighting with myself for one hour. I said that in the police report, too ... so I was fighting a whole hour, wondering should I really do it or not. Then after an hour I said to myself, now or never ... That's when I decided to do it. (Zoran, Simmering)

Amateurs and professionals use a different approach in their impression management. We hypothesise that the strategies vary according to the type of the offender rather than the interview setting (be it inside or outside prison). Still, the influence of the offender types and the type of offence on the impression management during an interview has to be looked at more deeply. In addition, further research is necessary to be able to compare the methods of impression management of the different types of offenders.

Triangulation and validation through crime-scene analysis

Triangulation of methods is a popular way to assure that the disadvantages of the different research paradigms are reduced and a holistic view can be achieved. It refers to combining various theories, methods, observers and empirical materials to produce a more accurate, comprehensive and objective representation of the object of the study (Silverman 2006: 291).

In our research project we applied triangulation of methods by conducting a quantitative analysis of the spatial aspects of 200 bank branches, by interviewing 41 incarcerated robbers and analysing their prison files and, as a final step, by a qualitative space analysis during which we visited 18 bank branches. Taking a look at the crime scenes, namely the victimised banks, was an integral part of validating the findings of our offender interviews.

We conceptualised our qualitative space analysis in such a way as to compare victimised bank branches (two-thirds of the sample) with those that had not been a target of a robbery (one-third of the sample). We also included the 'urban' aspect by dividing the sample into nine urban and nine rural branches. In 4 out of 12 cases it was possible to compare the findings of the offenders' statements with the actual crime scenes.

When we visited the bank branches we used a protocol as a general framework for our observation procedure. Furthermore, we interviewed the bank manager and the cashier using a short standardised questionnaire.

The protocol was used to standardise the observation procedure at each branch. The first step was taking photos of the surroundings and the insides of the banks as well as briefly summarising the access routes, the traffic situation, the parking situation and public transport. What possibilities are there to get away? What is the location of the nearest police station? In what kind of neighbourhood is this bank branch located? What kind of shops and buildings are found in this area of the city? Is it a middle-class district or the suburbs?

After capturing data about the surroundings the branch itself was analysed. The transparency of the bank, especially the proportion of glass in the facade, turned out to be an important factor for our analysis as a result of the offenders' statements. The degree of transparency, meaning a high proportion of glass windows in the front that enable a good view into the insides of a branch, proved to be a factor that many robbers took into consideration in their target selection and during the execution of their robberies. Interestingly the transparency had contradictory effects on the robbers' decision-making process and the target selection. Transparency was seen to be an appealing factor as well as a deterring one depending on the type of offender, their modi operandi and the means they had to control a situation. A high level of situational control enables the offender to react more appropriately in an unforeseen situation.

With regard to the design of the branch we collected data about the foyer, the number of and position of the cashier's desks and the overall design in detail. Furthermore, we observed the lanes that lead to the cashier (whether the route was narrow and angled or spacious and accessible without barriers).

Two factors are crucial for the robber to consider when committing a bank robbery: time and situational control. It is common knowledge among bank robbers that the duration of stay inside the bank should not exceed three minutes. After that period of time the likelihood that the police will have arrived at the crime scene is high. 'Situation control' is a feature every offender needs to take into consideration and includes the architectural, constructional and organisational aspects of the crime scene.

Crime scene evaluation is a highly appropriate method to test situational criteria and variables as criminogenic factors. In the case of bank robbery those factors include architectural, technical and organisational aspects. Technical factors include technical security measures such as CCTV cameras but also mechanical ones (doors).

A high number of offenders described in our interviews the easily accessible architecture of the bank counters as an appealing factor for committing a robbery. Over recent years the emphasis in the interior design of banks in Austria changed from a security-based design to a more customer-orientated design. The counters were moved near to the entrance to reduce the distance the customer needs to walk. At the same time the glass-partitions of the counters were removed. This implies that it is possible for the offender during the robbery to get behind the counter and grab the money, which accelerates the speed of the robbery. Furthermore, the offender is able to influence the amount of money taken, monitor the situation from a better angle and may be able to detect dye packs.

Another influencing feature quoted by our interviewees was the nature of the entrance door. Automatic entrance doors seem to be a deterring factor because robbers are afraid that they will get caught inside the bank during their robbery. By knowing that they have less than three minutes for the execution of the robbery before the police arrive at the crime scene they prefer to minimise the risk of getting caught. For example, one strategy to minimise the risk is to choose a branch with a mechanical door rather than an automatic one. Automatic doors are variables robbers cannot influence and thus the degree of situational control might be reduced and a successful completion of the robbery will be jeopardised.

Evaluation of the crime scenes also included interviews with the bank managers as well as the staff at the counters, who represent in Jock Young's model of the 'square of crime' the exact opposite of the offender: the actual victim (Young 1991). The accounts of the victims enabled us to reconstruct some of the modi operandi of our offenders. To include both the offenders' and the victims' perspective on the crime is an approach that enables the researcher to understand crime in a more comprehensive way.

One example was Nazif, a young migrant offender who was incarcerated in Gerasdorf, the juvenile penitentiary. He put himself across as an intimidating and even aggressive robber by claiming he had pushed away the cashier in a quite brutal manner during the robbery.

> *Nazif (N)*: And I said to her 'gimme the money!' and she just said to me 'we have no money!' Then I looked at her and I walked around the counter.
> *Interviewer (I)*: Mhm.
> N: Then ... I really only touched the woman, ... and she fell two metres. Honestly. I really didn't want it to happen ...

However, we did not find any evidence of his claim in the prison files (no sentence for assault or any other aggravating circumstances). In addition, when interviewing the victim of Nazif's robbery, his emotional accounts regarding his aggressive behaviour turned out to be an exaggeration.

> It was two young boys. I didn't even take them seriously, at first. The first thing I did was set off the alarm. Then I told him, I told him I had no money. Then he looked at me completely puzzled ... then he walked around the counter ... I just stood there ... then he pushed me aside a bit, 'cos I still stood there. I really had to contain myself not to overpower him. (Female cashier, victim)

Interviews with victims can provide the researcher with more exact information and additional insights into the circumstances of the offence. In the above case we were able to confirm our assumption about the category of 'gangsters' and their tendency to exaggerate. In our definition a 'gangster' (a subcategory of the type of 'intermediate robbers') is a young offender characterised by having a background of migration, previous convictions of property offences and a deviant circle of friends. His motivation is the need for money to support a 'partying lifestyle' of drugs and alcohol. Bank robbery is seen as a 'buzz' and a form of testing out boundaries. Furthermore, this offender type is highly influenced by the mass media.

Taking into consideration our research questions, which concentrated on the spatial factors of robbers' decision-making processes, the evaluation of the crime scenes proved to be a valuable method to validate our findings. Crime scene analysis enables a 'triangulated' view as the researcher is confronted with the actual manifestation of the offender's story.

Conclusion

Choosing the prison as a setting for conducting these interviews often brings along criticism concerning the reliability and validity of the interview data. One claim is that only unsuccessful robbers get in contact with the criminal justice system and therefore are imprisoned. However, Blumstein (1986) argues, that high-rate, serious offenders are more likely to be incarcerated. Therefore, in our point of view, the prison as a setting allows us to have access to a wide variety of offender types, even successful ones, especially in the case of the offence 'bank robbery', where the clear-up rates are relatively high (around 50 per cent).

Furthermore, we question the concept of natural, 'free' or unbiased settings for interviews in the social sciences. An aspect that remained completely overlooked in the criminological discourse is the question of whether the offender type rather than the setting (inside or outside prison) is influential on the accounts of the offenders. Further research is needed to compare the accounts of offenders outside and inside prison.

As researchers we can choose between different strategies to assure data quality and raise the validity of interview data. The most promising approach in our opinion is the triangulation of methods. In our research on bank robbery we found that validating the interview data was best achieved by a research design that used mixed methods. We carried out a quantitative analysis of bank branches in order to quantify relevant deterrent or appealing situational factors for robbers. During the research phase of qualitative interviews with incarcerated offenders we applied validation by evaluating the prison files. The use of prison files enables the researcher to detect 'flat' or 'open lies' and to get an insight into each individual case. They also contain valuable data (psychiatric reports, witness statements, etc.) that enable the researcher to be well prepared for the interview situation.

Finally we verified offenders' statements by visiting the crime scenes and examining situational factors. By evaluating the crime scenes it was possible to test situational criteria and variables as criminogenic factors. In our research into bank robbery those factors included architectural, technical and organisational aspects.

Following Young's (1991) model of the 'square of crime' we wanted to approach the crime from different angles. Thus we conducted additional interviews with the bank staff. By that we were able to collect the victims' accounts and could reconstruct some of the modi operandi of the offenders.

We believe that qualitative offender interviews are the most essential sources for access to the offender's perspective on crimes. Although it is often morally questioned if 'bad people' are trustworthy enough to tell 'true stories' their accounts provide us with very valuable data, especially if different methods of validation are being applied.

References

Bauer, J. (1999) 'Speaking of culture: immigrants in the American legal system', in J. I. Moore (ed.), *Immigrants in Courts*. Seattle: WA: University of Washington Press, pp. 8–28.

Blumenberg, H. (1966) *Die Legitimität der Neuzeit*. Frankfurt am Main: Suhrkamp.

Blumstein, A., Cohen, J., Roth, J. and Visher, C. A. (1986) *Criminal Careers and 'Career Criminals'*, Report of the National Academy of Sciences Panel on Research on Criminal Careers. Washington, DC, National Academy Press.

Bosworth, M., Campbell, D., Demby, B., Ferranti, S. M. and Santos, M. (2005) 'Doing prison research: views from inside', *Qualitative Inquiry*, 11 (2): 249–64.

Clavarino, A., Najman, J. M. and Silverman, D. (1995) 'The quality of qualitative data: two strategies for analyzing medical interviews', *Qualitative Inquiry*, 1 (2): 223–42.

Cromwell, P. (ed.) (2006) *In Their Own Words: Criminals on Crime*. Los Angeles: Roxbury.

Cromwell, P., Olson, J. N. and Avary, D. W. (1991) *Breaking and Entering: An Ethnographic Analysis of Burglary*. Newbury Park, CA: Sage.

Denzin, N. (1970) *The Research Act*. Chicago: Aldine.

Glaser, B. and Strauss, A. (1967) *The Discovery of Grounded Theory: Strategies for Qualitative Research*. New York: Aldine.

Goffman, E. (1959) *The Presentation of Self in Everyday Life*. New York: Anchor Books.

Goffman, E. (1961) *Asylums: Essays on the Social Situation of Mental Patients and Other Inmates*. New York: Anchor Books.

Hammersley, M. (1990) *Reading Ethnographic Research: A Critical Guide*. London: Longmans.

Hammersley, M. (1992) *What's Wrong with Ethnography? Methodological Explorations*. London: Routledge.

Jacobs, B. A. (1999) *Dealing Crack: The Social World of Street Corner Selling*. Boston: Northeastern University Press.

Jacobs, B. A. and Wright, R. (2006) *Street Justice: Retaliation in the Criminal Underworld*. Cambridge: Cambridge University Press.

Katz, J. (1988) *Seductions of Crime: Moral and Sensual Attractions in Doing Evil*. Oxford: Basic Books.

Matthews, R. (2002) *Armed Robbery*. Portland, OR: Willan.

Neuman, W. L. (2003) *Social Research Methods: Qualitative and Quantitative Approaches*. Boston: Allyn & Bacon.

Phillips, C. and Bowling, B. (2002) 'Racism, ethnicity, crime and criminal justice', in M. Maguire, R. Morgan and R. Reiner (eds), *The Oxford Handbook of Criminology* (3rd edn). Oxford: Oxford University Press, pp. 579–619.

Pogrebin, M. (ed.) (2002) *Qualitative Approaches to Criminal Justice: Perspectives from the Field*. London: Sage.

Presser, L. (2004) 'Violent offenders, moral selves: constructing identities and accounts in the research interview', *Social Problems*, 51: 82–101.

Silverman, D. (2005) *Doing Qualitative Research: A Practical Handbook* (2nd edn). London: Sage.

Silverman, D. (2006) *Interpreting Qualitative Data: Methods for Analyzing Talk, Text and Interaction* (3rd edn). London: Sage.

Strauss, A. L. and Corbin, J. (1990) *Basics of Qualitative Research: Grounded Theory Procedures and Techniques*. Newbury Park, CA: Sage.

Whittemore, R., Chase, S. K. and Mandle, C. L. (2001) 'Validity in qualitative research', *Qualitative Health Research*, 11 (4): 522–37.

Wright, R. T. and Decker, S. H. (1994) *Burglars on the Job: Streetlife and Residential Break-ins*. Boston: Northeastern University Press.

Wright, R. T. and Decker, S. H. (1997) *Armed Robbers in Action: Stickups and Street Culture*. Boston: Northeastern University Press.

Young, J. (1991) 'Left realism and the priorities of crime control', in K. Stenson and D. Cowell (eds), *The Politics of Crime Control*. London: Sage.

Index

Added to a page number 'f' denotes a figure and 'n' denotes notes.